FAITHFUL FIGHTERS

KATE IMY

FAITHFUL
FIGHTERS

*Identity and Power in the
British Indian Army*

STANFORD UNIVERSITY PRESS

STANFORD, CALIFORNIA

Stanford University Press
Stanford, California

Printed in the United States of America on acid-free, archival-quality paper

Library of Congress Cataloging-in-Publication Data

Names: Imy, Kate, 1987– author.
Title: Faithful fighters : identity and power in the British Indian Army / Kate Imy.
Description: Stanford, California : Stanford University Press, 2019. | Includes bibliographical references and index.
Identifiers: LCCN 2019004981 (print) | ISBN 9781503610026 (cloth: alk. paper) | ISBN 9781503610743 (pbk.: alk. paper)
Subjects: LCSH: Great Britain. Army. British Indian Army—History—20th century. | Soldiers—India—Social conditions—20th century. | Identification (Religion)—History—20th century. | Religion and state—India—History—20th century. | Nationalism—India—History—20th century. | India—History—British occupation, 1765–1947.
Classification: LCC UA668 .I49 2019 (print) | LCC UA668 (ebook) | DDC 355.30954—dc23
LC record available at https://lccn.loc.gov/2019004981
LC ebook record available at https://lccn.loc.gov/2019981259

Cover design by Kevin Barrett Kane

Cover image: First World War Sikh re-enactors at the Royal Pavilion War Stories Open Day, September 2014. *Source:* Royal Pavilion & Museums, Brighton & Hove. Reprinted with permission.

Typeset by Westchester Publishing Services in 10.75/15 Adobe Caslon Pro

For Kenneth

CONTENTS

ABBREVIATIONS

BL—British Library
EIC—East India Company
HHS—H. H. Somerfield Papers
HRC—Harry Ransom Center
ICC—Imperial Cadet Corps
IMA—Indian Military Academy
IOR—India Office Records, British Library
IWM—Imperial War Museum
KCIO—King's Commissioned Indian Officer
MSA—Maharashtra State Archives
Mss Eur—European Manuscripts, British Library
NAI—National Archives of India
NML—Nehru Memorial Library
PSA—Panjab State Archives
RATA—Royal Army Temperance Association
RIMC—Royal Indian Military College
SGPC—Shiromani Gurdwara Parbandhak Committee
TGM—The Gurkha Museum (Winchester, UK)
VCO—Viceroy's Commissioned Officer
WBSA—West Bengal State Archives
YMCA—Young Men's Christian Association

ACKNOWLEDGMENTS

This work would have not been possible without the tireless efforts of many scholars, archivists, family, and friends. Metropolitan State University of Denver and the University of Northern Colorado fostered my deep love of history. Rutgers University gave me the tools to develop this passion into a profession. Seth Koven, Bonnie Smith, and Indrani Chatterjee provided a lifetime's worth of invaluable guidance as well as incomparable models for being professional historians and mentors. The Institute of Historical Research, Fulbright Foundation, Critical Language Fellowship, Rutgers University, and the Mellon Foundation generously supported the research and travel for this project. Charu Gupta, Erica Wald, Margot Finn, Will Pooley, Eloise Moss, and Emilie Murphy made my overseas research extremely inspiring and rewarding. The Institute of Historical Research, University of Delhi, and American Institute of Indian Studies provided excellent forums for networking and scholarly collaboration.

Accessing these soldiers' stories would not have been possible without the hard work of many archivists around the world. In the United Kingdom I am grateful to the staff of the British Library, Imperial War Museum, National Army Museum, and Gurkha Museum. In Delhi, the staff of the Nehru Memorial Library, United Services Institute Library, and National Archives of India provided great assistance. Squadron Leader Rana Chhina of the United Services Institute and Professor K. C. Yadav of the Haryana Academy of History and Culture in Gurgaon were especially helpful and welcoming. I am also very grateful to the staff at the West Bengal State Archives, Maharashtra State Archives, Panjab State Archives, Gurkha Memorial Museum (Pokhara), Tamil Nadu State Archives, and the Uttar Pradesh State Archives, who helped me to better understand the wide geographical impact of the British Indian Army.

The editors, anonymous reviewers, and staff at Stanford University Press, especially Marcela Maxfield, Sunna Juhn, Brian Ostrander, and Sophie Gillespie, have been professional and supportive, providing tremendous guidance in the final stages of this project. I also received thoughtful feedback from reviewers and editors at *Gender & History*, *Twentieth Century British History*, and the *Journal of British Studies* on different incarnations of this work. Some of the research and insights in the sixth chapter have been published by *Gender & History* and the *Journal of British Studies* (Kate Imy, "Queering the Martial Races: Masculinity, Sex and Circumcision in the Twentieth-Century British Indian Army," *Gender and History* 27, No. 2 [August 2015]: 374–96; Kate Imy, "Fascist Yogis: Martial Bodies and Imperial Impotence," *Journal of British Studies* 55, No. 2 [April 2016]: 320–43). Parts of the second chapter are similar to findings in my article in *Twentieth Century British History* (Kate Imy, "Kidnapping and a 'Confirmed Sodomite': An Intimate Enemy on the Northwest Frontier of India, 1915–1925," *Twentieth Century British History*, 28, No. 1 [March 2017]: 29–56). Julie Stephens, Jennifer Mittelstadt, and Jenny Gavacs also gave me immensely helpful advice.

Many excellent Hindi and Urdu language teachers at Rutgers University, the American Institutes of Indian Studies in Jaipur and Lucknow, Language Must, Zabaan Language Institute, King's College London, and the East West Language Institute made it possible for me to utilize Hindi and Urdu sources. I am especially grateful to Nida Sajid, Renu Kumar, Zeba Parveen, Ziyaullah Siddiqui, Prem Singh Rajpurohit, Ahtesham Khan, Mohammad Raza Ali, Pramila Soni, and Shivi Saxena for their patience and expertise. Thank you also to the Critical Language Scholarship program for introducing me to so many remarkable scholars and intellectuals, including those just mentioned and also Adriane Raff-Corwin, Aparna Kumar, and Monika Bhagat-Kennedy.

Several generous colleagues helped me to develop this work at various stages. Courtney Doucette, Sara Black, Christina Chiknas, Danielle Bradley, Jasmin Young, Jen Wilson, Teresa M. Delcorso-Ellmann, and Dawn Ruskai provided invaluable feedback, assistance, and support that kept me going through the hard times. The Rutgers British Studies Center, the Rutgers Department of History, and Carla Yanni, Chris Bischof, Yvette

Florio-Lane, and Hilary Buxton helped me to better understand the nuances and complexities of British imperial history. I am grateful to many faculty, students, staff, and colleagues at the University of North Texas including the College of Liberal Arts and Social Sciences, the Department of History, UNT-International, the Office of Faculty Success, the Food Studies and Borders and Migrations mentoring groups, Harold Tanner, and the Military History Center for helping me to revise and complete this project. Several colleagues, including Nancy Stockdale, Sandra Mendiola Garcia, Rachel Moran, Clark Pomerleau, Marilyn Morris, Jen Wallach, Mike Wise, Talia Weltman-Cisneros, Alicia Re Cruz, and Andy Nelson, created a welcoming environment on campus and provided me with feedback on various chapters. Participants and organizers at various events generously engaged with my work by inspiring thoughtful questions, suggestions, and ongoing discussions. I am especially grateful to the North American Conference on British Studies, the Madison South Asia Conference, the Institute of Historical Research Directors' seminars and History of the Body colloquia, the Modern British Studies (Birmingham) conferences, the Southern Conference of British Studies, the Western Conference of British Studies, Vanessa Rockel, the Delaware Valley British Studies Center, the Rutgers Center for Historical Analysis, the Body in Colonial India colloquium (Goldsmiths), the "Empire, Armistice, Aftermath" (Singapore) conference, and the Western Association of Women Historians.

Most of all I am grateful for the love and support of my family—especially Kenneth, who helped me overcome hurdles both big and small—including the over two years of international travel necessary to complete the research for this work. Thanks also to PBT, Jack, Suzanne, Tom, Tara, Jason, Keith, Taryn, Brenda, David, the Polings, Nick, Megan, Kitty, Aimeé, Nikki, and Chuck. Your love, patience, and willingness to travel helped me survive in the surprisingly perilous world of academia. I am truly honored and grateful to have the support of wonderful friends, family, mentors, and colleagues. I will do my best to repay and emulate your kindness and generosity.

FAITHFUL FIGHTERS

INTRODUCTION

IN 2014, the Royal Pavilion in Brighton invited Sikh Britons to dress in First World War uniforms to commemorate the Pavilion's history as a wartime hospital for Indian soldiers (Figure 1). Wild and enthusiastic crowds—including many British women—chased and fawned over the uniformed men.[1] Celebrating the contributions of South Asians in the First World War has done much to correct the erasure of colonial troops in popular memories of the conflict. After all, there were more South Asian combatants and non-combatants in the First World War than Australian, New Zealander, South African, and Canadian combatants combined. Yet missing from this commemoration was an accurate reflection of the diverse South Asian soldiers who served in the Indian Army. Individuals who traced their heritage to Dogras from the Himalayan foothills, or Rajputs from western India, or Nepali men recruited as "Gurkhas" were noticeably absent. So, too, were any of the diverse Muslim communities whose presence in the colonial army was nearly double that of Sikhs. The desire to remember Indian loyalty and imperial service as unique to Sikhs reflects patterns of religious and military hierarchy that began long before the First World War. *Faithful Fighters* explores the Indian Army's attempts to racialize and militarize South Asian identities to secure the loyalty of its multi-racial, multi-linguistic, and multi-faith Indian Empire. Soldiers, in turn, shaped, rejected, or spread

FIGURE 1 First World War Sikh re-enactors at the Royal Pavilion War Stories Open Day, September 2014. The Royal Pavilion was built as a palace for King George IV but Queen Victoria sold it to the city of Brighton. It became a hospital for soldiers during the First World War. *Source*: Royal Pavilion & Museums, Brighton & Hove. Reprinted with permission.

colonial ideas to find a place for themselves in a world divided by nations and empires.

Faithful Fighters examines the cultural legacies of the British Indian Army from 1900 to 1940, as it fought to expand Britain's empire and combat anti-colonial rebellion in the twentieth century.[2] The first four decades of the century witnessed wars, international migration, and anti-colonial rebellions of unprecedented scale. These destabilized national and imperial borders as well as gender, national, and religious identities. As a result, the army was at the center of debates about rights to bear arms or cross borders, to access food and education, and to claim a religious or political identity. It would help to harden the gendered view of citizenship that emphasized military service and masculinity for self-governance. These became shared ideals across cultures, as many British Christians,

Hindustani Muslims, Punjabi Sikhs, Hindu Rajputs, Pathans, and Nepalis fought together in this colonial institution.[3] This "Indian Army" ranged from 150,000 to 250,000 in peace and swelled to 1.4 million combatants and non-combatants during the First World War. The war compelled soldiers to serve in battlefields as distant as the ports of Singapore, the trenches of France, the swamps of Mesopotamia, and the deserts of Arabia. Their efforts helped Britain to become the largest empire in world history. However, colonial rule blurred the lines between war and peace. Soldiers served as enforcers of colonial expansion in Britain's League of Nations mandates of Iraq, Jordan, and Palestine. They helped to militarize colonial borders near Afghanistan through brutal, expensive, and recurring campaigns. Soldiers also used violence to put down domestic rebellion in India. Each act of violence renegotiated and threatened to destabilize soldiers' devotion to colonial rule. Despite the army's military successes, soldiers wrestled with the mounting internal and external pressures of their service.

A major source of controversy within and outside the army was the recruitment theory of "martial races," which defined some religious, ethnic, and regional identities as inherently "martial."[4] Indian nationalists criticized the policy for fomenting racial and religious tensions and depicting some Indian men as effeminate and un-martial. It also enabled some soldiers to find commonalities with civilians in other occupied places. For example, many of the soldiers who were recruited to fight in Egypt, Afghanistan, and Mesopotamia were Muslim, as colonial perceptions held that such men were naturally militaristic.[5] Some soldiers developed sympathy for the Muslim anti-colonial activists they encountered. As far afield as Southeast Asia and the United States, Hindu and Sikh soldiers and veterans similarly met Indian exiles and revolutionaries who traveled around the globe to spread anti-colonial revolution. As anti-colonial activism intensified in the twentieth century, military officials believed that fusing soldiers' religious traditions with military duty would keep them disciplined and loyal. Imperial investment in soldiers' identities was meant to ensure long-term peace and unity. They hoped that soldiers' devotions to family, community, region, religion, or nation would not contradict or overpower their commitment to their professions.

The army's bureaucratic interventions into soldiers' lives increased in the twentieth century, but British officials had incorporated South Asian soldiers and their identities into military forces for centuries. Competition and warfare between English and French colonial ambitions brought South Asian soldiers into European forces by the eighteenth century.[6] The English East India Company's (EIC's) three distinct armies based in Bengal, Madras, and Bombay helped to protect, expand, and forcibly acquire areas vital to England's economic interests in India. These armies borrowed from existing martial cultures, recruiting patterns, and warrior communities in South Asia. For example, the EIC's Bengal army recruited Muslim and high-caste Hindu soldiers favored by Mughal (1526–1857) leaders. They made Urdu the official language of the Company ranks as it had been in the armies of these Muslim rulers. They also incorporated Nepali soldiers, who had served the Sikh Khalsa Empire (1799–1849), in Panjab.[7] One of the main differences between precolonial and Company service was that soldiers were under the exclusive command of European officers. This hierarchy carried over into the Indian Army and lasted until the First World War. At times, European officers attempted to break soldiers from their precolonial traditions by circulating Christian doctrine in the ranks.[8] Military attacks on Indian beliefs became common in periods of British evangelical fervor.[9] During the First Anglo-Afghan War (1839–42), soldiers traveled long distances without proper provisions, making them susceptible to disease, unsanitary food, and social scorn for breaking caste rules.[10] Indian soldiers had to wear leather chin straps and boots and forgo caste rules on service.[11] By the mid-nineteenth century, the Company imposed even greater restrictions on soldiers' service. The General Service Enlistment Act of 1856 mandated that Indian soldiers serve overseas, which in some communities meant a loss of caste identity.[12] Oversights or deliberate disregard for soldiers' needs led to frequent tension and hostility between soldiers and Company officials at a time when the EIC's hold over Indian territory and resources was growing stronger.

After another resurgence of British evangelical enthusiasm in northern India, a major rebellion broke out in 1857 that would spell disaster for the EIC. An entire regiment mutinied after Company officers arrested soldiers who refused to handle cartridges allegedly greased with pig and cow fat.[13] The Bengal cavalry followed suit soon after, inspiring the remaining infantry and artillerymen to rebel or disband. A large-scale revolt, known in nineteenth-century Britain as the Great Mutiny, spread across northern India from 1857 to 1858.[14] The uprising gained popular support in cities such as Agra and Lucknow, where there had been high-profile public debates between South Asian scholars and Christian missionaries.[15] British officials overlooked soldiers' varied complaints about land seizures, reductions in pay, missionary intervention, and mandates for overseas travel. Instead, they condemned the rebellion as an irrational response to the alleged greasing of cartridges, which invalidated the faith of Muslims and high-caste Hindus. After brutally suppressing the rebels, British officials legitimized their rule in India by claiming that India was composed of unfathomable religious diversity and violence that required a firm imperial hand to manage it. When the power of governing India transferred from the EIC to the British crown in 1858, Queen Victoria declared a policy of religious non-interference. The army, in turn, made some efforts to respect certain beliefs and practices, for example by replacing leather chin straps with pagris or turbans.[16] Promises of religious non-interference did not stop colonial officials from trying to control soldiers' identities to suit military needs.

The post-mutiny armies maintained some, but not all, of the EIC's organizing logic. The 1858 Peel Commission recommended diminishing the presence of high-caste Hindus and diversifying the recruitment of soldiers.[17] They did not aspire for true diversity. Military officials believed that the most loyal men during the "mutiny" of 1857 had been Punjabi Sikhs, Nepali "Gurkhas," and Scottish Highlanders, so they represented these men as the most "manly" and martial to encourage their recruitment.[18] By June 1858, seventy-five thousand of the eighty thousand South Asian troops in the Bengal army were Punjabis.[19] This tendency became institutionalized in the recruiting theory of "martial races."[20] Some believed that by identifying groups most prone to rebellion, they could either win them over or target them for violence to crush anti-colonial resistance. These recruiting strategies affected wider social and cultural debates within and beyond South Asia about racial differences between the "martial" and the "non-martial."[21] Military service became family tradition in some communities. Soldiers often served in the same regiments as their fathers, reinforcing the "inherited" nature of martial prowess.[22]

Imperial categories often struggled to encompass the complexity and fluidity of South Asian identities. Despite the similar regional origins of Sikhs and Punjabi Muslims, for example, British officials believed that their different spiritual convictions made them different "races." While many Nepalese and north Indian soldiers were Hindu, their physical, geographic, and linguistic differences marked their "racial" distinctions. Meanwhile, many communities and military officers emphasized linkages to warfare and martial cultures that predated colonialism, making these identities seem perennial and unchanging. By the late nineteenth century, British officials hoped that widely recruited communities would remain loyal and devoted to imperial rule. The Eden Commission reported in 1879 that the Punjab province was the "home of the most martial races of India" and "the nursery" of the best soldiers.[23] However, assumptions about militancy changed over time according to the needs of army recruiters and the economic conditions of prospective recruits.

The shift toward heavy recruiting in Punjab and the northwest related in part to fears of invasion, as well as British beliefs that the men found there were the most manly and martial. The so-called Great Game of colonial competition with Russia brought recurring campaigns into India's northwestern borderlands. After two Anglo-Afghan Wars (1839–42, 1878–80), the Government of India invested billions of rupees in the construction of railways, roads, and cantonment towns throughout the Punjab province.[24] This inspired the centralization of the military forces in India. By 1895, the old EIC designations of the Bengal, Madras, and Bombay armies were removed and replaced by a single Indian Army headed by a commander-in-chief in charge of four regional commands. The term Indian Army appeared officially by 1903.[25] This name remained in place until the independence and partition of India and Pakistan in 1947. Post-colonial India would retain the title, and much of the organizing framework, of the Indian Army.

In the years before, during, and after the First World War, the Indian Army simultaneously cultivated and challenged the possibility of

Indian national unity in the midst of rising nationalist and anti-colonial activity. *Faithful Fighters* therefore focuses on the *British* Indian Army as it existed in the first four decades of the twentieth century. After 1940, the colonial army was all but unrecognizable. That year, the army allowed Indian officers to command British soldiers—a severe blow to the inflexible racial hierarchy that had existed since the eighteenth century. During the Second World War, India's military forces swelled to 2.4 million people. Some of these soldiers abandoned the ranks and joined the anti-colonial Indian National Army. The period before the Second World War, therefore, is especially deserving of consideration because it reveals the army's vulnerabilities, as well as its influence in wider discussions about militancy and political change in South Asia. Soldiers' and civilians' experiences with and exposure to militarization were gradual and changed over time. Military cultures did not emerge fully formed at the outbreak of war in 1914 or 1939, or at the moment of independence and partition in 1947. Rather, in the period marked by the dissolution of the old regional armies in 1895 and the creation of the anti-colonial Indian National Army in 1942, the Indian Army was the primary site of debate and contention about what it meant to be a martial Indian man. In times of both war and "peace," the army contributed to mass militarization, influencing strategies of violent and non-violent resistance to, as well as collaboration with, colonial rule.

Faithful Fighters stands out from recent scholarly work on the Indian Army by considering not only how the army influenced Britain's and South Asia's ability to wage war but also how the army shaped colonial society in times of "peace." Cultures of the body and militant masculinity, for example, were formative in both the army and Indian nationalist movements. "Muscular Christianity" was an arm of British nationalism that emphasized the physical strength and endurance of British missionaries and soldiers who traversed the globe in the service of imperial Christianity. It was matched by "muscular Hinduism" in India, which supported cricket, football, and de-sexualized forms of yoga to develop Indian bodies to fight for the national project.[26] These trends demonstrate that intense cultural fluidity could exist between "colonizer" and "colonized." Yet proponents of muscular Hinduism also used these cultures to criticize imperial rule. Many English-educated Bengali politicians and intellectuals blamed colonization for creating physical decline and effeminacy, making Bengalis ineligible for military recruitment. They encouraged men to develop strong bodies to combat "degeneration" and undermine the accusation that they were too "effeminate" to rule India.[27] While both Indian nationalists and the army glorified strong martial bodies, they disagreed about what Indian men should fight to achieve.[28]

Focusing on military culture reveals how spiritual and political concerns were inseparably entwined, especially as anti-colonial politics and global war collided in the twentieth century. In 1905, British officials divided the Bengal province to streamline government bureaucracy. This gave greater political opportunities to the Muslim minority population who held numerous positions in the army.[29] Anti-colonial and nationalist actors interpreted this as an effort to undermine high-caste Hindus, who dominated the Indian National Congress (established 1885). This inspired division between extremists and moderates in the Congress and a sharp rise in militant anti-colonial activism. Following a famine in 1907, some anti-colonial campaigners journeyed to the agriculturally rich Punjab province, which served as the primary recruiting ground for Sikhs and Muslims, to inspire soldiers to mutiny. These political alliances frequently brought together Hindus, Muslims, and Sikhs who shared criticisms of British governance in India. The Government of India responded by moving India's capital to Delhi in 1912 to place greater political control in areas of military significance.[30] The First World War intensified these political and military tensions by sending South Asian soldiers to fight in every major field of battle—from Singapore to France, Mesopotamia to northwestern India, and from Arabia to East Africa. Racial hierarchies led British officials to worry about permitting Indian troops to fight in Europe and kill Europeans. Some Muslim soldiers were anxious about fighting against Muslim subjects of the Ottoman Empire or in Muslim holy lands. Many Punjabi Sikh veterans supported the international Ghadar (mutiny) movement to stir revolution in the army. During the war anti-colonial activists were optimistic that soldiers would join whole-heartedly in the anti-colonial struggle, in part by using the appeal of religious revolt.

By 1919, perceptions of the army's potential for anti-colonial collaboration changed dramatically when General Reginald Dyer commanded Indian troops to open fire against a demonstration in Amritsar, the holy city of the Sikhs in Punjab.[31] Widely regarded as the event that brought new vitality to Indian anti-colonial activism led by Mohandas Gandhi, the Amritsar massacre was also a brutal declaration that soldiers would remain loyal to the empire no matter their grievances. General Dyer's use of South Asian troops was intended to underline the divide between civilian anti-colonial rebellion and the loyal imperial army. The 1919 Anglo-Afghan War and rebellion in Waziristan (1919–20), meanwhile, undermined international anti-colonial activism with brutal campaigns along the Afghan border.[32] Amid these challenges, the Indian Army gradually desegregated its officer corps in a process known as "Indianization" in the 1920s and 1930s. This created further divisions by placing greater demands for loyalty on recruited men without reconciling the long-held religious hierarchies of the "martial races." As anti-colonial leaders like Mohandas Gandhi and the Ali brothers used religious imagery to challenge imperialism, the army's emphasis on "martial races" proved unstable. Military service inadvertently encouraged soldiers to see similarities with pan-Islamic, Hindu nationalist, and reformist Sikh activists who criticized and challenged imperial rule. As anti-colonial activism intensified, the army became more defensive in claiming the right to control soldiers' beliefs.

Faithful Fighters is the first study to interrogate how soldiers actually experienced and responded to British efforts to categorize and control their identities.[33] Several excellent scholarly works have highlighted the importance of the Indian Army in the global wars of the twentieth century.[34] Some have used post-colonial theory to interrogate soldiers' experiences of both world wars and the inadequacy of imperial record-keeping to capture soldiers' perspectives.[35] Others have questioned the racial and class hierarchies of military histories of the twentieth century by highlighting South Asian women, laborers, and low-caste sweepers who shaped the war effort.[36] Scholars have also transcribed soldiers' letters, explored the hybridity of British and South Asian military institutions, examined literary representations of soldiers' service, and tracked

Hindu ethics of warfare over centuries.[37] *Faithful Fighters* foregrounds soldiers' and civilians' experiences with militancy across categories of religious difference to understand how colonial rule and military service affected their identities in both war and peace. Some Sikh soldiers, for example, embraced army categories to gain employment and perform precolonial heritage through access to swords, known as *kirpans*. Certain Hindu men rejected British categories but also emulated the "martial races" to demonstrate their own military prowess. Focusing on the period before, during, and after the First World War illuminates these connections between military culture and colonial society. Soldiers participated in and shaped anti-colonial debates about bearing arms, accessing education, and crossing geopolitical borders. Anti-colonial rhetoric about food security, precolonial heritage, and religious purity, meanwhile, infiltrated military ranks. During this period, soldiers' imperial employment gave them the unique—and contentious—position of being desirable allies of both colonial and anti-colonial actors. Many of the ideas that underpinned army recruitment—including rigid codes of masculinity and hierarchies of religious difference—collapsed or were re-entrenched in the face of anti-colonial challenges. The fusion of religious identity with military prowess influenced soldiers and civilians from Hindu nationalist yogis to Muslim soldiers contemplating pan-Islamic activism. The idea of "religious warfare" was both encouraged by soldiers "from below" and used by nationalist, imperial, and community leaders to claim how, why, and when soldiers fought. *Faithful Fighters* tells the story of soldiers' battles between these contending forces and within themselves.

Taking a social and cultural approach to a colonial army in war and peace suggests that soldiers struggled to balance their multiple loyalties to family, community, nation, and empire. They needed to be "faithful" to many, often conflicting, devotions. Colonial officials, however, tended to read soldiers' political and social demands as religious complaints or antagonisms. Many scholars have rightly suggested that colonial rule hardened religious categories by legally defining caste, recruiting soldiers as "martial races," creating comparative studies of religion, and confiscating property based on European understandings of property rights. Casting "Hinduism," "Sikhism," and Islam as "religions" applied European, monotheistic frameworks to diverse beliefs and practices to make them legible to imperial bureaucracy.[38] These structures continued to influence some scholarly assumptions and popular discussions about the role of caste and "communal antagonism" in India during and after the colonial period. Imperial institutions such as the Indian Army spread the idea that religious difference was an insurmountable division within South Asian society and hardened these identities through bureaucratic categories.[39] Yet the colonial state's capacity to define identities exceeded its ability to actually control them. Soldiers simultaneously internalized and challenged colonial and anti-colonial demands for devotion.

It is important to "think with" and analyze the category of religion when discussing colonial institutions such as the Indian Army because twentieth-century soldiers lived and worked within the parameters set by their imperial service. Soldiers understood that casting their grievances as "religious" would earn them a more sympathetic—or at least responsive— ear from the colonial state. British officials, meanwhile, believed that they accommodated soldiers' "religious prejudices" by facilitating acts such as the fast of Ramzan (Ramadan) for Muslim soldiers and mandating purification ceremonies for Nepali "Gurkhas." What they actually did was respond to a wide variety of issues—including food shortages, labor contracts, anti-colonial violence, changing borders, education, and healthy recreation—that blurred the lines between secular and sacred, soldier and civilian. The story of the Indian Army was not about British officials tirelessly scrambling to accommodate religious diversity to prevent another 1857 rebellion. Rather, the army attempted to set the acceptable parameters of religion. This included defining which rites, rituals, beliefs, and practices could be incorporated into the army and which could not. The unintended consequence was facilitating interfaith discourse between British and South Asian men that both reinforced and challenged the religious and racial hierarchies of imperial rule.

Exploring military rituals reveals the complexity of soldiers' motivations for living, serving, and dying in the service of empire. The army attempted to discipline and train the loyal soldier by blending religious and military practice. Yet forging military identities meant making quick decisions about inclusion and exclusion: What was an irrational prejudice and what was a disciplined orthodoxy? Which beliefs and practices could be useful to build a loyal army and which were most likely to tear it apart? The army's efforts to control, regulate, and define soldiers' beliefs consistently wrestled with the rapid political, economic, and cultural transformations of the era. Soldiers used and manipulated national and imperial loyalties to suit their individual, community, and family needs, envisioning their own futures within and beyond colonialism. These affected wider debates about martial masculinity, racial regeneration, and religious unity in South Asia. Military leaders wanted to prevent soldiers from seeking allies among Indian politicians and activists who might better address their spiritual and secular needs. The threat of anti-colonial collaboration, however, gave soldiers powers and privileges not bestowed on Britain's non-military subjects in India. Imperial officials believed that military culture could overcome religious and racial difference and forge loyalty. Soldiers and civilians, in turn, embraced the army's religious militarism to create alternative, and sometimes anti-colonial, martial cultures. In many ways, widely recruited men could be the most threatening to military order.

The following six chapters identify and analyze army attempts to create stability in the army by controlling soldiers' identities before, during, and after the First World War. The first three chapters deal with Sikhs, Muslims, and Nepali "Gurkhas" who held the nominally privileged status of "martial races." Heavy recruitment gave them access to land, upward mobility, regular pay, as well as the opportunity to honor their beliefs and demonstrate their masculine prowess through military service. It also made them subject to traumatic wars and threats of political and social isolation. The last three chapters consider the simultaneous breakdown of "martial race" recruiting practices and the infiltration of military identities into British and South Asian society. This resulted in the further racialization of religion in conversations about access to food, education, and political representation across categories of religious difference.[40] Despite the army's attempts to isolate soldiers from colonial society, colonial society often emulated and shaped the army.

Chapter One considers a primary point of tension for South Asian soldiers—taking up arms and committing acts of violence to support imperial goals while challenging forms of militarism not sanctioned by the colonial state. This was especially true for Sikh soldiers, who carried a disproportionate burden to commit acts of violence due to their heavy recruitment. The colonial trope of the "loyal Sikh" meshed uncomfortably with soldiers' own desires to wear and carry *kirpans*. These swords or daggers were both religious objects and potentially threatening weapons. The contradictions of Sikh service were illuminated when the Indian Army used an excessive display of force near the Golden Temple of Amritsar during a Sikh holiday. In its aftermath, soldiers and civilians considered how to reclaim Sikh militarism to agitate for rights, privileges, and liberation from both colonial and nationalist leaders.

The slippage between loyalty and rebellion was also contentious for the diverse Muslim soldiers who fought in wars on behalf of Britain and the empire in Muslim-majority territories. Chapter Two examines how South Asian soldiers took part in the Third Anglo-Afghan War (1919), the rebellion in Waziristan (1919–20), and the dismantling of the Ottoman Empire during and after the First World War. Some soldiers rebelled by joining the pan-Islamic Khilafat movement. Others journeyed to Muslim-majority lands as part of military-funded pilgrimages to Mecca. There they served as both soldiers and de facto ambassadors and informers. South Asian Muslims faced few avenues for interwar peace and security. Those who lived on or near militarized borders faced even greater challenges of constant violence and political uncertainty. Many deepened their contract of loyalty with the imperial state to stake a claim for the future of their faith, at times interpreting pan-Islam as a pro-British identity.

Soldiers' connections to foreign powers sometimes could be sources of strength rather than weakness. Chapter Three follows the army's attempts to recruit soldiers known as "Gurkhas" from the nominally independent nation of Nepal. Nepalese soldiers enjoyed a distinctive reputation for being resistant to the Indian caste system and Indian anti-colonialism. However, their recruitment forced the colonial state to respond to Nepali concerns about soldiers who crossed the *kala pani*—or black waters of the ocean—for military service. Military officials viewed this as a "religious" objection and implemented a mandatory purification ceremony for Nepali soldiers before and during the First World War. Although there were many Indian Hindus in the army, the ceremony only applied to Nepalese troops. Their example demonstrates how caste rules could solidify, rather than undermine, soldiers' worth.

The introduction of a purification ceremony into military practice did not mean that British officials had a positive view of caste in the army. In fact, officers were often hostile to the caste rules observed by some Indian soldiers. Chapter Four explores the complex relationship between food and the military. Memories and tales of the 1857 rebellion convinced many twentieth-century British officials that caste threatened army stability. They made decisions about rations that both adapted to soldiers' perceived "religious" needs but also encouraged soldiers to give these things up to build strong bodies to serve the empire. Nonetheless, agricultural turmoil and famine were recurring features of South Asian life, affecting soldiers' view of military service and food. South Asian soldiers often borrowed from Mughal and Rajput ideas to express that they had eaten "the government's salt" and needed to stay loyal to it. Indian anticolonial activists, by contrast, made food a centerpiece of rebellion—made famous by Gandhi's periodic fasting and 1930 salt march. The army often used food to demarcate who was, and was not, entitled to eat the salt of the government.

Between the world wars, military officials emphasized differences between soldiers and civilians to fortify bonds with recruited men. The fifth chapter tracks how Indian military colleges and academies in the 1920s and 1930s solidified military culture by reforming army attitudes about education. Earlier army officials worried that education threatened soldiers' masculinity and martial prowess. Between the wars, officials hoped that loyalty could be learned. These enclosed spaces promised to facilitate racial as well as religious integration during the "Indianization" of the Indian Army. However, they isolated future Indian officers from the civilian population in a period of intense anti-colonial activism. Military education encouraged soldiers to see themselves as cosmopolitan leaders of an interfaith, commonwealth army and the rightful leaders of India. At times, these institutions went further by rewarding them for embracing British colonial and Christian values. As a result, many struggled to belong in either the empire or the nation.

Military education and indoctrination did not prevent soldiers from seeing validity in anti-colonial critiques. Instead, it idealized violent masculinity and religious militarism. Chapter Six reveals the unanticipated political consequences of military desegregation. Military cantonments in the 1930s had a tantalizing illusion of racial, class, and religious inclusivity. They facilitated intimate contact between British, Sikh, and Muslim men who sometimes shared political assumptions about the dangers of Indian nationalism. Military men vocally criticized colonial officials for failing to have the same disciplined control of Indian civilians that the Indian Army appeared to have over its soldiers. Some Hindu, Muslim, and Sikh soldiers and civilians shared common beliefs about the importance of martial prowess to forge a political identity. On the eve of the Second World War, some officers and soldiers found fascism more in line with their experiences of imperial military life than the city-based civilian governments dominating British and Indian politics in the 1930s. These men celebrated racial and religious hierarchies and political violence in ways that resonated in India in unexpected and tragic ways.

The army's adoption, incorporation, and modification of religious identities was never just about meeting soldiers' needs to prevent rebellion. Most colonial officials believed that stabilizing identities within the military would eradicate the tensions of religious and racial difference, creating a perfectly ordered imperial state. Soldiers, in turn, navigated changing imperial policies and shifting anti-colonial strategies to cope with—and extract privileges from—the conflicting agendas of imperialism and nationalism. At times they envisioned alternative post-colonial futures. The army hoped that creating unity in the army would secure the empire. Few anticipated that a strong army would militarize colonial society and hasten imperial decline.

CHAPTER 1

SPIRITUAL SWORDS AND
MARTIAL VIOLENCE

IN THE EARLY TWENTIETH CENTURY many Britons believed that Sikh men were the living embodiment of perfect soldiers. Major A. E. Barstow of the 2nd Battalion, 11th Sikh Regiment wrote in the 1920s that each Sikh was inherently "a fighting man" who could be counted as "the bravest and steadiest of soldiers." They were, in his view, "more faithful, more trustworthy" than other widely recruited communities known to the British as "martial races."[1] Another British soldier remembered that "the Sikhs were better than the others" because they were "more loyal."[2] British perceptions of inherent Sikh loyalty and superiority influenced wider debates about recruitment and martial prowess across religious communities in India. Creating the image of the loyal Sikh soldier idealized—and set up unrealistic expectations for—all soldiers. Both Sikhs and non-Sikhs struggled to live up to this effusive praise. Instead, British efforts to define Sikhs as both a religious community and a naturally loyal band of warriors inspired anti-colonial soldiers and civilians to challenge such paternalistic definitions of Sikh identity. Sikh soldiers' experiences of service, meanwhile, suggest that there were several unintended consequences of exalting a single community as inherently martial. In many ways, the imperial exaltation of Sikhs was the keystone of conflict in the twentieth-century Indian Army.

Twentieth-century British soldiers and officers had great confidence in Sikh soldiers because they believed that Sikhs had served in the Indian

Army consistently and loyally since the days of the 1857 uprising. This rebellion had started as a mutiny in the East India Company's Bengal Army and broke out into a wide-scale revolt across northern India. Its brutal suppression by British and Company forces resulted in the transfer of Indian territories to the British crown in 1858. Britain's victory would have been impossible without the contributions of soldiers from Punjab, Nepal, and the northwestern borders—including many Sikhs—who joined the British in putting down the rebellion. Twentieth-century military pamphlets claimed that devotion to the British made "the Sikhs as a body . . . loyal" in 1857.[3] These accounts of unwavering loyalty encouraged Sikhs to become the most disproportionately recruited soldiers in British imperial service. They made up 20% of soldiers despite being less than 1% of the population of India. As a result, they became the most paradigmatic "martial race" that British officials exalted as naturally loyal and "racially" fit to fight.

Sikhs' disproportionate recruitment reveals larger tensions within imperial employment. Scholars have rightly pointed out that exalting Sikhs was part of a grander imperial effort to "divide and conquer" India by fomenting dissent internally. Praising a minority community like Sikhs, according to this view, created both bitterness and aspirational jealousy among those not recruited as "martial races." Yet imperial rule was rarely stable or unquestioned, even by those exalted as the most loyal. This was no more evident than in the twentieth century, when anti-colonial rebellion and reformist activism rose sharply within and outside the army. British attempts to define and promote the image of the loyal Sikh reflected colonial fears of losing control of soldiers. In many ways, Sikhs' service in the Indian Army gave them the weapons to rebel.

DEFINING SIKHS, CREATING REBELS

Despite some British soldiers' assertions, there was no single definition of what Sikhs looked like, how they behaved, or what they believed. Regional and familial ties, alongside differences in class and employment, resulted in a plurality of Sikh identities.[4] Even Indian Army recruiting manuals acknowledged initially that not all Sikhs made ideal soldiers. The *Army Handbook for Sikhs*, published in 1899, identified class, caste, and regional differences that affected a soldier's martial potential. It maintained that agricultural Sikh Jats from northwestern India had the physical strength and indifference to Brahman dietary custom to be perfect soldiers. By contrast, it portrayed urban Sikh Khatris as reluctant farmers and Sikh Mazbhis as low-caste criminals.[5] The army attempted to overcome these differences by encouraging strict definitions of Sikh identity to transcend regional and caste differences and create the perfect soldier.

Civil servant Max Macauliffe, an "orientalist" scholar, greatly influenced army praxis through translations of Sikh texts and lectures to civil and military authorities. He claimed in 1903 that Sikh beliefs were a "comprehensive ethical code" that were valuable to the army because they inculcated "loyalty, gratitude for all favors received, philanthropy, justice, impartiality, truth, honesty, and all the moral and domestic virtues known to the holiest Christians."[6] Commander-in-Chief of the Indian Army, Lord Kitchener (1902–9), wanted Macauliffe's work translated into the "the ordinary Punjabi of the day" so that it could be disseminated "through every Sikh household in the country."[7] Although Kitchener and Macauliffe believed that Sikhs were naturally loyal, it was important to spread imperial interpretations of Sikh belief and practice to keep them that way. Kitchener was confident that Macauliffe's pro-empire accounts of Sikh heritage would stimulate Sikh recruitment by making Sikh men feel proud about military careers. He also praised the army's so-called class regiment system for isolating Sikhs from other communities in their own companies and battalions. This policy, in his view, allowed Sikhs to "keep up the purity of their religion" as was done in the nominally independent Sikh princely states of Nabha and Patiala.[8] This really meant that soldiers had to police their own behavior and identities—and that of their fellow soldiers—to gain a position and remain in the army. This military-sanctioned view of Sikh "purity" was an attempt to codify "Sikhism" as compatible with military service.

Controlling narratives of precolonial Sikh heritage was an important element of defining Sikh identity for the army. Many South Asian soldiers and cantonment workers emphasized lineages of military participation that predated 1857. For example, in 1919, Jam-Hat Singh knew that his family's military heritage preceded his grandfather's participation in the siege of Delhi in 1857.[9] He bragged to a British soldier that in 1750 his ancestors joined the Khalsa (elect) Sikh warrior fraternity, originally founded in 1699 by Guru Gobind Singh.[10] Emphasizing both 1857 and the Khalsa allowed Jam-Hat Singh to honor his family's precolonial and colonial military heritage simultaneously. Few Sikh soldiers understood their service to Britain as a clear choice between remaining "loyal" or "disloyal" to an unbroken history of imperial devotion. The Sikh Khalsa predated British presence in Punjab. It had gained political cohesiveness under Ranjit Singh and grew into an independent empire in the eighteenth and nineteenth centuries before falling to the East India Company in 1849.[11] Many soldiers joined British service in 1857 due to limited post-conquest financial opportunities, rather than inherent loyalty. Sikh heritage, therefore, both served and combatted British power. As anti-colonial activism took new forms in the twentieth century, Sikhs had to make choices about which loyalties to honor. Some Sikhs emphasized their devotion to the British after 1857 to gain greater concessions from the imperial state. Others hoped to revive Khalsa rule and the memory of the Anglo-Sikh Wars (1845–46; 1848–49) to campaign against colonialism.

Indian Army officers worked hard to demonstrate the continuity between British rule and the Khalsa. The Khalsa had marked its adherents by encouraging them wear the so-called 5 Ks. These included uncut hair (*kes*), comb (*kanga*), steel bracelet (*kara*), a short undergarment (*kachha*), and carrying a *kirpan*—sometimes defined as a sword or dagger. Of course, not all Sikhs were members of the Khalsa. Many professed Sikhs wore no external markers at all; many even cut their hair. Imperial admiration for the defeated soldiers of the Khasla Empire, however, meant that they were the "true" Sikhs in British eyes. One twentieth-century former regimental recruiting officer admitted that when young recruits claimed to be Sikhs but did not wear the five external markers of identity, they "were subsequently put through a course of instruction" and given initiation rites into the Khalsa warrior fraternity.[12] Sikh identity predated the formation of the Khalsa but British officials considered Khalsa Sikhs the most "pure." Military service, therefore, propagated Khalsa identity.

The army's investment in solidifying religious and military identities related in part to the contested state of the Punjab province. The frequency of droughts, plagues, and famines in Punjab early in the century compelled many peasants to join military service for subsistence. Regional hardships also attracted Christian missionaries who attempted to "uplift" Punjabis through material comfort and spiritual conversion but alienated and emboldened Indian reformist campaigns. For example, the Arya Samaj, formed in 1875, tried to counter missionary influence by reaching out to low caste and poor Hindus and Sikhs who felt socially and economically isolated by Brahmans.[13] Many Samajis joined imperial service and criticized Sikhs and Muslims for departing from "Indian" traditions.[14] Sikh reformers protested against the Arya Samaj by insisting that Sikh traditions, including the Khalsa, were distinctly Punjabi and Indian.[15] Organizations such as the Singh Sabhas (Sikh Societies) opened 121 branches in Punjab by 1899 and promoted Sikh culture and history to counter the threat of religious conversion.[16] The Tat (True) Khalsa, founded in 1899, emphasized the five markers of Khalsa identity.[17] The army's own efforts to emphasize the Khalsa and the 5 Ks made Sikh reformist efforts compatible with army culture. The terms "Khalsa" and "Sikh" became nearly interchangeable, which had not been true in the precolonial era.[18] Civilian debates both influenced and were influenced by the army's own efforts to fortify a loyal Sikh identity.

Encouragement of "pure" Sikh beliefs resulted in a spike in Sikh recruitment. Sikhs comprised 18% of the army in 1893 and between 20 and 30% by the First World War.[19] Lieutenant Governor of the Punjab, Sir Michael O'Dwyer, maintained that this was because Sikh soldiers fought for the sheer love of fighting.[20] Yet there was a complex pattern of social engineering at play, as demonstrated by Sir James Douie's *Provincial Geographies of India*. According to Douie, the Sikh population in India increased 37% in the first decade of the twentieth century despite widespread deaths from plagues and famines in Punjab during that period. This dramatic increase was also noteworthy because many Sikhs continued to be classified as Hindus on censuses because they did not wear the 5 Ks.[21] Some responded by adopting these markers to fit colonial categories and gain employment.[22] Douie predicted that "The future of Sikhism" was with those who claimed Khalsa identity.[23] Macauliffe and Kitchener's attempts to spread Sikh beliefs to every Punjabi household no doubt instilled many Punjabis with the sense that being visibly detectable as a Sikh could not only strengthen community bonds but also produce tangible economic and political opportunities.

Writing in 1911, Assistant Director of Criminal Intelligence David Petrie noted the peculiar situation resulting from British encouragement of Khalsa Sikh identity:

> The British Government, more particularly the Military administration, has put itself into a queer position as regards the Sikhs, who have been fostered and patted and taught to regard themselves as a great nation with great national traditions. This glorification of the Sikhs has been productive of curious results, because, while it has kept the banner of Sikhism flying to the great advantage of Government, it now appears to be likely to be used as an instrument to scourge us by a section of those for whose good it was primarily undertaken.[24]

There were, as Petrie recognized, indications that some Sikhs might use martial identity to challenge, rather than support, British power. In fact, fifty years after the uprising of 1857, Sikh soldiers were on the front lines of a potential rebellion. After the division of the Bengal province in 1905, the Raj deported many Indian politicians and activists perceived to be challenges to imperial rule. Many reached out to soldiers and veterans settled or stationed around the world. They found receptive ears in Punjab due to the prevalence of plague and famine. Punjabi Sikh leader Ajit Singh gained many followers from military families in agricultural protests in 1907 and 1908. The most turbulent resistance centered on Manjha region—the army's main recruiting ground for Jat Sikhs.[25]

Fears of military rebellion in Punjab inspired British officials to amplify their surveillance, which revealed recurring incidents of Sikh discontent.[26] According to one report, Lakha Singh, a Reservist sepoy of the 47th Sikhs, preached reformist ideas in the Sialkot Cantonment in 1907. Military officials suspected his association with a "school of new Sikhism," which took inspiration from the Singh Sabhas and Arya Samaj.[27] The superintendent of police in Bannu reported in May 1907 that Sikh sepoys attended Arya Samaj meetings and openly expressed their disdain for the government.[28] The regimental *granthi*, or Sikh scholar, of the 19th Punjabis,

Kirpal Singh, was recalled from leave when the rumor surfaced that he visited an Arya Mandir (Arya temple).[29] In 1907, two Indian soldiers and Arya Samaj members allegedly attempted to incite men of the 45th Sikhs at Peshawar against the government.[30] Facing fears of another 1857-level revolt, British officials believed that arresting Arya Samaj leader Lajpat Rai and Jat Sikh activist Ajit Singh would help quell discontent. Instead, it intensified Sikh agitation and hostility.[31] A meeting of Sikh *zamindars* (landowners) in Lyallpur urged men to contact their families in the army, start petitions for the release of Lajpat Rai, and give their European officers "trouble" until their demands were met.[32] The entwined activism of the Arya Samaj and Sikh reformers confused imperial narratives of unwavering loyalty and religious difference. Petrie worried in 1911 that Sikhs and Hindus continued to find great commonality. The only noteworthy difference between them, he believed, was Sikhs' refusal to use tobacco and their tendency to wear five markers of the Khalsa.[33] British recruiters were even more determined that the 5 Ks could distinguish the ideal Sikh recruit from the disloyal Arya Samaji.

Prewar anti-colonial activism in Punjab hints at why imperial officials like Kitchener and Macauliffe were so steadfast in their efforts to define Sikh identity. Military officers were certain that they could identify and segregate Sikhs from the rising tide of anti-colonial activism. They were shocked to find that Sikh soldiers were receptive to and makers of anti-colonial arguments. "Pure" Sikhs, to the British, marked themselves as members of the Khalsa to show their difference from Indian Hindus. "Impure" Sikhs, according to the imperial state, were liable to cultural fluidity and disloyalty. Sikh reformers participated in hardening Sikh identity to defend against religious conversion, social isolation, and economic inequality.[34] Sikh soldiers had to contemplate carefully whether their futures were most secure with the army, with the agricultural protests of the Punjab, or in reforming the Sikh community.

THE SIZE OF THE SWORD

No object embodied the tensions between rebellion and loyalty more than the *kirpan*. These swords or daggers were worn by men initiated into the Khalsa military fraternity. As one of the 5 Ks, *kirpans* helped military recruiters distinguish "pure" from "impure" Sikhs. Like Nepali soldiers' possession of curved blades known as *khukris*, *kirpans* were central to army life and culture.[35] Yet during a period of rising anti-colonial sentiment and uncertain Sikh devotion, colonial officials could not overlook that *kirpans* were material objects that could be used to inflict violence. While some men exalted *kirpans* as symbols of Sikh heritage, they also became tools of militant masculinity.[36] In fact, some Indian soldiers serving in China praised the use of swords by the Chinese Boxers during the Boxer rebellion (1899–1901).[37] Indian pan-Asian activists similarly glorified samurai swords during the Russo-Japanese War (1904–5). Swords, therefore, had wide cultural and political capital as anti-colonial weapons. Imperial attempts to define Sikh soldiers as the perfect "martial race" through *kirpans* encouraged expressions of militarism outside of colonial control.

British encouragement of the Khalsa 5 Ks created an interesting paradox: most South Asians were barred from bearing arms yet carrying them was a prerequisite of Sikh recruitment. The Indian Arms Act of 1878 had banned the possession of arms by those without a government license. In practice this disqualified many South Asian men and women from owning or carrying arms.[38] Bengali men famously fought to arm themselves with rifles claiming that an inability to do so was emasculating.[39] An editor of *Mahratta* echoed these views when condemning government restrictions on *kirpans*. He argued, "The right of bearing arms is the essence of freedom." Being denied weapons meant that "India has been emasculated—emasculated in every sense of the term."[40] Civilians resented that only soldiers and veterans recruited from the "martial races" had regular access to weapons. This, they believed, deepened the religious and racial hierarchy of colonial violence. Yet military officials relied on *kirpans* to tell Sikhs apart from Punjabi Hindus in the Arya Samaj. The army subjected its recruits to a military version of the *pahul* ceremony that initiated Sikhs into the Khalsa. Recruits had to drink sugar and water mixed with a *kirpan* from a common vessel in front of "five believers." Consuming this concoction, known as *amrit*, enabled Sikh men to prove their difference from Hindus and their independence from the caste system.[41] If a Sikh man did not adopt the customs of the Khalsa, then he would be ineligible for imperial service.

Unsurprisingly, the visibility and size of *kirpans* grew more ostentatious as anti-colonial activism intensified. In 1910, Sikhs circulated imagery that glorified the sword of Khalsa founder Gobind Singh. Broadsheets celebrated the use of the sword, Gobind Singh's teachings, and valor on the battlefield. One Sikh officer suspected that these offered a "historical remedy for bad times."[42] Another Amritsar man encouraged Sikhs to take up the sword to restore the glory of the Khalsa.[43] Fearing implicit threats, British officials cracked down on *kirpan* manufacture. They were surprised to find that Sikhs were not distributing these weapons on their own. In 1912, one deputy commissioner observed nervously that a Muslim at Bhera was manufacturing ornamental daggers claiming that they were *kirpans*. The commissioner worried that "These daggers appear to be used by Sikhs in religious ceremonies but any one whether Sikh or Musalman can obtain them."[44] British officials assumed that Sikhs would be inherently anti-Muslim because the rise of the Khalsa occurred in part as a struggle against the Mughal Empire. Imperial understandings of community difference did not recognize that, despite isolated incidents of violence, Sikh and Muslim communities had coexisted and collaborated in Punjab since the rise of the Khalsa.[45] The manufacture of *kirpans* by Muslims was an inconvenient reminder of that fact.

In reality, inter-community regional solidarities intensified due to shared hardships in Punjab. A special branch report from June 1907 noted anxiously that two Sikh sepoys visited a mosque in Kissa Khani Bazar, Peshawar. Once there they allegedly urged Muslims to convince the Amir of Afghanistan to send forces from Kabul against the British.[46] Around the same time, a "seditious leaflet" addressed to Indian soldiers appeared in the Dayanand Anglo Vedic and Islamia Colleges of Lahore. It called for "Sikhs and Pathans" to rise up, declaring, "You were once lions and have now become jackals," because their "motherland" had "hopelessly fallen into the hands of the enemy."[47] The manufacture of *kirpans* by Muslims reflected a trend of inter-communal solidarity. It embarrassed colonial officials that *kirpans* passed from Muslim to Sikh hands, making it Muslim neighbors and colleagues, rather than British authorities, who handed Sikhs their exceptional access to spiritual swords.[48] Military officials relied on the 5 Ks and the class regiment system to keep Sikhs "pure." Yet one of the 5 Ks was giving Sikhs the opportunity to build regional and political connections with other communities.

Colonial anxiety about *kirpans* revealed that the size of these devotional objects often mirrored Sikh power. Images in British military handbooks depicted eighteenth-century Khalsa Sikhs carrying long swords.[49] After the annexation of Punjab in the mid-nineteenth century, *kirpans* shrank in size from long swords to ornamental miniatures "1 or 2 inches in length."[50] *Kirpans* only grew slightly to around "2 or 3 inches in length" once Sikh soldiers became more widely recruited in the Indian Army. They still were worn "in miniature" on men's pagris or turbans in the early twentieth century.[51] Sikh scholar and activist Teja Singh condemned this trend, arguing that *kirpans* were meant to be "an active symbol, an instrument of offence and defence, and not a charm to be tied along with the turban-ends or stowed away in the back of the comb as it came to be done in the British days."[52] His emphasis on a comb and charm portrayed the *kirpan* as an object that had been effeminized and trivialized under the British. By contrast, he believed that *kirpans* were weapons that should "cut through armour . . . through men, horses, even elephants."[53] British disrespect for *kirpans*, he argued, began during the conquest of Panjab in the 1840s. Defeated soldiers, by his account, had to "pile their arms" at the feet of a British officer. Each soldier "came forward and, embracing his sword, uttered a groan, deep and long, and placed it on the pile in tears."[54] The *kirpan* became a symbol of the trauma of conquest and the loss of martial prowess. Service to the British, by extension, was about humiliation and defeat rather than martial continuity and inherent loyalty. Sikhs had frequent reminders of this fact; miniatures were even handed out as souvenirs at the Golden Temple of Amritsar, which was managed by a government-appointed official.[55] For both British officials and Sikh scholars, the size of the *kirpan* was directly tied to Sikh power. When the Khalsa was an independent empire, their swords were long and powerful; once Sikhs came under British rule, *kirpans* became miniatures.

The colonial celebration of Sikh masculinity chafed uncomfortably against Sikh men's desires to revive the practice of carrying large *kirpans* publicly. In response to British inquiries, the Chief Khalsa Diwan (Chief Khalsa Council), a major lobby for Sikh activism, found *kirpans* permissible if they were less than 12 inches in length.[56] Following this unofficial definition, police arrested one man in Amritsar for wearing a large *kirpan* in 1913. A riot ensued. Several Sikh organizations drafted official statements protesting "any limitation of the size of the emblems."[57] They referenced Queen Victoria's 1858 proclamation of religious non-interference and the importance of the *kirpan* for the Khalsa initiation ceremony. They attempted to define the debate as a "religious" issue to invalidate government intervention.[58] Deputy Commissioner King of Amritsar worried that "the possession of these weapons by Sikhs, especially those belonging to the forward party, is becoming increasingly common."[59] The "martial Sikh" was as contested as ever.

Protests about limiting the size of *kirpans* increased tensions between British officials and Sikh leaders. The honorary secretary of the Chief Khalsa Diwan consulted Sikh leaders in early 1914 and confirmed that *kirpans* under "one foot" were acceptable.[60] He also requested that "Sikhs wearing this religious symbol may not be harassed and hauled up in law courts under the Arms Act."[61] In this way, the Diwan agreed to compromise with government officials about limiting the size of the *kirpan* to one foot. They also used this concession to criticize the arrest of Sikh men. Due to this successful activism, on June 25, 1914, the Punjab government officially sanctioned the possession of *kirpans* "carried by Sikhs." This gave Punjabi Sikh men exclusive rights to swords.[62] After a few months of agitation the same rule extended to Burma and Delhi. However, due to the preexisting controversy about limiting size, no provincial governments gave official definitions of a *kirpan*'s maximum length.[63] As the Government of India soon realized, size mattered.

ACTIVISM AND ANXIETY DURING THE
FIRST WORLD WAR

Unequal military recruitment compelled Sikh soldiers to serve disproportionately in one of the most brutal conflicts of all time while debating within their communities about the morality of their service. In the first years of the First World War (1914–18) they endured the difficulties of trench life on the Western Front. These included poor food, inadequate sanitation, "shell shock," and massive death and casualties. Many later served in Mesopotamia, Egypt, or the Persian Gulf where they faced food and supply shortages, unfamiliar terrain, and debilitating climates. Home life was no less challenging: the war resulted in the heavy extraction of goods and wealth from the Punjab province.[64] Many men enlisted in the army after facing limited economic opportunities and the coercive recruitment policies of Punjab Lieutenant-Governor Michael O'Dwyer.[65] The *Morning Post* estimated that by 1916 the Punjab furnished 50% of wartime recruits despite being roughly 8% of the Indian population. Sikhs were one-third of these Punjabi fighters, even though they made up only about 10% of the population of the Punjab.[66] As more Sikh men ventured into notoriously ruthless battlefields, anti-colonial activists found many ready and willing collaborators. The war's brutality energized powerful critiques of imperial militarism. Debates about Sikh martial prowess, including the *kirpan*, would never be the same.

No Indian anti-colonial effort was as influential during the First World War as the Ghadar (Mutiny) movement, which attempted to overthrow British rule in India. Ghadar targeted Sikh regiments in the Indian Army, South Asian veterans in the United States, migrants in Southeast Asia, and prospective Sikh recruits.[67] It grew out of prewar agricultural protests and discriminatory migration policies in the United States and Canada. Intelligence officers observed that most Ghadarites were Sikh and over 50% were ex-soldiers.[68] They gained additional supporters after the return of a number of Punjabi Sikh emigrants who had sailed on the famous ship the *Komagata Maru* in 1914, which had attempted to challenge Canada's restrictive policies. Due to strict immigration laws, Canadian officials sent the ship back to India and forcibly relocated many would-be emigrants to Punjab. Passengers endured months on the ship with poor sanitation and food provisions. Experience of lengthy confinement inspired the migrants to riot at Budge Budge when they were forcibly returned to India. Many observed that the most highly recruited areas for the army also furnished a high number of emigrants to North America and East Asia.[69] Sikh soldiers sympathized with emigrants' plight and organized public meetings across India. Several sowars (cavalrymen) expressed their desire to join the returned emigrants in revolution by spreading their message to heavily recruited districts.[70] A Sikh *granthi* (religious scholar) suggested that conditions in 1914 were identical to those of 1857. He reminded a gathered crowd about the glory of the 1840s Sikh wars.[71] Ghadar success among soldiers shocked the imperial state.

Ghadar activists benefited from the rapid mobility of wartime, which enabled them to reach numerous Sikh soldiers.[72] They circulated in districts of India with prominent Sikh populations including Amritsar, Ludhiana, Jullundur, Ferozepore, and Gurdaspur during wartime festivals. *Gurdwaras*, or Sikh holy meeting places, in Hong Kong, Saigon, and Bangkok became centers for spreading Ghadar ideas to troops.[73] They contacted regiments such as the 25th and 26th Punjabis stationed at Hong Kong.[74] The 26th had to return from Hong Kong because they had been "infected with sedition." When they arrived at the depot in Ferozepore in 1915, returned emigrants from the *Komagata Maru* taught them to make bombs to challenge government interference in their religion. Sucha Singh, a reservist sowar (cavalryman) of the 23rd Cavalry at Lahore, encouraged his Lance Daffadar (cavalry corporal), Lachman Singh, to participate in revolutionary activity. However, Mul Singh, the regimental *granthi*, apparently dissuaded them from inciting a rebellion.[75] Not all efforts to prevent uprisings were so successful.

Ghadar activism turned violent during the Singapore Mutiny in February 1915. The revolt lasted seven days and resulted in the death of a few dozen British, Malay, and Chinese soldiers and civilians and the execution of nearly fifty South Asian soldiers.[76] At the time colonial officials focused on the "religious" motivations of Muslim troops of the 5th Light Infantry and inefficiencies among commanding officers. However, many soldiers identified Sikh soldiers and civilians, including those serving in the Singapore-based and Indian-staffed Malay States Guides, as leaders and instigators of the rebellion.[77] The Lahore Conspiracy Case investigated wartime "sedition" and concluded that many Sikh Ghadar agitators had stirred dissent among troops in Singapore.[78] Ghadar conspirators even planned a rebellion in Lahore to coincide with the Singapore Mutiny. To quell both disturbances, British officials employed spies to infiltrate Indian ranks.[79] Punjab Lieutenant-Governor Michael O'Dwyer, meanwhile, cracked down violently against wartime sedition.[80] The government executed twenty people for participating in the so-called

Lahore Conspiracy and sent fifty-eight overseas for transportation for life—the imperial equivalent of overseas imprisonment and exile. Soldiers and civilians recognized that these events represented threats to the Sikh community. Student Kalwant Singh wrote to soldier Ghamand Singh about his fear that the Lahore case spelled "disaster to the Sikh people." He asked "the Guru" for "help" because "It will be a long time before the Sikh people can raise their heads again."[81] A British censor detained the letter, fearing its impact on this widely recruited community.

Imperial accounts of Sikh participation in the war rarely mentioned their prominent role in the Ghadar movement. Instead, Sikh soldiers were among the most widely and visibly praised South Asian soldiers throughout the war.[82] Popular accounts often drew a straight line between Sikhs' support in 1857 and the First World War, erasing the years of rebellion in between.[83] One War Office film even foregrounded swords to depict Sikh soldiers' loyal service. It portrayed a "regimental durbar" of the 47th Sikhs in 1916 and included footage of Sikh soldiers unsheathing and offering their swords to their officers in a show of loyalty.[84] A symbol of potential anti-colonial militarism became a centerpiece of loyal service. Other men used swords to show their devotion to the war effort. Dafadar Nathan Singh of the 2nd Lancers wrote a Gurmukhi (Punjabi) verse from France that declared that "Once a Sikh takes the sword in hand / He has only one aim—victory."[85] Another soldier, Jemadar Chur Singh of the 47th Sikhs, took to heart his fellow soldiers' accusation that he had failed to be "a Sikh of Guru Govind Singh" because he sat "in fear inside the trench." In response, he grew angry, "drew his sword and went forward." A fellow soldier described Chur Singh's immediate death as his transition from coward to "martyr."[86] Many soldiers understood their wartime self-sacrifice as a form of nobility that helped them cope with and rationalize their difficult experiences.[87] By wielding their swords to do so, they combined prewar activism, Sikh lineages of martial prowess, and the Indian Army's military culture.

The army's tendency to publicize Sikh soldiers' service during the First World War convinced many Britons that Sikh soldiers were as strong and steadfast as ever. Reviving narratives of loyalty, including 1857, attempted to erase the attraction of anti-colonial ideas and the army's reliance on coercive recruitment. The army cast any soldier who questioned or rebelled against the empire as a betrayer of his community's "loyal" heritage. However, postwar Sikhs proved just as difficult to control.

THE *KIRPAN* IN POSTWAR SIKH ACTIVISM

After the war, British officials recognized Sikhs' difficult positions in India's postwar order. There was no denying that many Sikhs made exceptional contributions to the war. Yet some were central to the anti-colonial Ghadar movement. Sikh politicians in Punjab focused on the manpower contribution of the community and demanded—unsuccessfully—equal political representation with Muslims and Hindus.[88] Soldiers who returned, meanwhile, wrestled with traumatic battlefield experiences and homes that had been noticeably changed by the war. The Punjab province had endured drought, plague, and fluctuating food prices. Eight hundred thousand Punjabis died from influenza in October and November of 1918 alone.[89] The physical and psychological scars of war took years to heal. The postwar climate did little to ease their transition.[90] The passage of the Rowlatt Bills in 1919 increased soldiers' hardships by extending the anti-sedition Defence of India Act into the peacetime era.[91] This meant that the imperial state treated many returning soldiers like potential revolutionaries instead of venerated heroes.[92] Their reward for contributing to Britain's victory was finding their homes and communities devastated by inflation, disease, and political repression. Many soldiers redeployed their wartime militarism into renewed calls for anti-colonialism and religious revival. For many, the war had not ended: only the battlefield and aims had changed.[93]

In April 1919, many Sikhs entered into the holy city of Amritsar to celebrate the festival Baisakhi (Vaisakhi), which commemorated Guru Gobind Singh's formation of the Khalsa in 1699.[94] The end of the war, and the gradual return of many Khalsa Sikh men from overseas, made the celebration even more emotionally powerful. Amritsar possessed the famed Golden Temple and had been a center of Khalsa military expansion across Punjab in the eighteenth century. Yet this celebration was illegal due to recent bans on public gatherings after protests to the Rowlatt Acts. On April 13, 1919, General Reginald Dyer ordered fifty men of the

1/9th Gurkhas, 54th Sikhs, and 59th Sikhs to open fire on a large crowd at Jallianwala Bagh. Dyer's command killed 379 and wounded over 1,200 at a time when many Sikh and Punjabi soldiers were demobilizing or continuing to fight overseas.[95] A military attack on civilians near the Sikh Golden Temple during a commemoration of the Khalsa brought into question the army's exaltation of Sikh soldiers. Some agreed with the *Ghadar-Di-Gunj*, which declared that "The time to draw the sword has come."[96]

After the Amritsar Massacre Sikh protesters flooded into the holy city bearing swords. Governor Michael O'Dwyer had placed the city under martial law due to the protests, strikes, and violence against the Rowlatt Acts. Yet this influx of Sikhs was a more specific rebellion against the imperial occupation of a holy space and imperial efforts to define and control Sikh identity. General Dyer had received an honorary initiation as a Sikh at the Golden Temple *after* his leading role in the Jallianwala Bagh massacre.[97] Although Dyer and O'Dwyer claimed that the Sikh community supported martial law and the use of force against civilians, this influx of Sikh rebels told a different story.[98] The Amritsar superintendent of police recalled that "the city of the Sikhs was soon thronged" with Sikh men "armed with long *kirpans*." Over time, "their numbers, and with their numbers the size of their *kirpans*, began to increase."[99] The activists' main goal was to reclaim the keys to the Golden Temple, which continued to be managed by government-appointed officials.[100] The assistant director of criminal intelligence expressed concerns as early as 1911 that if Sikh reformers gained control of the temple it might threaten Sikh men's value as soldiers.[101] Nonetheless, the Government of India recognized their tenuous position after the war and massacre. They gave control of the Golden Temple to the newly formed Shiromani Gurdwara Parbandhak Committee (SGPC), which claimed the right to manage Sikh holy spaces (*gurdwaras*). The incident demonstrated that unified Sikh activism, armed with *kirpans*, could be a successful vehicle of change.

Sikh men's ability to carry large swords into Amritsar was a result of recent government concessions. The provincial governments in Delhi, the United Provinces, the North-West Frontier Province, and Burma followed Punjab in allowing Sikhs to carry *kirpans* without licenses. The Government of India recommended, but did not mandate, that all local governments adopt similar concessions in 1917.[102] Some provincial authorities, such as the Bengal government, did not grant exemption to *kirpans* due to the province's reputation as a center of revolutionary activity.[103] Sikh soldiers serving in military stations in provinces without an exemption, therefore, could not carry swords. Teja Singh lamented the contradiction: "Those who used the sword, those whose profession it was to wear arms, were not allowed to wear the Kirpan."[104] Yet the events of 1919 forced the government's hand. In September 1920 the Government of India granted all Sikh soldiers the right to wear *kirpans* in plain clothes and uniforms. Officially it was "in recognition of the loyal and distinguished services rendered by the Sikhs in the Great War."[105] The Chief Khalsa Diwan had recommended the provision and agreed that *kirpans* could be worn by Sikh soldiers only as long as the blades did not exceed nine inches, further reducing the length of swords from prewar recommendations.[106] Yet the stage was set for greater concessions, and further militarism, from Sikh soldiers and civilians.

The successful agitation at the Golden Temple, and the right to carry swords, inspired Sikhs to reclaim other holy spaces. Sikh *gurdwaras* (temples) had been centers of anti-colonial rebellion in outposts such as Hong Kong and Singapore during the war. Creating makeshift *gurdwaras* using tents, marquees, or hospital grounds also gave soldiers a sense of community while they were far from home. These spaces turned into potential sites of violence in India. *Gurdwaras* often had large and fertile plots of land and earned regular donations from pilgrims. Management of *gurdwara* funds could therefore be an important way to collect revenue and create change within the community. New political organizations such as the Central Sikh League started to agitate for change in *gurdwara* management by 1919.[107] In particular, many opposed the possession of *gurdwaras* by Sikhs who cut their hair and did not observe the 5 Ks.[108] Groups such as the Tat Khalsa pressured *gurdwara* managers (*mahants*) to embrace the Khalsa customs of the 5 Ks or be regarded as Hindus. Accusations of immorality soon undermined these managers' moral right to control holy spaces and members of the Sikh community started to assemble into groups known as Akali *jathas*. These *jathas*, or bands, identified as "Akalis," meaning "God's devotees" or "immortal soldiers." They organized along military lines and forcibly occupied *gurdwaras*.[109]

Unofficially, some British officers supported Akalis' reformist goals and viewed keepers of *gurdwaras* (*mahants*) as corrupt priestly figures. Others felt that single, if corrupt, figures were easier to manage than unpredictable populist movements. The Akali *jathas* were threatening because they represented an affront to law, order, and property, and occurred at a moment of intense anti-colonial non-cooperation.

The rise of Akalis and seizure of *gurdwaras* became violent when Narain Das, the manager (*mahant*) at Nankana, hired a private guard of Muslim Pathans—allegedly armed by the government—to defend the property from occupation in February 1920.[110] According to the Punjab government the Nankana *gurdwara* was "one of the richest in the Province." Narain Das, however, was "a notorious ill-liver."[111] On February 20, 1920, a group of "130 Sikhs" attempted to occupy the *gurdwara* courtyard but were "brutally massacred, the bodies being afterward burnt with kerosine [*sic*] oil."[112] Police arrested Narain Das and sent troops onto the site. The Punjab government reported that in response, "all the extreme and fanatic Sikhs of the Province flocked to Nankana."[113] The tension surrounding this event increased when Mohandas Gandhi and pan-Islamic activists the Ali brothers attended an October 1920 Lahore Sikh League meeting and paid tribute at Nankana.[114] The commissioner of Jullundur diminished the fear of interfaith alliances by expressing that Gandhi's tour "has had a good effect" because of his "denunciation of violence."[115]

Nankana contributed to the increased visibility and size of *kirpans*. In 1921, officials in the Punjab government worried that "certain classes of Sikhs have begun ostentatiously to wear large weapons 2 feet long."[116] The Punjab government responded by only issuing licenses to manufacturers who agreed to make *kirpans* that were nine inches or less.[117] Government officials targeted factories that manufactured longer *kirpans*, including one in Amritsar selling 18-inch swords, another at Bhera offering 22-inch weapons, and a Nabha location with *kirpans* as long as three feet (Figure 2). The governments of Burma, Bombay, and Bengal officially limited the size of *kirpans* to nine inches.[118] However, Sikh activists challenged imperial law. Scholar Teja Singh referenced "old Hindu books" such as *Agni Puran*, *Varah Samhita*, and *Devi Puran* to claim that historic *kirpans* were between one and a half and three feet in length.[119] Others consulted

FIGURE 2 Sikh men carrying long swords as part of the Fourth Akali Jatha at Jaito. *Source*: British Library IOR/R/1/1/4903, No. 53. Reprinted with permission.

Sanskrit, Punjabi, Urdu, and English dictionaries, often commissioned by the imperial state, to press for legal recognition of longer *kirpans*.[120] In 1923, two men appeared before the Punjab High Court for possessing 36-inch swords with curved blades of 28 inches. They maintained that *kirpan* and sword were "interchangeable and synonymous."[121] After consulting Monier William's Sanskrit dictionary, Platts's Hindustani dictionary, Bhai Maya Singh's Punjabi dictionary, and Macauliffe's work on Sikhs, the court decided that dictionaries frequently defined *kirpans* as swords. The Punjab High Court conceded that "the word (kirpan) can only be understood and read as meaning a sword, and therefore a Sikh possessing or wearing a sword has committed no offence."[122] *Kirpan* trials, therefore, revealed the limitations of imperial law. Imperial knowledge—in the form of translated texts and dictionaries—had long been used to control and bureaucratize South Asian identities. In this case, they helped those who challenged, rather than supported, colonial restrictions. These legal battles also made it nearly impossible to restrain violence from those with privileged access to weapons.

The colonial state's inability to control *kirpans* made it difficult to stop the occupation of *gurdwaras*. By March 1921, Akalis occupied multiple *gurdwaras* while "armed with axes and kirpans."[123] The viceroy explained that the *kirpan* made these events especially worrisome, since many were "almost as long as swords."[124] The Punjab police believed that the Akali movement was more important and dangerous than Mohandas Gandhi's unarmed followers because "The Akali has acquired the right to arm himself with an obsolete, but none the less formidable, offensive weapon."[125] Government officials responded by passing the Sikh Gurdwaras and Shrines Act of 1921 to establish a board of commissioners to investigate cases of disputed *gurdwaras*. The SGPC—which had taken up leadership in *gurdwara* management after the "keys affair" at the Golden Temple—protested the bill, limiting its effectiveness. The Sikh Gurdwaras and Shrines Bill of 1922 reiterated that the board would only have influence over "disputed" *gurdwaras*. It still met widespread resistance because so many Sikhs were still under arrest.[126] The same year, the Government of India issued a full exemption for *kirpans* "possessed and carried by Sikhs," just as the Punjab government had done in 1914.[127] This gave Sikhs the exclusive privilege to bear arms at a time when the vast majority of South Asians were debarred from possessing weapons without a license. Political pressures from Sikh reformers and activists succeeded at seizing concessions from the imperial state—but at a cost.

The universal exemption for *kirpans* contributed to further violence. In 1922, the superintendent of police in Punjab argued that since *kirpans* were "now indistinguishable from a sword," they had "occasioned considerable misgivings to other communities who have not been accorded the privilege of arming themselves with any form of sharp-edged weapon of offence."[128] Before the war, imperial officials worried that *kirpans* created bonds between Muslim manufacturers and Sikh purchasers. After the war, the exception made for Sikhs to bear arms allowed them to target non-Sikhs for violence. Access to *kirpans*, according to one Punjab official, allowed Sikhs to become "a privileged class" moving in "armed bodies, terrorizing passers-by by the open display of swords and battle-axes."[129] This even affected Sikh soldiers. In 1922, the wives and families of the 23rd Sikh Pioneers petitioned against sending the unit on field service out of fear of being subjected to Akali harassment when men were away.[130] This petition may have been a strategy to use imperial fear to prevent soldiers from leaving home so soon after the First World War. It also suggested that although military men often supported Sikh activism, they had lost their protected and exclusive access to violence.

SOLDIERS' AND VETERANS' POSTWAR ACTIVISM

Postwar martial enthusiasm disturbed British officials in part because it reclaimed symbols and strategies most associated with the Indian Army. In 1920 the SGPC and Central Sikh League transformed individual Akali *jathas* into a *dal* or army. By 1921 it consisted of about fifteen thousand men and doubled to thirty thousand in 1922.[131] Members wore a uniform of "black pugris [turbans] and large Kirpans."[132] They formed regular lines with a quartermaster in charge and marched to a "military whistle."[133] Hundreds and sometimes thousands of men marched together in formation, on horseback, and with flags, under the leadership of a "jathedar" (*jatha* commander) on their way to occupy *gurdwaras*.[134] Some arrived armed with large swords, carrying the Guru Granth Sahib (Sikh holy book), with their own medical corps and sanitary camps.[135] Many Akali Dal members even had been imprisoned in 1915 and 1916 for Ghadar activity. For unemployed or demobilized soldiers, participating in the Akali Dal extended the heroic suffering of war into a spiritual mission for their community.[136] It erased the moral ambiguities of imperial service and replaced it with a militant martyrdom.

As Akali forces grew, British officials in Punjab were shocked and awed by their well-organized activism. They gave credit for Akali successes to Sikh training in the Indian Army.[137] Some officers reasoned that military order and discipline were complicit in making Sikh protests more effective. This happened first through the deliberate "nationalizing" of Sikh beliefs and practice before the war. After that, Sikhs became inculcated in military order and discipline in wartime. By 1922, the Punjab police worried that the Akali Dal negatively impacted Indian Army recruitment. Jat Sikhs, recruited from agricultural communities in Punjab, had been "the backbone of the Sikh community" in the army but many were enlisting in the Akali Dal instead. In the Ludhiana district, a prominent recruiting ground, 240 of the 672 documented Akalis were pensioned or discharged soldiers.[138] Overall the numbers were less dramatic—the Government of India estimated that military veterans were only about 8% of Akalis.[139] Nonetheless, the culture and symbols of Britain's imperial military forces—originally adapted from the Khalsa—had been fully reclaimed and redeployed outside of the army.

Despite their relatively small numbers, Indian Army soldiers and veterans were influential and well-publicized participants in the Akali, *kirpan*, and *gurdwara* agitations. Retired Captain Sardar Ram Singh became an executive committee member and vice president of the SGPC.[140] In 1921, pensioned Havildars of the 35th Sikhs joined former Ghadar conspirators and ex-soldiers in Jullundur and Hoshiapur to make plans to murder British officials.[141] Others, such as Babu Santa Singh, a clerk in the 54th Sikh Regiment, and Ude Singh, a recruit in the 27th Sikh Regiment, resigned from their imperial employment to join the *gurdwara* reform movement.[142] One *jatha* (band) consisted entirely of one hundred former soldiers.[143] The pensioners' *jatha* used the symbolic power of loyal servicemen to highlight the injustice of British opposition to Sikh political activism.

Soldier and veteran Akalis blurred the lines between devotion and rebellion. Subedar Amar Singh released a statement underlining the pensioners' feelings of loyalty, at times echoing colonial tropes. He claimed that most of the marching veterans belonged "to families whose blood has seen continuous military service since the unhappy times of the Indian Mutiny."[144] The men, he explained, had served on battlefields around the world during the war, including Afghanistan, Neuve Chapelle, and Ypres. They endured entrenchment in the "icy water" in France and dehydration from 135-degree temperatures in Mesopotamia.[145] Twenty-four of the one hundred Akali pensioners had been wounded in action. One lost a leg and two others went blind from poison gas. Almost all, he asserted, possessed medals, titles, and honors. Amar Singh recognized the value of drawing a parallel between Sikhs who suffered in the war and those who continued to fight in *jathas*. His claims of loyalty did not convince military officials, who suspected that he distributed SGPC pamphlets "designed to affect serving Sikh soldiers."[146] However, mobilizing the narrative of Sikh loyalty and the spectacle of suffering was a useful strategy to pressure the colonial state and gain civilian sympathy.

Within the army many soldiers supported the Akalis without renouncing their imperial employment.[147] Fifteen soldiers of the 57th Rifles, and several more in Mesopotamia, received sentences of imprisonment ranging from four to ten years for insisting on wearing *kirpans*. They received commands to remove their *kirpans* despite the Government of India's recent concession for soldiers to wear them.[148] Other military men faced arrest and went on hunger strikes after they wore the Akali uniform of *kirpans* and black *pagris*.[149] Soldiers from the 19th Punjabis and the 36th, 27th, 15th, and 14th Sikhs faced courts-martial for political activism in 1922.[150] Many, no doubt, saw Akali activism as consistent, rather than at odds, with the martial Sikh identity encouraged by the Indian Army. While military officials wanted to believe that Sikh activists were merely doing what they had learned from British training, soldiers brought the Akali uniform of dark *pagris* and long *kirpans* into British institutions. Cultures of militancy were not dictated solely by British power.

The Akali movement reached a height of militarism in 1922 as a result of the incident at Guru-ka-Bagh. Twelve miles from Amritsar, a man named Sunder Das was in charge of two Sikh shrines attached to profitable arable land and a small plot sacred to Guru Arjan Dev, known as Guru-ka-Bagh.[151] In August 1922, police arrested five Akalis after they cut down some branches to provide "fuel for the Guru's free kitchen."[152] Once the men faced conviction for theft, the SGPC encouraged Sikh agitation in the area. The colonial state arrested many SGPC leaders as a result. Soon after, Akalis went to widely recruited villages and dissuaded men from enlisting in the Indian Army or returning from leave. They organized two separate *jathas* (bands) consisting of entirely military pensioners to march in protest. What started as an attempt to reclaim holy spaces became a way to protest imperial policing and recruitment. One colonial official recalled that men assembled at the Golden Temple in Amritsar—near Jallianwala Bagh—and marched to Guru-ka-Bagh through "admiring multitudes" while wearing "a special uniform." According to one British observer, these incidents became an "unspoken appeal" to soldiers "to quit service and join his brethren at Guru-ka-Bagh."[153]

A more militant thread of the Akali agitation, called the Babbar Akali, went further in seeing the *kirpan* as a centerpiece of armed anti-colonial revolt. At a fair in Jind State, army veteran Kishan Singh "Gargaj" made a speech declaring that "wielding of [the] sword was the religious duty of the Sikhs when other means had failed." He advised the rural population not to fear the police but to "arm themselves with kirpans."[154] In 1923, Karma Singh Daulatpur recited a poem in Hoshiarpur that encouraged adherents to "Catch hold of the double-edged dagger, So the Babbar declares aloud. Sharpen both the edges on the whetting stone. Without the dagger, freedom cannot be won."[155] By 1923 the Government of India declared that the Babbar Akalis were an unlawful organization and crushed them ruthlessly. They stationed infantry and cavalry troops in the Doab region, used airplanes to distribute propaganda, and punished military pensioners for having sympathy with or harboring suspected members.[156] Of the ninety-one Babbar Akalis tried in the Babbar Akali case, three died in jail, twelve were sentenced to transportation for life, and thirty-eight received varying terms of imprisonment. Seven were executed in jail February 1926.[157] British officials feared that the army's encouragement of Sikh martial devotion had created a powerful force that they could no longer contain. The colonial state responded defensively by targeting Sikhs with violence and humiliation.

BETWEEN HEROISM AND HUMILIATION

Arrests became a primary means of challenging the Akali movement. Humiliation and confinement, some British officials hoped, would prevent Sikh men from claiming the masculinity associated with militancy and activism. Within one year, forty people were convicted of keeping or selling *kirpans*. The total number of arrests for possession of *kirpans* ranged between 1,000 and 1,500.[158] Some of the rumors and reports about these arrests undermined Sikh claims to masculine and moral legitimacy. For example, Hindi and Urdu newspapers alleged that Sikh prisoners had their long hair pulled or torn in prison. Others faced "savagery" from Pathan guards satisfying their "heart's craving" by violating Sikh activists sexually with "pieces of wood."[159] Homophobic fears of violating and penetrating the martial male body echoed fears of male intimacy and same-sex desire in the Indian nationalist movement. The spectacle of arrest and the implicit sexual violence of confinement turned Akalis' militant sacrifices into potentially humiliating and emasculating traumas.[160]

Much to the chagrin of Sikh protesters, the rate of arrest increased rapidly during and after Guru-ka-Bagh. The number of Akalis arrested per day quickly rose from 40 to 60 to 80, peaking between 100 and 130. Due to their swelling numbers, British officials held imprisoned Akalis in temporary jails consisting of "an open-air barbed-wire enclosure" that accommodated "hundreds of prisoners." This policy echoed imperial strategies of confining plague victims, refugees, "criminal tribes," or prisoners of war in militarized enclosures.[161] Yet these Sikh men—including army veterans—were not formal combatants or categorized as contagious or "criminal." Instead, the colonial state confined those earmarked as martial for exhibiting excessive militarism. Ultimately, police held thousands of Akalis "in barbed-wire pens" and cut off their rations.[162] This left Akalis in the uncomfortable position of choosing between hardships. They would either continue to endure arrest for occupying *gurdwaras* or face social condemnation for failing to embody heroism and martyrdom. Many agricultural laborers and landowners felt torn between their obligations to till the land and SGPC pressure to keep up their holy struggle.[163]

The spectacle of arrest also extended into the nominally independent "native" or "princely" states, raising questions about the reach of British imperial power. Patiala was a princely state surrounded on all sides by the militarily significant Punjab province. The Maharaja of Patiala, Bhupinder Singh, carried honorary ranks in the Indian Army and was regarded as one of the most prominent Sikhs in India. When the Government of India extended exemptions for *kirpans*, he issued restrictions on *kirpans'* size and shape. He mandated that all *kirpans* had to be purchased from the Arms Manufacturers of the State to avoid confiscation.[164] By contrast, in the neighboring Sikh state of Nabha, the Indian Army defied the ruler's sovereignty by putting down Akali activism.[165] Maharaja Ripudaman Singh abdicated in 1923, sparking widespread rumors that British officials had orchestrated his abdication because of his sympathies to the Akali cause.[166] In protest, Sikhs in and around the princely states assembled a massive *jatha* at Jaito and continuously read from Sikh texts to pray for the restoration of Ripudaman Singh. They hoped this would amend the "indignity imposed upon the Sikh Faith."[167] This widened the scope and aims of Akali politics. It was no longer about maintaining and controlling holy spaces, or protesting arrests, but advocating for the sovereignty of Sikh leaders. Jaito became a regular destination for *jathas*. In 1924, on the anniversary of the Nankana tragedy, five hundred people assembled into a large *jatha* with axes, swords, spears, and clubs. They charged at the police and military when ordered to halt.[168] Soon, numerous *jathas* arrived at Jaito. The Indian Army helped to crush yet another protest in a princely state nominally held by Sikh rulers. The violence of this *jatha* strained relations between the SGPC, the Akali Dal, and the Government of India. British efforts to control Sikh militarism transcended imperial borders.[169]

A selection of photographs taken of Akali *jathas* in Jaito in 1924 demonstrate the centrality of the *kirpan* in colonial efforts to break the will of renegade Sikh men.[170] Once the Nabha police arrested the Akali *jathas*, many were held in barbed-wire pens, as became customary in British-held territory during and after Guru-ka-Bagh (Figure 3). However, the photographs also depicted the men lined up, stripped down, and holding their *kirpans* waist high (Figure 4). This forced posture conveyed defeat and humiliation, not unlike the scene of the defeated Khalsa Empire in 1849 described by Teja Singh. Their *kirpans*, officially recognized as a part of Sikh identity and an exempted "religious" object, took center place. In other images, the fully clothed members of the Nabha police held the chains of stripped and handcuffed Akali prisoners (Figure 5). Other photographs depicted Nepali "Gurkha" soldiers of the Indian Army wearing their own "spiritual" swords—*khukris*—while fighting to put down Sikh rebellion (Figure 6). These non-Indian troops bore their weapons in the service of the British at a time when Sikh *kirpans* embodied the uncontrollability of Sikh militancy.

Photos of the arrested men contrasted the way that the Akalis represented themselves prior to their confinement. The men often marched in uniforms and columns, presenting themselves as a well-organized and disciplined military body (Figure 7). Official photographers, however, made these men adopt humiliating forced poses and lay their *kirpans* bare before an imperial gaze. This played on men's fears of public humiliation.

FIGURE 3 Members of the Akali Jatha, including those carrying the Guru Granth Sahib (Sikh holy book), are held in a fort behind barbed wire. *Source:* British Library IOR/R/1/1/4903, No. 14. Reprinted with permission.

FIGURE 4 Six members of the Akali Jatha hold their kirpans waist high while in confinement. These images were likely used for police records. *Source*: British Library IOR/R/1/1/4903, unnumbered. Reprinted with permission.

These photos could be distributed and shared, making their emasculation visible to their communities. Imagery of defeat deprived Akali activists of being masculine participants in a holy struggle of bravery and strength. Instead, colonial photography depicted them as naked, humiliated, and overpowered. Although the Government of India gave Sikhs nominal exemptions to carry swords without restriction, those present in a Sikh princely state, not fully under colonial control, still endured restrictions and humiliation inflicted by British power. Their challenge to imperial interference resulted in a loss of masculinity—and threatened the loss of martial prowess—for the Sikh community more widely.

According to the Punjab government, subsequent *jathas* at Jaito convinced most Sikhs that "neither the religious nor the political aims of the Sikhs were likely to be attained by direct action."[171] By summer 1924 the Akalis began to lose prestige. The Akali movement declined in 1925, owing in part to the success of the last of several Sikh *gurdwara* bills and the

FIGURE 5 A member of the Nabha police holds a handcuffed Akali prisoner
in captivity. *Source*: British Library IOR/R/1/1/4903, No. 62. Reprinted with
permission.

FIGURE 6 A long line of Nepali "Gurkha" soldiers surrounds the members of the Akali Jatha. Some of them have visible *khukris* attached to their belts. *Source:* British Library IOR/R/1/1/4903, No. 45. Reprinted with permission.

FIGURE 7 The Akali Jatha at Jaito marches in formation and with flags. *Source:* British Library IOR/R/1/1/4903, No. 30. Reprinted with permission.

increasing restlessness of the population with the movement.[172] The Sikh
Gurdwara and Shrine Bill, which passed in the Legislative Council on
July 7, 1925, gave Sikhs legal control over disputed shrines. This cre-
ated ambiguity and the potential for further tension and violence when
Hindus or Muslims laid claim to "disputed" holy spaces alongside Sikhs.
The bill recognized the SGPC as a representative of Sikhs in matters
related to *gurdwaras*. It also attempted to formally define Sikh identity.
Anyone who declared themselves a Sikh and a believer of Granth Sahib
and Ten Gurus could be considered a Sikh in imperial bureaucracy. Those
who wished to participate in temple management needed to declare themselves as officially separate from Hindus.[173] Punjab Governor William
Malcolm Hailey believed that this would pacify the Sikh community and
absolve the government of blame. Those invested in the issue, he believed,
would be left to "quarrel among themselves."[174] This decision to let activists
"quarrel among themselves" revealed that the movement caused considerable embarrassment among British officials and highlighted institutional shortcomings. Akalis successfully challenged the government's
will, and ability, to resist reformist demands. Sikhs' attempts to define
themselves according to the Khalsa—rather than their relationship to the
empire—enabled them to challenge imperial legislation about property
and governance. It resulted in the hardening of Sikh identities and the
use of threats and intimidation against those who feared losing their favored status. The government's response also created the conditions for
further regional and interfaith tension.

The 1925 Sikh Gurdwara and Shrine Bill hardened the definition of
"Sikh" and gave further institutional backing to loyalist, military-minded
Sikh men. For the Sikh soldiers who hoped to return to military service
after participating in Akali agitation, Nepali "Gurkha" presence reminded
them that they were replaceable. Being stripped or confined in barbed-
wire pens deprived them of the claims to masculinity that they hoped to
gain from both military service and militant activism. Those who chose
their own interpretations of what it meant to be Sikh, or protested the
government's ability to intervene in such decisions, might even be regarded
as "Hindu" and become marginalized as disloyal and un-martial.[175] Government definitions of Sikh identity created greater tensions between

those willing to cooperate with British power and those who continued the militant activism and inter-community solidarity in which so many prewar Sikh soldiers had actively taken part.

SWORDS OF DISSENT

Despite the tentative colonial sanction to permit *kirpans* after the First World War, British officials grew increasingly anxious about their own swords. In 1926 the Punjab government altered the inscription on a Lahore statue of Sir John Lawrence, a conqueror of Punjab, due to pressures from Mohandas Gandhi to have it removed. They changed the inscription from "will you be ruled by the pen or the sword?" to "With the pen and the sword I have served you."[176] Acknowledging colonial violence through weapons of war in the years after Amritsar was, at the very least, politically irresponsible. Yet the army's control of real swords, such as *kirpans*, continued into the interwar period. A 1912 edition of a military pamphlet had described *kirpans* as miniature objects representing "an emblem of the weapon which his ancestors used with great effect in bygone wars." The 1932 edition of the same pamphlet, by contrast, described the 5 Ks and called the *kirpan* "a short sword."[177] It did not acknowledge the nine-inch concession for soldiers to wear *kirpans* after the First World War. Instead it reiterated that *kirpans* were "usually worn in miniature in the hair," making it unnecessary "to wear the larger Kirpan."[178] A few years later the 4th Battalion of the 11th Sikh Regiment mandated that "Kirpans will not be worn."[179] Once Akali organizers focused their attention on formal political parties rather than a violent populist movement, the army was comfortable reinstituting its control over *kirpans* and, by extension, Sikh militancy.

The intense period of Sikh activism before, during, and after the First World War suggests that late colonial enthusiasm for the "loyal Sikh" came from a hard-won battle that divided the Sikh community internally. British officials emphasized continuity and loyal service between 1857 and the First World War to undermine the very recent incidents of Sikh activism. They encouraged Sikh practices and beliefs most associated with the Khalsa to isolate and demographically engineer loyal soldiers. This separated Sikhs who wore the 5 Ks from "slow converts" who did not. It also distinguished Sikhs from those allegedly disloyal colonial subjects who participated in the Arya Samaj. Those who used these identities to challenge colonialism, such as the Babbar Akalis, would bear the brunt of colonial attacks against non-sanctioned militarism. These hard divisions did not always work as many men took British employment and critiqued imperial rule simultaneously. Nonetheless, Sikhs in the army became the quintessential "Sikh" in the imagination of many British soldiers, administrators, and civilians. These men may have appeared more steadfast in their devotion, and were more recognizable as "Sikhs" through the 5 Ks, only because postwar activism had shaped Sikh identity around both colonial and precolonial ideas of martial prowess. The colonial state proved adaptable in incorporating aspects of Khalsa identity into the army, and delegitimizing whatever did not fit.

The brutality and seeming irrationality of the Amritsar massacre exposed the depths of imperial racism, the overreaction possible after a traumatic war, and the excessive militarization of the Punjab province.[180] It was also a defensive effort to claim soldiers' loyalties despite challenges from anti-colonial activists. Using South Asian troops to violently suppress domestic rebellion came off the heels of successful efforts of groups such as Ghadar to stir mutinies among the troops during the First World War. While British officials like Dyer and O'Dwyer viewed themselves as public school disciplinarians retaining control over their "boys" through violence, South Asian soldiers were not powerless actors forced to accept this subservient position.[181] They used imperial bureaucracy to undermine or reform government legislation. This forced imperial administrators to become reactionary to their demands: provincial authorities and courts disagreed on interpretations of colonial law while district commissioners made arrests that contradicted the Government of India. British officials held themselves responsible for the discipline and organization of soldiers' activism but British administration lagged behind the rapidly changing postwar world. British law could not help but appear irrational and antiquated.

Kirpans proved to be more than just symbols of heritage, devotion, or masculinity. Those who bore them claimed the power to inflict violence— both real and imagined—aggressive and defensive. Weapons could change hands outside the supervision of state authority or be carried illegally after being secured by legal means. Real Hindus, Muslims, Christians, and Sikhs continued to struggle over their ability to serve in the military, occupy holy space, bear arms, or defend themselves from violence. These tensions increased because of anti-colonial activism, postwar traumas, and changing government policies. Increasing a single community's access to arms due to their perceived loyalty and penchant for military service brought real violence to soldiers and civilians alike. It also revealed the imperial state's impulses to confine, arrest, humiliate, and brutalize even those considered the most "loyal." Militarism could not exist without violence. Army attempts to draw clear lines between tamed militant loyalty and overzealous ferocity were destined to fail.

CHAPTER 2

BORDERS, BOUNDARIES, AND BELONGING

THE COLONIAL NARRATIVE about the "loyal Sikh" attempted to define a diverse community to suit imperial rule and military recruitment. Army understandings of Muslim soldiers proved just as fraught with contradiction, compromise, and contention. Before and during the First World War, Muslim soldiers' service took them to places like Egypt, Mesopotamia, and Afghanistan where they found opponents of imperialism who shared their faith in Islam. Many soldiers had family connections to these regions or showed political support for Muslim rulers. Yet soldiers and civilians whose identities fell under the umbrella of "Muslim" did not have a single political vision for the future. Rather, prewar activism and wartime service exposed them to the true diversity of Islam globally. Imperial officials, meanwhile, hoped to differentiate the loyal from the disloyal because Muslims made up at least 35% of soldiers in the army.[1] This gave soldiers of the same faith vastly different experiences of war and peace. Some benefited from a nominally exalted status as a "martial race." Many others remained targets of colonial violence. At a time when colonial officials racialized Sikh soldiers as naturally loyal, they shifted uncomfortably between their own understandings of Muslims as loyal or disloyal, useful or dangerous. British officers, soldiers, and administrators struggled to understand the difference between devotion and extremism, shaping the choices and destinies of Muslim subjects and allies around the world.

ISLAM IN THE INDIAN ARMY

The Indian Army's treatment of its South Asian Muslim soldiers was fraught with contradiction and mutual collaboration long before the outbreak of war in 1914. East India Company armies collaborated with Mughal military elites and absorbed Mughal styles of warfare and discipline in the eighteenth century.[2] Muslim recruits held prominent military positions throughout the nineteenth century, especially in the cavalry. During the uprising of 1857, some high-ranking Muslim elites hoped to revive Mughal rule. In response, colonial officials dispossessed individuals and institutions associated with Mughal power. They also limited the mobility of "fakirs," or Muslim ascetics, because some had helped to stir anti-colonial sentiment among troops in 1857.[3] The imperial state categorized many Muslim communities as "criminal tribes" to regulate their movements or justify violence against them.[4] Former mutineers and persecuted groups sought refuge in the northwestern borderlands adjacent to Afghanistan, where anti-colonial networks developed and thrived.[5] The army pursued reprisals and violent campaigns in the region to prevent borderland communities from seeking alliances with Russians in Afghanistan. This so-called "Great Game" resulted in three Anglo-Afghan Wars (1839–42, 1878–80, 1919) that militarized and destabilized the northwestern borders.[6] The region had a Muslim-majority population, many of whom felt called to military service due in part to the lack of opportunities.[7] This made the Indian Army anxious about, yet dependent upon, its diverse Muslim subjects.

Frequent exposure to Muslim soldiers led some officials to praise Muslim men and romanticize their alleged "martial" qualities. Indian Army officer Francis Yeats-Brown of the 17th Cavalry praised "the tradition of loyalty and true religion" among soldiers who represented "the best traditions of Islam."[8] Francis Thackeray Warre-Cornish exalted the "warlike clans" of "Punjabi Musalmans" and Pathans who rode "with the Koran strapped to their saddle-bow."[9] General Andrew Skeen, the Chief of the General Staff (1924–28), acted disdainfully toward Hindu soldiers while giving preferential treatment to Muslim recruits.[10] Some of these men reinforced the colonial trope that these men were desirable because they were naturally violent and untamed.[11] British officials often admired

Muslim men as fierce warriors but also worried that their supposed martial prowess might become uncontrollable.

The colonial state tried to stabilize military recruitment by fortifying political bonds with elite South Asian Muslims. However, the early years of the twentieth century only brought greater uncertainty. For example, the partition of the Bengal province (1905–12) gave Bengali Muslims a majority in a newly created province of East Bengal. The Morley-Minto Reforms (1909) created separate political representation for Muslims. However, the decision to reverse the Bengal partition alienated many Muslim subjects who looked for political answers and alliances outside of India.[12] The Ottoman Sultan became a symbolic and aspirational ally for some, since he was the caliph, or head, of global Islam. Many Indian Muslims supported him during the 1911 and 1912 Tripoli and Balkan Wars. Police officer F. C. Isemonger cynically described this sympathy as motivated by the desire for "wars of the Cross against the Crescent."[13] This imagery of religious war overlooked how pan-Islamic unity was an attractive alternative to European imperialism rather than strictly about religious animosity.[14] Nonetheless, the pamphlet *Our Indian Empire* similarly cast soldiers' divided loyalties as purely religious issues. It warned British soldiers that Muslim men from India's northwestern borderlands were "ignorant and fanatical" and liable to be tempted by those who preached "religious wars" to "destroy the 'infidels.'"[15] In the years before the First World War, military praxis cast soldiers' "warlike" traits and faith as possible sources of anti-colonial rebellion.

In reality, army anxieties about "fanatical" dissent far outpaced actual incidents of religious violence. For example, in 1908 one man named Shah Alam attacked an Indian officer, reportedly stating during the attack, "I am a Ghazi and will kill Sahibs and all of you who are servants of unbelievers." However, this incident undermined rather than confirmed colonial fears of so-called religious rebellion. The Punjab government claimed that Shah Alam's case could be considered "a case of abnormality amounting to weakness of intellect."[16] Their evidence was that he had given conflicting reports about his intentions after his arrest. He was imprisoned in the Andaman Islands penal colony in 1909 for committing "a murderous fanatical attack on a native officer." By 1913, Shah

Alam became "insane" with an affliction of "religious mania," according to the medical officer. They reported his suicide in 1915. Imperial diagnoses of insanity often were specious since many colonial officials considered South Asians insane if their behavior challenged European mores.[17] Yet even in the midst of the First World War officials recognized that Shah Alam's "religious mania" was an "abnormality." It was worth recording because it was exceptional. Nonetheless, military pamphlets warned soldiers *en masse* about "fanatical" martial Muslims. Army tendencies to exalt the martial races—including many Muslims—did not sit well with broader imperial condemnation of certain Muslim subjects as "fanatics." These underlying tensions intensified, but also opened a space for alternatives, during the First World War.

ISLAM AND THE WAR

Muslim soldiers' potential connections to other Muslims outside of India became a central anxiety during the First World War. Germany's Kaiser Wilhelm II (1888–1918) held imperial ambitions in Northern Africa and the Middle East. He had visited Constantinople, Jerusalem, and Damascus before the war and adopted the honorific title "Haji" to imply that he had completed a Hajj pilgrimage.[18] This proved significant when Wilhelm allied with the Ottoman Sultan, Mehmed V, who claimed the position of caliph. By November 1914, shortly after the Ottoman entry into the war, the Sultan formally blessed a proclamation of jihad signed by twenty-nine religious authorities. It was presented to political, military, and religious dignitaries and read publicly.[19] This continued a pattern of Ottoman leaders using jihad to fortify bonds between subjects, including non-Muslims, in times of war.[20] However, their German allies spread a more explicitly anti-British interpretation of holy war to the Muslim subjects of the British Empire. They circulated anti-British propaganda and organized Muslim prisoners of war into bands of "jihadi" warriors. Several events indicated that some Indian soldiers might be receptive to these appeals: in 1915 the 5th Light Infantry, composed of many Muslim troops, mutinied in Singapore.[21] The same year the 130th Baluchis refused to set sail for Mesopotamia, citing religious objections. Members of the 15th Lancers opposed fighting near Muslim holy places in 1916.[22] Many officials blamed German agents and the all-Muslim composition of some Indian Army forces for these incidents.[23] However, Muslim soldiers' experiences with war went far beyond reductive depictions of jihad. In fact, the vast majority of Muslim troops served without incident. The existence of real plots to use Islam as a unifying force of rebellion nonetheless shaped British strategies for maintaining soldiers' loyalties.

Indian soldiers and civilians took active roles in campaigning against Britain during the war for reasons beyond German manipulation or religious enthusiasm. During the "Silk Letter Conspiracy," for example, Maulana Obaidullah Sindhi, a Sikh convert to Islam, implored the Amir of Afghanistan to support the struggle for Indian independence.[24] These efforts started as early as 1909, but gained notoriety in 1915 when he participated in a plan to invade British India from Afghanistan.[25] Indian revolutionary Raja Mahendra Pratap and several Indian prisoners of war furthered these efforts by participating in the 1915–16 German mission to Afghanistan to convince the Amir to go to war against British India.[26] The revolutionary Ghadar party even declared a provisional government and named Sindhi home minister.[27] They condemned Muslim soldiers for fighting against their "Moslem Ottoman brethren" and urged them to "emancipate India and Egypt from the injustice and bondage of the English."[28] Letters purporting to be from influential Muslims in and beyond the Ottoman Empire circulated widely among Indian soldiers in France.[29] British wartime Director of Information John Buchan memorialized this period in the 1916 novel *Greenmantle*. His view of the conspiracy included antisemitic implications that the plot was a German-Jewish conspiracy to exact revenge against Russia for the pogroms.[30] However, calls for pan-Islamic unity—and soldiers' responses to these appeals—cannot be understood exclusively as European political calculations. It was part of a longer effort to negotiate the terms of Muslim soldiers' service and colonial rule in South Asia.

Class and regional ties also influenced soldiers' abilities to process the war and interpret the meaning of their service. Colonial officials attempted to fortify bonds with Muslim elites to ensure the stable recruitment of soldiers during the war, especially in the Punjab province. Punjab had long been a primary region of recruitment and provided 75% of wartime re-cruits. While Punjabi Sikhs were the most disproportionately recruited soldiers from the region, Punjab was a Muslim-majority province. Punjabi Muslims were the true backbone of the Indian Army and were frequently deployed in overseas campaigns.[31] As a result, the army and colonial offi-cials worked hard to retain stable relationships in the region throughout the war. Organizations such as the Punjab Muslim Association, founded in 1916, and the Punjab Zamindar Central Association cultivated loyalty among prominent, landed men from military families.[32] This was not sim-ply the result of imperial calculation. Members of both groups disparaged communist and Hindu-led anti-colonial movements, which they believed threatened the interests of Muslim landowners with connections to mili-tary power.[33] Men recruited from the province were encouraged to stay loyal, while returning veterans faced social and political pressure if they criticized the war or imperial rule.

Religious appeals actually helped to keep some soldiers in the army during and after the war. The Ahmadiyya movement, inspired by Muslim reformer Mirza Ghulam Ahmad, argued that Muslims were right to fight for Britain despite the protestations of the Ottoman Empire. Pamphlets drafted by Ahmadiyya supporters entered without censorship into trenches and military cantonments. Some Indian soldiers condemned Ahmadiyya advocates as either "false" Muslims or Christians in disguise.[34] Others found their arguments convincing. Echoing Ahmadiyya ideas, one *maulvi* (Muslim religious scholar) named 'Abd al-Hakim wrote an Urdu pam-phlet that described Muslim service in the army and police as a "religious duty."[35] He condemned political leaders who encouraged Muslim men to step down from imperial service. Doing so, he believed, only strengthened the Hindu majority and cost Muslims their political voice and material opportunities. Such arguments did not make 'Abd al-Hakim blindly un-critical of imperial rule. He acknowledged that British officials confiscated Muslim lands and dismantled Mughal power after the uprising of 1857. However, he celebrated the Indian Army, and implicitly the theory of martial races, for believing that Muslims made good soldiers.[36]

Secular arguments sometimes blended seamlessly with religious jus-tifications. 'Abd al-Hakim affirmed that there was nothing in the Koran that made it unlawful for Muslims to fight in the army. Instead, the Koran encouraged Muslims to support their lawful rulers, no matter their faith or region of origin. Muslims and Christians needed to stand together and support one another, he contended, due to their shared monotheistic traditions.[37] 'Abd al-Hakim challenged wartime and postwar pan-Islamic sentiment by suggesting that Indian Muslims were strongest if they united under British rule. He worried that if Muslims fought for independence, they would alienate their British allies and lose political rights, employ-ment, and representation. Soldiers' difficult decisions to be "loyal" or "dis-loyal" to the British during and after the First World War was about far more than religious extremism or German plots. They engaged head-on with the complexities and hardships of life under imperial rule.

INDIA, ISLAM, AND HIJAZ

'Abd al-Hakim's warnings came at a time when British imperial rule ex-panded in Muslim-majority regions, providing real opportunities and challenges for Muslim soldiers. Britain had declared a protectorate over Egypt in 1914 to secure access to the Suez Canal. They reached an un-derstanding with France to divide Ottoman lands in the Sykes Picot agreement (1916), which became official in subsequent treaties (1919–23). Indian Army officers eased this transition by allowing Muslim troops to oversee shrines and gravesites in recently conquered areas including in the Mesopotamia and Palestine mandates.[38] This made it possible for soldiers to envision themselves as pious protectors of their faith rather than sin-ners who fought for a Christian empire against fellow Muslims.[39] If the British Empire was to survive its own rapid expansion, Muslim soldiers needed to become British imperial ambassadors of Islam rather than rebels in a pan-Islamic revolution.

A few weeks after the ceasefire with the Ottoman Empire, Everard Digby, a reserve officer of the Scinde Horse, believed that he had the key to Muslim soldiers' loyalty: he proposed sending them on pilgrimage to visit the holy cities of Mecca and Medina. Soldiers' already-planned returns to India from battlefields along the Eastern Mediterranean made it conve-nient for them to stop at Mecca and Medina on the way. Such events were not without precedent. British Christian soldiers similarly participated in pilgrimages to holy sites such as Bethlehem.[40] Digby speculated that "every Mohammedan soldier of the Egyptian Expeditionary Force, if asked whether he would like to go on the Hajj now that he is in Mecca, would, I think without exception, jump at the suggestion." He mentioned that several soldiers had actually asked him if they could do so. Such a pilgrimage, he contended, would "catch the imagination of the whole Muhammadan World" and prove most valuable for the "masses of India." Digby elaborated:

> At the end of the greatest war in the world's history, the greatest Muhammadan Empire in the world, though ruled by men of alien Faith—after defeating, with the help of Muhammadan troops, the next greatest Muhammadan Power, the ruler of which was for centuries the Caliph—is so solicitous of the spiritual welfare of its Muhammadan citizens that, unasked, it makes special arrangements for a large proportion of its Muhammadan veterans to perform the Haj.[41]

Digby's stroke of political genius, he believed, would assuage postwar concerns about Britain's conquest of a Muslim power. It would undermine criticisms of the potential destruction or dissolution of the caliphate, quelling revolutionary sentiment in India, Persia, Afghanistan, and Egypt. He felt that this would prove Britain's commitment to being the world's "largest Muhammadan Power."[42] By October, King George V showed his support for the proposal and it received approval before the end of 1918.[43]

Pilgrimages became important investments in soldiers' beliefs at a time when anti-colonial revolution seemed like a real possibility. The secretary of the Military Department hoped that pilgrimages could "be put to excellent use for propaganda purposes in India."[44] He responded to the general fear that wartime experiences and pressures from home had inspired many Indian Muslim soldiers—especially those serving on the Western Front—to embrace a more devout and moralistic worldview that at times supported anti-colonial activities.[45] A few who served in Muslim-majority lands developed sympathy and contacts with international Muslims.[46] What made these political pilgrimages useful rather than dangerous, however, was that many soldiers, unlike the civilian leaders of pan-Islamic activism, actually felt *unsympathetic* to Muslim civilians in occupied regions. For example, Abdul Rauf Khan of the 21st Combined Field Ambulance described the civilians in Mesopotamia as "thoughtless and careless."[47] Anwar Shah of the Camel Corps in Egypt lamented the presence of prostitutes during the holy festival Eid, during which Egyptian men celebrated drunkenly with less pious "Hindustani" soldiers. He longed to return to "Our country!"[48] Another Punjabi Muslim soldier looked forward to serving in France because "The people far surpass the Egyptians."[49] By the end of the war, the General Headquarters in Egypt was not worried about revolutionary pamphlets circulating among South Asian troops because "contempt for Egyptians" appeared to be "general."[50]

Few soldiers recognized that wartime traumas of violence, dislocation, and economic turmoil may have been the root cause of the "undesirable" traits among the Muslim men and women they encountered. In Egypt, for example, the influx of British, Australian, New Zealander, and South Asian troops increased illicit trades in alcohol and prostitution. The crucial defense of the Suez Canal required heavy recruitment for the Egyptian armed forces and Labour Corps, the latter of which was frequently starved, beaten, or imprisoned for resisting imperial labor demands. In early 1919 the British army's imposition of martial law included burning villages and aerial bombardment. Indian Army men, in turn, frequently carried out policing duties that gave Egyptians little fondness for them in return.[51] Many soldiers became disillusioned by civilians who appeared irreligious and immoral only after enduring homelessness, geopolitical collapse, and logistical failures. The lived realities of war in Muslim-majority lands precluded many South Asian soldiers from being optimistic about pan-Islamic unity. Pilgrimages, therefore, became a way to define Muslim unity within, rather than against, the British Empire.

The Army Department admitted that a goal of the pilgrimages was to popularize "service in Egypt and Palestine amongst Indian Moslem soldiers."[52] This was crucial as the British gained control of the League of Nations mandates in Mesopotamia, Palestine, and Transjordan. South Asian soldiers, meanwhile, enjoyed the opportunity to meet Sharif Hussein, who held tentative power over the holy cities of Mecca and Medina and hosted the Indian soldiers as guests during their visit.[53] British officials had backed Hussein's family in the Arab Revolt (1916) against the Ottoman Empire. As the Ottoman-appointed Sharif of the city of Mecca, he gradually took control of the Hijaz, a region of western Arabia adjacent to the Red Sea and Suez Canal that contained the holy cities. During the war, Hussein was unpopular in India due to his claims to be the rightful caliph. One anti-British pamphlet alleged that "Muhammedans would not acknowledge such a Caliph who would be of low rank, especially when he was a slave of the infidels."[54] Indian hostility intensified after Sharif Hussein arrested several prominent South Asian Muslim leaders, including members of the Silk Letter Conspiracy, who forged anti-colonial alliances during wartime pilgrimages.[55] British officials tried to salvage Hussein's reputation by improving the conditions of the Hajj pilgrimage during the war. They even co-funded Indian civilians' pilgrimages in 1917.[56] Sending soldiers on pilgrimage after the war, however, proved to have a slightly different goal. British officials wanted their South Asian soldiers and Arab allies to understand the postwar world—and Muslim men's roles in it—in the same, pro-imperial, way. They hoped to make pan-Islam into a pro-British political identity.

MILITARY PILGRIMAGES

Approval for military pilgrimages came just three months after the completion of the regular yearly Hajj in late summer 1918. The planning met many complications, revealing further tensions between wartime aims and postwar occupation. Large parts of the Hijaz railway had been destroyed by Britain and its allies during the war to cut off Ottoman supply lines. The railway had originally opened in 1908 and was funded in part by South Asian Muslims who saw it as a way to modernize the Hajj and strengthen the Ottoman Empire.[57] Most postwar officials sidestepped British complicity in its destruction.[58] Nonetheless, it meant that soldiers had to travel to Jeddah by sea and then journey the rest of the way to the holy cities by road.[59] The overland journey took thirty-six hours over twenty-three miles on camels and donkeys.[60] Ignoring logistical difficulties and postwar debts, the War Office sanctioned sending two thousand soldiers on a "minor" pilgrimage outside of the regular Hajj season.[61] They set sail in January 1919. This clandestine military occupation of the holy cities of Islam attempted to transform Indian perceptions of these soldiers from impious infidels into distinguished Hajis.

Military pilgrimages proved initially popular among soldiers. Eight thousand expressed a desire to go on the first voyage.[62] By January 1919, the first ship, *Jehangir*, carried forty-six Indian officers and 1,200 other ranks from Suez to Jeddah on a four-day journey.[63] A second party of forty-five officers and 1,095 other ranks embarked from Suez on *Abbas-aieh* in mid-February.[64] A third, smaller party of one officer and sixty-three other ranks left Suez on February 22.[65] The perceived success of this first combined "minor pilgrimage" led to soldiers' official participation in the formal Hajj seasons from 1919 to 1921. Demobilization, continuing military campaigns and occupations, and political maneuvering in and around Hijaz ensured that soldiers continued to fight, and pray, in the region long after the formal end to the First World War.

During their journeys men blurred the lines between religious pilgrims and imperial soldiers. According to Subedar Major Sirdar Khan, they marched in formation in "white clothing with naked feet and heads."[66] Those who participated in the early 1919 pilgrimage had permission to wear "the 'Ihram,' or pilgrim's cloak."[67] They also visited the Ka'aba to perform the major rites and ceremonies of Hajj.[68] Others felt restrained by military discipline. On one journey the men were prohibited from traveling around the city in parties of fewer than ten and without a noncommissioned officer. They similarly could not purchase "pistols, daggers and rifles" although many desired to do so.[69] During the formal Hajj of 1919, military officials instructed the men to wear uniforms to improve their discipline.[70] They marched in uniform to the Koh-i-Nur but removed their boots before entering.[71] Soldiers' presence, meanwhile, worried civilians. By 1920, according to the Army Department, there was a "Widespread rumour in India . . . that we have Indian troops in Hijaz through whose help King Hussain is maintaining his position."[72] Civilians speculated that soldiers arrived in uniform because they were an occupying army. When soldiers returned to Hijaz for another pilgrimage in 1920, uniforms were neither worn nor taken.[73] Still, the arrival of trained and experienced soldiers made it difficult to interpret such men as religious pilgrims rather than another invading force. These pilgrims could, if the situation called for it, serve effectively as invaders and conquerors. Their day-to-day encounters with civilians similarly represented an economic and physical occupation of the holy cities that would not have felt dramatically different from wartime.

Despite some restrictions, Muslim soldiers enjoyed privileges and comforts that exceeded normal experiences of Hajj. Sharif Hussein provided mules and camels for transport and accommodations in barracks and tents while they were *en route* to Mecca.[74] Hired guides escorted them to places of religious interest.[75] Their treatment mirrored that of foreign dignitaries. Leading officials in Jeddah—including the governor and military commander—greeted soldiers' ships on arrival.[76] An honor guard of Arab policemen, the whole Mecca garrison, and their band also greeted them at the landing pier.[77] Indian officers dined with Hijaz Minister of War General Mahmud Pasha.[78] Sharif Hussein visited the soldiers in their barracks and met with each Indian officer in the palace. He kissed each of them on the head, and shook all of their hands.[79] By the second and third pilgrimages in 1919 and 1920, he kissed every low-ranking soldier as well.[80] Indian officers enjoyed gifts of the previous year's "Holy Carpet," which had covered the Holy Ka'aba.[81] Although there was a water shortage in Mecca during the regular Hajj of 1919, the troops did not feel the strain because military authorities gave them high-quality water.[82] Soldiers had separate entrances to holy places "to avoid a crowd and the mixing of clothing."[83] Hakim Said Hasan, an Indian police inspector, believed that civilians "received the troops with open arms and they did not consider them as ordinary pilgrims but as the guests of their King." The men socialized with local teachers, managers, and officers of the Arab Army.[84] Most civilian pilgrims faced repeated inconveniences and dangers to their health and safety—often regarded as normal sacrifices for a religious journey. Soldiers, by contrast, enjoyed the opportunity to be distinguished guests in the Muslim holy lands.

Soldiers' special treatment stemmed not only from Sharif Hussein, but through their imperial service. When the Arab government could not regulate shopkeepers, soldiers conducted their transactions through the British agent at Jeddah to minimize "extortion by local money changers."[85] Safeguards against their spending freed the men to make, according to police inspector Hakim Said Hasan, "voluntarily liberal and appropriate donations to various charities in Mecca." These included donations to the poor, widows, building canals, schools for Indian children in Mecca, and to the "mullas" who attended to them throughout their journey.[86] British officials' ability to provide financial safeguards enabled soldiers to become pious patrons of the Muslim poor.

Despite imperial and local privileges, soldiers endured some difficulties. Tainted water, dysentery, mosquitos, plague, and heatstroke were common threats.[87] Their participation in formal pilgrimages in late 1919 and 1920 meant that they "constantly mingled with the 70,000 other pilgrims from all parts of the East," to the dismay of medical and military officers.[88] Captain J. M. Shah of the Indian Medical Service condemned the state of the accommodations in Mecca, which included poorly drained latrines with prevalent mosquitos. Despite soldiers' superior accommodations compared with most pilgrims', according to Shah, "The sanitary condition of these buildings" was "appalling" and the air quality "foul and vicious." He concluded that poor infrastructure left the local population "debilitated, anaemic and malaria-stricken."[89] He scrutinized the administration of the city, which implicitly criticized Sharif Hussein. Shah felt that the medical conditions of Medina were so dire that "The establishment of a British hospital at Mecca, in my opinion, is an absolute necessity." This was an imperial obligation because of the "large number of Indians who are residents there" and the thousands of Indians who visited annually.[90] The commander of the Egyptian Expeditionary Force agreed with Shah's proposal.[91]

As Shah's observations suggest, these pilgrimages made Indian men both pilgrims and de facto intelligence agents in the region. This was a deliberate policy: as soon as the War Office approved the proposal for pilgrimages, Colonel Wigram at Buckingham Palace requested that Indian officers send reports of their journeys to King George V.[92] Senior Indian officers commanding each party presented reports and letters about the behavior of the Sharif. The British agent at Jeddah similarly shared information about Hussein's actions. Captain Ajab Khan gave politically useful details about possible disputes or a civil war between Hussein's four sons.[93] Others offered logistical information about the water supply into the holy city and various maps of Hijaz.[94] In addition to drafting their reports, these men also enjoyed greater leadership opportunities. Since no British officer was permitted to enter the holy city, Indian officers were left "entirely responsible" for the soldiers.[95] Subedar Major Sardar Khan commanded the men from when they left Jeddah until they arrived at the port.[96] At a time when Indian nationalists demanded more political rights and opportunities for advancement in the army, Muslim soldiers took leading roles in shaping the military, religious, and political future of a region of vital imperial and religious importance.

Pilgrimages also highlighted institutional inequalities. Captain J. M. Shah of the Indian Medical Service alleged that IMS officers outranked every Indian man in the army because they held British commissions. He described himself repeatedly as a "British Officer" because of his rank. This implicitly re-entrenched imperial hierarchies and caused some animosity among the Indian officers.[97] Men enmeshed in different colonial institutions also had frequent differences of opinion. Police inspector Hasan praised the accommodations and the leadership of Indian medical and military men.[98] He found the soldiers to be "nice and gentle." By contrast, Shah was more critical of the accommodations, provisions, and health precautions. He disparaged the quality of rations and soldiers' behavior. He found that before the Hajj men were excellent in "bearing, discipline, and general behavior." After performing the Hajj, the temptations of Mecca "lead some of them away from the path of virtue."[99] Shah's "British Officer" rank could not be threatened by his candid reflections, unlike police and Indian Army men whose livelihoods depended on their ability to pacify military families and British officers. Shah's apparent ability to remark more freely about the flaws of the journey emphasized the inability of other South Asian men to do so. South Asian Muslim men could take important roles in the pilgrimage but they were still colonial subjects. Their ability to author a report was still burdened by colonial needs and expectations.

PAN-ISLAM AND THE IDEAL MUSLIM

One of the unique features of the military Hajj was that it allowed soldiers to cultivate a pro-imperial, pan-Islamic identity. Sharif Hussein told them that Mecca was a place "for every MUSLIM . . . from any part of the world."[100] He also celebrated soldiers' service to Britain during the First World War as "the cause of Just and Right." Captain Salamat Ulla Khan echoed this sentiment not only by praising their journey as "the great bond of Muslim brotherhood" but by giving thanks to the "British Government."[101] This celebration of Muslim brotherhood between British allies helped legitimize, rather than undermine, British intervention in the region. It established a seemingly consensual ground on which imperial rule expanded with the support of Muslim subjects and allies.

Sharif Hussein attempted to solidify his connection with Indian soldiers by expressing anti-Ottoman views. He blamed the Ottomans for the "crooked and narrow" streets in his own city, the lack of latrines and sanitation, the absence of schools and "badly arranged markets," and the "general ignorance" of the people. He maintained that the Ottomans had received £150,000 annually in pilgrimage quarantine dues but had not improved accommodations.[102] They also failed to protect precious objects during the war which threatened "the prestige of Islam."[103] Hussein contrasted Ottoman mismanagement of the pilgrimages with the attentive treatment he provided to Indian soldiers.[104] This helped him to rationalize his wartime actions. He maintained that he supported the British because the blockade had caused starvation among the people of Mecca. When the Ottomans failed to send food aid, he started to negotiate with Great Britain, which saved the people from famine.[105] Just as War Office officials failed to mention Britain's role in the destruction of the Hijaz railway, Hussein omitted that the *allied* blockade contributed to widespread hunger in Hijaz. Focusing on the Ottomans' unwillingness to give aid emphasized how his alliance with the British saved the day. Like Indian officers, Hussein expressed gratitude for "his Britannic Majesty for having helped him at a hard time." He felt "indebted to him to his dying day."[106]

Hussein was candid in sharing his opinions with Indian soldiers because he believed that they were "good Muslims."[107] He contrasted them to the Young Turk Party, whom he found irreligious for drinking liquor and committing adultery. Turks apparently taunted men who prayed or kept the fast of Ramzan. Liquor shops thrived near the railway station in the vicinity of Medina. Meanwhile, "women of bad character of the Jewish nation had settled in Medina for immoral purposes and the laws of the Shra' [*sic*] were quite ignored."[108] This latent antisemitism protected Arab women from accusations of immorality. It also criticized westernization without explicitly offending his British allies. Hussein nonetheless lamented Ottoman officials' decision to build schools for girls and educate them "on European lines," which left boys "in the dark." He opposed making Mecca "like a European city with theatres and cinemas." He did so by investing money in military schools for boys.[109] He even allowed Indian pilgrims to visit these military schools, where they were greeted with enthusiastic speeches and songs.[110]

Sharif Hussein viewed military pilgrimages as an opportunity to cultivate a specific vision of international Muslim masculinity. This came at the expense of the Ottoman Empire and the modernizing Young Turks. His anxieties about alcohol, sexual decorum, and "Jewish" women hinted at the fragile postwar environment. The war brought dance halls, hostels, and brothels to amuse troops and laborers. The soldier-pilgrimages proved to be a counter-revolutionary force of peacetime. They hardened expectations of conduct that had been abandoned during the war. By singling out the South Asian troops as "good Muslims," Hussein praised men who were trained by British officials as exemplars of religious belief and moral discipline.

Hussein admired Indian soldiers for being "good Muslims," but soldiers were not impressed by the Muslims they encountered in Hijaz. Subedar Major Sirdar Khan reported that "For keeping the places clean Arabs were told off."[111] Captain Ajab Khan received help from the Hijaz police to protect soldiers' camps from civilians and Arab mendicants. Soldiers grew weary about the "crowds and crowds" of beggars. Ajab Khan found the Bedu camel men on the journey from Mecca to Jeddah "a very unmanageable creature" who required bribes.[112] Meanwhile, some soldiers questioned Sharif Hussein's morality due to his failures as a ruler. Subedar Major Jalal Khan of the 2/19th Punjabis regarded the Sharif as a "great man" as well as caliph, but noted that "the majority of the Indian Officers were not of the same opinion."[113] Captain Ajab Khan believed that Hussein was "popular among his subjects and is loved by and loves every one of them."[114] Yet he remained more skeptical about the governance of

Hijaz more generally. He found the Hijaz government "very backwards in its modes and ways of governing." Hussein was "a very nice self-willed man of old type" but the officials around him were "given to corruption and malpractices."[115] Matters grew especially strained when police searched Indian soldiers in their armpits and between the legs, which he characterized as a "dishonourable thing."[116] Hussein may have praised Indian soldiers for being good Muslims but his actions and administration caused them to feel physically disgraced and demoralized. Soldiers regarded themselves as moral, disciplined, and civilized compared to the apparently immoral, ungodly, and materially minded Muslims living in the holy lands, including Sharif Hussein.

In the eyes of his Indian observers, Hussein failed most in his treatment of South Asian civilians. Ajab Khan explained that while soldiers had "free access" to holy sites, "poor Indian pilgrims" had to beg for the gate-keepers to let them in. Soldiers "resented" the "cheating of the poor Indian pilgrims."[117] At times soldiers even responded with "violence and rioting."[118] Ajab believed that most Indian pilgrims' experiences in Mecca were "pitiable." "Sick Indian Hajis" lay outside hospital gates for hours and had to pay high prices for medicine. He believed that "a bold move on the part of the Government of India" was necessary to correct the current state of affairs. He recommended appointing a British agent at Jeddah and several Indians to oversee the plight of Indian pilgrims.[119] Once again, Indian military men depicted British presence in the holy lands as a necessary source of stability, even when it meant granting further access to and control over South Asian bodies and autonomous Muslim rulers.[120] The treatment of Indian civilians was not just about pilgrimages but was also a matter of protecting the Indian diaspora. Indian officers estimated that between half and three-quarters of the population of Mecca were Indian or of Indian heritage.[121] Since Britain was "the greatest Moslem ruling power in the world" they needed to protect "the interests of our Moslem fellow-subjects at these holy places." Appointing a British representative and establishing a charitable hospital in Mecca and Medina, he believed, would help to ease Indian soldiers' hardships.[122] Like the medical officer Shah, who referred to himself as a "British officer," Ajab Khan spoke of British intervention in terms of "our" responsibilities to "our" subjects. As a Punjabi Muslim soldier, he identified with imperial power, as well as with imperial Muslim subjects.

Ajab Khan's defense of imperial intervention reflected his own role in fostering support for British rule among Muslim subjects. He was an honorary captain of the Indian Army, a title bestowed to Indian soldiers at the end of their careers. He had been a Subedar in the Hong Kong Regiment and the 76th Punjabis and earned the 1st Class Indian Order of Merit for gallantry in Mesopotamia.[123] This distinguished career gave him political clout. The viceroy nominated him as an unofficial member of the Imperial Legislative Council and as part of the Punjab Muslim Association deputation that met with the secretary of state in Delhi. In 1918 he was nominated to the viceroy's Legislative Assembly for 1918–19 to represent the Punjabi military classes.[124] Sending prominent Punjabi Muslim men like Ajab Khan to Hijaz and Mecca helped to diminish dreams of anti-colonial pan-Islamic unity. These men's criticisms of Sharif Hussein, and sympathies with Indian pilgrims, were useful for British imperial authorities. Their reports justified further British presence and, if necessary, military intervention.

Like British leaders, Sharif Hussein had his own political reasons for supporting the pilgrimages. He hoped that facilitating Indian soldiers' pilgrimages would gain him important allies in the turbulent postwar world. However, Indian soldiers contributed to Britain's *lack* of confidence in him. British officials decreased their subsidy to Sharif Hussein after the war ended. This hurt his power as a ruler and diminished his ability to impress South Asian soldiers.[125] Soldiers noted that their accommodations became less lavish each year.[126] During the 1920 Hajj, soldiers observed that "the welcome they received in the HEDJAZ was . . . not so spontaneous or pronounced as that accorded to them on previous pilgrimages."[127] They viewed this as another indication of Hussein's poor leadership rather than a signal of Britain's decreasing financial support. By 1920, the Indian Army believed that the pilgrimages were less politically necessary. In 1921, the War Office requested to revert to prewar arrangements.[128] The only one who disagreed was Winston Churchill, who was secretary of state for the colonies. He wanted to see the procedure expanded rather than phased out. According to J. E. Shuckburgh, Churchill wanted to make it possible for "all British Moslem soldiers who desire to make the pilgrimage during their leave."[129] However, the War Office declared that, after 1922, soldiers needed to carry out the Hajj as they had done before the war—as civilians at their own expense.[130] By March 1922 the military pilgrimages ended.[131]

The military Hajj played a crucial role in Britain's decision not to aid Sharif Hussein when he faced invasion in 1924. Ibn Saud of Nejd, one of Sharif Hussein's major rivals, had also been Britain's wartime ally and resented Sharif Hussein's claim to be caliph. When he invaded Hijaz, British officials did not intervene. They rationalized that it was a local issue that should be solved by regional powers. Indian soldiers' tepid response to Sharif Hussein, and their disgust at the treatment of Indian pilgrims, contributed to imperial skepticism about his political value and leadership. Hussein invested considerable funds for Indian soldiers' pilgrimages yet his rule would barely outlast their existence. Pilgrimages did, by contrast, help to strengthen British goals at a tenuous postwar moment. Soldiers and veterans who may have become nationalist or pan-Islamic sympathizers traveled overseas to engage with a Muslim ruler. This convinced some that Muslim leadership in the holy lands did not necessarily guarantee the best interests of Indian Muslims. As men trained in British military discipline, some viewed—or reported—that British imperial rule could be a source of health, rationality, and fair governance. This inspired them to *encourage*, rather than question, British intervention in the region. Wartime and postwar experience "telling off Arabs" and condemning poor Hijazi beggars and Bedu camel men from Egypt to Mesopotamia led some soldiers to believe that Islam was in need of redemption. As Britain's de facto Muslim ambassadors, they put their faith in the empire.

MAKING THE DISLOYAL PATHAN

International travel gave some Muslim soldiers a measure of appreciation for the potential benefits of imperial service. Closer to home, however, the fate of Muslim subjects was far more tenuous. The borders of northwestern India were unstable during and after the First World War due to recurring threats of foreign invasion and the tendency of anti-colonial revolutionaries to seek alliances in the region. Recurring military campaigns destabilized life and society for many military and civilian residents. At a time when the army funded soldiers to carry out of one of the five pillars of Islam, it also waged brutal military campaigns against other Muslims believed to be too martial and too Muslim. This parallel story of wartime and postwar Muslim identity exposes how violence often underpinned constructions of the perfect Muslim soldier.

During the First World War, northwestern India remained a primary site of imperial insecurity. For example, in 1915, Afridi soldier Mir Mast allegedly climbed out of the trenches in France, walked over to the Germans, and offered to join their ranks. Once accepted, he reportedly drew maps of the overland route into India to help German and Turkish spies launch an invasion through Afghanistan.[132] Such exceptional stories fueled the imperial perception that Muslim men recruited from the northwest were the most likely to betray British rule in India. In fact, it was the constant threat of military violence that made life complicated for both soldiers and civilians. Pathans, also known by the colonial state as Pushtuns, Pashtuns, Pukhtuns, Pakhtuns, and Afghans, were the ethnic majority in northwestern India, in present-day Pakistan.[133] According to British authors, Pathans occupied a space that was both praise-worthy and contemptible for being an unconquerable "frontier." A pamphlet providing "Hints for Soldiers" regarded Pathans as naturally "brave and warlike" because they were raised in "an inhospitable land of bare mountains, where only the hardiest survive."[134] According to British officials this rugged masculinity made them a desirable "martial race." At the same time, British officials worried about the revolutionary potential of the region and the men who lived there.

Pathans' ties to northwestern India and Afghanistan turned them into targets of violence and scapegoating during the war. British officials executed three men of the 130th Baluchis in Rangoon and sentenced two hundred other Pathans to various terms of imprisonment after they were insubordinate and killed a British officer in 1914.[135] After the incident the viceroy was convinced, "There is no doubt that there is a strong disinclination among certain classes of Pathans especially Afridis to fight against Turks or their allies."[136] What he did not acknowledge was that Rangoon was a locale that had considerable prewar and wartime anti-colonial activism.[137] As early as 1907 officials worried about "unrest" among the Punjabi soldiers stationed there, even though Punjabis were long associated with being unwavering and reliable.[138] The 130th Baluchis, therefore, may have responded more to successful international revolutionary networking than general "religious" objections. Similarly, many Pathans in the 20th Infantry deserted from the Persian Gulf, a region known for its harsh climate and poor provisions. Officials cited that their reasons were a disinclination to fight against Muslim soldiers, eliminating the possibility that they had many other concerns about their imperial service.[139]

Incidents of desertion led military officials to modify the recruitment and service of Pathans. They initially singled out "trans-frontier" Pathans in 1915 whose livelihoods and family ties to Afghanistan caused them to transgress the boundaries of British and Afghan territory. They depicted these men as "fanatics" with an overzealous commitment to Islam. Charles Townshend carried this bias against his soldiers with him into the Mesopotamia campaign, contributing to his defeat at the famous Siege of Kut-al-Amara in 1916.[140] By 1916 all trans-frontier Pathans were withdrawn from Mesopotamia. In October 1917, this ban extended to Pathans who lived near or beyond the Indus River. Official reasoning was that such men displayed "religious prejudices" about fighting against Ottoman forces.[141] Pathan and Afridi soldiers, in turn, exchanged news about men who had deserted.[142] News of desertion deepened the unease of those who were already far from home, felt the mounting pressure of imperial suspicions, and had to cope with some of the most difficult military campaigns. By 1918, individual incidents of desertion all but guaranteed Pathan demobilization. When 12 Pathan men deserted from the Egyptian Expeditionary Force (EEF) between January and July 1918, it led to the withdrawal of all 132 trans-frontier Pathan men. The remaining 3,500 Pathans of the EEF were put under "special watching."[143]

Desertion was not simply a matter of "prejudice" or piety. It often coincided with other wartime challenges. Muslim men constituted one-third of the soldiers who served from Egypt to the Persian Gulf. There they endured extreme heat, unsanitary provisions, large insects, and unfamiliar terrain.[144] This was a region of the world where few soldiers—regardless of their religious beliefs—wanted to serve. Soldiers who lived through the Siege of Kut in April 1916, for example, endured cholera, dysentery, and poor provisions. They faced a lack of vegetables and eventually a compulsion to eat horse meat.[145] Desertions were most common during periods of low morale. This was the result of homesickness, poor food, culture shock, poor command, racism, and high casualties, which similarly inspired desertions among Europeans. Despite these challenges, Pathans proved integral to important campaigns. They were among the first to arrive in Mesopotamia in 1914 and participated in raids led by T. E. Lawrence in the Arab Revolt.[146] By 1918, rates of desertion were much lower, totaling only thirty in the entire Egyptian Expeditionary Force. This decrease coincided with improved logistics and a series of Ottoman surrenders in Mesopotamia, including the conquest of Baghdad.[147] While some soldiers no doubt combined their many wartime grievances with their personal feelings of spiritual devotion, this should not be understood as the sole or even most important factor influencing soldiers' choices to desert. Colonial officials nonetheless continued to presume the inherent religiosity of South Asian men, which led them to read soldiers' grievances as "prejudices" or "fanaticism."

Tales of Pathan disloyalty became a common and oft-repeated cliché in accounts of Muslim troops in the war. Cavalry officer F. James recalled that, "A party of Pathan soldiers, escorting a convoy, decided to desert to their homes in Afghanistan with their rifles and ammunition."[148] Rajput soldier Amar Singh was certain that "the Muhamedan [*sic*] soldiers have proved greatly wanting in loyalty toward the British government. The chief culprits have been the Afridis and Pathans from the trans-frontier areas of India."[149] One Hindu politician similarly maintained that "trans-frontier Pathans have been discredited." He used this to argue for expanding recruitment in the army beyond the martial races.[150] For non-Muslim Indian politicians and soldiers, spreading the narrative of Pathan disloyalty discredited the army's prejudicial recruiting practices. If Pathans' loyalties were uncertain, they contended, then why were they recruited so widely? The censor of Indian mail, meanwhile, believed that Punjabi Muslims were reasonable soldiers but Pathans were far too hasty.[151] In 1918, the Military Secretary to the India Office, General H. V. Cox, confirmed that the trouble "amongst Indian troops in Mesopotamia, Egypt, or France has practically been restricted to Pathans, especially trans-frontier Pathans." He believed that "the Musalmans of India (other than Pathans) have been generally reliable."[152] Cox believed that "war weariness"—rather than "religious prejudice"—played the dominant role in Pathan soldiers' dissatisfaction. Whatever the perceived cause, the result was continuing to regard Pathans as particularly unreliable.

In reality, Pathans faced specific challenges that exceeded the hardships of the average soldier. Many Pathan men joined the Indian Army due to endemic poverty across northwestern India and Afghanistan.[153] Those who resided in areas outside of British control received more frequent threats to their land and families during the war, increasing their desire to return home.[154] Most were prevented from doing so due to imperial fears that returning soldiers would stir rebellion and unrest along the borders.[155] Widespread poverty was due, in part, to the instability engendered by the frequent military campaigns in the region. It had been a long sore-spot of the British rule in India. Various communities faced coercion, propositions for alliances, or forcible subjugation in their efforts to play Afghan, Russian, and British authorities off one another. Throughout the war, Bengali, pan-Islamic, German, Persian, Egyptian, Ghadar, Irish, and Russian revolutionaries wanted to use the Afghan capital of Kabul as a launching pad to invade British India. After the Bolshevik Revolution, communist revolutionaries referred to Muslims in Persia, Afghanistan, and northwestern India as "Oppressed Peoples of the East." British wartime fears of German and Ottoman plots bled seamlessly into postwar anxieties about communism, pan-Islam, and anti-colonialism.[156] Pathans were left to face difficult and immediate choices about where to invest their loyalties. Anti-colonial revolutionaries called them foolish traitors if they served the British. Military officials scaled back on their employment. The constant threat of violence and economic deprivation made it impossible for Pathans to join any military force or political alliance without considering their immediate needs for safety and security.

Even after the European ceasefire in 1918 Pathans endured imperial violence. The Third Anglo-Afghan War (1919) began when the Amir of Afghanistan, Amanullah, tried to launch an invasion into India. His predecessor and father, Amir Habibullah, had remained neutral during the First World War but was assassinated by revolutionaries. Amanullah's invasion was a culmination of wartime revolutionary activism led by Indian Ghadar activists, the Indo-German Mission, and Maulana Obaidullah Sindhi of the "Silk Letter Conspiracy."[157] Ultimately, the invasion failed and Amanullah negotiated a separate peace for Afghan independence within a few months, leaving his Indian allies with nothing.[158] The war ushered in no less than three years of conflict among Pathan tribes living in Waziristan along the Indo-Afghan border.[159] The difficulty of the conflict and prolonged experience of war led to mass desertions.[160] Pathan soldiers returning from war or facing demobilization, therefore, returned home without jobs and facing the uncertainties of local military attacks with few assurances from either Afghan or British authorities. The colonial state, meanwhile, continued to demonize them as inherently uncivilized, fanatical, and disloyal.

The brutality of the Third Anglo-Afghan War and its aftermath blurred the distinctions between war and peace—a common feature of living in a militarized imperial borderland. Mrs. Lilian Starr, who worked in a missionary hospital in 1920, recalled that the Peshawar Hospital made "quite a collection of British bullets" that had been "removed from Afghan patients."[161] Military officials believed that conventional warfare could not succeed in tribal areas and turned to aerial assaults. This inspired terror among the many civilians subject to it.[162] One British newspaper recorded that "All prisoners testify to the demoralising effect of our aerial attacks upon men who have faced rifle and gunfire in the past with undaunted courage."[163] Another man lamented the foreign aircraft that pierced "dwellings with falling fire." He raided British military stations (cantonments) to kill British officials for revenge.[164] British military pamphlets, meanwhile, warned British soldiers that they would face murder or assault if they ever encountered Pathans, contributing to a lack of empathy for those subject to military violence.[165] Thus, India's northwestern borders remained an active war zone not easily returned to a peaceful state by 1918, 1919, or even 1920.

Rather than acknowledging the traumas of protracted wars, British officials accused Pathan militias of succumbing to the "call of Islam" whenever their behavior challenged imperial control.[166] This was due in part to the defeat and disintegration of the Ottoman Empire. This increased South Asian anti-colonial support for the Khilafat movement, led by the Ali brothers, which attempted to protect the Muslim caliphate.[167] The Third Anglo-Afghan War, meanwhile, convinced some Muslims that India was *Dar-al-Harb*—the realm of war. Pious followers of Islam, according to this view, should either stay and fight or migrate to regions of the world under Muslim control. The newly independent Amir of Afghanistan, Amanullah, promised to support pilgrims and migrants with land and food.[168] This inspired a mass migration of South Asian Muslims into Afghanistan called *Hijrat* in May 1920. Facing acute postwar economic and political challenges, tens of thousands of South Asian Muslims migrated to Afghanistan. British cavalry officer Francis Yeats-Brown recalled that it was impossible for Indian soldiers to remain "indifferent to that strange pilgrimage into Afghanistan which so closely affected the land and families of our men."[169] Confirming imperial fears, some pilgrims joined up with Bolshevik revolutionaries and Indian nationalists in Kabul. The majority simply found hardship, theft, and starvation. Afghani officials struggled to accommodate the pilgrims and two-thirds returned home with less financial stability than when they departed.[170] Pathan men were scaled back from their imperial positions at a time when pan-Islamic and communist movements in the northwest called on them to abandon India for a promise of spiritual and economic salvation.

While military pilgrimages to Mecca and Medina made colonial rule appear almost all-knowing and all-powerful, imperial borderlands told a different story. Postwar uncertainty led British officials to single out the "dangerous" Pathan as a threat to India, hardening preexisting imperial narratives of Pathans being wild, cruel, and untamed. British Private J. P. Swindlehurst revealed the pervasiveness of this view by 1920. He wrote in his diary, without giving a specific example, that if a Pathan man had a "grievance fancied or real" it would result in "nothing short of killing." He even copied entire sections from military handbooks alongside passages from Rudyard Kipling into his diaries to capture the fantastic and romantic qualities of these men.[171] When he observed that three Pathan cooks were "quite decent straightforward men" he assumed that this was because "they had been disciplined."[172] Despite his positive encounters, he fell back on colonial rhetoric. For some soldiers, imperial discourses spoke louder than personal experiences. This made it easier to participate in and facilitate violence against populations demonized as fanatical.

BRITISH SOLDIERS AND BORDER CROSSINGS

Many British army men like Swindlehurst failed to overcome institutional suspicion of Pathans despite positive interpersonal encounters. However, some Indian Army officers developed a surprising degree of sympathy, and intimacy, with the men they commanded. This was the case for First World War veteran Captain Reginald Abel Lewis Moysey of the 1/22nd Punjabis, who allied with Pathans against the colonial state. In 1920 and 1921 he lived in the northwestern cantonment of Rawalpindi "in a tent away from any other officer" and became "very intimate with" Pathan soldiers. Rawalpindi's superintendent of police heard that Moysey planned to "employ Pathans" to raid the supply depot's guards and "obtain their rifles."[173] Half of the garrison spent a night guarding the points that Moysey "and his gang" were expected to attack.[174] Moysey had returned to India at the height of the Hijrat movement, during which Indian Muslims migrated to Afghanistan. He served beside Muslim troops in the First World War and during the brutal conflicts in Waziristan. Unlike Pathan soldiers, who faced court-martials, dismissal, or accusations of excessive religious feeling for unusual or suspicious behavior, Moysey crossed British imperial borders repeatedly without immediate retribution. His case suggests that Britons could be far more attracted to and invested in narratives of "Pathan militancy" than most actual Pathans, deepening the racialized violence of imperial rule.

At first, Moysey's intimacy with Pathans and threats to raid cantonments resulted in no formal police or military punishment. He spent the summer of 1921 serving with the 2nd Battalion, 21st Punjabis in Waziristan. This took him even farther into India's northwestern borderlands.[175] Later that year, he became embroiled in a series of illegal incidents. In September 1921, a young Pathan man roughly seventeen years old named Nur Hussein Shah was arrested for violating the Indian Arms

Act. Moysey, who was about twenty-three years old, was Nur's official guardian.[176] Superintendent Hadow arrested Nur Hussein Shah "with difficulty" for running around with an automatic pistol. Moysey "forcibly released" him from police custody.[177] Moysey was reduced in rank from a captain to a lieutenant and received authorization for resignation on November 19, 1921.[178] Police recaptured Nur Hussein Shah to serve a prison sentence under the Arms Act in the Rawalpindi jail.[179] Even though imperial wartime concerns fixated on the dangers of Pathan soldiers, it was the British officer who used violence to free a young Pathan man from British captivity.

It did not take long for British officials to speculate on the reasons for Moysey's behavior. Superintendent Hadow claimed that "There is very little doubt that Moysey's mania is unnatural offences and that this boy is his particular paramour."[180] Deputy Commissioner H. A. Smith argued more explicitly that Moysey was "a confirmed sodomite," which "adds to the undesirability of letting him stay in India."[181] By the twentieth century the colonial state had an ambivalent view of same-sex contact between men. Allegations of homosexuality, at times, provided distractions from accusations of imperial mismanagement or scandal.[182] Many colonial officials even assumed that Muslim soldiers from the northwest had sex with one another due to the perceived scarcity of women. Some believed that this was a sign of their robust strength and rugged masculinity.[183] Despite the illegality of "sodomy" in colonial India, soldiers were rarely prosecuted. Condemning Moysey as a "confirmed sodomite," however, ignored his other possible motivations. This echoed the disregard for anything other than religiously motivated disloyalty among Muslim troops.

Moysey had a very different explanation for his behavior. According to Moysey's account, Nur Hussein Shah was a pious young man who saw a bird carrying entrails near a mosque.[184] Nur opened fire at the bird to "prevent the desecration of this holy place." Moysey admitted that he "released" Nur from prison as soon as he heard about the incident. Police apparently brought forward a "false charge" by alleging that Nur shot at them. The young man received a sentence of one year imprisonment and a fine for violating the Arms Act. This was reduced to eight months after an appeal. Moysey claimed that he wanted to submit the matter to the

High Court but could not afford to do so because he spent every penny "defending an innocent man" who had merely "acted in the defense of the sanctity of a place of worship and would not pay the Police money to let him go."[185] Moysey's forcible release of Nur, he insisted, was only to undermine police corruption. According to Moysey's story, Nur was just a young man who protected his holy place. This fit well within the logical framework of a colonial state that was paying for Muslim soldiers to perform the Hajj. British officials wanted to present themselves as protectors, rather than opponents, of Islam. On the surface, Moysey's defense of Nur seemed to embody that policy.

Moysey's statement—so self-righteous in preventing a holy desecration and condemning police corruption—did not account for how or why Nur Hussein had a pistol. He also omitted what measures he took to free Nur from police custody. Most importantly, his statement was also a declaration for how and why he was kidnapping Judith Birdwood, the ten-year-old daughter of General Sir William Birdwood.[186] In late November 1921, two days after securing his resignation, Moysey confided to a fellow officer that he planned to attend a dance hosted by General Birdwood without an invitation. He intended to abduct "the General's youngest daughter" and take her "into independent territory." Moysey threatened to blackmail the viceroy and marry Judith off to a Pathan man if his demands for cash and transportation were not met. His main object was to "secure the release of" Nur Hussein Shah.[187] Despite being tipped off about the plan in advance, General Birdwood and Deputy Commissioner Smith did not believe that it would actually take place.[188] Moysey arrived at 10:45 P.M. with a motor car, grenades, a revolver, a pistol, and extra cartridges and magazines.[189] When he climbed into Birdwood's garden, police tried but failed to arrest him. His car was "put out of action and the bombs and revolver removed."[190] Police laid "traps" near his car and bungalow and arrested him.[191]

British officials decided not to pursue an attempted kidnapping case against Moysey to avoid a scandal. They only sentenced him to two months' rigorous imprisonment—the equivalent of hard labor—for releasing Nur from prison.[192] However, the India Office, Punjab government, and superintendent of police remained fearful that Moysey possessed "an intimate knowledge of Pushtu" and had "many Pathan friends." He had even crossed borders "disguised as a Pathan."[193] They worried that he would continue "to assist trans-frontier raiders and to organize their activities." Pathan soldiers, they contended, might take retribution against the officer who had foiled his plan.[194] This response implies that Moysey may have been more than just a "sodomite" inflicted with "mania." The deputy commissioner admitted that Moysey's "attitude towards Government" had "never been loyal." The Punjab government, in turn, requested his deportation in December 1921—a severe punishment for a former officer.[195] His two-month imprisonment expired in January 1922 and he arrived in London on the P&O steamship *Egypt* in February.[196]

Despite all of the rumors and evidence about Moysey's intentions to raid the cantonment, have sex with Pathan men, arrive armed at a general's place of residence, blackmail top officials, forcibly release a man from police custody, and kidnap a general's daughter, he only faced two months in prison and deportation from India. He had done so by threatening to defile two prized symbols of British rule—the body of a white general's daughter, and that of a potentially recruitable young Pathan man. A sentence of rigorous imprisonment indicates the severity of his crimes; it was rarely inflicted upon British officers. This judgment was also small compared to Nur's eight months for violating the Indian Arms Act. At the end of it all, Moysey could still return to Britain and live an ordinary life, a choice quite absent for South Asian men who fell afoul of the colonial state. However, Moysey was not content to return to England and maintain an illusion of peace.

In May 1922, three months after returning to England, Moysey applied for a passport to Persia.[197] Unsurprisingly, the Foreign Office, the director of military intelligence, and the commissioner of police were unwilling to grant it.[198] The India Office provided ample evidence of his antics and denied his access to any country near northwestern India.[199] However, denial of a passport did not prevent Moysey from returning to India. He visited the Afghan Legation in London in April 1923. Shortly thereafter he allegedly disguised himself as a lascar seaman, boarded a ship to India, and crossed into Afghanistan "disguised as an Afridi tribesman."[200] By September 1923, officials found Moysey in Jalalabad wearing

"Afridi clothes" and saying "his prayers fluently as a Mussulman."[201] He arrived in Kabul using his stepfather's surname, Rattray, as his own.[202] He claimed that he had resigned from service in the Indian Army to serve the Afghan government and was awaiting orders. British officials in Kabul believed that "A knowledge of the character of the man does not warrant the placing of any credence on his statements." They suspected that he was a spy.[203] They arrested him at Landi Khana in November 1923.

Rather than simply sending Moysey back to England, the viceroy and secretary of state for India arranged to have Moysey shipped to Penang, Malay States, to live on a rubber plantation under his brother's supervision. Moysey agreed not to return to India for five years under the terms of the European Vagrancy Act. He was banned from doing so under the Frontier Security Regulation.[204] These acts, like deportation and rigorous imprisonment, were extreme pieces of legislation only selectively used against Europeans. Using them against Moysey suggests that he represented a considerable threat to the colonial state that exceeded the potential embarrassment of disgracing and condemning a former officer.[205]

Despite the exceptional nature of Moysey's case, his attempt to kidnap a general's daughter reflected the state of imperial uncertainty during and after the Third Anglo-Afghan War and Waziristan campaign. What made the plot surprising was that it was carried out by a British actor. In 1920, the year before Moysey's failed kidnapping of Judith Birdwood, a group of raiders tried but failed to abduct the wife of a Colonel Foulkes after killing her husband.[206] British periodicals often recounted such activities with fascination, noting for instance that "Wars, feuds, murders and abductions, are the order of the day" in northwestern India.[207] Author Alfred Ollivant believed that "kidnapping is common all along the Frontier," adding that it was usually South Asian money-lenders or British officers who made the most frequent victims.[208] Most famously, a group of raiders led by Ajab Khan Afridi kidnapped teenaged Molly Ellis after killing her mother in 1923. Like Moysey, their main goal was to use her to secure the release of their imprisoned comrades. The Ellis case sparked international outrage.[209] Some claimed years later that it "nearly involved Great Britain and Afghanistan in hostilities."[210] Moysey's case, by contrast, was carefully silenced to avoid a scandal. Some of the information about his alleged sexual intimacy with Nur was even scratched out of some versions of official records.[211] British authors' tendencies to portray kidnapping as a perennial part of the "wild frontier" overlooked the specific context of the Third Anglo-Afghan War (1919). Between 1919 and 1920 alone, over six hundred raids took place, resulting in the death of nearly 300 Britons and the kidnapping of 463.[212] Moysey's decisions to plan raids, kidnappings, and border crossings were consistent with ongoing acts of war.

Moysey's "intimate" attachments to Pathan soldiers likely gave him a different perspective than most soldiers and officers. Calls for Khilafat and Hijrat may have seemed logical to a man who lived and worked in a Muslim-majority region and fought beside Pathan soldiers in the First World War. He also had the privileged position to use threats of violence to express his political sympathies. Unlike his South Asian colleagues, he did not have to live in a perpetual state of institutional suspicion that condemned men as revolutionaries, "criminal tribes," or "fanatics." British officials remained reluctant to categorize Moysey as a habitual offender no matter how many laws, social norms, and borders he transgressed. They hoped that relocating him to other parts of the empire would reduce his propensity for political danger. In the end, Moysey's actions created further suspicions of Indian revolutionaries. Colonial officials gained new fear that they would enter "disguised as seamen" and carefully scrutinized passport procedures for Indian travelers and workers at ports because of a British soldier's antics.[213] His cultural fluidity and intimacy was built on a foundation of racial privilege that resulted in disproportionate punishments for those he claimed to protect.

In many ways, Reginald Moysey more closely resembled imperial definitions of Pathans than any South Asians. He crossed borders, planned raids and kidnappings, slept in tents, spoke several languages, and recited Muslim prayers "fluently" and with uncommon vigor. By being masculine and chivalric, cruel and unrestrained, Moysey embodied the imperial perception of the Pathan soldier. The fact that he was British allowed him to appropriate imperial markers of risk and danger. Few actual Pathans, who faced demobilization, ongoing military campaigns, and constant imperial suspicion, would have been able to challenge the imperial state as consistently and repeatedly as Moysey did without facing violent retribution. His immersion in imperial discourses, his status as a British officer, and his access to Pathan soldiers gave him the tools to undermine British authority. By contrast, Nur Hussein Shah endured a lengthy imprisonment for violating the Indian Arms Act. Other Indian men faced years of imprisonment for threatening to kidnap British women.[214] Moysey's attempt to kidnap Judith Birdwood resulted in no documented punishment. Muslim soldiers and veterans, by contrast, had little choice but to prove their loyalty or face violent consequences.

SITUATING BORDERS

Facing Khilafat and communist activists, potential invasion during the Anglo-Afghan War, religious migrations such as Hijrat, and the conquest of new "mandates," the Indian Army doubled-down on their investment in their Muslim soldiers. Officers hoped that, rather than joining "disloyal" rebels like Moysey, or venturing to the Afghan borderlands, soldiers would view the army as a path to economic and spiritual salvation. Yet soldiers of the same faith could have vastly different experiences of war and peace. Pathans endured consistent challenges of poverty, institutional suspicion, and military invasion. Their experiences contributed to greater uncertainty in the militarized northwestern borderlands. This became a boon for some Punjabi Muslims. Although they had also faced similar difficulties of famine, plague, and influenza, the army increased, rather than decreased, Punjabi recruitment and made political alliances with influential men in the region. Some even helped forge an idea of what it meant to be both a practitioner of Islam and a *participant*, rather than subject, of the British Empire. British investments in Islam attempted to create a carefully selected corps of South Asian Muslim allies who could serve, defend, and even identify with imperial rule. This was essential for enabling the colonial state to carry out acts of violence against others.

Examining the treatment, recruitment, and experiences of Muslim soldiers in the Indian Army suggests the fluidity not only of colonial identities but also between victims and perpetuators of imperial violence. Sometimes soldiers could be both. Individuals earmarked for military service often carried out extreme acts of violence on behalf of the colonial state. At the same time, they often came from communities or regions deeply affected by military invasion, few economic opportunities, limited mobility, or institutional discrimination. Soldiers most affected by the militarization of colonial borders helped to spread violence to Britain's League of Nations mandates in Palestine, Transjordan, and Iraq and to expand imperial influence in regions not officially under British tutelage, such as Hijaz. The militarization of borders deepened the racialization of geopolitical division, shaping every aspect of soldiers' lives.

The imperial state functioned not only by dividing Sikhs, Muslims, and Hindus from one another, but by dividing communities internally. The differences between Punjabis, Afridis, and Pathans were often fluid due to intermarriage, migration, and changing identities. Their actions also confounded imperial logic. Some who identified as Pathans continued to serve loyally in the army while some Punjabi Muslims fought against imperialism until independence. Imperial investment in or condemnation of these communities shaped—but did not determine—their economic and political futures. The imperial state saw some soldiers' connections to foreign powers, such as Afghanistan or the caliphate, as indications of their uncertain loyalties. However, being a soldier with national or spiritual devotions outside imperial control did not always result in institutional condemnation. At times, the colonial state even invested in Hindu "religious" rituals at a scale comparable to the military Hajj. This was based, like their Muslim counterparts, on their geographic position and perceived value to the empire.

CHAPTER 3

PURIFYING THE SOLDIER

BRITISH OFFICIALS WORRIED about securing Muslim soldiers' loyalties due to their international connections to people and places from Hijaz to Afghanistan. By contrast, some considered soldiers from a nominally independent nation as some of the most steadfast. During the First World War, at least sixty-five thousand soldiers of the Indian Army were Nepalese soldiers, recruited in the army as "Gurkhas." Many British officers praised the wide recruitment of Nepalis even though they were not formal subjects of the British Empire. This was the result of British "martial race" discourses, which regarded Nepali men as pro-British Hindus and Buddhists who were resistant to caste restrictions, antagonistic to Indians, and unsympathetic to Indian nationalism.[1] Despite this confident rhetoric, Nepali soldiers, like Sikhs, proved to be more than an unambiguous force of blind loyalty. Like Pathans, their transborder connections presented unique challenges and opportunities to the imperial state. As anticolonial and nationalist critiques intensified across South Asia, Nepali soldiers found themselves at the crossroads of the conflicting agendas of nations and empires. Those who traveled overseas in military campaigns faced the very real threat of social and political isolation if they were fortunate enough to return.

Despite British tendencies to exalt Nepali soldiers for their difference from Indian Hindus and resistance to the caste system, caste restrictions would *enable* the Indian Army to secure recruits and preserve diplomatic relations with Nepal. In particular, the *pani patya* ceremony was a method of allowing Hindus who had crossed the oceans to rejoin their communities. By the First World War it became mandatory for Nepali troops but not for Indian Hindus. The army's willingness to preserve the purity of Nepali men drew attention to the fact that they were less sympathetic to similar demands from Indian soldiers. This military ritual also revealed British anxieties about anti-colonial politics, international diplomacy, South Asian labor, and the entanglement of religion and militarism. For soldiers, the cost of securing employment and purity was greater wartime hardships and uncertain political futures.

THE *KALA PANI*

Before the First World War, British officers stressed that Nepali soldiers had fewer cultural objections to military life than Indian Hindus. The 1915 handbook on "Gurkhas" pulled from 1830s East India Company texts to prove this point. It maintained that Nepalese soldiers "see in foreign service nothing but the prospect of glory," while high-caste Indian Hindus "can discover in it nothing but pollution and peril from unclean men."[2] Repeating the same arguments about Nepali soldiers over the course of nearly a century continued the orientalist trend of portraying colonial subjects' beliefs and practices as fixed and unchanging. The reality was much more complex. Nineteenth-century Nepalese military leaders had cultivated a form of "military Hinduism" that combined European discipline and Kshatriya (warrior) identity. This included disdain for many civilian religious and dietary customs, earning them further praise from British officers.[3] At the same time, Nepali soldiers' need to maintain or reject caste requirements in the twentieth century was shaped by textual warnings about caste purity, economic opportunity, displacement trauma, fears of social isolation, and very real threats of political backlash. It was not simply a perennial religious complaint. The Indian Army's eventual inclusion of the *pani patya* purification in military practice responded to the fact that there were both preexisting and evolving concerns about crossing the oceans.

South Asian discourses about crossing the *kala pani*—Sanskrit for black or dark waters—stood at the intersection of various social and cultural concerns about migration and mobility. According to Vedic teachings, crossing the oceans made travelers impure and forced them to lose their caste status. Colonial officials sometimes deliberately exploited this fear with the punishment of transportation, which sent prisoners to confinement on the Andaman Islands.[4] These Vedic warnings usually applied only to Brahmans, so only a few elite, South Asian Hindus took special precautions throughout the eighteenth and early nineteenth centuries. Some maintained rigorous diets onboard ships or participated in ceremonies to be readmitted into their local communities.[5] However, the fears of the "black waters" spread beyond Brahmans as South Asian indentured servants journeyed to the Caribbean in the nineteenth century. Their experiences with high casualty rates and rampant diseases during months-long sea voyages on cramped and unsanitary ships raised the fear of crossing the oceans. It increasingly connoted not only losing high-caste status, but displacement, homelessness, fragility, disease, and suffering for both Hindus and non-Hindus.[6] Service in the Indian Army similarly deepened anxieties about crossing the *kala pani* across faiths. Soldiers journeyed overseas during campaigns such as the Second Opium War in China (1856–60) and in Mediterranean campaigns against Russia. Their failure to return merely confirmed their families' fears, according to interwar novelist Mulk Raj Anand, that "all who went beyond the mountains or across the black waters were destined for hell."[7] During the First World War, South Asian Muslims even articulated fears of the oceans that echoed their Hindu comrades. A Punjabi Muslim Havildar, Fazl Mehdi, described families' "ceaseless anxiety" about their "soldier sons across the sea."[8] Another South Indian Muslim soldier worried in February 1915 that the "calamity" of the war caused him to "cross the seas," leaving him "sacrificed" beneath the snow of France.[9] Indentured labor and international military service opened up an array of South Asians—including low-caste laborers and non-Hindus—to the dangers of crossing the oceans. Secular fears were adopted into and intermingled with concerns about outcasting Hindu travelers, but the Indian Army continued to regard it as a religious complaint that could be assuaged with a formal ceremony.

In Nepal, crossing the black waters carried its own political implications. Many Nepali soldiers recruited as "Gurkhas" were Buddhist rather than Hindu. Nonetheless, Nepali political leadership had close connections to Brahman elites who ensured that soldiers were subject to Hindu caste rules. In particular, the position of Rajguru was created to mediate between the Kshatriyas (warriors) and Brahmans (priests) brought into contact during the expansion of the precolonial Nepalese state of Gorkha, for which "Gurkha" soldiers were (mis)named. These alliances created rituals, religious patronage, land transfers, and loyalty bonds that helped to spread Gorkha rule in the eighteenth and nineteenth centuries. The Rajguru remained the head of the Brahman family that served as pandits (priests) to Nepal's ruling Rana dynasty into the twentieth century.[10] The Rajguru generated state income from fines inflicted on those who broke caste rules, including soldiers returning from overseas service.[11] Therefore, it was politically important to ensure that all Nepali subjects, including soldiers serving in the Indian Army, honored the mandates of the Rajguru. Individual soldiers did not necessarily ascribe to caste-specific beliefs about the *kala pani*. They nonetheless had to maneuver between religious and secular authorities in Nepal, Britain, and India as soon as they joined the colonial army.

MAKING "GURKHA" SOLDIERS IN
ANGLO-NEPALESE RELATIONS
British recruitment of Nepali soldiers, like the debate about the *kala pani*, developed in response to the peculiar relationship between the British Raj and Nepal. The term "Gurkha" was an English alteration of the name Gorkha, the small regional hill state led by a Rajput Chetri aristocracy that bordered Bengal during the rise of the East India Company.[12] The Company employed Nepali soldiers after the Anglo-Nepalese War in 1814–16.[13] Despite the single moniker of "Gurkhas," recruits were ethnically, linguistically, and religiously diverse. They came from a variety of castes and classes, including the hill ethnic groups, low-caste populations, children who were the result of intermarriage between high-caste Hindus and hill communities, and poor Brahmans and Kshatriyas.[14] Some had even served the Sikh Khalsa empire, leaving a linguistic trace in the Nepali word for mercenary (*lahure*), after the Sikh capital of Lahore.[15] British recruitment, however, fostered the idea that these recruits were

ethnically homogeneous and encouraged a more unified culture.[16] British Resident in Nepal Brian H. Hodgson had encouraged the recruitment of Nepali soldiers in the 1820s and 1830s, but fiscal cuts, campaigns in Afghanistan, and fears of another war with Nepal halted these projects.[17] British admiration for Nepali soldiers remained.

The 1857 rebellion revived Nepalese recruitment. Nepalese Prime Minister Jung Bahadur Rana led ten thousand Nepalese troops into battle in the hopes of gaining territory that had been ceded in 1816.[18] His military support did not mean that he welcomed long-term European cultural and economic influence. He restricted the movement of Nepali soldiers into India until his death in 1877.[19] When Bir Shamsher Rana rose to power in Nepal through a coup against his uncle in the 1880s, the British found a mutually beneficial ally. Nepal's new leader was eager to gain British political support. British Commander-in-Chief Lord Roberts, meanwhile, believed that it was important to recruit the "type" of men—including Nepali "Gurkhas"—who had served the British in 1857 and the Afghan wars. The Nepalese prime minister earned British support and weapons in exchange for permitting Nepali recruitment.[20]

The contested nature of Rana dynastic rule often left soldiers to become targets of political backlash. In both India and Nepal, the Hindu reformist group Arya Samaj challenged Brahman influence and found success in prominent military recruiting areas of northern India.[21] One method of diminishing Brahman influence, they contended, was embracing foreign travel. In Nepal, the Arya Samaj's critiques of Brahman power threatened the delicate balance between secular and monastic power, represented in the alliance between the Rana dynasty and the Rajguru. Nepali men—including soldiers and veterans—who tried to import Arya ideas from India threatened to upend this careful alliance of secular-religious authority. Some were imprisoned by the Rana's influential pandits.[22] Soldiers also paid indemnities to the Nepalese state for overseas service to Britain, which made them important funders and sources of legitimacy for the Rana dynasty. Soldiers' participation in ceremonies such as *pani patya* helped the Nepalese state to retain its authority over the employment, migration, and mobility of its subjects.

When Prime Minister Chandra Shamsher Jung Bahadur Rana seized power from his brother in another coup in Nepal in 1901 he realized the political significance of soldiers' travels. He was the first Rana ruler to have received an English education and he frequently wore English-style clothing in public.[23] He collaborated with British officials by granting permission for military recruitment, becoming an ally on India's northern border and permitting British influence over Nepal's foreign policy. In exchange, Chandra Shamsher hoped to import and manufacture arms and to retain political sovereignty and British recognition as an independent state. Yet some British officials, especially Viceroy Lord Curzon (1899–1905), regarded Nepal as a "Native State" of India, which was only nominally independent.[24] Chandra Shamsher's apparent openness to British influence left him subject to critiques from Nepali intellectuals, migrants, and discharged soldiers who alleged that he had lost his masculinity through his adoption of European norms.[25] In turn, he used rigorous dietary codes in his daily life and travels to signify that he had forsaken neither masculinity nor self-control.[26] He similarly ensured that Nepali soldiers maintained strict diets during their international military service. Many Nepali soldiers developed conflicting loyalties and ambivalent views of providing military service to a bordering imperial power that could—and often did—threaten Nepal's independence. They had similar ambivalence about a dynastic ruler who faced charges of internally colonizing his own people.[27]

Complicating the relationship between India and Nepal was that Nepal also bordered China, another expansionist state. Nepal sent regular diplomatic missions and gifts to China after a military defeat in the eighteenth century. The British government in India, meanwhile, sometimes saw China as an attractive ally against Russia. Yet British fears of Chinese intervention into the Himalayas resulted in sending further weapons and support to Nepal.[28] In 1900, the British Raj took an even more aggressive stance. It called on its South Asian forces, including Nepalis, to join the international coalition fighting against an anti-European rebellion in China. The so-called Chinese "Boxers" (Society of Righteous and Harmonious Fists) had entered Beijing in June 1900, setting off a massive international contest for imperial influence. The Boxers challenged European imperialism through attacks against Christianity and foreign intervention.

In response, an international alliance of British, German, Japanese, Russian, French, American, Italian, Austrian, and South Asian troops intervened with military force.[29] Fighting in China in 1900 compelled Nepali men to cross the *kala pani* and wage war against one of their major diplomatic partners in the service of another, threatening the delicate political balance of the region. Nepalese Prime Minister Bir Shamsher protested against Nepali soldiers' participation due to their need to cross the *kali pani*.[30] When Chandra Shamsher came to power the following year, he agreed that this would result in the outcasting of Nepalese men.[31]

British officials refused to accept the prime ministers' resistance to Nepali service in China. They argued that Nepali troops had crossed the waters without social condemnation when they went to Malta in 1878 during the Russo-Turkish War and in their frequent trips to Burma thereafter. When Indian Hindus such as Dogras journeyed to Egypt, the Nepali troops resented being left out of the campaign.[32] Viceroy Lord Curzon was especially confused. He claimed that high-caste Indian Hindus such as Dogras, Rajputs, and even Brahmans served in Abyssinia, Mauritius, and Egypt without objection.[33] British discourses continued to maintain that Nepalese soldiers should have been more resistant to caste rules than Indian Hindus, yet the latter were proving to be indifferent to caste rules compared to Nepalese men. The Nepalese state's resistance undermined "martial race" discourses. However, British officers suspected that Nepalese authorities were nervous about maintaining their relationship with China because it had supported the new regime after the inter-familial coup.[34] They only blamed the crossing of the *kala pani*, British officials believed, to create a less politically contentious objection to sending soldiers overseas.

To curb anxiety about crossing the *kala pani*, Bir Shamsher proposed sending a Nepalese pandit (priest) to inspect the water supply on the troop ships for China. The British Resident of Nepal believed that having a respected authority sign off on the water supply would eliminate protests and objections from Nepal.[35] Viceroy Lord Curzon detested the idea of establishing a precedent for "*gurus* turning up from all sorts of unsuspected quarters."[36] Yet British officials finally agreed to have ships inspected and Nepali troops successfully set sail for China. Ironically, soldiers demonstrated less concern than British or Nepalese authorities about maintaining their caste purity. Subedar Gumbirsing Pun of the 6th Gurkha Rifles forced his men to drink salt water from the ocean when they complained about needing to use their pre-approved water sparingly.[37] The result was favoring military discipline over the potentially harmful impact on men's health and purity.

Nepali soldiers who served in China also encountered Indian Hindus whose critiques of imperial service were rarely confined to crossing the *kala pani*. Rajput officer Amar Singh and Rajput soldier Gadadhar Singh emphasized troops' brutality against Chinese civilians and the racism that they endured from Europeans and Americans.[38] Gadadhar Singh even wrote about pan-Asian sympathies after admiring the Chinese Boxers and Japanese soldiers.[39] As Hindus, all of these soldiers might have taken the opportunity to write at length about the social and ritual struggles of crossing the black waters. Their emphasis on other matters, however, suggests that soldiers had many overlapping secular and sacred concerns during their travels. Eliminating caste-based complaints about crossing the *kala pani* would continue to be more of a priority for military, religious, and secular authorities than soldiers themselves. The tense relationship between India, China, and Nepal meant that soldiers were often stuck between the conflicting political agendas of various powers in the region. Finding common ground and collaboration by monitoring soldiers' caste was meant to protect secular authorities from larger social and cultural criticisms about militarism, state governance, imperial service, and diplomacy. British orientalism and Nepalese political calculation, however, would continue to foreground religious causes and remedies, even in the midst of unprecedented overseas military mobility.

PREWAR IMPURITY

Unsurprisingly, having ships inspected by a "guru" in 1900 did not save Nepali troops from social scorn when they returned home from China. By 1906, British military officials heard that some local pandits, especially near the capital of Kathmandu, refused soldiers' attempts to pay for purification ceremonies. Soldiers asserted that food and drink arrangements had been "strictly in accordance with Hindu rights and customs."[40] Yet only *soldiers* were being refused absolution: a group of Nepalese students returned from Japan in 1906 without being excluded from their communities.[41] In fact, this period saw tens of thousands of South Asian civilians relocate for education and employment around the world. When civilians crossed the seas for these reasons, friends, families, and local powers could find ways to welcome them home. The story was different for soldiers. Being a soldier in the Indian Army was far more contentious and politically divisive than being a student in Japan or a laborer in the United States. The refusal to readmit soldiers suggests that the problem of crossing the black waters was not just about religious warnings, but uncertainty and suspicion about fighting for the British.

British and Nepalese officials disagreed about whether or not pandits' outcasting of Nepalese soldiers after 1906 was a new or perennial phenomenon. Lieutenant Colonel D. C. F. MacIntyre of the 1/4th Gurkhas believed that soldiers experienced no difficulty when they went to Malta, Perak (Malay States), or England. He could not understand why soldiers faced difficulties after returning from China.[42] The officer commanding the 1/7th Gurkha Rifles similarly maintained that in his sixteen years of service he never heard of any Nepali soldiers being penalized for going overseas even though "thousands" of men had done so.[43] It was his understanding that soldiers who crossed the waters regularly reported to village headmen or paid local priests a quantity of between two and four *annas* when they returned.[44] As long as soldiers verified that they had not broken caste rules, they were able to restore their purity.[45] Nepalese Prime Minister Chandra Shamsher had a much different perspective. His impression was that *all* of the men who traveled to Malta were rejected by their relatives and could not enter their villages. He gave the specific example of Colonel Run Jung who visited England, lost communication with his wife, and was exiled to Calcutta. Chandra Shamsher believed that *none* of the Nepalese soldiers who crossed the *kala pani* in the service of the Indian Army were ever readmitted to their former social or caste status.[46]

Criticism from Nepal caused fractures among British officials. Some suggested that the issue had become "overblown" because of the involvement of Chandra Shamsher. Others echoed Curzon's desire in 1900 to avoid setting "an awkward precedent."[47] The debate finally reached the British Foreign Office, which recommended, with the support of the

Nepalese prime minister, keeping the matter as contained as possible. British and Nepalese officials agreed to coordinate a *pani patya* purification ceremony for the battalion receiving the most criticism: the 1/4th Gurkhas. Other Nepalese troops had served in China but did not receive a similar concession.[48] A. R. Martin of the British Army Department condemned the decision as "an entirely new and bigoted procedure."[49] The British Resident in Nepal, Major J. Manners-Smith, worried that this decision would result in "a certain amount of priestly interference" during every subsequent overseas campaign.[50] The most immediate beneficiary of the controversy was Sir Chandra Shamsher, who became an honorary colonel of the 4th Gurkhas and an honorary major-general in the British Army in 1907.[51]

The *pani patya* dispute did not hurt British perceptions of Nepalese soldiers. In 1907, officers of the 3rd Gurkha Rifles praised Nepali men for having "few caste prejudices," which they believed exemplified their efficiency as soldiers.[52] Writing the year after the international backlash about the 1/4th's travels to China, this regimental history echoed the cliché that Nepalese soldiers were preferable soldiers to Indian Hindus because of their willingness to overlook caste restrictions while on service.[53] This proved different from the reality. Many officers had pointed out that Indian Brahmans, Rajputs, and Dogras served overseas without difficulty. By contrast, Nepalese service was contentious because of caste criticisms. Whether or not Nepali soldiers agreed with and participated in criticisms about crossing the *kala pani*, they became an institutional burden *because* of caste. Military discourses perhaps exalted Nepali men at the expense of Indian Hindus to sway soldiers' loyalties. British condemnation of caste implicitly criticized the Rajguru and the prime minister of Nepal. Portraying soldiers as having few caste objections encouraged them to see themselves as independent of Nepalese religious and political authority.

Creating an artificial distinction between Nepali combatants and a caricature of the "prejudiced" Indian Hindu may have attempted to prevent sympathy with Hindu-dominated political movements. Debates about *pani patya* occurred shortly after the 1905 partition of the Bengal province. Many Indian nationalists saw this event as an attempt to splinter the Indian National Congress and diminish the role of Bengali Hindus in imperial politics. In addition to the Bengal partition, a series of revolts in the Punjab in 1907 threatened the army's recruiting base in India. In 1908 alone, the number of Gurkha Rifles regiments doubled from five to ten.[54] This gave Chandra Shamsher considerable bargaining power as a contractor of Nepalese labor. British praise for Nepalese "efficiency" and indifference toward "caste" attempted to control the narrative of soldiers' service. In British minds this would ensure that the Indian Army maintained sufficient recruits despite growing anti-colonial challenges.

As more Nepalese troops joined the army, their need to travel overseas also increased. Thirty men of the 1/2nd Gurkha Rifles traveled overseas between 1901 and 1911 for campaigns or ceremonies in China, Somaliland, or England. Members of the 1/1st Gurkha Rifles went as far as Australia.[55] However, the travels that garnered the most attention—and most severe backlash—were those related to Britain's king-emperor. By 1913 rumors became rampant that Rifleman Durga Mal (Thakur) of the 1st Battalion 2nd (King Edward's Own) Gurkha Rifles had gone to England with the Indian Coronation Contingent in 1902 to honor King Edward VII. After his return, local authorities forced him to live as an outcaste for two years. He wrote to the adjutant of the 1/2nd Gurkhas that as soon as he wore "the King's Coronation medal" he was "condemned from my caste, nation and country for ever."[56] A medal that was once a mark of distinction became a token of social and political shame.[57] Similarly, Honorary Captain Santbir Gurung of the 2/2nd Gurkha regiment became an outcaste for going to England in 1910 as Orderly Officer to the King-Emperor.[58] According to Nepalese officials, such ceremonies were "unofficial duties" that were not necessary or appropriate for Nepali men's service in the Indian Army.

The prewar dispute went as far as King George V, who was the colonel-in-chief of the 2nd Gurkhas.[59] Once the king was involved, British officials reiterated that the whole matter was simply a religious issue. The commanding officer of the 1/2nd Gurkhas defended his men by stating that they held no "Brahminical views" that would prevent them from traveling overseas.[60] The King's Equerry, Major C. Wigram, suspected that Prime Minister Chandra Shamsher was "very susceptible to Brahminical influence."[61] Sir James DuBoulay, private secretary to the viceroy, agreed with Wigram that "Nepal seems to be a priest-ridden country." He found Chandra Shamsher, by contrast, sympathetic to Britain's secular diplomacy.[62] The Nepalese prime minister confirmed these impressions by blaming the "conservatism of priests and people of Nepal."[63] Blaming Brahmans became a simple way for British and Nepalese leaders to agree upon a single problem and possible solution. This prevented them from asking deeper questions about why Nepalese soldiers received the most criticism for travels to China and England specifically.

The British Resident of Nepal soon tested the prime minister's commitment to secular diplomacy. In October 1913 he asked Chandra Shamsher to grant a general exemption to all Nepalese soldiers traveling overseas on service. He assured the prime minister that the Government of India would arrange food and drink that would not violate their caste rules. He also reminded Chandra Shamsher that the Rajputs who went overseas were "as orthodox in the matter of the Hindu religion and caste observances as your Gurkha subjects." However these soldiers' prestige had increased, rather than decreased, due to their success in overseas campaigns.[64] This struck a tenuous balance between assuring officials that the Government of India was steadfast in maintaining soldiers' purity, but also urging Nepalese soldiers to be less "orthodox" than their Indian counterparts. This was a deliberate effort to exploit the "martial race" assumption that Nepalese soldiers resisted and were hostile to the caste rules of Indian Hindus. The colonial state praised Indian Hindus to pressure Nepalese men into thinking that their martial prowess was threatened by the comparison.

Chandra Shamsher was caught between the need to appear amenable to military demands, to respect the authority of the Rajguru, and to avoid appearing "prejudiced." In 1906 he gave an impassioned speech declaring that overseas employment was crucial to the future development of Nepal. He encouraged people to welcome men back into the community because having strong, well-trained soldiers was necessary for the strength of the nation. He cited passages from the "Mahabharata" that exalted past heroes who journeyed overseas.[65] By 1913, however, he was careful to distinguish between his "personal views" and those of "the priesthood and the people." He reminded the British Resident that before the matter of the 1/4th Gurkhas was settled in 1906, pandits, social elites, and civil and military officers convened to discuss the matter. The 1/4th Gurkhas only gained permission for the purification ceremony because they had been on active duty. Durga Mal and Santbir Gurung, by contrast, were considered unauthorized travelers. He believed that other men, such as Subedar Major Hasta Bir Ghartim, were never readmitted into their caste and communities. He worried that British eagerness to blame Brahmans and demand full exemption for all soldiers meant that "the British authorities concerned did not think it worth their while to give due consideration to such an important matter." This resulted in "serious consequences to the unfortunate sufferers."[66] Chandra Shamsher agreed with British officials that the main issue was the "priesthood." However, he also criticized British authorities' tendencies to minimize soldiers' grievances.

By January 1914, Chandra Shamsher was willing to approach the Rajguru and Brahman elites about authorizing the grant of *pani patya* to all soldiers who proceeded overseas. However, British officials developed their own apprehension when Brahmans demanded a list of names of soldiers who had traveled overseas.[67] L. W. Reynolds feared that providing a list would leave men "punished more severely." In fact, the *majority* of men who went overseas since 1900 had not actually been outcasted, so "it would appear better to let well alone."[68] British officials worried that a bureaucratic tool of keeping track of soldiers' movements could be used to persecute soldiers for "religious" transgressions. Word had spread quickly that people could extract money from returning soldiers. The rate charged to men increased from a few *annas* to as much as Rs. 7.[69] Many officers, including the officer commanding the 1/4th Gurkha Rifles, developed the opinion that *pani patya* was "a form of blackmail."[70]

Eventually, some British officers blamed Nepalese soldiers, rather than Nepali leaders, for the controversy. Indian Army Commander-in-Chief Beauchamp Duff (1913–17) assumed that Captain Santbir Gurung "deliberately set himself to flaunt his journey to England in the faces of the priests" who "know their advantage and will cling to it." This "direct challenge" could not be overlooked if the pandits wished "to maintain their hold on the people at large."[71] The officer commanding the 2/7th Gurkha

Rifles similarly suspected that Rifleman Durga Mal and Captain Santbir Gurung had simply refused to pay the fines.[72] In fact, Durga Mal and Santbir Gurung may have felt confident refuting such mandates *because* of military discourses about caste. It was, after all, a pervasive military cliché that Nepali "Gurkhas" did not care about caste rules and that *pani patya* was simply "blackmail." Soldiers' journeys, meanwhile, exposed them to Dogras, Rajputs, and Brahmans who faced no difficulties despite their identities as high-caste Indian Hindus. Working in a military culture that condemned "Brahman" influence no doubt shaped men's feelings about the need—or lack thereof—to subject themselves to the fines and social restrictions of local authorities. British officials blamed Nepalese soldiers for "flaunting" their travels and refusing to pay fines. Yet they implicitly encouraged such behavior by questioning and undermining Brahman authority and urging Chandra Shamsher to do the same.

By early 1914, the army believed that it had solved the problem of soldiers crossing the *kala pani*. They proposed sending all Nepali soldiers who went overseas since 1902 to a single location to receive *pani patya*.[73] They insisted that Nepali soldiers "stick to an approved and uniform narrative" about maintaining caste rules overseas to avoid "too many inconvenient questions."[74] Men's individual experiences and impressions of the journey were to be erased beneath a standardized script, removing all value from the ceremony for those who believed that it was a social and spiritual necessity. This made the whole procedure only a bureaucratic inconvenience and a diplomatic formality.

By June 1914, the foreign secretary to the Government of India revealed the extensive measures taken to ensure soldiers' absolution. First, the government collected evidence purporting that men had not violated caste rules. They issued "certificates to this effect" to each soldier. Next, the commanding officers of Gurkha regiments supplied lists of men willing to appear before a tribunal at Kathmandu to obtain *pani patya*. Once they appeared they would gain state support and be absolved of all fines inflicted on them. The government of Nepal agreed to pay "such indemnities" on their behalf. All men willing to participate reported to the Resident at Kathmandu.[75] On September 18, 1914, Lord Crewe, the secretary of state for India, sanctioned the measures proposed.[76] In total, about eighty-four men planned to journey to Kathmandu. They would receive full compensation for their travel, leave, and fees to participate in the ceremony.[77] British and Nepalese officials shared confidence in transforming this local practice into a military ritual. They hoped that this would eliminate future criticisms and bring institutional stability to soldiers' service. However, the 1914 provisions would quickly be overshadowed by—and become a precedent for—the thousands of Nepalese troops who traveled overseas during the First World War.

PANI PATYA FOR THE SICK AND WOUNDED

In October 1914, the discussion of *pani patya* took a dramatic turn after nearly a year and a half of intense debate. Of the seventeen Gurkha battalions impacted by outcasting for overseas service, eight were preparing to return overseas in the First World War.[78] One Government of India official hoped that because of the war, the Nepalese authorities might "reconsider their decision as regards general absolution and to let bygones be bygones."[79] Major General F. J. Aylmer, adjutant general in India, argued more explicitly that "the case should be dropped till the War is over."[80] For British officials, the war necessitated looser restrictions than peacetime. They believed that the Nepalese government and the Rajguru should have granted complete exemption to soldiers. Nepalese authorities disagreed. They recognized that Britain's need for troops was a political opportunity. The Indian Army and the Nepalese state ultimately coordinated unprecedented efforts to regulate Nepalese bodies through the religious-military ritual of *pani patya*. Soldiers returning home from the First World War would not be able to return to Nepal until they had gone to Dehra Dun, an Indian military station hundreds of miles from the nearest port. There they received *pani patya* from a paid pandit in a military camp. The Army Department issued certificates verifying soldiers' purity after the ceremony was complete. Fragile regional tensions kept non-colonial soldiers in the service of Britain and hardened performances of their faith under military discipline.

When war began in 1914, eighteen thousand Gurkhas were already serving in the Indian Army. A total of between sixty-five thousand and two hundred thousand Gurkhas served by the war's end.[81] Recruiters in

Nepal received lucrative payments during the conflict. This meant that men's status as "volunteers" was often questionable. "Volunteers" often included prisoners who frequently deserted. British officials in India handsomely rewarded the Nepalese government with a promise of Rs. 10 lakhs annually for its contribution of soldiers.[82] The massive contribution of Nepali soldiers accelerated discussions of *pani patya*. Unlike the long, drawn out debate of 1913 and 1914, it took just over a week for the adjutant general in India, F. J. Aylmer, to issue instructions about *pani patya* to all commanding officers. Nepali soldiers returning from overseas would not be able to enter Nepal prior to receiving the ceremony.[83] Those who already returned to remote stations had to proceed to a larger station to participate. All others had to go to Dehra Dun, a hill station in northern India with a large number of Nepalese settlers.[84]

Wounded Nepalese soldiers started to arrive in India by January 1915 and military and medical authorities had their instructions to reroute Nepalese troops to Dehra Dun by March.[85] By April 1915, over 120 men had received *pani patya* from seventeen Gurkha Rifles battalions, exceeding the number for the entire period of 1902–12.[86] In June 1915, military officials issued the certificates, signed by the adjutant general, that claimed that soldiers had not broken their caste and were eligible for *pani patya*; 624 men had done so by month's end.[87] Despite British officials' concerns in 1913 that *pani patya* was a form of "blackmail," they helped to extend it to all Nepalese soldiers. This made it mandatory even for those who were Buddhist rather than Hindu and for those who never faced criticism or excommunication. This increased the religious authority of the Rajguru, who was paid by the Nepalese state.[88] British officials often condemned Brahman influence on soldiers but they dramatically extended their power to secure Nepali recruits and win the war. According to the orientalist logic of the Indian Army and the religious-secular authority of Nepalese leaders, soldiers' refusal to participate in a caste ceremony left them subject to military and political punishment. This forced Nepalese soldiers to endure additional challenges during an already earth-shattering war.

Making *pani patya* mandatory resulted in a massive bureaucratic effort to ensure that soldiers had not broken caste rules overseas. In reality it simply created a paper trail asserting that this was true. Many hospitals assembled boards of enquiry to portray accommodations for Nepali soldiers as flawless. The board at the Meerut General Hospital described meticulous arrangements for gathering water, washing, cutting hair, and burning bodies.[89] Those at the Lady Hardinge Hospital in England stated that Nepali troops were "fully satisfied with existing arrangements" because food was "prepared by competent Hindu cooks and water given to them by Hindu water-carriers."[90] At Barton-on-Sea Nepali soldiers apparently had "no complaints" about food, drink, smoking, or sleeping because "They realise that they are on service."[91] Captain E. H. Lynch of the 2/8th Gurkha Rifles at Milford-on-Sea reported that the men had "no complaints of any kind whatsoever." One unnamed "Gurkha officer" apparently assured him that "all arrangements made were excellent and could not be improved on."[92] This Nepalese combatant, like the many unnamed men who had "no complaints," may have worried that their requests would be dismissed as mere "prejudices." After all, British officers condemned Durga Mal and Santbir Gurung for "flaunting" their overseas service while also praising Nepali men for their supposed indifference to caste. Any soldier who complained would have been singled out for not behaving as a "Gurkha" soldier "should." British officers would have been equally unlikely to report soldiers' grievances, fearing backlash for failing to accommodate their men. However, some officials admitted that on-the-ground arrangements did not matter as much as the diplomatic manipulation of these practices. One official claimed that "The trip to England is likely to give the Gurkhas a little trouble to go back into their caste" but if it did "there is a penance for every sin committed against caste rules, and this also can be atoned for."[93]

Statements from hospitals did not give a clear indication of the lived reality of life in war, which often betrayed caste proscriptions. Nepalese soldiers served for years in locations such as France, Egypt, Mesopotamia, and Gallipoli, where circumstances were notoriously sparse and unsanitary. Extreme weather, sandy beaches and deserts, hastily constructed latrines, and rotting food were regular features of soldiers' service. Lieutenant Colonel F. S. Poynder of the 9th Gurkha Rifles recalled that soldiers in all fields of battle experienced extreme dietary hardships that included eating "tinned meat or biscuit" or the "ration bread given to the British troops." As opposed to hospital claims that Nepali soldiers had high-caste Hindu cooks, the reality was that the men themselves usually had to serve as cooks while short on sanitation and supplies.[94] Military policy and diplomatic negotiations based decisions about whether or not soldiers had maintained their "purity" overseas on the ideal—and likely overstated—arrangements in hospitals.

Adding further complexity to the implementation of mandatory *pani patya* was that military bureaucracy lagged behind soldiers' movements. Rifleman Nandbir Lama of the 2/10th Gurkha Rifles was sent to Takdah instead of Dehra Dun due to a mistake by the Railway Medical Transport officer.[95] Satu Khatri, a Naick of the 2nd Kashmir Imperial Service Troops, made it to Nepal on sick leave from German East Africa without performing the ceremony.[96] Nepalese and British officials ordered him back to Dehra Dun.[97] This forced sick and wounded men to make additional journeys and to take time away from their recuperation after enduring long overseas voyages. At times, the army accommodated irregularities, such as when Subedar Major Jaman Sing Gurung, 1/6th Gurkha Rifles, was too ill to make it to Dehra Dun. They sent him special instructions for *pani patya* and a certificate verifying that he had not broken his caste.[98] In August 1915, Rifleman Nandbir Lama disembarked at Bombay from France and was sent directly to his regimental center without stopping at Dehra Dun. He forwarded a letter to Dehra Dun enclosing the necessary fee and earned absolution.[99] However, special accommodations were not the norm. In August 1915 the prime minister had a list of twenty-two men of the 3rd Kashmir Imperial Service Rifles who returned to Nepal without receiving *pani patya*.[100] Their commanding officer stated that they did not want to return to Dehra Dun because they were certain that "it would cost them a good lot." They preferred to stick to longer-held military policy of doing it "in their own country."[101] The adjutant general in India ultimately ordered all of these soldiers to proceed to Dehra Dun to receive *pani patya* no matter where they were or what they desired.[102] Soldiers' own wishes to remain at home, to renounce the importance of the ceremony, or to continue living in their community without having faced any penalty for doing so, were overruled by military bureaucracy. The army feared backlash from the prime minister of Nepal, who acted, ostensibly, in the best interest of soldiers.

Some officers attempted to make arrangements more convenient for soldiers even though military bureaucracy made it almost impossible to do so. In May 1915 the officer commanding the war hospital in Meerut announced the arrival of "a Darjeeling type of Gurkha classed as a Limbu." This man believed that his caste and region of origin exempted him from needing *pani patya*. He felt so ill that he became "very anxious to reach his home in Takdah" rather than being rerouted to Dehra Dun. The commanding officer argued that this was a "particular case" because the soldier was so weak and requested not to go. The man wished "to see his relative before he died." The officer sent him to his military base as requested. However, in response to the incident, the officer commanding overruled the soldier's self-identification. He was certain that "the man was a Gurkha, his father living in Dankhuts" and therefore he needed to be sent to Dehra Dun. When the man arrived at Takdah he was nearly unconscious and died shortly thereafter.[103] The bureaucratic handling of *pani patya* resulted in difficult—and life-threatening—conditions for Nepalese men. Some attempted to renounce British claims to set the parameters of "Gurkha" identity. They preferred to forgo the ceremony and visit family rather than subject themselves to additional travel. Some British officers attempted to accommodate the men when they had the power and opportunity to do so. Bureaucratic rigidity made it increasingly difficult. Higher officials criticized their actions by deciding which medical or military authority had the right to define men as "Gurkhas"—without paying attention to the declarations made by men themselves.

Many soldiers pushed back against bureaucratic stringency. Some soldiers from Kashmir and Jammu proposed making their own arrangements for the ceremony closer to home.[104] They received support from a *panchayat* (local council of five).[105] They argued, controversially, that Kashmir was a "Hindu State" with "many learned pandits" and "several sacred places." They believed that this made it an appropriate place to receive *pani patya* instead of Dehra Dun. The "learned pandits" would adhere to the proscriptions found in "the Dharm Shastras (Hindu sacred books)," saving "the State from unnecessary expenditure."[106] However, Chandra Shamsher flatly denied the validity of pandits not deputed by the Rajguru and instructed soldiers to proceed to Dehra Dun. He added, with a hint of threat and intimidation, "I hope you will kindly see it done to avoid future troubles."[107] Nepalese authorities therefore cracked down on the right of localized civil (*panchayat*) and "religious" authority (pandits) to determine procedures for reaffirming soldiers' status in the community—even when Nepalis lived in Kashmir rather than Nepal. This was coordinated, and sanctioned, by the secular Nepalese government, acting on behalf of and in cooperation with, the Rajguru and the Indian Army.

The institutionalization of *pani patya* during the war resulted in a power shift between Nepalese authorities. Unlike the years prior to the war, the Rajguru agreed that "granting Patyas shall in future be regulated by the State."[108] The Indian Army's involvement extended the influence of the Nepalese government over "religious" matters. Chandra Shamsher deprived local authorities of the right to demand that soldiers pay fines or participate in local ceremonies. The only legitimate ceremony became the one administered in Dehra Dun under the Rajguru. Men could prove their purity only by producing their military certificates to Nepalese authorities. Anyone who attempted to get money from men faced political consequences, upending localized systems of power. Nepalese soldiers, and the Indian Army, helped to centralize a religious-state procedure carried out by a prime minister who consistently maintained his secular proclivities.

MASS-PRODUCING "PURITY"

By 1916, entire battalions, rather than periodic bursts of sick or injured Nepalese soldiers, were returning to India. The 2/8th, 1/5th, 1/6th, 1/4th, and 2/2nd Gurkha Rifles all departed from Egypt in mid-February 1916.[109] By the hundreds, men planned to make their way not only to Dehra Dun but also to cantonment towns like Bakloh and Lansdowne.[110] Nepali soldiers remained under strict instructions not to return to Nepal before they received *pani patya*. To meet their needs, Pandit Yagya Prasad Upadia, agent of the Rajguru, visited Peshawar and Bakloh while Pandit Vishwa Natha, working at Dehra Dun, traveled to Lansdowne.[111] As with the sick and wounded, the returning soldiers needed to present certificates that maintained that they "have kept inviolate their caste whilst serving overseas."[112] In just the first week of March 1916 the adjutant general supplied over 1,700 certificates.[113] The next week he supplied an additional 700.[114] The *pani patya* ceremony had expanded to an unprecedented scale through the support of the Indian Army and Government of India.

As with the sick and wounded, soldiers' return to India resulted in many unanticipated challenges. The married men of the 1st Peshawar Division were unable to request leave to visit their families until they received their certificates. Similarly, the men of the 1/6th were held in "segregation" at Karachi until they received their own.[115] Three battalions serving with the Mesopotamia Expeditionary Force planned to return in August 1916 to stations at Dehra Dun, Dharamsala, and Maymyo (Burma). The 2/10th's return to Burma was troublesome because, instead of sending the battalion to Dehra Dun, they commissioned the pandit to cross the sea and meet them in Burma.[116] The army considered Burma a part of India and soldiers received an exemption for that journey. However, this did not extend to the pandit. Because of institutional debate and delay, it took almost a full month for him to arrive. In the meantime, soldiers could not participate in Dussehra festivities, despite their enthusiasm to celebrate after a long time overseas.[117] Bureaucratic mandates about soldiers' "religious" needs resulted in them being unable to take part in one of the most popular holidays for Nepali soldiers. It took until September 21 for the Government of India to coordinate the necessary food and drink for the pandit to arrive on a steamship.[118]

Enabling travel for pandits, rather than sending all Nepalese troops to Dehra Dun, continued for the duration of the war. The priority remained giving men the ceremony as soon as possible so that they would not "contaminate" their communities in either Nepal or India.[119] The officer commanding the 1/6th Gurkhas received permission from Chandra Shamsher to let his men take *pani patya* at Kakool instead of Dehra Dun because it took twelve days out of the men's six weeks of leave. When he tried to get permission from the Indian Army, higher officials reprimanded him.[120] By war's end, British officials came around to what Chandra Shamsher was already sanctioning. He agreed to send a representative of the Rajguru to Manmad, Maharashtra. British officials hoped that a similar procedure could be adopted at other locations. They recognized that moving entire battalions through Dehra Dun was impractical.[121] During demobilization in March 1919, Chandra Shamsher confirmed that he would send multiple agents of the Rajguru from Nepal to administer *pani patya* to troops at their respective stations.[122] Although the Indian Convalescent Section at Dehra Dun closed in August 1920, a camp at Dehra Dun continued to grant *pani patya* until 1922.[123]

Once Chandra Shamsher gained authority from the Rajguru to oversee all matters related to the *pani patya* for Nepalese soldiers, he was much more flexible in allowing concessions for troops. British officials, by contrast, proved stricter in their firm interpretation of how *pani patya* should be implemented. At one point, British officials even suggested arresting men who failed to adhere to their ever-changing guidelines. This would have meant imprisoning soldiers who had served the empire in the horrific conditions of the First World War. Their failure to participate in—or understand—this massive military ritual left them vulnerable to the disciplinary actions of the imperial state. Ultimately, the prime minister of Nepal suggested that arrests would not be necessary.[124] The Nepali prime minister's control of *pani patya* gave him greater political agency and strengthened his relationship with the British Raj.

SOLDIERS' DISCONTENT AND THE ENDURANCE
OF *PANI PATYA*

As early as 1916, Nepali soldiers expressed their discomfort with the mandatory *pani patya* even though it was enforced by both British and Nepalese authorities. Accounts of desertions from Dehra Dun became increasingly common. Two men, Krishna Bahadur Rana and Loke Bahadur Adhikari, alleged that they had been led away by a "coolie" recruiter who planned to send them as laborers to Mesopotamia. Officials found Khadga Singh Gurung of the 2nd Gurkha Rifles at the war hospital at Dehra Dun. He had abandoned his regiment, re-enlisted, spent two-and-a-half months in training, and gone to Turkey.[125] The concentration of Nepali troops at Dehra Dun made it easy to get "lost in the crowd" and rejoin another regiment. Getting another employment opportunity was more appealing than seemingly endless delays. Indian revolutionaries also took opportunities to network with the large numbers of Nepalese men at Dehra Dun and reached out to them directly.[126] Conspirators of the international Ghadar ("mutiny") movement drafted multiple pamphlets aimed at Nepali men. One Hindi-language pamphlet encouraged soldiers to kill their officers. Another encouraged them to join the Germans and drive the British out of India.[127] The officer commanding the 3/8th Gurkha Rifles reported that disaffection spread quickly at the "Panipatia Institute" at Dehra Dun, making this site of "religious purification" into a threat of political contagion.[128] The entwined narratives of Nepali soldiers' inherent loyalty and indifference to caste unraveled in Dehra Dun.

Nepalese soldiers' willingness to abandon their posts at Dehra Dun was not simply a result of the plots of Indian nationalists. Like soldiers of all nationalities, Nepalese troops were shaped and tested by the rigors of war. As early as February 1915, three Nepali men were shot on parade for deserting from the trenches.[129] By November, depression was common among Nepali soldiers in the York Place Hospital in Britain. One man even committed suicide.[130] In Egypt, a Pathan Dafadar, Ali Mardan, recalled in 1916 that one Nepali soldier "went mad" and wounded three Indian officers before firing "indiscriminately" in the trenches.[131] Lieutenant General Sir James Willcocks, the first commander-in-chief of the Indian Corps in France, found Nepali soldiers' results in battle extremely disappointing even though the British press praised them repeatedly.[132] Mulk Raj Anand reproduced Indian soldiers' bitterness about Nepali soldiers' apparent special treatment and exaltation. One Dogra character in his 1939 novel *Across the Black Waters* lamented that British audiences only "admired their loyal Sikhs and Gurkhas." Indian Hindu soldiers wondered if the treats sent to Indian troops were actually meant for Nepalese men.[133] Yet for these soldiers, discontent and bitterness did not need to come from external political plots. It was a natural expression of having a prolonged experience with a difficult war.

Two letters purporting to be from Nepali soldiers arrived at the Foreign and Political Department and hinted at the discontented state of these men. One letter addressed to Nepali Lieutenant General Baber Shamsher Jung Rana Bahadur argued that Nepali soldiers were upset because their leave had been interrupted when they arrived at Dehra Dun. The letter declared that "The subjects of our Gurkha Government are exhausted." They believed that "We have got no justice by being enlisted in the British Army."[134] Another letter attributed to the men of the 3/5th Gurkhas complained that they "have been done up" and were nothing more than "earth and dust."[135] Top officials in both Britain and Nepal, who coordinated recruitment and *pani patya,* were convinced that the letters did not really come from Nepalese men.[136] The officer commanding the depot of the 2/8th Gurkha Rifles suspected that the first letter was certainly written by a "malcontent who has abetted irregularities by Gurkha soldiers, particularly in cases of leave." The senior medical officer, by contrast, attributed these feelings to Nepali soldiers who had served in the northwestern borderlands between India and Afghanistan.[137] These soldiers, no doubt, recognized the implications for Nepal's own political sovereignty of fighting protracted wars along India's borders. This brought their experiences of fighting in the arduous battlefields of the First World War much closer to home. In addition, Nepali soldiers were subject to delays and institutional uncertainty when they returned to India. Many had already endured long journeys after being recruited by less-than-voluntary means. Their forced relocation to Dehra Dun or long waits for the arrival of a pandit reinforced their lack of control. Military *pani patya* made them more "pure"—and more powerless—than other soldiers serving in the Indian Army. The price of a religious mandate was losing personal freedom.

In the years after the war, several British officers reflected on the exceptional procedure of *pani patya,* revealing the institutional uncertainty that it engendered. Major General Nigel Woodyatt rationalized that it was the only way to avoid Nepal's strict penalties for traveling overseas. He believed that without it men would have been subject to "excommunication of the severest type." Their families, he argued, would have refused "to eat, drink, or smoke with him." This was known as "*huqqa pani band* (lit. smoking and water stopped [*sic*])." Woodyatt celebrated Chandra Shamsher for convincing the "priesthood" to grant dispensation to all men serving overseas by persuading "the spiritual head in Nepal" to send a representative to Dehra Dun.[138] For Woodyatt, the situation was a straightforward matter of a secular Nepalese authority circumventing "religious" proscriptions. His interpretation did not acknowledge that the prime minister, and the Indian Army, had actually hardened and widened the *pani patya* ceremony. Compared to Woodyatt, Colonel L. W. Shakespear was far more critical of army participation in *pani patya*. He described the matter as a "trouble" regarding "the religious aspect of Goorkhas crossing the sea." He believed that this started with the 1913 scandal over Subedar Major Santbir Gurung, rather than in debates about South Asian troops in China. He denigrated the wartime procedure: "it would have been far less expensive to Government had the Pandit been directed to visit all Goorkha Regiments." It seemed irrational to send "large numbers of men from port to Dehra first, and then having to pay all their rail fares back to distant stations."[139] For Shakespear, mandating *pani patya* wasted funds and resources and created undue hardship for soldiers. He believed that this could have been more effective regimentally. Few questioned the necessity of *pani patya* even though its inclusion in military praxis was new to the twentieth century.

The military *pani patya* lived on despite postwar cynicism. H. R. K. Gibbs described the ceremony as being expertly streamlined by the time of the *Second* World War. It took place at Regimental Training Centres and each man paid two *annas* to be granted a certificate verifying his purity. A similar ceremony, Bhor Patiya, was performed to readmit men who had "unwittingly broken caste rules." Men who failed to do so faced imprisonment, heavy fines, and outcasting. Despite these arrangements, Gibbs was quick to note that "While the Gurkha is certainly not given to making an undue fuss over his food requirements it must be remembered that the Laws of Nepal are founded on very orthodox Hindu caste laws and are strictly enforced in Nepal under pain of loss of caste."[140] The perceived stringency of "Hindu caste laws" and the Nepalese government's "orthodox" interpretation allowed British officers to continue to regard Nepali men as exceptional soldiers. Meanwhile, officers like Gibbs maintained the prewar tendency to blame the Nepalese government for inflexibility. This was the opposite of officers who had commended Chandra Shamsher for his secular concessions after the First World War.

British recruitment of Nepali soldiers during the First World War enabled a new "treaty of friendship" between Nepal and the British Raj in 1923. However, a formal agreement for Britain to recruit Nepali soldiers only occurred in 1947, when the British departed from newly independent

India and Pakistan.[141] Chandra Shamsher benefited personally from his contributions to the war with a promotion to full general in the British Army in 1919. He also enjoyed awards of Grand Cross of the Order of St. Michael and St. George, in addition to the large annual financial subsidy.[142] The recruitment of Nepali soldiers ensured the survival of the *pani patya* ceremony, even as it fell out of favor in Nepal. One military official believed that "Religious prejudices are generally fading into the background in modern Nepal" and *pani patya* was left to the discretion of individuals by the 1960s.[143] However, General Surndra Bikram, a quartermaster general of the Nepalese forces in 1960, found it strange that *pani patya* was still an official policy for Nepali soldiers serving with British forces. He said that officers in the Nepalese Army rarely went through with the ceremony when returning from overseas "and wondered why British Gurkhas still bothered to do it."[144] British officials remained reluctant to make it voluntary unless there was an explicit ruling from the Nepalese government.[145] Thus, British military officials, who consistently condemned the "prejudice" and stringency of "religious" authorities, were the most lasting proponents of the *pani patya* ceremony. Even in the 1960s, when Nepalese officers deemed the procedure all but irrelevant, British military leaders still maintained that it had political value. British military institutions, more than the "religious" forces they frequently condemned, were the most bound to and politically inflexible about "religious" practice.

BLACK WATERS

Writing on the eve of the Second World War, novelist Mulk Raj Anand recognized the importance of South Asian soldiers' anxieties about crossing the oceans. In *Across the Black Waters*, the Indian protagonist Lalu was surprised when he arrived in France without enduring "some calamity." He had not forgotten the "legendary fate of all those who went beyond the seas." Lalu knew that if his father was alive he would have regarded the war as a "curse" and "prophesied disaster for all those who had crossed the black waters."[146] However, Anand gave little consideration to Nepalese troops. One character in the novel resented the rumor that Germans perceived all South Asians to be "Gurkhas with kukhries in our mouths, savages who will creep up to them, take them by surprise and kill them."[147] This portrayal of Nepalese soldiers as creeping "savages" with knives in their teeth—rather than sharers in the burdens of the black waters—hints at the tenuous relationship between Nepali soldiers and the Indian nationalist movement. After the war, Nepali soldiers became famous and notorious for their role in suppressing anti-colonial rebellion, most prominently during the massacre at Amritsar in 1919 and its aftermath. Their ethnic and regional difference from Indian Hindus made them visible symbols of British efforts to suppress anti-colonial dissent.[148] Yet their services proved far more complex. Hailing from a nominally independent nation state with few opportunities for political and economic advancement, Nepali men were contracted by the prime minister of Nepal to ensure diplomatic and military favors from the British Empire. Indian nationalists' belief that Nepalese soldiers were martial savages was inseparable from their perceived value to the British. Yet their employment left them subject to British, Indian, and Nepalese political expectations. Freedom and independence had a much different meaning for them.

The mandatory *pani patya* ceremony emerged from the unexpected challenge of maintaining control over soldiers in the early twentieth century. British and Nepalese officials' ability to persuade Nepalese troops to travel to China made British officials optimistic, if also short-sighted, about formalizing religious practice. It was the ultimate colonial fantasy: using British military discipline to bring order to South Asian "religion." Yet this strategy would make one of the "martial races," praised for their lack of adherence to "Hindu" customs, institutionally bound to one of the most extensive religious ceremonies carried out by a European military institution. This was at a time when Indian Hindus had demonstrated— through their own global travels—that they were far less "prejudiced" and "beholden" to caste than British officials assumed. The massive institutional policy of *pani patya* ensured that *all* Nepalese soldiers, rather than just an unlucky few caught for their transgressions, would have to atone for their service to Britain. They moved thousands of men on long journeys from Bombay to Dehra Dun, or Burma to Kathmandu, so that religious needs, as policed mostly by secular authorities, could be granted institutional rationality. Military authorities turned a limited and localized practice into a de facto process of military quarantine. This gave British and Nepalese authorities unprecedented access to the bodies and beliefs of Nepali soldiers. *Pani patya* separated Nepalese men physically from Indian "Hindus" and used strict medical precision to protect soldiers from the contagions of mobile military life. Soldiers' difficulties at Dehra Dun, and their openness to anti-colonial ideas, revealed that the procedure did not quite work as intended. Segregation was not a surefire way to secure loyalty and purity. In many ways it intensified anti-colonial feeling.

Nepali soldiers emerged from the First World War disillusioned by the hardships of their service and resenting their imperially and nationally sanctioned inability to return home. Some decided not to return to Nepal and instead settled in cities such as Dehra Dun and Banaras. These cities became important sites of resurgent Nepali nationalism that emphasized warriors who fought against, rather than for, the British.[149] Nepali migrants' abilities to belong in either the Indian nation or the British Empire proved limited. After their immense wartime sacrifices, these men remained citizens of Nepal with no access to the limited benefits of being an imperial subject. They were ineligible for interwar opportunities for upward advancement such as military colleges and academies that were gradually opening to Indian soldiers and veterans.[150] Anti-colonial and nationalist movements also excluded them. Despite these constraints, Nepali soldiers made choices to desert during the war, draft letters of discontent, petition for ceremonial exemptions, or abandon their regiments in Dehra Dun. Chandra Shamsher, in turn, ensured that they would endure additional hardships for their service to the British. Independent citizenship did not bring them personal freedom. The realities of global war, limited employment opportunities, and racialized labor contracts left them subject to the whims of both empires and nations. Nepali soldiers and veterans who resided in India had to contend with being viewed as a mercenary enemy bearing *khukris* in their mouths. Their choices were carefully observed by imperial, national, and anti-colonial actors who all claimed to represent their best interests.

The danger of crossing the *kala pani* for Nepali troops was leaving home, entering into a global contest between nations and empires, and finding themselves adrift in a divided world. Despite their reputation as the model "Hindus" of the Indian Army, Nepali troops were no more or less inclined to fight or rebel than their Indian counterparts. However, the institutional support—or mandates—that they received for their beliefs and practices reveals that the Indian Army was capable of accommodating certain religious practices if they were useful to the imperial state. Meanwhile, they considered the demands of many others—including Indian Hindus—as simply "religious prejudices." One soldier's "prejudice" was another soldier's path to martial belonging. Caste rules helped to secure Nepali service to Britain. Many other soldiers became imperial outcast(e)s.

CHAPTER 4

THE GOVERNMENT'S SALT
FROM FAST TO FAMINE

DURING THE OPENING MONTHS of the First World War, General Sir James Willcocks, who commanded the Indian Corps in France, condemned South Asian soldiers captured at the First Battle of Ypres. He regarded them as "of no use" and thanked god that "we are rid of them, they were altogether a very poor and disgruntled lot."[1] Officers of the Indian Army had long prized South Asian soldiers recruited from India's so-called martial races because they believed that these men had long military traditions that made them ideal warriors. By contrast, Willcocks blamed the dietary demands of high-caste Brahman soldiers for making them useless as combatants. Before the war he described Brahman diets as "the chief stumbling-blocks to their being classed with the best corps."[2] He characterized their food needs as "so binding on them" and celebrated officers who could "break through any of the traditions."[3] Army certainty about the logistical burden of Brahman diets stemmed in part from the long-held colonial narrative that caste transgressions caused the uprising of 1857. Indian soldiers of the Bengal Army in 1857, so the story went, rebelled because military officials soaked their cartridges in beef and pig fat to violate the religious practices of Hindus and Muslims. This legacy of supposed betrayal left the Indian Army both steadfast and paranoid about what its soldiers consumed. For soldiers, eating or not eating military food was far more complicated.

Military officials' certainty about the religious causes of 1857 made them confident that securing religiously appropriate food would prevent rebellion in the twentieth-century army. Willcocks reinforced this perception in France by calling the Government of India "very wise" for "scrupulously observing every detail relating to their religious customs, especially as far as their food was concerned."[4] Yet soldiers' food needs and desires changed over time according to more than perennial religious "custom." In a period of widespread famine, for example, joining the army could be an escape from deprivation. The army's plentiful rations helped soldiers to avoid hunger and build strong bodies. Soldiers' steady employment gave them exceptional access to food that, in many ways, isolated them from civilian experiences of imperial rule. It also divided them from one another. Whether they were Hindus, Muslims, or Sikhs—or Nepali "Gurkhas," Punjabis, or Rajputs—the army's understanding of religious difference provided an institutional sanction to provision them unequally. A careful examination of military food practices before, during, and after the First World War reveals that the most "martial" soldiers could become the most logistically burdensome, and those deemed the most "prejudiced" could be the most open-minded. Soldiers' access to food, more often, exposed them to the inequalities of imperial rule. They accepted or rejected military food based on their shifting understandings of religious devotion, dietary necessity, or maintaining connections with their families and communities back home. For the colonial state, food was the cornerstone of making a martial man.[5]

THE GOVERNMENT'S SALT

Debates about food in the army long predated the First World War. Hinting at this longer tradition, Major R. T. I. Ridgway of the 5th Battalion Pathans contended that soldiers saw themselves as "*nimak-halal*—[*namak halal*] had eaten the salt of the Sirkar."[6] *Namak halal* literally meant lawful or righteous salt. It derived from the Arabic practice of serving a guest who consented to a bond of mutual protection by accepting bread and salt.[7] Mughal rulers in South Asia used this phrase to grant honors or gifts and maintain alliances. Warrior lineages such as Rajputs evoked *namak halal* when they fought to death for those whose salt they had eaten.[8] The

forces of the East India Company (EIC) took up the practice of referring to soldiers' pay as "salt" or *namak* and passed this on to the colonial
Indian Army.[9] Food was inseparable from soldiers' understanding of
their military service. This combined regional, occupational, and religious
rationales for loyalty.

During the First World War, soldiers repeatedly evoked "salt" to justify military service across religious categories of difference. One Punjabi Muslim soldier wrote to his comrades that they had "been eating the
salt of the British Government" for "three or four generations" and needed
to fulfill their obligations without shame.[10] Subedar Mir Dast, a Pathan
of the 55th Rifles and Victoria Cross winner, encouraged his fellow soldiers to "Show great zeal in your duty and be faithful and eat the salt of
the government with loyalty."[11] A Sikh soldier composed a melancholy
song beseeching that "Perchance the Guru may save us, but what will be
will be! We have eaten the salt of the Sirkar, before, when times were
good: Let us fight like valiant soldiers and pay the debt with our blood."[12]
Sepoy Chutar Singh reminded Sowar Rajan Singh that "You should always remember to be loyal to him whose salt and water you have eaten."[13]
Soldiers' willingness to evoke not only loyalty to the government, but also
"the Guru" or to "three or four generations" of their families, indicates
that military service was a complex mix of economic, familial, and community obligations. Soldiers' constant need to remind themselves and their
families why they were fighting indicates that "the government's salt" was
neither a universally acknowledged nor an automatically convincing reason to fight in brutal imperial conflicts.

What can account for soldiers' repeated invocations of "salt"? They em-
phatically were not declarations of unwavering loyalty to the Indian
Army. Rather, they reveal that imperial service required careful justifica-
tion and constant reaffirmation. Soldiers and officials were often insecure
about the role of food in forging soldiers' loyalty. Commander-in-chief
of the Indian Army Lord Kitchener (1902–9) expressed his hope in 1903
that soldiers would always follow the injunction "to fight for him whose
salt thou has eaten."[14] Others campaigned for soldiers to break this pledge.
In 1907, a man named Sawan Singh claimed to be a former Lance Duf-
fadar of the 25th Punjab Cavalry when he appeared at the Strangers'

Home for Asiatics in London, a halfway house and recruiting station for South Asian soldiers and sailors. He distributed an Urdu pamphlet that condemned those who stayed "loyal to the British" because they had "eaten their salt." Soldiers, the pamphlet claimed, were "so blinded that you cannot even comprehend where it is that the English got the salt which they give you to eat." It reasoned that "they have got the salt by taking from you. . . . It is the English who are eating *your* salt."[15] This pamphlet inverted the logic of loyal service. It maintained that as long as British officials extracted food and money from India, soldiers owed them nothing.

Sawan Singh's pamphlet recognized that British power in India relied on profitably extracting food to feed its expanding empire.[16] For-profit agricultural exports started in the eighteenth century under the EIC, which contributed to the death of ten million people in famine-stricken Bengal.[17] Periodic famines plagued India at the end of the nineteenth century in what historian Mike Davis called "Late Victorian Holocausts."[18] Their severity caused the population of India to decrease in the 1890s.[19] Dadabhai Naoroji, the first South Asian member of the British Parliament, argued that British rule was responsible for draining India of its resources and causing famines. One Indian civil servant similarly used the Famine Commission Reports of 1880 and 1898 to demonstrate that twenty-two famines had occurred during 130 years of British rule in India.[20] Military arguments about soldiers' loyalty to the government's salt chafed uncomfortably against the agricultural devastation of imperial rule.

The army worked hard to ensure that soldiers did not feel the pangs of hunger and food scarcity that burdened Indian civilians. Late nineteenth-century railway and canal work in the Punjab province created a "new agrarian frontier" in the so-called canal colonies. This area had long attracted military veterans and pensioners given "wasteland" as compensation for military service in the conflicts of 1857 and Afghanistan (1839–42, 1878–80). Canal work brought renewed agricultural productivity to the region. However, railroads also increased prices for foodstuffs sold in international markets.[21] By the turn of the twentieth century, controversial agricultural policies increased agricultural output for export but diminished emergency reserves.[22] Another devastating famine broke out in Punjab during the winter of 1907–8. The periodical *Free Hindustan* blamed Britain's "murderous commercial policy" for the hardships in and around dominant recruiting areas.[23] Indian independence advocate and syndicalist socialist Henry Hyndman argued that the extent of famine under British rule was unknown to both Hindu and Muslim rulers of India.[24] Many soldiers who came from peasant backgrounds in Punjab were receptive to arguments about imperial responsibility for the hardships of hunger. By 1907, the Government of India aggressively tracked "sedition" among South Asian soldiers. Intelligence officers reported that soldiers complained of being too busy fighting on frontiers and overseas to cultivate their own land.[25] Fighting for the government's salt felt less powerful when military service failed to protect soldiers from food insecurity.

SOLDIERS' DIETS

Food scarcity in Punjab made military recruitment appealing and controversial for soldiers who craved stable diets. One British officer admitted that new recruits made the best advertisements for future recruiting because they demonstrated "what regular exercise, good pay, free rations and clothing did for them."[26] Some soldiers sidestepped the criticisms of imperial food practices by viewing the army as a path for, rather than impediment to, food security. The army, in turn, sharpened its arguments about what the ideal soldier—and martial man—should eat. Officials who defined martial diets attempted to make imperial food into something that could strengthen—rather than weaken—Indian men. Many argued that only eating like a soldier could give men the martial prowess to fight for—or in some cases against—imperial rule.

Ironically, it was very difficult to define and secure an ideal military diet. Food rituals for British soldiers proved to be as complex as any South Asian restriction. In *A Common-Sense Health Lecture* of 1911, a former military man warned British soldiers to avoid "tainted meat, unripe or overripe fruit, badly cooked vegetables, and messes hawked by natives." He encouraged soldiers not to "drink in excess" because impure water was more dangerous than the battlefield. Especially damaging was milk in bazaars, which "swarm with enteric germs." Soldiers should not "take water from natives" because men employed by army regiments apparently "fill their bags at any available source."[27] British officials racialized dirty food as a problem particular to India. Yet food was a recurring imperial concern. The *Hints for Soldiers Proceeding to India* discouraged soldiers from consuming dirty milk, syrups, impure water, and unripe or rotten food. Enteric fever, it alleged, was traceable to "dirty liquids." Flies, meanwhile, spread diseases that could only be purified by boiling all liquids.[28] British soldiers recalled that when flies got on food it was a "quick way to get diarrhea," so cookhouses were inspected daily. Cooks had to wash their hands in "Pinky Parney" (potassium permanganate).[29] These extensive efforts were intended to keep British soldiers clean and healthy. The logistical burdens of feeding British men did not result in accusations that Christianity or European science made British soldiers unfit to serve. Instead, medical and military officials institutionalized these complex food rituals as "common sense."

Debates about South Asian soldiers' diets proved more contentious, if not necessarily more logistically difficult, than their British counterparts. One point of controversy was meat. Many Muslim, Gurkha, Rajput, and Sikh men ate meat but it was an infrequent luxury in most Punjabi homes. By contrast, military officials delighted in offering a weekly quota of meat on active service.[30] Influential civil servant and "orientalist" Max Macauliffe argued in 1903 that when Sikhs started eating meat "they became muscular, vigorous, strong, and fit for martial duties." When Hindus stopped eating meat, he asserted, "they became prey to foreign invaders."[31] The perceived importance of meat made it possible for British officials to increase the meat ration for South Asian soldiers in China from eight ounces per week in 1902 to twenty-eight ounces per week in 1906—ten ounces more than their British counterparts.[32] Such extravagant dietary provisions were due, in part, to the need to incentivize prolonged service overseas.[33] Nonetheless, it reinforced British perceptions that soldiers' strength depended on meat-heavy diets.

The army's glorification of meat eating did not go unnoticed in Indian society. Some nationalist leaders echoed the army in praising meat-heavy diets to build martial men. Indian troops' meat supplies usually consisted of chicken, lamb, or goat. However, some Indian activists such as

Swami Vivekananda encouraged Hindus to eat beef. Vivekananda believed that doing so would make Hindus as strong and masculine as British, Sikh, and Muslim soldiers.[34] However, many high-caste Hindus, including some leaders of Indian nationalist movements, emphasized the purity of the vegetarian diet and the stain of consuming beef. They increasingly made vegetarianism a cornerstone of the nationalist project through protests about cow slaughter.[35] A group of Sikh Kukas brought a degree of notoriety to the anti-cow-slaughter movement when they killed butchers in Amritsar. Some Sikhs continued to abstain from eating beef even though British civil servants like Macauliffe insisted that Sikh canonical writings said nothing against it.[36] By contrast, cow protection societies gained support from members of the Indian National Congress, who at times encouraged rioting against Muslim butchers.[37] British officials tended to diminish imperial culpability in such protests by casting them as perennial Hindu-Muslim antagonism.[38] However, a 1907 political meeting in Bombay highlighted the army's role in cow slaughter. Participants alleged that the army slaughtered ten million cows to feed British soldiers at a time when 95% of the South Asian population starved.[39] In 1910, one man named Daya Ram protested both "the slaughter of cows by Mahomedans" and "the feeding of British troops on cows."[40] The ubiquitous beef diets of British soldiers required the habitual slaughter of cows. While the army was quick to label such objections as irrational "religious prejudice," such criticisms implicitly censured British rule and military occupation.

In 1909, a retired major, W. H. Kemp, revealed how the army continued to be inflexible with diets, despite nationalist, religious, and famine-related criticisms. Kemp had worked for the Army Veterinary Department and estimated that 1,190,000 female cows were killed annually to feed British troops. He worried that "we are blindly shutting our eyes to the fact, that we are permitting a vast number of animals which are the sole source of supply of the bullocks and cows, to be destroyed for the production of the beef consumed by a large European, and a small Mohamedan community." He suggested substituting male buffalo so that the majority of the population could still get access to milk products.[41] Lieutenant Governor of the United Provinces, Sir J. P. Hewett, was not convinced by

Kemp's arguments despite being responsible for addressing famine relief. He was more worried that replacing cows with buffalos would call attention to and revive the cow protection movement.[42] This, he believed, would be "most embarrassing" and so he rejected Kemp's proposal.[43] British and South Asian soldiers benefited from an abundant military food supply during periods of intense famine and food shortage. British officials' fears of reigniting a "religious" issue, however, led them to ignore their part in creating and exacerbating food shortages.

Indian soldiers' published accounts of military life unsurprisingly avoided these controversial aspects of army food and instead focused on anecdotes of luxury or hunger. Many recalled the bonuses and special feasts that they received on service.[44] Khan Bahadur Risaldar Shahzad Mir Khan delighted in the fact that the same money could buy three times as much bread in Afghanistan as in India.[45] Jemadar Abdur Razzak, a Muslim soldier from Vellore in the 1st Madras Lancers, opened his memoir by recounting the rations he received on a troop ship to Malabar. These included rice, flour, dal, ghee, sugar, potatoes, onion, a bottle of rum, pepper, a bottle of brandy, a bottle of port wine, a jar of lime juice, soda, and lemonade. When he visited England as part of the honor guard of Queen Victoria he enjoyed many "rich meals."[46] Both men's published memoirs no doubt delighted readers with the apparent culinary luxuries of the army. Yet their works did not shy away from incidents of uncomfortable shortages. Compared to his gluttony in Afghanistan, Shahzad Mir Khan recalled that food was so scarce in the Himalayan borderlands that he resorted to overpaying merchants and hunting. On an expedition to Africa, he remembered that it was "impossible to eat a square meal" because of the intense heat and the expense of water.[47] A Rajput officer, Amar Singh, similarly complained to his diary that during a visit to Rawal Pindi in 1901 "The food arrangements were that I nearly starved myself." He could find no decent water to drink, the bazaar sold only "dirty sweets," and "the servants had nothing to cook things in."[48] Soldiers' accounts of military service, therefore, painted a very uneven picture. The army could at times give soldiers access to dietary extravagance. It also made them suffer due to shortages and poorly managed resources. While some men used these accounts of shortage and hardship to emphasize their own resourcefulness and stoicism, their testimonies also suggest that the army did not always deliver on its promise to reimburse soldiers' service with "salt." Their hardships also indicate that religious mandates were only some among many food issues affecting military service.

Soldiers' inconsistent access to food was a boon for anti-colonial activists. The pamphlet at the Strangers' Home for Asiatics emphasized that British soldiers got three servings of meat per day but Indian soldiers had to eat "dal & chapatis." The result was making their faces "the colour of the Earth."[49] The author believed that "If you too had food like the English, you would not be so black and worn-out. For you & the English are both from the same original stock—you are both Aryans." The pamphlet combined Aryan race theory with an environmental determinism that defined access to food as a marker of "racial" purity. Identifying South Asians as Aryans, the author suggested that soldiers' inferior food marked them as racially unfit with "black" skin. This racialized argument portrayed service in the Indian Army as a source of weakness and racial degeneration rather than strength and physical prowess.[50] Despite the army's claim to provide soldiers with "the government's salt," food proved to be a source of unease as much as comfort. The army's ever-changing demands for meat diets, sanitary food, or privation forced soldiers into many politically, socially, and physically uncomfortable situations. This left unending possibilities to critique military service.

BRAHMAN DIETS

Soldiers experienced many dietary challenges but much of the army's anxiety about South Asian soldiers' food centered on the perceived dietary stringency of high-caste Brahmans. Hindus made up roughly 40% of the army—a low proportion considering that they were nearly 70% of the population of India.[51] Brahmans formed less than 2% of soldiers in the early twentieth century. This was a dramatic reversal from the early nineteenth century, when high-caste Brahmans and Rajputs made up roughly 80% of the soldiers of the Bengal Army.[52] One reason for the demographic shift was that Brahmans became the central scapegoats of the 1857 rebellion. High-caste Hindu and Muslim soldiers, so the story went, revolted after being forced to open the greased cartridges of the Enfield rifle with their mouths.[53] As a result, subsequent British officials denigrated high-caste Hindus—but not Muslims—as incompatible with military service due to their perceived stringency. The reality was that Hindu and Brahman soldiers repeatedly changed what they ate according to military demands. Army narratives about Hindu and Brahman unsuitability for military service, however, used food to define masculine and martial prowess and undermine food-based critiques of imperial rule.

The army's criticisms of Brahman diets were a relatively new feature in the late nineteenth and early twentieth centuries. Some EIC officials in the eighteenth century had believed that Brahman diets increased rather than decreased these men's value as soldiers. Brahman soldiers who served in EIC armies ate no meat, cooked their own food, ate alone, and carried pre-prepared fried breads and sweetmeats.[54] Officials regarded these measures as suitable ways to maintain endurance against the sanitary and climate challenges of army life and recommended that European troops do the same.[55] However, evangelical chaplains and medical officials condemned soldiers' formerly praiseworthy culinary habits as religious prejudices.[56] After the 1857 uprising, the Peel Commission (1858–59) recommended recruiting fewer high-caste Hindus, deepening institutional biases. Late nineteenth- and early twentieth-century military officials went further to single out Brahman customs as harmful to the army. One military memoir included a detailed story about Sita Ram, a Brahman soldier, shunned socially after drinking water from the hands of a low-caste girl. He only regained his social status by paying large penalties to a Brahman priest. This tale reinforced criticisms of "Brahmanical priests" common among British administrators and Indian authors such as Premchand. Scholars have rightly debated the veracity of this memoir but it nonetheless proved influential for military praxis: it was republished several times in the twentieth century and circulated widely in army exams and newspapers.[57] This story of Brahmans corrupting and polluting soldiers became a well-worn imperial cliché.

In reality, there were many conflicting military accounts of how Brahman soldiers actually behaved. The 1897 *Handbook for the Indian Army* on Brahmans asserted that Brahman physiques were either emaciated or bloated. It accused Brahmans of embezzling funds meant to supplement other soldiers' diets.[58] EIC administrator Brian Hodgson wrote in the 1830s that high-caste Hindus saw in overseas service "nothing but pollution and peril from unclean men." His observations were republished in the 1915 army handbook on Nepali "Gurkhas."[59] *The Hints for Soldiers Proceeding to India* contended in 1912 that to some Hindu soldiers "the mere glance of a man of inferior caste makes a meal uneatable; if his shadow fall upon the cooking vessels the contents have to be thrown away."[60] Major S. H. E. Nicholas, 95th Russell's Infantry, argued similarly that the Ahir men of his regiment were martially fit because "it does not matter if your shadow falls" on their food "as certain classes would have you believe." The only exception was that if Rajput or Brahman soldiers were sitting nearby, "they might feel compelled to play up to religious prejudice and treat the food as polluted."[61] High-caste men previously valued for their conscientious health and sobriety embodied prejudice and irrationality according to army officials in the twentieth century. By the time of the First World War, only one regiment of the Indian Army bore the name "Brahmans."[62]

Despite repeated assertions about Brahman aversion to impure shadows, Captain C. Watson Smyth, who served with the 1st Brahmans, viewed things differently. In 1911 he maintained that he had "never seen a Brahman throw away his food because the shadow of a man of another caste had fallen on it" even though he walked nearby when men were cooking in camp.[63] He believed that "caste prejudices sound formal when put down in cold print, but in reality they are very elastic." He undermined the depiction of elaborate rituals quoted in several military handbooks. Brahmans, he found, were officially obliged to bathe and change into a dhoti or loincloth before cooking and eating but they rarely did so, especially in cold weather. On service, Brahmans gave "up the purifying bath."[64] Smyth did not describe how coercion, including social and professional pressure, may have influenced such flexibility. Nonetheless, he undermines the criticism that Brahmans were inefficient soldiers because of food. Even James Willcocks, who condemned Brahman habits during the First World War, attested that they "abandoned" their "most treasured customs" prior to the conflict.[65] In reality, the army ensured soldiers' compliance. Smyth explained that "the strict rule is that no Brahman must eat meat." However, before Brahmans were enlisted, military officials made them promise to consume it. Men were forced to do so monthly in front of an Indian officer.[66] By successfully compelling Brahman soldiers to eat meat, Smyth described a situation in 1911 very different from the pervasive anxieties about greased cartridges.

Indian soldiers also frequently mentioned how they gave up dietary stringency while on service. Gadadhar Singh, a Rajput of the 7th Rajputs, served in China during the 1900–1901 "Boxer" rebellion. Shortly after returning he published a Hindi-language travelogue and war testimony that recounted a conversation with an American soldier who condemned Indian soldiers' strict habits. He argued that in times of war Hindu soldiers gave up their restrictive diets, living and eating communally. Communal dining, he believed, brought out the truest expression of religion.[67] Gadadhar Singh's view of inter-community dining reflected his participation in the Arya Samaj, a reformist society that was influential among Punjabis during periods of famine. Samajis encouraged inter-caste dining to embrace, rather than alienate, low-caste Indians who might turn to Christian missionaries for social inclusion and economic advancement.[68] For example, participants at one Arya Samaj meeting in Lahore alleged that Christian missionaries adopted Hindu dietary customs to gain the trust of Hindus and convert them to Christianity. By 1910 "interdining" was discussed widely in Arya Samaj newspapers.[69] Soldiers like Gadadhar Singh no doubt found easy parallels between the army's anti-Brahman attitudes and the Arya Samaj's calls for Hindu reform. Even though the army became suspicious of the Arya Samaj's anti-colonial undercurrents, many soldiers, officials, and reformers agreed about the desirability of reappraising Hindu dining habits on the eve of global war.

Debates about Brahman diets became important because Britain relied heavily on their participation on and off the battlefield during the First World War. The War Office claimed to recruit Brahmans as hospital cooks and active-duty body burners to carry out the ceremonies and proper procedures for Hindu soldiers, even though some of these rites normally were performed in India by low-caste Hindus.[70] While officials portrayed Brahmans as too "prejudiced" for military service, other widely recruited Hindu soldiers relied on Brahmans to maintain their own dietary purity. Officers believed that most Hindu combatants—including Nepali "Gurkhas" and Dogras—preferred Brahman cooks.[71] Urdu-language military propaganda proudly declared that high-caste Brahmans carried all food items into Hindu soldiers' kitchens.[72] By assigning Brahmans subservient, non-combatant tasks, the Indian Army depicted Brahman men as not quite martial or manly enough to fight. This military perception was much at odds with Hindu and Brahman soldiers' many sacrifices and difficult wartime experiences.

As both soldiers and non-combatants, Brahmans played key roles in India's immense contribution to the war. Ratan Lal, an army clerk at the post office in Basra, wrote to the Urdu periodical *Jat Gazette* that he had no trouble keeping his "religion" intact overseas. He assured readers that many people in the Mesopotamia campaign made do without meat by receiving vegetables, sugar, milk, flour, and condiments appropriate for their diets. There was even one "Brahman cook" for every fifteen men. Writing in 1918, when some of the logistical failures of the early war had diminished, Ratan Lal urged men to take up military service without reservation.[73] Other men admitted that soldiers made important wartime sacrifices. Gugan Singh of the 20th Deccan Horse wrote to Mular Singh, the editor of the *Jat Gazette*, describing one incident when the lieutenant-governor of the Central Provinces visited his regiment. The official asked a soldier named Dalip Singh "whether he removed his boots when he took his meals." Dalip Singh responded that he and his fellow soldiers "had given up all that sort of thing in the war." They were even willing to eat with French and Englishmen. To this the lieutenant-governor reportedly responded "Bravo! that is as it should be."[74] Hindu soldiers could earn open praise for altering their diets.

At times, wartime flexibility left soldiers to answer to their families and friends back home. M. L. Tilhet wrote to Pyari Lal Tilhet that many soldiers in Egypt who formerly rejected food when "the shadow of a passer-by had fallen on it" had started eating "from the hands of sweepers" to avoid starvation. Tilhet evoked the well-worn cliché about those certain "other" Hindu men who rejected food tainted by a shadow and depicted his choices as a matter of life and death. Yet he went further: a "Doctor Lieutenant, by caste a Brahman" apparently "abstains from nothing" and advised others to do the same.[75] Historian David Omissi has suggested that Tilhet referred to the Brahman doctor to diminish his own transgressions. This example also suggests that Brahman men who lived or worked in Europe were not as stringent in their practices as British authorities often assumed. In fact, such men, under greater scrutiny from colonial officials, often played active roles in encouraging dietary flexibility.

It should have been impossible for military officials to categorize "Hindus" as universally bad for military discipline due to their diversity and the frequency with which they used their beliefs to *rationalize* rather than challenge martial actions and wartime diets. Rajput officer Amar Singh recalled meeting boats of sick and wounded soldiers, some of whom had been prisoners of war in Kut. "There was hardly any flesh on them," he recalled, but the men were reluctant to eat the mule provided. Amar Singh told them that "their various Maharajas had sanctioned their eating it" and that "if I had been with them I would have done the same." Amar Singh carried a social position and military rank superior to the majority of men he encountered and no doubt influenced some of the former prisoners for that reason. Yet he also explained that "our people" had "eaten animals in the old days when they were in a siege and that in a great famine even our own greatest Rishi [holy man] [Veswamitra] Jee had not only eaten dog's meat but had offered it to the Gods as this was written in our Puranas [Hindu sacred texts]." He assured them that when they returned home, no one would question what they had done but would look upon them "as heroes."[76]

Amar Singh's story captures the tensions of competing accounts of Hindu wartime diets. On the one hand, he suggests that Indian leaders such as Maharajas had long sanctioned flexibility in the face of hardships, including wars. Dietary elasticity was itself an acceptable response to the extreme conditions of food shortage. On the other hand, men who refused to eat mule meat wanted to remain steadfast and uphold religiously sanctioned food purity. No less noteworthy is Singh's eagerness to smooth things over for the army by convincing soldiers to make do, rather than protest their food. Indian Army officer Francis Yeats-Brown recalled a similar story of a "Hindu officer" who was a prisoner of war in Turkey and set an example to his men "by eating beef, in order that they should not starve."[77] Men policed themselves and their fellow captives. At the same time, various spiritual and secular authorities including Hindu officers, "various Maharajas," and the heroes of the Puranas redefined acceptable wartime behavior. These Hindu soldiers and Hindu beliefs widened, rather than limited, the possibilities of martial service.

There were a few well-known cases of Hindu men whose wartime behaviors did cause logistical difficulties. The officers of the 9th Bhopal Infantry allegedly celebrated their soldiers' capture after they had disagreements about Brahman soldiers' diets.[78] This included the oft-repeated story about non-Brahman shadows passing over their food. H. V. Cox's report on the conduct of the 3rd Brahman Regiment in Mesopotamia suggests an alternate reading of these soldiers. Cox believed that the men of the 3rd Brahmans objected to communal dining in a deliberate effort "to get the regt. passed as unfit to remain at the front owing to caste prejudices."[79] This was spearheaded by two Havildars (noncommissioned Indian officers) who attempted to prevent the introduction of group messing into the regiment. As Cox suggests, their primary goal was to be relocated away from their harsh wartime locale in Mesopotamia. The problem was not "prejudice" but rather soldiers' ability to self-consciously deploy military assumptions to influence where and how they served in battle.[80] Men played into stereotypes about Brahman particularity to set the terms for their service. Their plan worked. The regiment was transferred from Mesopotamia to another destination.[81] The men of the 9th Bhopal Infantry may have similarly played into colonial stereotypes to influence where they served or to resist other difficult aspects of military service. It was more likely *institutional* prejudice that ensured that the final regiment bearing the name "Brahman" was partially disbanded by 1917.[82]

Soldiers' wartime experiences indicate that there was no emblematic Hindu or Brahman soldier who embodied their communities' dietary needs. Some men endured hardships to preserve their beliefs, even if this meant starving as prisoners of war. Others felt that it was acceptable to forgo normal restrictions in wartime. Hindu men had conversations with one another outside of British supervision to define and refine their understandings of appropriate behavior. This was true for low-ranking

POWs, elite Brahman doctors, and Rajput officers. Other soldiers used British discourses of prejudice to set the terms of their service. Military assumptions about the particularity and logistical difficulty of Hindu diets was especially misplaced due to the fact that wartime food was logistically difficult for *all* soldiers, including those whom British officials regarded as the most "martial."

CATERING TO THE "MARTIAL RACES"

British officials frequently criticized, and eventually disbanded, Brahman soldiers for supposedly dietary reasons. Yet they were often willing and able to cater to the needs of soldiers of the "martial races." For example, twentieth-century military publications attributed a level of "common sense" to Muslim diets. The *Hints for Soldiers Proceeding to India* rationalized that pigs were forbidden because they "are filthy feeders all over the east" and frequently caused disease. The pamphlet described the fast of Ramzan, the careful preparation of *halal* meat, and the avoidance of alcohol as logical countermeasures to the challenges of the tropical sun, much as British personnel had described Brahman diets in the eighteenth century.[83] The culture of scientific rationality and sobriety that denigrated Brahman diets as "prejudices" in the twentieth century left space for the dietary needs of Muslim troops and other soldiers deemed "martial." Meeting widely recruited soldiers' dietary needs could help recruitment and deepen alliances with military men. It could also prevent soldiers from complaining, rebelling, or wondering if Britain's enemies would be more sympathetic to their needs and desires. Food became a reason not to recruit Brahmans at the same moment that the army committed unparalleled efforts to feed other South Asian soldiers.

According to British officials, Nepali soldiers, recruited as "Gurkhas," were valuable soldiers because they apparently had few dietary restrictions. Although some were Hindu, they were "broad-minded" and "freer from prejudice than most followers of that creed," according to British officers.[84] However, the army coordinated extensive logistical efforts to manage Nepali soldiers' food during the war. The officer commanding the 2/9th Gurkhas explained that "Rations are taken from India for the whole period of absence and batmen are specially sent to cook food."[85] An Indian Medical

Service officer reported similar measures: "Food is cooked by good caste Hindus in a Hindu cook-house, and distributed by good caste Hindus and Gurkha convalescents. No Mohamedan is allowed in the Hindu kitchen." British officials provided aluminum dishes cleaned "by a Hindu waterman."[86] They collected live animals from France, Spain, Switzerland, and Corsica and assigned a representative from each regiment to slaughter goats "in the manner required by their religion." The meat was then carefully labeled and marked to ensure that each regiment received the appropriately slaughtered meat.[87] Nepali men also slaughtered their own meat "in a Hindu slaughter-house."[88] Even though reported measures usually fell short of the reality, they indicate that British officials made significant effort to provision certain soldiers if they considered such measures necessary. This did not make Nepali troops ineligible for service or earn them the distinction of being bad for military discipline.

In fact, army officials widely publicized their efforts to honor South Asian diets. The Government of India distributed twenty thousand copies of "The Commemorative Pamphlet for the Brighton Pavilion Hospital." Ten thousand went to the troops and ten thousand to institutions in India such as schools and libraries.[89] Written with English, Urdu, and Gurmukhi (Punjabi) sections, the pamphlet described extensive arrangements for soldiers' food in hospitals. These included the construction of "no less than nine kitchens" to accommodate "each of the different castes" with "Indian methods of cooking." The hospital created "Special arrangements for the killing and storing of meat for separate castes." While the English section of the pamphlet included ethnographic descriptions of the differences between "Hindu" and "Muslim" diets, it also asserted condescendingly that Indian cooks "had to be taught to cook standing up" and had "never heard of gas, far less seen it." The Urdu section, by contrast, was more specific in assuring its readers about the expertise of the British and Indian staff overseeing soldiers' care. It listed their names, ranks, and length of service in India. Both versions stressed that "The food of the Hindus is handed out from the store to the different head cooks by a high caste Brahman." Both versions also reiterated that men of different castes were kept completely separate with personal space for washing their own utensils. The pamphlet asserted that when the king and queen visited the hospital "a high caste Brahman testified to the excellence of the food and the arrangements regarding it."[90] Once again, Brahmans took prominent roles in representing and catering to the "martial races."

In addition to producing commemorative pamphlets, Indian hospitals helped to encourage favorable impressions of the army's food arrangements. Soldiers who had exceptional access to food and spare time in hospitals praised the dietary provisions in their letters home. In one letter, Said Ahmad Khan of the 26th Punjabis Tank praised the Kitchener Indian Hospital in Brighton for providing "Food and drink . . . of the best" quality.[91] Maratha soldier G. Lowan stated that arrangements in the Kitchener Hospital were "perfect" and just as good as "if we were at home."[92] Yet these declarations cannot be taken as representative of soldiers' general experiences of war. The Urdu section of the commemorative pamphlet for the Brighton Pavilion Hospital explained that soldiers received assistance writing letters during their free time. The army made sure that soldiers spread word of their exceptional treatment.

Publicized accommodations for soldiers in hospitals far exceeded what was possible in war. Lt. Col. Allanson, serving with a Gurkha Regiment at Gallipoli in 1916, complained about "The food difficulty." The problem was not religious oversensitivity but rather the failures of British logistical management. Food was cooked two miles away, which meant that it was "thoroughly messed about by orderlies" to the point that it was "almost uneatable."[93] Lt. Col. W. R. B. Williams of the 2nd Battalion 7th Gurkhas similarly recalled that it took months for food from India to make it to the battlefields of the Mesopotamia campaign.[94] Conditions were notoriously sparse during the Siege of Kut-al-Amara in 1915 and 1916. Officers made it mandatory for all South Asians to eat horsemeat by April 1916.[95] This was objectionable for soldiers of all faiths serving in the campaign, who already endured shortages of meat and vegetables and general malnutrition. Up to eleven thousand perished from scurvy in the latter half of 1916.[96] After the war, the men of the 1/7th Gurkhas who served in Kurdistan in 1919 endured frequent diarrhea and dysentery.[97] Military failure to provide clean and healthy food was a recurring source of anguish.

The army's competence dealing with and distributing food was central to their ability to sell the war effort to the home fronts in Britain and

India. According to army discourses, British officials were paternalistically devoted to providing proper food for their soldiers. This made soldiers' traumatic experiences—including food shortages—seem unavoidable or exaggerated when soldiers came home telling stories of woe. Many soldiers, no doubt, related to one Sikh soldier who lamented in 1915 that he was experiencing "a devil's war" that was not worth the effort because his parents "have food enough and to spare."[98] The soldier's emotive cries suggest that the government's salt no longer seemed like a fair trade for wartime suffering.

FASTING THE GOVERNMENT'S SALT

British officials widely publicized what soldiers *did* eat but many men were more preoccupied with what they did *not* eat. The outbreak of war in 1914 coincided with the *Roza*, or the month-long fast, of Ramzan, affecting approximately 35% of soldiers in the army who were Muslim.[99] The fast was one of the five pillars of Islam and required participants not to eat or drink anything—including water—from sunrise to sunset for the month-long fasting period. After sunset, individuals broke the fast with light snacks, and then woke up just prior to sunrise to eat again. At the end of Ramzan, many communities celebrated Eid-al-Fitr with celebrations and feasting. In recruiting manuals, British officers worried that this cycle of fasting and feasting was bad for soldiers' health and presented a logistical challenge. In addition to the month-long fasting period, soldiers required three weeks to recover and rebuild their strength.[100] At the outbreak of war, the army contemplated whether or not to allow Muslim soldiers to complete their fasts or make them prepare their bodies for war. Their decision, and Muslim soldiers' demands to honor the fast, reflected the continuing centrality of food for soldiers' service.

One factor influencing Ramzan in war was British uncertainty about Muslim soldiers' willingness to fight against the Ottoman Empire, or in Muslim holy lands.[101] Muslim soldiers could not help but be influenced by Indian anti-colonialism, German and Ottoman propaganda, rumored and real desertions among certain Muslim troops, and mutinies allegedly stirred by religious concerns. Making matters worse, the United States Embassy reported that Indian Muslim prisoners of war in Turkey received extremely conscientious treatment regarding their fasts and diets.[102] In the Mesopotamia campaign, soldiers heard frequent rumors that the Ottoman army treated Muslim troops more favorably, contributing to their desires to desert. British officials, by contrast, secured written permission from religious leaders in India to compel Muslim soldiers to eat horsemeat during the Siege of Kut.[103] Denying soldiers the ability to carry out the fast of Ramzan, therefore, provided yet another unfavorable contrast to Britain's wartime enemies. Geopolitical factors gave the fast of Ramzan significant political and military importance. Yet soldiers' own understandings of the fast were also shaped by the longer relationship between food, faith, and martial devotion.

Muslim soldiers had long wrestled with honoring the fast during military service.[104] One European author observed that "Some Muslims when sick would not break the fast to save their lives."[105] Mrs. Meer Hasan Ali, the English wife of an Indian Muslim government employee, believed that there were important exceptions. In *Observations on the Mussulmans of India*, written in 1832 and republished in 1917, she noted that "the sick, the aged, women giving nourishment to infants . . . and very young children . . . are all commanded not to fast."[106] Recruiting officer Major W. Fitz G. Bourne echoed this view in 1914 by stating that the sick, aged, pregnant and nursing women, young children, and travelers were "exempt" from fasting.[107] By 1915, recruitment manuals adjusted the list in a slight but significant way, adding that "Soldiers on service and travellers are also exempt."[108] Military pamphlets included soldiers alongside pregnant women and the aged who were granted exemption for their perceived weakness. Soldiers' lack of choice might prevent them from demonstrating their strength, stamina, piety, and masculinity. It could also become a financial burden. According to a pamphlet by Ja'far Sharif, a language teacher to the Madras government, republished in 1921, those unable to fast during Ramzan were required to free a slave, feed sixty beggars, or fast independently for sixty days.[109] If enforced, each of these would have been a serious financial burden for low-ranking soldiers. Many joined military service for the promise of a reliable income and sent money home to support their families. Paying absolution for not fasting would have negated the material inducements of military service.

Ramzan also played an important role in debates about early twentieth-century physical morality. Mohandas Gandhi famously believed that fasting had "biomoral" value by using the power of physical emptiness to shed light on the world's violence and injustice.[110] Gandhi acknowledged that Muslim colleagues found it easy to take up "fasting as a means of self-restraint" due to their experience with Ramzan.[111] These arguments supported the view of Muslim reformer Mirza Ghulam Ahmad, whose teachings entered without censorship into military ranks before and during the First World War. Ahmad taught that "Fasting is necessary for the perfect purity of the soul" and could aid in the "spiritual progress of man."[112] Nur Mohamed, a Pathan of the 38th Central India Horse, echoed this view when confronted with a man who mocked him for keeping the fast. He replied that "The life which we are now leading is one which God would not inflict even on a dog, as it is a time of unspeakable hardship with death always at hand, and perhaps by the grace of God we may gain heaven by reason of our self-denial in having kept the fast."[113] Soldiers used the self-denial of fasting to find power and purpose amid wartime destruction.

With concerns about incurring financial burdens, family shame, or demonstrating a lack of piety and virility, Muslim soldiers had many complex reasons, in addition to the immediate political context, for continuing their fasts during the war. Some judged each other harshly for failing to do so. Badshah Khan told soldier Torai Khan from the Meerut Stationary Hospital that he was praying for "the welfare of all Muslims" because some, including many Punjabis, "did not even keep the fast."[114] Pir Dil Khan, a soldier serving at the front with the 129th Baluchis, worried that a letter had come in from either Mecca or Medina condemning all Muslims who "eat the fast [*sic*] and do not pray."[115] Driver Lal Din requested that Manlair Karim Bakhsh send him "the orders about keeping fasts over here."[116] Zabu Shah assured his mother from the trenches that "Today we are keeping the fast. We had to give it up for a fortnight, but today we have begun again."[117] Dealing with the stress of war, anticolonial activism, pressures from home, and their own anxieties about spiritual devotion, men often judged one another for failing to keep up the holy struggle within themselves.

The wartime debates about Ramzan proved especially complicated after the Singapore Mutiny in February 1915. Soldiers of the 5th Light Infantry had wrestled with the decision to fast during the war. When news of the war reached the regiment during Ramzan in August 1914, the British officers asked Indian officers whether the men would be willing to quit fasting, even though the regiment was not ordered to mobilize.[118] Subedar Major Khan Mohamed Khan, the highest-ranking Indian officer, conferred with the regimental *maulvi*. This appointed religious scholar decided that the men should quit the fast. One soldier, Sepoy Fazal Rahman, disagreed and developed "a great following in the regiment." He was discharged from the regiment for being, as the Subedar Major alleged, "much too religious."[119]

Fazal Rahman's protests did not represent a simple excess of "religious" feeling. Food was a central source of discontent for soldiers in Singapore prior to the premature end of Ramzan in 1914. One issue was the unsympathetic nature of the Subedar Major who, according to the medical officer, had a "tendency to obesity." By contrast, the Subedar Major referred to the other men as "thinner and weaker." Despite this discrepancy in stature, British officers relied on the "obese"—and higher paid—Subedar Major to act as the voice of Indian soldiers regarding matters such as rations and fasts. Prior to the controversy over Ramzan, he had ignored soldiers' complaints that the vegetables were of bad quality. He did not intervene when men were issued live chickens instead of goat meat at the same weight, including beaks and feathers. In India, men purchased their own milk and fresh meat as well as curry. In Singapore, the price of meat and milk was too expensive, and it was difficult to find familiar spices and flavors.[120] Concerns about food access far from home weighed on soldiers' minds when the Subedar Major agreed to end the fast prematurely. An indifferent superior officer and an inadequate food supply made the self-sacrifice of Ramzan one of soldiers' few opportunities to ensure their spiritual and physical well-being.

British and Indian officials recognized that food played an important role in agitating the regiment before the Singapore Mutiny. A number of men fell out of a parade shortly before the mutiny citing physical weakness. The commanding officer, Lieutenant Colonel E. V. Martin, brought sepoy Yusaf Khan before the British military and medical officers, as well as the Subedar Major, and ordered him to strip. He said that Yusaf looked like "a living skeleton," which proved that the men were undernourished and should not be subject to excessive physical duties.[121] In addition to being banned from finishing the fast, soldiers were inadequately fed and unable to supplement their diets. Existing challenges of exhausting physical labor and serving far from home were exacerbated by the humiliation of having their bodies put on display for the scrutiny of high-ranking officers.

Soldiers' inability to make choices about what they ate—or did not eat—intensified the unfavorable aspects of military service. While many soldiers' bodies grew strong through government support, men also felt that their bodies were subject to divine authority. Control over eating or not eating the salt of the government gave Muslim men the power to make what they consumed, and how they served, divine. The army, in turn, would alter their perspective of fasts in light of soldiers' demands. Rather than seeing Ramzan as a logistical burden, they accepted it as a legitimate form of community belonging that could solidify, rather than undermine, military discipline and loyalty.

THE LOYAL FAST

The fast of Ramzan had "biomoral," economic, and religious value but it also represented an opportunity for men to celebrate and feel connected to their communities. Compared with the daily food-related anxieties of army life, Ramzan gave Muslim soldiers special luxuries when they broke the fast each evening. It was customary for soldiers to enjoy extravagant feasting during Eid, which immediately followed the fasting period. Mrs. Meer Hasan Ali argued that Eid was "one of the greatest heart-rejoicing days" and was "a sort of reward for their month's severe abstinence."[122] Soldier Abdul Ali Khan recalled that during one wartime Eid 1,500 men gathered together for food and tea. "We had sports and such a display of joy," he explained, "that I cannot describe it. All the Sahibs thanked us for what we had done."[123] For Fazl Ali Khan, the importance of Ramzan was not merely in the fast itself, but in the joy and celebration that followed. Deprived of the opportunity to fast, soldiers likely felt that they also would have also missed their chance to celebrate. Military officials hoped that bringing Ramzan and Eid into military life might secure soldiers' gratitude and loyalty.

Many soldiers saw honoring the fast as a necessary prerequisite for their wartime service. Havaldar Ahdurehman Khan wrote from France to the newspaper *Akbar-i-Jung* that in preparation for Ramzan, the Jemadar, Nawab Khan, approached the commanding officer about having a temporary mosque erected. When sanctioning the request, the commanding officer asked that they "don't forget your Sirkar [government] in your prayers." When the fast ended, seven hundred Muslim men gathered to celebrate. One regimental havaldar offered prayers for the victory of their king-emperor, utter defeat of the Germans, and a safe and victorious return of Indian soldiers to India.[124] Abdul Ali Khan remembered similarly that at one celebration they offered prayers "for the victory of our King."[125] The *Nottingham Evening Post* reported that at the 1915 Eid celebration in Woking, England, the *maulvi*, Sadr-ud-din, spoke to the fifty South Asian Muslim soldiers assembled there. He addressed them "in Hindustani" and emphasized "the righteousness of the cause in which they were engaged."[126]

Military officials also allowed Ramzan to shape troops' movements. An officer of the 40th Pathans explained that "The period during which the Indian Corps was being re-organized was purposely timed at Sir James Willcocks's request to coincide with the Fast of Ramazan."[127] Willcocks, who so fervently critiqued Brahman soldiers' dietary needs, found it possible to bend military maneuvers around Ramzan. Soldiers often emphasized their piety as well. In 1915, Pathan soldiers attended a musical gathering after a hard-fought period on the front lines in France. In order to keep the fast, they declined the refreshing lemonade offered by the local French mayor. Forgoing refreshment after a lengthy period of difficult fighting allowed them to reframe their wartime suffering for divine ends, while also potentially offering a critique of war service. They voluntarily abstained from military luxuries to find honor and discipline in their wartime experience. Unlike their Brahman counterparts, Muslim soldiers were not condemned as "prejudiced" for these choices. Officers facilitated their actions and regimental histories celebrated their piety.[128]

Military efforts to accommodate soldiers during Ramzan went beyond the battlefield as soldiers disseminated stories of their experiences. Havildar Ghufran Khan, writing from the Pavilion Hospital in Brighton to Subedar Zaman Khan, called the arrangements for Ramzan "excellent" because fasting men were given their own ward.[129] In separate letters to the *Akbar-i-Jang*, Havildar Mohamad Sofid and Savar Abdul-Rahman enthusiastically reported that the hospitals in Brighton provided wounded and sick soldiers with such luxuries as "two bananas, one pound of milk, sugar, one orange and other fruits" for breaking the fast in the evening, as well as a supper of meat, bread, and rice and a light meal before daybreak that included milk and sugar.[130] Special arrangements for Ramzan and Eid enabled soldiers to enjoy exciting diets and more diverse foods from home. This was a direct contrast to battlefields and overseas military stations, which left soldiers with difficult access to appropriate and diverse food and led to both self-policing and harsh judgment between men. During Eid, however, they wrote down and circulated their gratitude for military arrangements in periodicals and letters home. This reproduced and disseminated their appreciation, making arrangements for Ramzan a useful investment in Muslim loyalty.

Military engagement with the fast of Ramzan deepened the contract of *namak halal*. The fast was not simply a devotional act prescribed within religious texts, or a logistical challenge to be overcome by British officials. Events in Singapore showed that food and fasting could become a source of discontent, if not mutiny. But more often, the fast of Ramzan, and Eid, created opportunities to cultivate positive support for the war. Overseas feasts and fasts provided soldiers with rare opportunities to unite in rigorous shared suffering or remember home with familiar food. Dramatic events such as the mutiny of the 5th Light Infantry were not necessarily directly caused by the cancellation of the fast. But such acts unsettled soldiers' feelings of comfort and stability during their overseas service. Their concerns about Ramzan related to several specific pains and hungers—for military solidarity, religious devotion, the comfort of home, and the desire for satisfying food. Military officials' eventual decision to provide careful and thoughtful arrangements for the fast of Ramzan cultivated a corps of steadfast martial Muslim men heading into the turbulent postwar world. It also underlined that other soldiers—and diets—still did not belong.

POSTWAR DIETS

The army's willingness to include Ramzan in military life contrasted with their continued suspicion of Hindu diets and praise only for Hindus who changed their habits. Willcocks acknowledged that soldiers frequently had to make do "without any of their accustomed food," but that they enjoyed doing so for the opportunity to win a medal.[131] Another British officer argued that the war brought positive change because many Dogra soldiers would not touch onions or carrots, but they grew "accustomed to these excellent vegetables during the Great War." He was pleased to find that "practically all Dogras will eat them now, and that the prejudice against them is dying out." A distinguished subedar major even introduced "cultivation of the carrot into his own village."[132] The army had publicized its efforts to honor soldiers' dietary preferences during the war but postwar British officers admitted that soldiers were expected to accept dietary modifications. Postwar officers depicted soldiers' willingness to change as an indication of the army's cosmopolitan culture and open-mindedness. This did not necessarily prevent soldiers from enduring continued discrimination.

Like their British counterparts, some South Asian soldiers celebrated the war for creating greater dietary flexibility and inter-community solidarity. Jemadar Tek Chand's letter to Chhotu Ram in Rohtak was published in the Urdu periodical the *Jat Gazette* in 1918. He claimed nearly one quarter of the soldiers gave up exclusive dietary practices during the war. Similar integration should happen, he asserted, among "Hindu castes"—which to him included Sikhs, Jats, Brahmans, Rajputs, and Dogras—so that eventually Hindus and Muslims could do the same.[133] S. M. Jafri, an Indian YMCA worker, recalled that one Indian cavalry officer in France encouraged his fellow soldiers to "forget our absurd prejudices of castes and religions. There is no such thing as caste."[134] Soldiers embraced the idea that they had transcended the dietary "prejudices" so long condemned in the army. Unlike those prewar soldiers who were often sympathetic to arguments about cow protection or imperial agriculture, postwar soldiers felt proud that they were "unprejudiced," and hence martial.

Postwar praise for dietary modification was a thinly veiled indication that anti-Hindu biases continued to be prominent in the army. The *Sepoy Officer's Manual*, revised in 1922, argued that "in matters of cooking and feeding, the uneducated Indian Musalman is not free from the prejudices of the Hindu." It encouraged keeping Muslims in their own companies and regiments to keep them from "the doubtful influence of their Hindu comrades."[135] Similarly, the manual encouraged the organization of Rajputs from the United Provinces into class regiments because they "are much more under Brahmanical influence and possess many of the faults of that class."[136] A major in a Sikh regiment argued in 1928 that "every effort has been made" to protect Sikh soldiers from "the contagion of Hinduism."[137] Concerns about "Hindu," or more specifically Brahman, diets "infecting" Rajputs, Nepalis, Sikhs, or Muslims suggest that diets were fluid and permeable across religious differences. Nonetheless, Nepali "Gurkhas," Rajputs, and Dogras continued to be considered ideal "martial races" who were resistant to caste rules about dining. This meant that, to the British, a tiny minority of Brahmans continued to be the embodiment of "the contagion of Hinduism." This outlook pandered to those "martial races" of Sikhs, Muslims, and "exceptional" Hindus who dominated Indian Army ranks. These men, minorities in India, could feel socially and martially superior to high-caste members of Indian society. As "unprejudiced" meat-eaters who gave up "prejudices" against foods like carrots and onions, soldiers could point to their diets as the reason for their martial superiority. This artificial distinction overlooked how members of all of these communities had demonstrated religious objections, logistical burdens, and sacrifices to serve the war effort. Food remained an essential way to define who was martial, even as soldiers' diets continued to change.

Anti-Hindu attitudes became especially prominent during the Indianization of the Indian Army, which gradually opened officer ranks to South Asians after the First World War.[138] Many high-caste Hindus—including Brahmans—had the educational and financial advantages to afford military schools and academies. Yet they experienced several challenges from British leaders. Indian Hindus who gained admittance to the Royal Military College at Sandhurst (UK) faced difficulty not with dietary "taboos" but in finding food that was flavorful and familiar. Men such as Joyanto Nath Chaudhuri and K. S. Thimayya attended exclusive international boarding schools and were familiar with the bland British food served at Sandhurst. They sought out Indian restaurants in London in the mid-1920s to have some spices and dishes that reminded them of home. On some occasions Sandhurst employees avoided serving Indian cadets "mutton and eggs" for religious reasons.[139] Yet they were also adamant that they would not cater to Indian diets. The letter congratulating S. P. P. Thorat on his admission to Sandhurst in December 1924 stated that all cadets "will, while at the Royal Military College, belong to the ordinary College Mess and no special messing arrangements can be made on their behalf."[140] Being an officer of the Indian Army, according to Sandhurst, meant conforming to British military diets. Indian identity—according this view—embodied particularity and divisiveness and was inherently at odds with British standards.

Military efforts to create a standard military diet free from "prejudice" did not mitigate British prejudices about Indian food. S. P. P. Thorat recalled that after being posted to the 1st Battalion, 14th Punjab Regiment in 1927, "We were forbidden to bring Indian food or play Indian music even in our own rooms."[141] Such bans often extended to officers' clubs as well. Commanding officers insisted that Indian food and Indian music had no place in the "Indian" Army.[142] Jagjit Singh Aurora remembered that Indian meals were limited to two lunches per week; all remaining meals were British food. When he tried to suggest that the cooks in Singapore fry rather than boil some of the vegetables, he was transferred from his post as messing member. Indian Catholic officer Stanley Menezes attended Officer Training School at Lahore and Bangalore and similarly faced disappointment when he requested vegetarian food. He ended up receiving "potato cutlets at breakfast, potato cutlets at lunch, and potato cutlets for dinner" because "the cooks had not been trained to do anything vegetarian."[143] As an Indian Christian, Menezes demonstrates how Indian officers' diets were influenced by more than strict religious mandates and could, in fact, be influenced by regional or national identities as well as personal preferences. Ultimately, Menezes ate meat instead of enduring culinary boredom. In J. N. Chaudhuri's unit, Indian food was only served at Sunday lunch. After a long struggle the 16th Light Cavalry finally introduced a "mildly curried" vegetable dish at every meal. Some men found alternative food arrangements by congregating around the married quarters and relying on the culinary skills of married soldiers' wives, or meeting at the tent of the temporarily attached Indian medical officer to devour curry secretly.[144] Sikh instructor and musketry training teacher Subedar Dalip Singh even distributed "excellent Indian food" to those soldiers and officer cadets who might otherwise miss culinary diversity.[145] The problem for many men was less about stringent dietary "prejudices"—which many willingly gave up—than in finding a diverse and flavorful array of options within the army.

Indian food also became a symbol of British discontent with the incursion of South Asians into "British" spaces between the world wars. The 1932 *Hints for Soldiers Proceeding to India* warned soldiers that:

> All men of the Indian Army are strict in the observance of their religion, and are often debarred by it from accepting eatables or even water from one who is not of the right creed or caste. If you offer them anything and your offer is declined, do not take offence. The reason is almost certain to be that religious prejudices forbid the acceptance.[146]

William Homer, who served with the 2nd Battalion Royal Fusiliers in India between the wars, used this reasoning when explaining his own limited contact with Indian soldiers. He remembered that "we were always a little bit apprehensive: could you offer them a cigarette? Wait a minute, are they the sort that smoke or are they the sort that don't smoke? Uh, what about a drink? Some of them won't drink this, some of them won't drink that, some of them won't accept food. So, I feel that . . . the Indians didn't make enough—they were prevented by their own culture—from becoming friends with us. I think. Yes."[147] Institutional clichés about the Indian men's unwillingness to engage socially with British soldiers discouraged many from attempting contact. Even those well-meaning British officers who welcomed Indian officers into their units maintained apprehension about their diets. General Thimayya recalled that when he was attached to the Highland Light Infantry in Bangalore, British soldiers expressed their anxiety that "We mustn't be snide about Indians in front of you. Mustn't give you beef."[148] This careful treatment, a mixture of condescension and irritation, made career Indian officers feel that they were unshakably different and incapable of fully belonging in the army because of British prejudices about Indian food. Making Hindu soldiers and officers feel off-balance and defensive put extra pressure on them to prove their loyalty and belonging.

FOOD WARS

Army anxiety about South Asian soldiers' diets could never be separated from changing understandings of loyalty, devotion, and rebellion. This was especially true as food became central to anti-colonial critiques of imperial rule. Most famously, in March 1930, Mohandas Gandhi led an historic 230-mile, twenty-four-day march from his ashram in Ahmedabad to the sea at Dandi. He and his followers protested the government's monopoly over India's salt by illegally making their own. He chose salt because it was a commodity that all South Asians used for daily sustenance. Everyone—no matter their gender, caste, or economic stability—could illegally make salt without resorting to violence.[149] Gandhi's march blended a critique of exploitative imperial food policies with moral arguments about diet. This brought him international sympathy during a worldwide economic depression. The march's success gained momentum from the already potent imagery—evoked powerfully in 1924—of Gandhi's rail-thin body fasting to challenge the pains of imperialism.[150] Gandhi's march, in many ways, represented everything that the Indian Army was not: egalitarian, nonviolent, and anti-colonial. However, by combining moral and economic arguments about the imperial monopoly over food, the Dandi March engaged with the longer debates about food and the army. Many soldiers believed that it was their duty to fight for, rather than against, "the government's salt" long before Gandhi made his own.

The "government's salt" was deeply ritualized as military officials categorized and quantified what food was most appropriate for fighting men. The lived reality of military life consistently fell short of imperial promises. Soldiers faced food shortages, poor sanitation, and bland rations. British officials continued to blame "the contagion of Hinduism" and recall half-remembered stories of 1857 to justify their military hierarchies.

Yet Hindu accommodations were hardly exceptional compared to the fast of Ramzan for Muslims, or providing "pure" food and drink for Nepalis. The army's continued anxiety stemmed from a lack of control over Indian bodies. They tried to regain it by shaping the narrative of soldiers' service. Britain's willingness to preserve and protect soldiers' diets through rigorous bureaucratic management was meant to demonstrate the respectful treatment of the army and empire toward Indian subjects. Meanwhile, soldiers could embrace colonial narratives about their own lack of "prejudice" to give them an outlet for wartime and postwar frustration with civilians who criticized their professions or failed to understand their difficult wartime experiences.

By the 1930s, a wide range of Indian anti-colonial activists, ranging from members of the Indian National Congress to Indian communists, insisted that soldiers did not owe the loyalty of their "salt" to an exploitative imperial government.[151] The Indian Army, in turn, all but disappeared from anti-colonial debates about food. When the Indian National Congress Working Committee drafted a food-based "appeal," they did so to "Police Brethren," rather than to soldiers. Yet they used familiar arguments: "You may be doing these things thinking that you were doing your duty to those whose food you eat, but the result is that you take sacrifices of your country-men, you drag the country into slavery."[152] The *Police Patrika* similarly demanded that policemen stop cooperating "with the sinful administration" because "You eat the salt of Mother India," rather than the British government.[153] These arguments echoed those put forth in the 1907 pamphlet found at the Strangers' Home for Asiatics when soldiers were deeply embedded in anti-colonial networks. Soldiers' erasure from these debates, however, suggests that for many interwar anti-colonial activists, colonial soldiers were beyond saving.

CHAPTER 5

A NATION AT ODDS WITH NATIONALISM

AFTER THE FIRST WORLD WAR many British and Indian officials recognized that the Indian Army was in dire need of reform and rejuvenation. In particular, the old pattern of closing off the officer corps to South Asians seemed drastically outdated after a war in which Indian troops were an integral part of Britain's victory. Returning to the deeply hierarchical society of colonial India, however, military officials reasoned that radical religious integration was a prerequisite of racial desegregation. In 1922 the Prince of Wales Royal Indian Military College (RIMC) opened in Dehra Dun to educate South Asian boys in the manners and discipline of British officers. A central tenet of the RIMC was "to eliminate gradually as many class prejudices as possible without wounding religious susceptibilities." One method of achieving this was by having all of the boys dine together so that "a Sikh may be next to a Pathan or a Pathan next to a Dogra" (Figure 8).[1] The college's interfaith dining scheme convinced officials that the school provided a "sound and healthy basis" for "unity, patriotism and common endeavor," which were "the essential complements of successful 'nationhood.'" They hoped that this would "permeate not only the Indian Army of the future, but through it the country at large."[2] The implication was that South Asian communities were inherently divisive. The army, by contrast, envisioned itself as a source of interfaith harmony.

FIGURE 8 Young men sit together for a meal at the Royal Indian Military College. Military officials stressed that they would sit together regardless of their religious differences. *Source*: Prince of Wales Royal Indian Military College Dehra Dun. British Library IOR/L/MIL/17/5/2283, opposite page 5. Reprinted with permission.

The encouragement of "national" unity in the 1920s army bore little similarity to prewar army attitudes. The 1912 recruiting handbook *Our Indian Empire*, given to all British soldiers, explicitly described India as "not yet a nation" because of "sharp distinctions of caste" and "religious jealousies." It considered India "a mere patchwork of races."[3] The encouragement of unity and nationhood also contrasted the army's exclusive "martial races" recruiting practices and class regiment system that carefully isolated Hindus, Christians, Muslims, and Sikhs. By the 1920s and 1930s, however, British military officials attempted to use education to create loyal and disciplined Indian soldiers and officers who would find more in common with one another than with their civilian communities. This would require fusing "martial race" assumptions with the "muscular Christianity" of British public schools to create a unified military culture of strong, devout, and sober men of empire.[4] Few anticipated that educational, religious, and racial integration would shock and destabilize, but also re-entrench, army hierarchies.

TEACHING LOYALTY

Despite shifting institutional priorities, some British and South Asian soldiers and officers regarded education and martial prowess as incompatible. Former Indian Army officer (1905–24), and British fascist, Francis Yeats-Brown recalled that "In my day . . . it was considered rather smart to be illiterate . . . indeed, I have heard the opinion advanced by worthy Indians of the old school that reading is bad for the brain, and, to tell the truth, I am sometimes disposed to agree."[5] A Punjabi Jat interviewed by M. L. Darling agreed with this view. He had attended the Khalsa College but believed that "The army makes a boy punctual, up-to-date, and strong; the school makes him punctual, up-to-date, and weak."[6] A survey of 216 retired Punjabi men from the army taken between 1934 and 1938 revealed that 157 out of 216 veterans had never been to school.[7] Many British officers since the late nineteenth century assumed that not educating soldiers would keep them safe from the corrupting influence of western education. This prevented boys from growing "soft," "effeminate," and inclined toward anti-colonial ideas. Avoiding education, they believed, enabled soldiers to maintain their rural and agricultural values as well as their strong bodies. Ignorance, many military men assumed, was essential to the strength and stability of the army.[8] Yet by the first decades of the twentieth century this worldview proved unsustainable. Some imperial administrators believed that educating soldiers could help to achieve, rather than undermine, army goals.

By the early twentieth century Viceroy Lord Curzon (1899–1905) came to the conclusion that certain types of education could fortify British alliances with elite Indians and strengthen the army. He opened the Imperial Cadet Corps (ICC) in 1901 after the Maharaja of Cooch Behar pressured military officials to train his son for a military career.[9] The ICC targeted wealthy landowners and princes for military training to solidify the relationship between military and landed elites. One unintended consequence was that it exposed elite men to the endemic racial inequalities and poor treatment of the Indian Army.[10] The ICC became defunct during the First World War but its existence widened the possibility of valuing rather than condemning army education. When war broke out in August 1914, the army committed Rs. 61,032 to improve education for Indian troops.[11] Military officials wanted to ensure that every soldier—from the lowest ranking "sepoy" to the upwardly mobile Indian officer—had sufficient knowledge to perform his duty and defend against the corrupting ideas of disloyal outsiders. In many ways, this institutional shift reflected changes that already occurred within the *British* Army. Fears of Irish nationalists and concerns about soldiers' bodies and souls inspired British officials to invest in military education, religious reform, and social improvements for British and Irish soldiers in the nineteenth century.[12] As in Britain, the goal of military education in India was to keep soldiers disciplined and loyal.

Several prewar precedents anticipated the shift to using education to improve soldiers' military training and discipline. The army began circulating the pro-imperial military publication *Fauji Akhbar* in 1909 to give soldiers something to read and discuss other than vernacular presses that sometimes criticized imperial governance.[13] The *Fauji Akhbar* had Urdu, Hindi, and Gurmukhi (Punjabi) editions and maintained a decidedly secular tone. Occasionally it referred to the support that Sikh *granthis* (religious scholars) gave to soldiers in battles, or asked for prayers for men who had died.[14] Yet army officials also believed that more overt religious education also was necessary. By 1911, the Army Department worried that South Asian recruits were educationally and politically "backward." The secretary of state for India suspected that "the chief, if not the only way of tampering with his loyalty lies, in our opinion, through his religious principles."[15] Soldiers' lack of education, the argument followed, left them exposed to manipulation by religious authorities.

The perceived threat of religious rebellion also contributed to an increasing emphasis on education in the army. Officials critiqued the fact that many regiments lacked official "religious teachers," even though chaplains were common for British soldiers. Instead, soldiers often took it upon themselves to hire civilians through "regimental subscriptions."[16] Army officers feared that "itinerant priests" entered into military spaces and administered ceremonies without any supervision from British officers. This, they believed, exposed soldiers to "sedition-mongers."[17] Examples included men such as Granthi Bhagwan Singh in Hong Kong and Canada, Indar Singh of Hong Kong and California, and Kirpal Singh of the 19th Punjabs in Jullundur, who encouraged dissension among South Asian troops. Balwant Singh, a former Lance Naik of the 36th Sikhs, apparently journeyed to Hong Kong, Vancouver, and California as both a Muslim *faqir* (ascetic) and a Sikh *granthi* with the goal of "preaching sedition."[18] The lack of official religious teachers gave soldiers the power to invest in the teachings and worldviews that were most appealing to them. Army officials worried that this might not always include imperial loyalty.

Regularizing religious education, many officers hoped, would eliminate "religious" sedition. Officers of the 127th, 129th, and 130th Indian Infantry believed that their soldiers were "ignorant, superstitious, and much under the influence of their spiritual leaders." They felt that if the army directly paid religious leaders the army would gain "a hold upon him."[19] By 1912, after some debate, the India Office sanctioned the Army Department's proposal to raise the monthly payment of all religious instructors to Rs. 15 per month. The Government of India agreed to approve requests for religious teachers whenever regiments requested them. In 1913 alone there were eleven documented requests for regimental religious teachers. Requests continued to flow into the Army Department during and after the First World War.[20] During the war, "religious teachers" advocated for soldiers in matters as varied as diet, surgery, burial, and securing places of worship.[21] Yet they would not succeed in the army's primary goal of ensuring loyal service.

The war revealed the limitations of using religious teachers to undermine anti-colonial activism. The regimental *maulvi* (Muslim religious scholar) of the 5th Light Infantry, for example, did not prevent the 1915 mutiny in Singapore. He supported British officials' plans to cancel the fast of Ramzan (Ramadan) but did not pacify the men after doing so. Instead, soldiers such as Sepoy Fazal Rahman criticized the *maulvi* for "interfering with their religion."[22] He viewed the *maulvi* as an impediment to, rather than agent of, spiritual fulfilment. The *maulvi*'s lack of spiritual authority led many soldiers to become devotees of Nur Alam

Shah, a self-styled *pir* or holy man who lived in Singapore's large Kampong Java mosque. A secret agent described Nur Alam Shah as "a very seditious and fanatical man" who preached against the British Government and assisted mutineers.[23] British officials alleged that Nur Alam Shah was an important force in inciting unrest among soldiers.[24] Soldiers' resentment toward the inadequacy of hired men may have only further infuriated those who were already discontented.

Despite the regimental *maulvi*'s compliance in prematurely ending the fast of Ramzan he faced accusations of disloyalty after the mutiny. The main case against him was that soldiers had offered "an undue amount of praying in the Mosque prior to the mutiny period" according to the general officer commanding.[25] The mutiny occurred just before the 5th Light Infantry was set to leave Singapore for active service. This could have easily explained the "undue amount of praying." However, the *maulvi* failed to report Sepoy Manowar Ali's vocal prayer for "the victory of the forces of Islam" in the regimental mosque. Officials retroactively interpreted this as an indication of his pan-Islamic loyalty to the Ottoman Empire and a sign of the unrest to come.[26] The *maulvi*'s failure to report the prayer, in their eyes, made him either disloyal or incapable of predicting which utterances could be mutinous. Several soldiers defended the *maulvi* but he was nonetheless "returned to India for disposal."[27] The *maulvi*'s history of loyalty and opposition to "extreme" men such as Fazal Rahman and Manowar Ali did not save him from losing his job. His inability to prevent the mutiny made him institutionally irrelevant.

The inability of army religious teachers to prevent rebellion during the war made many soldiers and civilians question their utility in peacetime. One Indian politician recommended eliminating them to decrease the army budget. He found them unnecessary when soldiers were in India because they had "mosques or temples available within reasonable distance of his camp."[28] Military officials believed that these men had become less important to army stability. The secretary of state for India felt that "the activities of *Sadhus*" had decreased by 1922. He argued that "this form of agitation is practically dead."[29] Of the 170 documented attempts to tamper with the loyalty of the troops between 1920 and 1922, only 13 were categorized as "speeches or fatwas" by "Mullas, Maulvis, Granthis, and

Sadhus."[30] Nearly three times as many attempts came in the form of "seditious pamphlets and notices." This convinced the viceroy that the press was the chief means of spreading dissent to the troops. Religious teachers remained in most regiments despite postwar concerns about army expenditures because the financial investment in them were low. Most were paid less than the lowest-ranking soldiers.[31] Fears about the negative impact of the press, however, meant reevaluating once again the best method of educating soldiers to be loyal. The ongoing fear of colonial rebellion inspired British officials to invest more comprehensively in soldiers' education.

EDUCATING THE SOLDIER

Prewar concerns about education emasculating soldiers were overpowered by changing army goals and priorities. By the 1920s, the debate about education had shifted due to pressures and challenges of opening officer ranks to South Asian soldiers. This process, known as Indianization, was a result of mounting Indian nationalist criticisms about racial hierarchy in the army and the expense of maintaining a British officer corps in India. It gained momentum during the war, when leading politicians such as Indian National Congress president Satyendra Sinha (1915–16) and India Secretary Austen Chamberlain (1915–17) emphasized the need for Indianization.[32] The admission of Indians to the Royal Military College at Sandhurst started in 1917, enabling Indian men to train as "gentleman cadets" and compete for positions as officers alongside British men. This coincided with Secretary of State Edwin S. Montagu's famous declaration promising to increase Indian presence in imperial institutions. However, army officials believed that most Indian gentlemen cadets did not or could not adapt well to officer life. During the 1920s and 1930s, the army increased its military educational institutions for South Asians to address their perceived shortcomings.

Several institutions facilitated the army's slow investment in Indianization. The Prince of Wales Royal Indian Military College opened in Dehra Dun in 1922 to educate South Asian boys in British military education and discipline starting around age twelve. Successful graduates competed for positions at Sandhurst, from where they could secure commissions as officers. Similar institutions, called King George's Royal

Indian Military Schools at Jhelum and Jullundur, opened in 1925. These catered to boys from military families who might become soldiers rather than officers.[33] By 1932, the Indian Military Academy (IMA) trained future Indian officers in India rather than at Sandhurst. Each institution adopted similar methods of cultivating the "right" type of young man and boy by encouraging men to blend the nineteenth-century "martial race" ethos of the Indian Army with the "muscular Christianity" of British public schools. This "hybrid" or "cosmopolitan" version of martial masculinity proved to be a prerequisite for gradual military desegregation in India.[34] The decision to extend education to both aspiring officers and low-ranking soldiers indicates that institutional policy about education had evolved tremendously due to interwar political and economic pressures.

The Indian Army supported interwar educational initiatives because it would address the perceived "educational backwardness of the martial classes."[35] The army often recruited members of the same family, which cycled a pattern of poor education through generations. Soldiers moved too frequently across military stations to give their children access to regular schooling. This put military sons at an educational disadvantage compared to children whose fathers were engaged in civilian occupations in city centers.[36] Military education, therefore, might protect soldiers' families from economic hardships and nationalist critiques of army service. It also could help soldiers' children to develop, according to the Army Department, "the spirit of loyalty, obedience, and citizenship in boys who, it was hoped, would one day serve in the army of their country."[37] They would circumvent prewar concerns about effeminacy by emphasizing "agricultural, technical and industrial training."[38] If successful, this would have prevented educated soldiers' sons from seeking non-military employment, losing touch with their agricultural and military roots, or finding sympathy with nationalist activists.

Unsurprisingly, British officials modeled South Asian military education on British precedents. Nineteenth-century Boys' Brigades, and later off-shoots such as the Boy Scouts (established 1908), attempted to reform boys from a young age by training them in military discipline and Christian morality so that they could pursue imperial careers.[39] Public schools in

Britain retained class-based exclusions that isolated the future elite from British society. By contrast, the Indian Army encouraged all aspiring rank-and-file boys to receive public-school-style education. This, they believed, would turn them into perfect soldiers. One educational commissioner argued that "if an Indian boy has been educated in a secondary school of the English type, there is every reason to believe that he can be turned into a good type of British officer."[40] This applied to low-ranking soldiers as well. The King George's Schools provided education for boys—particularly soldiers' sons—starting around age ten or eleven.[41] The first two opened at Jhelum and Jullundur (established September 1925) and maintained the strict segregation that boys would find in the army. Jhelum offered positions to three hundred Muslims from highly recruited communities, including Hazaras, Pathans, Punjabi Musalmans, Baluchis, and Brahuis.[42] Jullundur had over two hundred spots for Sikhs, Dogras, and West Punjabi Hindus.[43] While some debated opening a school in Bombay for Marathas, the next King George's School opened in Ajmere to cater to Rajputs and Jats in 1930.[44] These schools educated boys of the "martial classes" and emphasized strong martial bodies through rigorous physical standards for height and weight.[45] Boys received ample quantities of food including spices, butter, eggs, limes, fresh fruit, rice, and sugar.[46] Nepali men and boys could not enjoy these opportunities because they were not British subjects.[47]

The King George's Schools were unique for attracting boys who would join the army as low-ranking "sepoys" rather than officers.[48] Boys could be directly enlisted into the corps of their fathers after graduation. Those whose fathers died or were on more than 50% disability pensions received free tuition and maintenance.[49] This led some officials to worry that "the character training given at the schools is excellent" but the standard of general education was ill-suited for any career outside of the army. Ultimately this did not matter. The Army Department admitted before the Legislative Assembly that every boy enrolled at Jhelum or Jullundur was obligated to join the army after graduating.[50] These institutions were meant to strengthen the economic and employment prospects of soldiers' families. What they became were childhood training facilities for future soldiers.

The curriculum of the King George's Schools outlined what 1920s British officers felt would best equip future recruits for an army career.

The courses of instruction included squad drill, saluting, Boy Scouts training, physical training, and sports. Physical training taught boys "a high standard of mental and physical fitness." This encouraged "team spirit" and "the idea of playing-the-game for the game's sake." Sports helped boys to develop "a cheerful attitude" as well as alertness, concentration, and "perfect control of mind over body." Also essential was teaching boys "Esprit-de-corps, cleanliness and good conduct" through hygiene, sanitation, and physiology. Citizenship lessons instructed boys on "the privileges and obligations of a citizen of the British Empire." In order to communicate effectively in the army boys learned to read and write "in the vernacular script." They also learned Urdu in Roman, Persian, or Hindi script, as well as English. This was a dramatic reversal from the prewar encouragement of illiteracy among the rank-and-file. Instead, literacy became a way to defend men and boys against itinerant preachers who, British officers suspected, whispered in their ears about anti-colonial ideas. Boys also learned important lessons about loyalty through "Indian History," which emphasized Indian contributions to the First World War. Heroic tales of the war were meant to "arouse a spirit of patriotism"—or "Imperial patriotism"—and teach them "the past history of the unity for which they are earmarked."[51] Military education therefore re-wrote the turbulent history of the First World War. Soldiers' critiques of war service and participation in Ghadar and pan-Islamic activism were erased beneath clear-cut accounts of unwavering imperial loyalty.

By the 1930s *all* enlisted soldiers received education. Men had to demonstrate that they were "educationally fit" before enlistment. After joining, they received education in "Conduct, regimental history and esprit de corps." Geography taught them "the danger to which India is exposed by sea and land." Histories of the "British navy and British and Indian armies" would, in theory, convince soldiers that British rule was essential for defending India. These lessons emphasized "law and order" and "the benefits which he derives as a citizen of the British Empire." Just as important was a man's duty "taking part in its defence."[52] The official version of "Indian History" emphasized the dangers of invasion "as proved by the invasions of the past." To challenge nationalist accusations that

British officials fomented division, soldiers learned about "the dissentions and misery with which the country was afflicted when stable government did not exist." Lectures on "the history of particular races" developed "racial pride" and "esprit de corps." Finally, Indian history lessons attempted to demonstrate that India had enjoyed "political, agricultural and economic development" since 1858. The British, according to this interpretation, provided "security from invasion" and "the establishment of good government, law and order."[53]

The army's history lessons encouraged soldiers and aspiring soldiers to think that India without the British would be chaotic and tumultuous. British rule, by this account, was an unbroken lineage of stability and reform. Soldiers' education sustained a narrative of the great benefits that British rule provided to India. According to this view, calls to end imperial rule merely placed soldiers—and India—at risk of invasion and internal division. Military education, therefore, gave soldiers the tools to debate with Indian nationalists and anti-colonial activists. When imperial opponents claimed that the empire divided and destabilized South Asia, soldiers could come ready with defensive arguments about strength and unity. Loyalty, they believed, could be learned.

The most aggressive efforts to spread military education emphasized training elite boys who hoped to become King's Commissioned Officers. Efforts began in earnest with the construction of the Royal Indian Military College at Dehra Dun. The commander-in-chief approved the scheme during the 1921 Legislative Assembly and the Prince of Wales was present for its opening in 1922. The inaugural group consisted of thirty-seven boys aged fourteen to seventeen.[54] The school filled the buildings formerly occupied by the Imperial Cadet Corps, which had trained the elite sons of princes and landed aristocrats. By 1923, seventy boys had enrolled for courses of instruction lasting six years.[55] In 1925, officials were confident that Indian applicants for Sandhurst who trained at the RIMC were superior to those educated elsewhere. They expanded enrollment to 120 students.[56] The initial intention of the college was to train boys for Sandhurst but by the 1930s they competed for positions at the IMA at Dehra Dun. Those who graduated from either academy became eligible for officer commissions.

Debates about the RIMC reveal how Indianization and military education attempted to rebuild Indian boys in the image of British officers. A committee led by General Sir Charles Monro in 1920 emphasized the importance of potential candidates being "caught young" to allow boys to be "subjected to training and other influences calculated to ensure the production of the stamp of man required."[57] As at other schools, RIMC boys participated in games, gymnastics, and other physical training, which brought "a wonderful change in their physique, manliness and agility."[58] On average, boys joined at twelve and left as young men between the ages of eighteen and twenty, dedicating, like their low-ranking counterparts in the King George's Schools, most of their young adult years to British military training and discipline.[59] Part of making boys acclimate to military life was to have them think of the college as their home and the army as their family.[60] Lt-Col H. L. Haughton, Commandant, RIMC Dehra Dun, explained that he wanted to "know every boy inside out" including "his weaknesses." The adjutant, Risaldar Sardar Khan, became "like a father and a mother to the boys."[61] The idea of the army being the ma-baap (mother/father) of recruits was a well-worn imperial trope. British officers often felt that soldiers were their "children." However, these institutions enabled South Asian men, such as Risaldar Sardar Khan, to take up the parental role. They also allowed the army to develop this familial relationship from a much younger age. The RIMC could even deny young men permission to attend festivals, ceremonies, or marriages back home— further isolating them from other familial or non-colonial social connections.[62] The only South Asian teachers permitted at the RIMC were three religious teachers and two vernacular teachers. The remaining instructors and leadership positions were all held by British officials.[63] The interwar Indian Army operated under the assumption that an Indian officer's loyalty and military effectiveness depended on isolating him from South Asian society and making him, insofar as possible, into a British man.

Building boys into officers emphasized "cosmopolitan" sensibilities.[64] The college trained cadets to "move with confidence" in European or South Asian society without causing "embarrassment." Learning English was essential. The RIMC insisted on English-medium education because it prepared boys to communicate effectively at Sandhurst.[65] Emphasis on

English remained in place even after the IMA opened in Dehra Dun.[66] Mandating English helped to perpetuate the increasingly common view that English was a "neutral" alternative to languages such as Hindi and Urdu, which were sometimes claimed as exclusive "religious" modes of expression for Hindus and Muslims, respectively. Former British officer Yeats-Brown wrote more cynically that "nowadays it is obvious even to the stupidest yokel that promotion and pay depend on knowledge of English."[67]

Military emphasis on cosmopolitanism blended the army's "martial race" recruiting with British public school discipline, at times with contradictory results. For example, widely recruited communities had the least access to English-language education, making them less successful on the English-language exams. One educational commissioner nonetheless defended the continued emphasis on educating rural men and boys from military families for officer training because they were "brought up in the disciplinary instincts of the soldier, and the right of preference should be given to those who have followed this profession for generations."[68] Military officers had previously claimed that illiteracy helped to keep such men strong and steadfast—the key to becoming a perfect soldier. These older ideas meshed uncomfortably with official desires to use English education to inculcate imperial devotion. Paradoxically, interwar upward mobility depended on both a lineage of loyal military service and a strong proficiency with English. Men had to simultaneously perform a "pure" martial race identity, while also having sufficient western education to be fluent in English. Military education embodied the interwar army's crisis of identity.

SUCCESSES AND FAILURES OF INDIANIZATION

Throughout the 1920s and 1930s many wondered if the Indian Army was sincere in its commitment to Indianization due to various half-measures and failures. Prominent politicians such as Motilal Nehru and M. A. Jinnah participated in these debates, signaling their importance for plans of national development. Yet few could agree on the best method of increasing the number of South Asian men in the officer ranks. The Daly College at Indore had opened during the First World War to train King's Commissioned Indian Officers (KCIOs) but closed in 1919.[69] The moderate Indian politicians of the newly created Indian Central Legislative Assembly wanted to ensure long-term success by guaranteeing that ten spots at Sandhurst were reserved for South Asians starting in 1918.[70] After the Sandhurst Committee report (1926), headed by General Andrew Skeen, Indian candidates gained twenty vacancies at Sandhurst annually.[71] Vacancies for Indians at Sandhurst rose to thirty by 1931.[72] Yet there were frequent disagreements between moderate Indian politicians, the War Office, the Foreign Office, and the army's higher command about the success of these measures. Some alleged that the rapid increase in South Asian cadets doomed them to failure due to cultural differences. Between 1918 and 1930, only 153 of 175 vacancies for Indian cadets at Sandhurst were filled. Only eighty-six received commissions and just seventy-one continued to serve in the army.[73] Indian cadets, meanwhile, complained about being subject to the disciplinary control of a retired British officer "guardian" who restricted their mobility and encounters with white women in Britain.[74] Despite their education and training, Indian cadets also found it difficult to integrate with their British counterparts.[75] The high financial and emotional costs of sending South Asian men to England for military education resulted in limited successes and threatened Indianization.

Economic and nationalist pressures urged the acceleration of Indianization despite recurring challenges. Initial "test" plans to Indianize the officer corps included creating eight "Indianized" units. In these units, the newly trained KCIO trained at Sandhurst and gradually replaced the longer-held position of Viceroy's Commissioned Officers (VCOs). VCOs had been the separate hierarchy for Indian soldiers prior to Indianization. Every battalion had twenty VCOs who served as company and platoon commanders for men from the same community. Promotion to VCO ranks was slow: it took roughly sixteen years to become a naik, fifteen additional years to become a havildar, and an additional nine and then six years to become a jemadar and subedar, respectively. These last two VCO ranks gave Indian men, often aged in their sixties, the rough equivalent of the lowest British officer ranks of lieutenant and captain.[76] During Indianization, however, young, often elite, KCIOs gained leadership positions over men with different regional and religious identities and longer records of service. Despite the long-held tradition of British Christians doing the same, the army worried that this caused dissension between Indian communities. Even more contentious was that the "Indianized" units with KCIOs eliminated VCOs, getting rid of men who had served as intermediaries between officers and soldiers. It also eliminated the possibility of low-ranking men rising through the ranks.

Indianization demonstrated that class, as well as racial, barriers needed to be removed for successful military integration. Training to become a KCIO at Sandhurst was cost-prohibitive for the vast majority of soldiers. The fees for taking the exam alone were very high: men had to pay over Rs. 7 to take the exam and Rs. 50 to receive their certificate of admission. This was three times the monthly salary of the lowest-ranking South Asian soldier.[77] Class tensions underpinned mutual suspicion between the elite Indian KCIOs and the soldiers they were meant to command. Soldiers felt voiceless without having VCOs to advocate for them, while Indian KCIOs struggled to find a place in British officer society. KCIOs also received higher salaries than VCOs, which meant increasing army costs considerably.[78] By 1931, the commander-in-chief was under the impression that the eight "Indianized" units had become "unpopular." Nonetheless, the worldwide economic depression hastened political reform, and the number of Indianized units increased to fifteen in 1931.[79] The IMA opened the following year, in 1932, following the suggestion of the Indian Military College Committee under Commander-in-Chief (1930–35) General Philip Chetwode. The opening of the IMA represented a culmination of the Indian Army's many conflicting demands to Indianize while also training men to be loyal imperial subjects.

The IMA became an "Indian Sandhurst" to train Indian men as KCIOs. It occupied the buildings of the former Railway Staff College in Dehra Dun, near the RIMC. Its existence meant that South Asians and Anglo-Indians were no longer eligible for admission to military colleges in the United Kingdom, including Sandhurst.[80] This was ostensibly to avoid hurting "esprit de corps" by creating a hierarchy between officers trained at Sandhurst and those trained at the IMA. Yet institutional inequalities persisted. IMA cadets received a course of instruction twice as long as what was mandatory for British cadets at Sandhurst. Selection was a mix of open examination, recruitment from among actively serving Indian Army men, and hand-picked candidates selected by the commander-in-chief, who tended to come from the "martial races." These methods were an improvement over the rigorous nine-step selection process that aspiring Indian cadets faced at Sandhurst.[81] However, there remained hierarchy, social distance, unequal pay, and lack of promotion for KCIOs trained at the IMA compared to British King's Commissioned Officers trained at Sandhurst.[82] The aim of Indianization had been to racially integrate the officer corps and allow Indians to become officers equal in rank to their British counterparts. Educating British officers at Sandhurst and Indian officers at the IMA instead represented a deeper and more systematic educational segregation.

Some Indianization institutions proved successful in their original aims after the opening of the IMA. Between 1923 and 1931, the RIMC graduated about eighteen boys per year, of whom thirty-six were admitted to Sandhurst.[83] After 1932, the RIMC became a feeder for the IMA. An educational commissioner praised RIMC candidates for being the best prepared for interviews.[84] During the first IMA competitive examination in October 1932 three of the four young men to earn perfect scores on their interviews came from the RIMC.[85] Six of fifteen admitted to the IMA for the inaugural class did as well.[86] The following spring, three of the top five finishers in the exam overall were RIMC-trained.[87] In fact, the IMA's inauguration in 1932 gave RIMC boys a more clear sense of their future careers. Those accepted to the IMA had their names listed in the *Dehra Dun College Magazine*. The magazine also honored former RIMC students such as Lieutenant Ali Asghar Khan, who graduated in 1922. When he passed away at Srinagar while posted to the 1/7th Rajput Regiment in October 1932, boys read about his being a "charming fellow" from the "very best stock." Boys at RIMC participated in the IMA's opening ceremony, played games regularly against the academy's "Gentlemen Cadets," and felt more comfortable moving to an institution that was in the same town, rather than halfway around the world.[88] The opening of the IMA in 1932 proved that the army's educational efforts were working—just not in the way initially intended. The racial and religious hierarchies of the army, meanwhile, took new shape.

CHRISTIANIZING OFFICERS

The desire to train Indian men as officers revealed some unintended contradictions in army policy. Moderate Indian politicians wanted to integrate a racially and religiously hierarchical army. British military officials hoped to limit Indianization to widely recruited communities. Yet the need to turn South Asian men into British-style officers inherently privileged those educated and trained in British educational institutions. This elite education was inaccessible to most soldiers and their families, apart from a few well-connected and landed men. Indianization, therefore, favored those who already had elite status. Making it through the rigorous selection process usually required men to be well-immersed in the ethos of muscular Christianity that underpinned British public schools and military institutions. Becoming an Indian officer obliged men to assimilate into a British-Christian military tradition—a distinct cultural position from the "martial races" long prized for their non-European cultural "purity." In an era of rising anti-colonialism, this often meant being a cultural outsider in India.

Exposure to Christian training proved relatively common among aspiring Indian Army officers. IMA graduate Dinesh Chandra Misra went to Christian schools including St. Andrews High School in Gorakhpur and a mission school in Lucknow. There he had to pass tests about the catechism, despite being a Chaturvedi Brahman.[89] Kristen Kumar Tewari, who received his commission during the Second World War, attended a former Christian college in Lahore.[90] IMA graduate Ketoli Chengappa Medappa was a graduate of a Bishop Cotton school and earned the top score on the October 1937 exam. The Bishop Cotton schools in Bangalore and Simla proved to be popular destinations for aspiring IMA men: future colonels and generals such as D. C. Basapa, R. N. Batra, and Dharitri Kumar, and men killed in action such as Captain C. P. Jimmy Machia were also Cotton alumni.[91] Many alumni who earned top marks on the IMA exams even adopted European names: Dharitri Kumar went by "Monty," Codanda Ponnappa Machia went by "Jimmy," and future General Kodandera Subbayya Thimayya went by "Timmy."[92] Other Christian schools had similar success. Khwaja Wasiuddin, a future high-ranking officer whose father was governor of the North-West Frontier

Province, studied at St. Gregory's High School and the RIMC before finishing second overall on the IMA exam.[93] K. S. Thimayya went on to be chief of army staff in independent India. He attended St. Joseph's College in Conoor, run by Irish priests, before transferring to the Cotton School in Bangalore and attending Sandhurst.[94] The military and imperial cultures of English-medium education, sport, sobriety, and morality permeated Christian schools and colleges across India. These institutions trained South Asian men to become exemplars of muscular Christianity without necessarily being Christian.

The prevalence of IMA candidates graduating from Christian schools related to the fact that well-off South Asian parents often sent their children to Christian or mission schools because they offered the most elite education. Many such schools had well-known reputations for securing their pupils high positions in civil and government employment. Some parents also believed that, rather than trying to convert children, Christian schools offered moral training and religious dialogue that secular education did not.[95] They did, of course, expose Indian students to Christian teachings. The first Cotton School, for example, was founded in 1865 by Bishop Cotton and became known as the "Eton of the East." It was revitalized under the leadership of the Society for the Propagation of the Gospel in Foreign Parts after 1907 and became home to Asia's first Scouting Troop in 1909.[96] This twentieth-century institution embodied the Indian variant of muscular Christianity that underpinned much of the army's cultural ethos. Subjects such as English literature inculcated Christian morality through narratives of upward mobility and self-improvement.[97] This too, was a central tenet of enlistment, officer training, and promotion in the Indian Army. The most elite future officers were well-versed in how to present themselves as paragons of duty, sobriety, and devotion. This gave them qualities of leadership that were detectable to the British and South Asian men assessing their viability as potential officers. Those whose body language, demeanor, or communication skills would have been out of place at a British Sunday church service would be at an immediate disadvantage.

The pervasiveness of British-Christian educational culture in the Indian Army gave Anglo-Indians and Indian Christians unexpected access to the benefits of Indianization. Anglo-Indians, sometimes referred to as

Eurasians, were born in India and often had full or partial European parentage. They were permitted to compete for IMA positions intended for South Asians.[98] This gave them opportunities in an army that largely excluded them in the twentieth century. Most low-class Anglo-Indians could not take low-ranking positions in the Indian Army due to the preference for so-called martial races. They had to be relatively well-off to return to England to enlist in the British Army or to receive officer training at Sandhurst. When Anglo-Indians had the chance to compete for positions at Sandhurst they were not very successful. Only one Anglo-Indian gained admission but he was dismissed before graduation.[99] Indian Christians, meanwhile, had been isolated from the army for decades. Eighteenth- and nineteenth-century East India Company officials had recruited Indian Christians and Anglo-Indians to replenish its military labor supply.[100] British officers in the late nineteenth and early twentieth centuries, by contrast, categorized Indian Christians as "pariahs"—or outcaste Hindus. Outside of wartime they rarely had opportunities to join the army—even then the labor corps was far more common.[101] They did not even receive their own chaplains.[102] Martial race assumptions had become so well entrenched that one major of the 17th Lancers balked at a Muslim cavalry soldier's desire to convert to Christianity. The major apparently declared that "A clerk could be a Hindu and join other gods to God as much as he pleased, but not a combatant of the 17th Cavalry."[103] Becoming Christian in the years before the First World War resulted in the loss of martial status. This was a situation much different from the pre-1857 army, in which many evangelical British officers attempted to convert South Asian soldiers.[104] It reflected the anti-missionary sentiment more common in the army after 1857. During Indianization, however, the pendulum swung back. Indian Christians and Anglo-Indians found a degree of institutional relevance once again. Many still faced racial and class discrimination in Britain, among British officials, and in Indian nationalist circles. Yet the Indian Army was, for a time, willing to acknowledge that Christians could be Indians, and that Indian Christians could be martial—identities long excluded in military praxis.

Like those who trained in Christian schools, Indian Christians and Anglo-Indians enjoyed high rates of success on the competitive exams, especially for the interviews. Interviews were conducted by two Indian Army officers with command experience plus one civil official, usually from the education department, and one "Indian gentleman" nominated by the governor-general.[105] These interviewers, either intentionally or subconsciously, scored candidates in such a way that made a Christian soldier's faith, education, and ethnicity the best preparation for becoming officers. In the spring of 1939, three out of the top ten finishers overall on the exam were Christian—including two Indian Christians and one Anglo-Indian.[106] By the fall, seven out of ten Indian Christians, and four out of five Anglo-Indians, received passing scores in their interviews.[107] Christian candidates were small in number but they tended to do better on average than candidates of other faiths. Some Indian politicians criticized the highly subjective nature of interviews but military officials maintained that they were necessary to "ascertain whether the candidate is suitable in respect of personality and other matters for the position of a commissioned officer in the Indian Army."[108] Racial assimilation in the Indian Army favored those most exposed to a British Christian tradition, leaving behind many of the so-called martial races. What British military officials never imagined, however, was that Indian officers might outperform their British counterparts in both military discipline and Christian devotion.

CHRISTIANIZING SOLDIERS

South Asian soldiers' and officers' immersion in muscular Christianity was not an unambiguous triumph of imperial Christianity. In fact, at the very moment that British institutions spread Christian military education to South Asians, the Christianity of British troops was as uncertain as ever. A "Committee of Enquiry upon Religion" believed that the First World War had negatively affected spiritual devotion in the British army and nation. The Committee's report, published in 1919, shared one military respondent's view that "The soldier has got religion, I'm not so sure that he has got Christianity."[109] One aspect of this change, they speculated, was that the British educational system emphasized material wealth, rather than moral improvement, and exposed students to non-Christian philosophical traditions. Education in Britain allowed British men to lose their faith while officials in India were using education to help South

Asian soldiers solidify theirs. Institutional anxieties about British Christianity shaped and were shaped by the racial integration of the Indian Army. Both shared intersecting concerns about soldiers' bodies, loyalties, and moral commitment to imperial rule. In fact, the interdenominational culture of "muscular Christianity" in the army would influence and be influenced by the westernized education of interfaith Indian officers.

Prior to the twentieth century British officials in India believed that Christianity was the only thing keeping British soldiers from going down a path of destitution and debauchery.[110] The increased educational standard of British men, and the decrease in Irish and Scottish recruits, contributed to more positive attitudes toward soldiers in the twentieth century.[111] Several official regulations also explicitly reinforced the Christianity of British soldiers. It was a bureaucratic impossibility for soldiers to be anything other than Christian; "Jewish" was included in the long list of possible "denominations."[112] Pamphlets for soldiers frequently referred to "we Christians" and failed to give descriptions about Christianity when cataloguing other beliefs. If soldiers "do not know all about" Christianity, one pamphlet contended, then they "ought to."[113] Hiring chaplains also fell under the discretion of military leadership, and British soldiers were marched to church on Sunday. Army regulations gave precise instructions for the distribution of bibles, prayer books, and furniture in churches. They even accounted for the Indian laborers present during church services who served as prayer room attendants and punkah pullers prior to the adoption of electric fans.[114] Other forms of inequality also existed. Many cantonments had churches for religious minorities such as Catholics, Presbyterians, and Wesleyans but they were often farther away from the barracks, forcing non-Anglican soldiers to make long marches in the hot Indian sun.[115] This created feelings of isolation and inequality for the non-Anglicans who made up around 30% of the British forces in India, mirroring the divisions between "martial races."[116]

British soldiers' chaplains were also treated according to a religious hierarchy.[117] Catholic and non-Anglican chaplains routinely earned less than half that of Anglican and Presbyterian chaplains.[118] Due to insufficient pay, Roman Catholic priests tended to be "foreigners who are content with a humble standard of living."[119] William Keatinge, the principal

Roman Catholic chaplain for soldiers, worried that "The foreigner never really understands the British soldier and the British soldier has very little use for him."[120] Despite the higher rate of pay for Anglicans, J. Bell of the Indian Ecclesiastical Establishment complained that his pay was "inadequate for a European."[121] This prevented him from enjoying the "standard" assumed for his position and from maintaining the expected class-based moral superiority over enlisted men. Officer cadet Maurice Boxall, whose father was an Anglican priest, complained to his parents that one Canon Brooks at Quetta gave sermons that were "appalling." More damningly, Brooks had "a very Cockney accent & my candid opinion of him is that he is a fool."[122] At a time when British officials worried about the "ignorance" of Indian soldiers and their "religious teachers," British soldiers and officers expressed similar concerns about the insufficiency of Christian leaders. Making matters worse, soldiers of all denominations found it difficult to access chaplains due to frequent travel and chaplains' obligations to civilian communities.[123] Many British soldiers, in turn, viewed religious designations as little more than bureaucratic formalities. Some changed their denominations to get extra leave or to avoid pushy chaplains.[124] The army's own ambivalence about Christianity resulted in greater emphasis on discipline and sobriety than doctrine, which dimmed the enthusiasm of many devout chaplains and soldiers alike.[125]

British officials increasingly favored interdenominational socialization to overcome soldiers' religious indifference. This created important models for interfaith integration during Indianization. Despite lingering institutional suspicion toward missionaries, army officials supported the Royal Army Temperance Association (RATA), the Salvation Army, the Sandes Soldiers' Homes, and the Young Men's Christian Association (YMCA) to inspire health, sobriety, and unity among soldiers.[126] Men found food, tea, coffee, and light and airy surroundings that helped to redirect their desires to commit "sins." One soldier even remembered the Salvation Army as "the most wonderful organization ever."[127] Denominational blindness was essential to the success of these initiatives.[128] Soldiers praised chaplains who planned interdenominational gatherings in theaters or tents, which freed them from the discomfort of the Sunday church parade.[129] The questionnaire provided to prospective chaplains even emphasized that chaplains should live "piously, soberly and honestly." Although each chaplain should be "a loyal churchman," they should also be "tolerant and broad-minded in respect of unessential matters of doctrine and ritual."[130] Christianity in the army prioritized the cultivation of clean and sober men who, above all, could set a good social and moral example without squabbling over denominational differences.

During the First World War some chaplains believed that this interdenominational Christian brotherhood should include South Asians. Despite initial military resistance, some missionaries even served as de facto recruiters for Punjabi Christian soldiers.[131] Certain members of the YMCA encouraged ideas of "race-brotherhood" among British and South Asian troops.[132] Makeshift YMCA "huts" hosted musical performances, games, food and drink, and other amusements. They also provided lectures on sex and hygiene and courses on reading and writing. This mirrored the amenities that British soldiers in India had long received from the Salvation Army, the RATA, and Sandes Soldiers' Homes. These spaces also opened up the possibility of interracial discussions of faith. One Indian YMCA worker in Marseilles, S. M. Jafri, described a Risaldar (an Indian cavalry officer) who interrupted a musical performance to give a speech about how "education" and "unity" were crucial for "the advancement of our country." The Risaldar praised the YMCA for providing lectures on education. Equally important, he believed, was for soldiers to know that "Religion also must not be a matter of difference and disunity." All people, whether "a Hindoo or a Mohammedan, a Christian or a Jew, a Parsi or a Buddhist," should "not look down upon a man of another religion with prejudice and enmity." He believed that once Indians overcame "differences and ill feeling" they could become "a united and progressive people."[133] Such sentiments made it possible to imagine that the war, and the YMCA, was making interfaith and interracial unity a reality.

The YMCA's interracial socialization between soldiers largely ended with the war. British military officials eagerly took advantage of American funds and resources to support British and South Asian troops during a global conflict. This continued to be true for British, but not Indian, soldiers. The RATA closed down in the 1920s because the YMCA proved so successful among British men.[134] Yet the army was reluctant to make the same interventions for South Asian soldiers back in the highly segregated society of colonial India. Postwar life returned many Indian soldiers "home," where military officials assumed that they would be able to reintegrate smoothly despite their traumatic experiences and years abroad.

The YMCA's successes hint at why some Anglo-Indians and Indian Christians, as well as non-Christians trained at Christian schools, became allies rather than outsiders during Indianization. In the 1920s and 1930s, interdenominational Christian institutions enabled British soldiers to have frequent encounters with Anglo-Indians and Indian Christians. One soldier, William Homer, remembered going horseback riding with an Anglo-Indian girl named Dorothy, whose British father ran the YMCA at Nainital and whose mother was an Indian Christian. Meanwhile, the YWCA in Delhi often held dances where soldiers could meet nurses and other British, Anglo-Indian, and Indian Christian women. Homer recalled fondly that he skated, rode horses, and "made love" with one woman named Kathleen Joy who was staying at the YWCA.[135] Rather than threatening their physical strength and morality, soldiers' encounters with British, Anglo-Indian, and Indian Christian women gave them a sexual outlet that was perceived to be safer and cleaner than a brothel. For Charles Francis Crossland, however, Christian sex did not always mean interracial harmony or physical purity. While serving briefly with the Royal Army Medical Corps in India during the 1920s he found that the YMCA was one of the only ways of meeting women. Nonetheless, he described encountering widely held beliefs that Eurasian women were "loose" as a result of their interracial heritage. He, in turn, spent most of his time in the venereal ward.[136] Perhaps for these reasons, the YMCA, YWCA, and Salvation Army became less popular by the 1930s. According to William Homer, these places were best for getting tea, a bun, and a magazine, but by and large the "Practice of visiting . . . had gone." He remembered: "that's the last place you'd go to, you see, no sensible soldier would go to the Salvation Army for a cup of tea . . . we'd got other things to do."[137] With plenty of "amenities," and competing institutions for soldiers' time and recreation, interwar British soldiers relied less heavily on chaplains and religious organizations to find comfort and distraction.

Indian officer S. P. P. Thorat described a very different recreational situation for Indian officers and soldiers that underlines the slippage between religious and racial hierarchies in the interwar army. He found that sports were one of the few ways that non-Christian Indian men could spend their downtime. The YMCA allowed British soldiers to dance or have carefree sex with women. By contrast, Thorat claimed to avoid "the company of girls. In fact I rather shunned them."[138] More than likely, this meant that Indian officers had to be more clandestine with their non-married or extra-marital sexual encounters through brothels, as had been the case for British soldiers and officers in earlier decades. Christian organizations' investment in British soldiers' recreation prevented the army from having to invest more funds to keep them amused. All British soldiers, however, had access to Christian spaces whether they genuinely professed the faith or not. Indian officers, recruited for their "martial race" beliefs, faced institutional sterility. Being Christian, or embracing Christian education, opened certain channels of recreation and upward mobility to some Indian men. After attending integrated Christian schools, however, Indian officers who were not Christian found that their religious differences guaranteed racial exclusion. No matter how fully they embraced the army's marriage of the martial races with muscular Christianity, they still did not fully belong.

MARCHING TO TEMPLE, MOSQUE, AND *GURDWARA*

The asceticism of army life for interwar Indian officers meant that many found new value in religious instruction. Thorat remembered that "men took keen interest in religion" because "of the complete lack of any amenities." Religious teachers delighted the men with "mythological stories and legends."[139] Thorat, by contrast, found the army's approved "Pundits, Granthis, or Maulvis" disappointing and uninspiring. He condemned them for having "little knowledge of the scriptures" and providing "sermons" that were "elementary."[140] Like British officer cadet Maurice Boxall, who condemned his "cockney" chaplain, Thorat saw the army's religious teachers as embarrassingly ill-informed. Nonetheless, religious education played an important role in Indianization. The army's ethos of muscular Christianity shaped South Asian soldiers' training, encouraging

Anglicized and militarized interpretations of their beliefs that were compatible with army service.

For the interwar army, "religion" was just another subject in the comprehensive program of military education. The King George's Schools for aspiring soldiers set aside "definite hours" for religious instruction. The primary goal was to "read extracts from his sacred works and to correspond with his own people."[141] This taught soldiers to spread loyal interpretations of their faith. Officers and religious teachers, meanwhile, encouraged soldiers to make "sound judgments" so that "there may be no conflict between a soldier's conscience and his military duty."[142] They did so by vetting their religious teachers carefully. At the RIMC, Maulvi Mohammed Akram Khan was "a pensioned Dafadar" who had been part of the 13th Lancers. He instructed "the Muhammadan Cadets in the Quran." Pandit Bala Datt Pandey, who instructed the Hindu cadets, was a havildar major in the First World War in France. He also served as an interpreter for the 23rd Labour Corps. He spoke "English well and teaches from the Ramayan and Mahabharat"—two texts that emphasized the duty of spiritual warfare. Sikh Granthi Dalip Singh was a "pensioned Havildar" from the 29th Punjabis who served in France, Palestine, and Mesopotamia. He doubled as the musketry instructor and was a "well educated man" who instructed Sikh boys from the Granth Sahib.[143]

These carefully selected religious teachers all had military experience and gave boys and men mandatory instruction on textual interpretations of belief, distancing them from regional or familial practices. Pensioned teachers had financial incentive to keep their teachings as pro-British as possible.[144] They were also subject to military discipline and answerable to Indian officers.[145] Reading religious texts in military spaces under the guidance of pensioned religious teachers equipped soldiers to challenge anti-colonial interpretations of belief and practice. Prior to the First World War anti-colonial activists used texts such as the *Bhagavad Gita* to justify a divinely sanctioned fight against imperialism.[146] By contrast, the army trained South Asian soldiers to believe that their service to the empire was a fulfillment of their moral duty.

Religious education in the army was not completely dictated by imperial officials. Indian politicians frequently pressured military authorities to incorporate religious instruction into army life. One politician encouraged the government to include "religious training" at institutions such as the RIMC because "religion also influences morals."[147] This shaped official strategies and rhetoric about creating military unity through religious difference. RIMC Commandant Haughton explained that "We have a Sikh teacher, a Maulvi and a Pandit. There is a Gurdwara, a mosque and a temple. Every Friday afternoon is given over to religious instruction."[148] Religious teachers ensured that every day before evening meals, boys went to "Gurdwara, mosque or temple."[149] Edwin John Watson, former president of the RIMC, similarly recalled that boys were "paraded by religions" and then "marched off to their various temples, the Sikhs to the gurdwara, and the Hindus to the temple and the Muslims to the mosque."[150] Boys received "Compulsory religious instruction" from 1 to 2 P.M. and could attend daily evening prayers. This no doubt gave Indian boys the same sense of obligation and duty that many British soldiers and officers felt about their own mandatory worship. Those who had to march to a religious space every day were unlikely to wander off the college grounds to search for additional sources of devotion.

Military officials believed that religious arrangements were so important that a pamphlet for the RIMC included images of the college *gurdwara*, mosque, and temple.[151] These were likely meant to reassure families that their boys' morality and faith would not get left behind in their English military educations. Like interdenominational Christian spaces, these were "attractive modern buildings of orthodox design" equipped with "electric lights and fans."[152] Some even had the "protection" of barbed wire enclosures. These images (Figure 9) also reveal the idealized marriage of religious and military order. In addition to being clean and well-landscaped, the buildings apparently lacked civilian worshipers. Soldiers could feel they were participating in a spiritual duty without being tempted by chats with non-loyal individuals. Military religious spaces gave British officials the illusion of control over soldiers' beliefs.

A major goal of religious education during Indianization was to build interfaith unity among aspiring officers so that they could lead soldiers from any religious background. Educational training pamphlets maintained that "toleration of the religion of his comrades and respect

FIGURE 9 The Masjid on the grounds of the Royal Indian Military College. Boys had predefined times for worship. *Source*: Prince of Wales Royal Indian Military College Dehra Dun. British Library IOR/L/MIL/17/5/2283, opposite page 7. Reprinted with permission.

for their beliefs is the duty of every soldier."[153] Lt-Col H. L. Haughton, Commandant, RIMC, explained further that:

> We are getting a very good co-operative spirit in the college, and the boys are all beginning to understand one thing:-that any sort of intrigue or caste feeling or back-biting will not be tolerated. That sort of thing is absolutely fatal in any army. At Dehra Dun there is plenty of room for every boy to practise his own religion perfectly freely without there being any class feeling or intrigue amongst them. I must say that I am very pleased with the spirit which the boys have shown. From the start I rub into them that the college is the Prince of Wales's Royal *Indian* Military College, that they are candidates not for the Punjabi army, or the Bengali army, or the Madrasi army, but for the *Indian* Army, and that they have got to remember that they are Indians first, whatever their caste.[154]

In contrast to the "class regiments" that so carefully segregated Hindus, Muslims, and Sikhs, the RIMC celebrated national unity and religious integration. This made it the opposite of the King George's Schools, which segregated future recruits according to religious differences. Haughton revealed that it was still necessary for the army to sort out "religious" differences: "If we have any little cases of enmity amongst the boys, we take them to the gymnasium and give them boxing gloves and make them settle their differences like that."[155] In military schools, religious difference was addressed with interpersonal violence. This inherently privileged the biggest and strongest boys who would be best able to defend their position. It also taught them to view the whole matter as a game of sport. Religion, the army believed, should come second to physical fitness and military discipline. A boy's ability to defend his faith with his fists no doubt distorted how boys felt about their beliefs and their martial professions. Religious worship became a performance of military masculinity that served, rather than undermined, a soldier's devotion to the army.

MARCHING TO CHURCH

The fusing of religious devotion and military discipline resulted in an unexpected opportunity for Indian officers to participate in and influence Christianity in the army. In particular, the church parade, or "parade service," was a prominent symbol of Christianity and imperial duty. British soldiers, dressed in their finest and armed with weapons, caused what former British officer Thomas Nickalls called an "awful clatter" as they marched each week to receive the divine wisdom of the chaplain appointed to their particular military station.[156] This ceremony remained in place even as the Indian Army became "Indianized" and South Asian men took leadership roles in the armed services. Indian officers marched to church alongside their British counterparts. Marching to temple, mosque, or *gurdwara* at military colleges and academies prepared them to participate in, and ultimately show the limitations of, the martial Christianity of their British counterparts.

Soldiers' participation in the church parade was well-entrenched in army policy. Army regulations required all British "other ranks" (non-officers) to attend "Divine service" by marching to and from their places of worship under the charge of a non-commissioned officer of the same denomination.[157] Men needed to do so "with arms." The church pews even had built-in notches to keep soldiers' weapons in place during the service.[158] Toco Moses Stevens and William Homer, who served in India in the 1930s, remembered that soldiers marched to church to commemorate an attack on Christian worshipers in church by Indian mutineers in 1857. Marching to church fully armed was a ceremonial declaration that the incident would never happen again.[159] Twentieth-century soldiers participated in the church parade to reproduce British narratives of the mutiny through the physical ardor of marching to church. Yet South Asian soldiers were among Britain's closest allies in India in the interwar period. Publicly performing a ritualized memory of the mutiny could be an embarrassing anachronism rather than a symbol of strength and resilience.

Despite the symbolic and ceremonial value of the parade, military and church officials disagreed about whether church parades exerted a positive or harmful influence on the men. A group of Anglican bishops in India condemned "the strictness of the ceremonial parade on Sunday mornings." This made "the parade service unpopular and to some extent unprofitable." They conceded that the parades had military value but they were also "burdensome to the men" especially "in warm weather and in stations where the barracks are at a considerable distance from the church." Equally embarrassing was that British officers rarely attended. This resulted in "a bad effect on the minds of the men."[160] Some soldiers took extensive measures to avoid participating. Signalman H. H. Somerfield, for example, repeatedly sneaked out of church. He even contemplated becoming a Muslim, in part to avoid marching to church on Sundays.[161] William Homer, who served with a British battalion in India in the 1930s, recalled that the church parade "always spoiled Sunday" because "We all resented it."[162] Many clergymen ignored these protests. The Catholic Archbishop of Simla argued that the parade was an imperial necessity because "the individual and the nation recognise the duty of publicly worshipping God."[163] Some Anglican chaplains agreed that the "Parade Service is an official acknowledgment to Almighty God that as a Nation and Empire we believe in Him." They found this ceremony "even more necessary in India than elsewhere."[164] Parades forced soldiers to come together and listen to the words of a chaplain, bringing devotion into the purview of military duty. It created an illusion of strength and unity in a colonial space known for its religious and racial diversity. This spectacle offered soldiers' bodies to nation, empire, and Christianity, but did little to ensure the faith of individual British soldiers.

Chaplains' fervent defenses of the church parade reveal that Indian schoolboys' marches to temple, mosque, and *gurdwara* would have also worked remarkably well as symbols of imperial unity. These ceremonies promised to turn Indian men from potentially seditious and unreliable "sepoys"—whose mutinous potential lived on in church parades—into disciplined, loyal, and capable officers. Military colleges and academies, in short, taught Indian men to pray like a soldier. The days of drifting to a nearby mosque or raising a regimental subscription to hire a wandering mendicant were gone. The army worked hard to make religious devotion disciplined and controlled as a part of military and imperial duty. Sometimes this duty included marching for Christianity itself. When IMA graduate Brigadier Sukhwant Singh was attached temporarily to the 2nd Welch: "on a couple of occasions I marched the troops to the Church and listened to their prayers." He added, however, that "I regularly attended my own prayers at Gurdwara Mai Than" in Agra.[165] By placing his own "prayers" at the *gurdwara* alongside the "prayers" of the church parade, Sukhwant Singh suggested that each ceremony had the same relative value for the men who participated in them. Beliefs were meant to be practiced and respected at certain times in conjunction with military duty but never distracting from it.

In reality, the church parade did less to warn mutineers than to draw attention to British officers' shortcomings. Another officer, Jazwan Singh, used the downtime before the parades to get to know the enlisted British men of his regiment. This contrasted with the absentee British officers whom clergymen deplored.[166] Indian officer Dinesh Chandra Misra believed further that participating in the church parade was an opportunity to demonstrate his martial superiority. Misra attended the weekly church parade despite being a Brahman. This confused his commanding officer, who misunderstood Misra's military duty as Christian devotion. The commanding officer declared his wish that "my countrymen, young officers, would be as devout Christians as you are."[167] Although Indian officers' participation in the church parades was optional, religious and military training allowed them to see it as just another duty to their profession. Some even enjoyed the opportunity to outperform British officers and men. While British soldiers lamented the cumbersome burden of church parades, South Asian men saw them as a way to demonstrate that they were disciplined, strong, and capable men, worthy of leading the armed forces and the nation.

Indian officers' ability to master and appropriate imperial Christianity both upended and reinforced the goals of Indianization. British officials hoped that military schools and academies would build a cadre of loyal, interfaith soldiers ready and capable of combating anti-colonial rebellion and winning global wars. Just as often, they drew attention to British soldiers' shortcomings. Indian men, by contrast, proved willing and able to adapt to the changing needs and preferences of military institutions—even if that meant accepting subtle Christianization and further isolation from their civilian communities. Their ability to do so made them liable to adopt the army's assumptions and biases about selective recruitment, stringent codes of masculinity, and religious hierarchies. The army's educational programs exposed children, young men, and soldiers to a lifetime of military indoctrination that fused religious devotion with military masculinity, often with unintended consequences. British efforts to institutionalize South Asian soldiers' beliefs would not prevent British institutions from crumbling. In fact, these tensions intensified as the world became more economically and politically divided. British and South Asian religious and military cultures became more formalized and institutionalized as the world faced destabilizing financial collapse and another apocalyptic war.

CHAPTER 6

MARTIAL MASCULINITY IN THE
FASCIST UTOPIA

IN THE SUMMER OF 1937, working-class British soldier H. H. Somerfield
spent many hours in India with Christian, Sikh, and Muslim men. Together they visited cinemas, trekked the foothills of the Himalayas, stayed
in guest houses operated by British women, and discussed "sodomy"
with a Hindu café owner. They even rented state-of-the-art cars and
relaxed in fan-equipped clubs and dance halls.[1] By the 1930s, working-
class British and South Asian soldiers enjoyed greater access to the creature
comforts of military service long preserved for the white officer elite. This
convinced some that the army and empire had finally made good on its
promise to provide opportunities that transcended racial and class difference. However, this interracial sociability and recreational pleasure was
only an illusion of inclusivity. Somerfield, and many other soldiers in the
Indian Army, were not optimistic about the future of the British Empire,
instead anticipating and fearing its rapid decline. They joined a growing
chorus of colonial and anti-colonial activists who contrasted the clean
and ordered spaces of military cantonments with the chaos and deprivation of interwar India. The illusion of stability proved to be short-lived.

Interwar military service provided an attractive—and misleading—
alternative to the global economic depression of the 1930s. The worldwide collapse brought sharper critiques of imperial rule as well as greater
incentives to join the Indian Army. Despite continuing campaigns by

Indian nationalists and anti-colonial activists, the Conservative-led National Coalition Government in Britain planned to retain India at all costs by 1931. Plans for economic growth and productivity focused domestically on Britain to combat the depression. This left uncertainty about Britain's role in India. The army was expensive due to Indianization reforms and continuing military campaigns along the northwestern borders. Despite the British government's pledge to keep India, many in and beyond Britain wondered if holding on to India was still morally or economically justifiable.[2]

As global prices for agriculture plummeted, the Indian economy stalled, hurting India's overseas exports and domestic employment opportunities. This emboldened communist as well as class, caste, and religious critiques that attracted individuals seeking protection from or rebellion against imperial capital. Mohandas Gandhi gained global sympathy with his 1930 salt march and tour of the United Kingdom in 1931. However, his pledge of nonviolence and growing connections to Europeans and Americans alienated him from many Indian nationalists and anti-colonial activists who criticized his cosmopolitan, middle-class ethics. Communists, untouchables, peasants, and borderland communities across India developed their own anti-colonial, and often anti-Gandhi, political organizations.[3] Meanwhile, the North-West Frontier Province erupted in renewed rebellion. This was exacerbated by shrinking economic opportunities, inspiring even more deadly imperial assaults in the region. For many anti-colonial activists, Gandhi's nonviolence felt too conservative and tame to bring radical change to India.[4] Since war and violence were recurring features of India's colonial history, many believed that militancy was a necessary antidote.

Amid the chaos and political infighting of depression-torn India, the Indian Army felt calm by comparison. Military service came with a guarantee of employment, housing, and food. As a result, soldiers made fast and decisive choices about where to invest their loyalties. Could they, given their employment histories, become nonviolent protesters for peace and independence? Would they retreat to the northwestern borderlands in search of armed allies? Could communism give full expression to their anxieties about limited economic opportunities? For many British and

South Asian soldiers, the army had made them upwardly mobile. This gave some a feeling of personal investment in the future of imperial rule. Many felt embittered by their isolation from the inner circles of colonial and anti-colonial power in both Britain and India. The army, by contrast, gave them relatively elite status, including education. Soldiers were prepared to fight for what they believed they had finally earned from the colonial state. Anti-colonial activists, by contrast, believed that the fight should be against imperial governance itself. The future of militancy in India was uncertain and widely contested.

MARTIAL HINDUS

By the 1930s the glorification of militancy pervaded Indian politics far beyond the "martial races." Many high-caste Indian Hindus came forward to take the Indian Military Academy (IMA) entrance exams and compete for positions as officers to demonstrate that they, too, could be martial. This confused some military officials, who had long associated Indian Hindus—outside of a few widely recruited exceptions—with being non-martial. In fact, many Hindus spent decades redefining the public face of Hinduism. Hindu nationalists increasingly attacked the theory of martial races and the idea that the "effeminate Bengali"—or Mohandas Gandhi—represented Hindu identity.[5] Many believed that military service could prove Hindus' martial worth and, in turn, their capacity to lead an independent Indian nation. Their understanding of who belonged in the nation, however, was as contested as ever.

Several influential Hindu reformist campaigns encouraged Indian Hindus to view military service and militancy as inseparable from masculinity. The Hindu Mahasabha (Greater Hindu society), founded in the first decades of the twentieth century, sought to improve Hindu physiques and martial spirit. Members popularized the Kshatriya (warrior) dharma through volunteer corps and military schools. *Akharas* (gymnasiums) also offered wrestling, body-building, and stick fighting to develop strong civilian physiques capable of fighting for the nation and reversing the so-called degeneration of colonialism.[6] Author and nationalist Vinayak Damodar Savarkar famously described the 1857 uprising as a war of independence in 1907. He increasingly adopted anti-Muslim attitudes and became a major supporter of the violent youth organization RSS (*Rashtriya Swayamsevak Sangh*), founded in 1925, which encouraged militant ultra-nationalism among Hindus.[7] The anti-Hindu *Mother India* by American author Katherine Mayo, released in 1927, alleged that Hinduism was too corrupt and effeminate to be left unchecked by colonial rule. This inspired a defensive response about the purity of Hinduism and the masculinity of Hindu men.[8] When Mohandas Gandhi and the Indian National Congress resumed non-cooperation in 1929, many condemned Gandhi's thin body as weak and effeminate, despite his advocacy of health and exercise.[9] Gandhi's physicality, his opponents contended, perpetuated the imperial view that Hindus were physically incapable of serving in the armed forces, defending against invasion, and fighting for independence. The Hindustan Socialist Republican Army, by contrast, targeted British officials for assassination after 1928. It became especially popular due to young revolutionary Bhagat Singh's execution by the state in 1930. He became a martyred hero, and a militant alternative to Gandhi, for Indian nationalists. His sharp western dress, martial extremism, and use of bombs and pistols encouraged styles of militant masculinity that challenged colonial and nationalist tropes about Indian degeneration.[10] Although women were active campaigners in various anti-colonial movements, mainstream nationalism increasingly defined the fight for citizenship through militant masculinity, which often implicitly excluded women from being more than symbols of political power.[11]

Debates about Hindu masculinity often focused on the lack of official military training for young Hindu boys and men. These arguments became common in the mid-1920s due to the lack of success of Indian cadets at Sandhurst. For example, in 1926, renowned politician and Nehru family patriarch Motilal Nehru proposed "instituting military classes" in "most secondary schools." He believed that "military discipline" should be a standard part of the curriculum to make secondary schools more similar to British public schools.[12] Other Indian politicians, including members of the Hindu Mahasabha, similarly stressed military education. One politician wondered why schools failed to have cadet corps or rifle clubs to encourage boys to take up military careers. Their absence enabled Indian students to earn advanced degrees but become "scholastically, physically or socially" unsuitable for the army.[13] Others encouraged the army to build additional military schools for boys to encourage "military spirit among the people of the country."[14] Many British officials agreed that additional schools would help train boys for military life from a younger age.[15] British military education for boys, they argued, was essential for building national and military leadership in India.

By the 1930s, Indian politicians increasingly condemned the army's inability to acknowledge Hindu masculinity. The Indian Military College committee debates in 1931 proved especially contentious when negotiating the terms for the formation of the IMA. Politicians Sir Abdur Rahim and Mr. S. N. Mukarji worried that only "martial races" would be eligible. This was harmful because it barred strong men from military service because of their region or religion, creating "serious slur on the manhood of a large class of India's population." They contended that the issue was not that "non-enlisted classes" in regions outside of northwestern India did not want to serve in the army but that "they are definitely debarred from doing so." The result, they argued, was that many men embraced "anarchist and revolutionary activities" including "deadly agrarian and communal riots."[16] The army, in their view, was fomenting rather than curbing anti-colonial violence across the subcontinent by denying men the ability to serve in the army. This attack on masculinity, they felt, merely pushed young men into the hands of anti-colonial revolutionaries. Few considered that the glorification of militancy within the army and colonial society was actually to blame. Instead, they accused the British of "preventing the growth of martial spirit and leadership." This ensured that India was dependent on remaining "either under the heel of Britain or under the heel of the enlisted classes" for generations to come.[17] Not only were Hindu men fit and willing to serve, they argued, but the widely recruited Sikhs, Muslims, and Punjabis had developed arrogant attitudes and unearned access to power because of their exalted status.

Perhaps no individual was as critical of the army's recruiting practices as Hindu Mahasabha leader B. S. Moonje. Moonje served as an official and non-official member of various Sandhurst and Indian College committees, shaping Indianization.[18] His 1931 minute paper rivaled the length of the entire Indian Military College committee report. In it he expressed that the army perpetuated "the myth of the artificial distinction of martial and non-martial classes." This proved, in Moonje's view, that the government exercised "the policy of 'Divide and Rule.'" Rather than creating stability, the army spread "the poison of communalism in the body politic of India," which "emasculates large sections of the people." He agreed with other politicians who felt that existing army recruitment practices created "swelled-headedness in those who are generally enlisted in the Army." The army claimed to represent national unity through its interfaith arrangements at schools and colleges. However, Moonje believed that failing to change recruiting practices "perpetuates the system of a mercenary Army which is the inevitable concomitant of a foreign government."[19] As such, he articulated an increasingly common argument among Indian nationalists: that soldiers in British military service were merely mercenaries who enlisted for a paycheck. This narrative ignored the army's reliance on military-religious rituals and education to make service desirable for soldiers. Yet Moonje echoed soldiers who used precolonial identities to claim martial status. He identified as a Maratha and defended the martial heritage of his community. He praised the martial qualities of Madrasis, Beharis, Bengalis, and Telugus who were frequently excluded from military recruitment.[20] Moonje's arguments about discrimination in the army no doubt resonated for many communities who felt excluded from military service. Yet his exaltation of Indian martial prowess often explicitly excluded non-Hindus.

Moonje's participation in the Indian Sandhurst and Indian Military College committees allowed him to shape interwar debates about education, military training, and martial masculinity.[21] As a leader of the Hindu Mahasabha, he was also invested in the cultivation of martial Hindu men. The same year that the IMA opened its doors in 1932 the non-government Shivaji Military School opened in Pune. This academy was largely unsuccessful but it encouraged Moonje to build a similar military school appealing exclusively to Hindus. He made preliminary plans in 1935 before it eventually opened its doors in 1937 as the Bhonsala Military School.[22] Moonje declared that the primary goal of his school was "to bring about Military regeneration of the Hindus."[23] It was intended for "all Hindu boys" who would be welcome "whatever caste they may belong." All boys were considered Kshatriyas (members of the warrior caste). "No caste distinctions" would be acknowledged. For Moonje, "perfect Social and Religious equality" would be the result. The place of non-Hindus, of course, remained ambiguous. Moonje explained that boys would develop "ideas of common Brotherhood and common Nationality" by learning to defend "their Religion, Culture," and the "honour of their Womanhood and the country."[24] Emphasizing brotherhood, national unity, and the defense of women borrowed from well-worn Indian nationalist tropes about the primacy of masculinity in the anti-colonial struggle.[25] The singleness of "their religion," however, suggests that "common nationality" was inseparable from having a shared religious identity. Despite such implicit exclusions, British military men supported the martial regeneration of Hindus to gain more recruits. Former Indian Army Commander-in-Chief Sir Philip Chetwode (1930–35) took a leading role in Indianization and oversaw the establishment of the IMA. He refused to comment on Moonje's condemnation of "the class composition of the ranks" because it was the responsibility of the British and Indian governments and military leaders.[26] Nonetheless, he reportedly invested personally in Moonje's academy, supporting religiously segregated martial training for Hindus.[27] IMA examiners similarly encouraged potential candidates to attend University Training Corps at Indian colleges so that they could learn military values long before applying.[28]

Despite Indian Army encouragement, schools and military training programs founded by Hindu nationalists often contradicted army goals. One man at the opening of an Officers Training Class declared that "India belonged to the Hindus and that it was their plain duty to do all in their power to protect it." The man believed that it was necessary to foster "Unity and discipline" to "retaliate on those who attacked Hinduism."[29] The idea that "India belonged to the Hindus" could be interpreted as both an anti-colonial statement and an implicit threat against religious minorities. Moonje even claimed that military training would take lessons from "the Maha Bharat days." Muslims in India, he suggested, should be viewed as "guests" rather than members of the nation. If they misbehaved, they would be "dealt with according to Shastras."[30] Many members of the Indian National Congress alleged that Moonje held anti-Muslim attitudes.[31]

The martial regeneration of the Hindus, for Moonje, meant preparing for a potential war against Muslims. Despite his immersion in colonial debates about education, his school trained boys physically and morally for the purpose of "attaining Swaraj."[32] "Swaraj" had many different meanings but it increasingly connoted the fight for national independence. Moonje's vision of the nation, however, was one in which Muslims needed to "behave" according to the whims of Hindu leaders.

Interwar debates about military education in the Sandhurst (1926) and Indian Military College (1931) committees were meant to streamline Indianization. What they revealed, however, was that many Indian Hindus continued to feel isolated from and discriminated against in the army. Non-official schools and training corps developed alongside the army's military educational institutions and challenged the army's monopoly over martial masculinity. As a result, they often criticized widely recruited religious minorities. However, at the very moment that Indian politicians felt most isolated from the Indian Army and determined to emphasize their own martial cultures, the army became more, rather than less, inclusive of Indian Hindus. Civilian pressures to revive Hindu masculinity succeeded at convincing the army to make good on its claims to be an interfaith institution. This did not, however, mean an end to faith-based discrimination.

HINDUS AND INDIANIZATION

When Dinesh Chandra Misra applied for a position at the IMA he felt out of place because he was a Brahman. Sharing his memories with the Imperial War Museum decades after his retirement, he estimated that roughly 80% of the young men present for interviews came from the Punjab or the North-West Frontier Province. His IMA interview panel consisted of three British officers and two South Asian Muslims. One of the Muslim men apparently asked Misra if he came from a "class of bigoted pundits" and suggested that he find a white-collar job. Despite this challenge, Misra earned a perfect score on his interview and enrolled at the IMA in 1933. This made him one of the earliest cadets of the IMA. When reflecting on the process, Misra spoke highly of the British officers whom he believed "gave intelligent questions," while "the Punjabis [maybe] didn't know much, one didn't even know the English language and the other was a doctor in uniform."[33] This barely concealed hostility toward what he felt was the unjust exaltation of Muslim men stayed with Misra for decades after he left British imperial service. He remained skeptical about Muslim qualifications and continued to feel like a mistreated military minority because he was a high-caste Hindu. Yet Hindus were actually frequent beneficiaries of Indianization. Being more representative, however, did not eliminate institutional bias.

Hindus became officers in the Indian Army far more than most Hindu politicians and soldiers recognized. Elite Hindu men and boys had the educational and financial advantages to afford British military schools and academies. Army fears in the 1920s that the "martial classes" were educationally "backward" compared to other communities meant that their rates of success lagged behind so-called "non-martial" communities in competitive entrance exams. The IMA examiners noted this trend by 1935, suggesting that there was an "increasing desire of the well-to-do business and professional classes to launch their sons on a military career." They worried, however, that "these boys come from classes with no martial traditions." If they had family connections to imperial institutions it was in the civil service rather than the army. Examiners regarded this lack of military heritage as a "pre-existing handicap." Nonetheless, some boys impressed the interviewers because they were "well developed physically and mentally." They condemned others who came forward with only "lip interest" in being a soldier, as demonstrated by their failure to pursue sports or military training at universities. They speculated that such boys regarded the IMA as just another job opportunity. Examiners added somewhat defensively that "In no case, however, was a likely youth who appeared suitable on personal and independent grounds refused a chance merely because he came of a class that had not previously engaged in military service; on the contrary, several candidates of this type were awarded very good marks."[34] The army was careful, despite its observations about "non-martial" applicants, to defend itself against charges of discrimination.

The IMA examiner's comments about "non-martial" and "business" communities were thinly veiled references to Hindus, who regularly did well on the IMA exam despite evidence of institutional biases against them. Only two Hindu men finished in the top ten in the inaugural exam and they were both Punjabi. Subsequent Hindu performance was high overall but they tended to do poorly on the highly subjective interview portion of the exam. Of the top forty finishers on the first exam, four of the five who received the lowest interview scores were Hindu.[35] In 1934, the candidates who received the highest scores without passing the exam were all Hindus who failed the interview. This included one Punjabi Hindu who finished ninth overall but was ineligible for entry because of his low interview score. Nonetheless, by that year, Hindu success rates had increased: six out of the top ten finishers overall were Hindu.[36] In spring 1935, when examiners made their long statement about "well-to-do business and professional classes," eight out of the top ten finishers were Hindu.[37] All of the top five and seven out of the top ten were Hindu in the fall of 1935. The following spring six of the top ten were also Hindu.[38] The examiners monitored community breakdowns of applicants starting in 1937. This demonstrated that Hindus were frequently top scorers on the exam but had lower rates of success in the interview. That year, eleven of fifteen Muslim candidates received qualifying scores in their interviews while only twenty out of thirty-nine Hindus did.[39] The following year only 53% of Hindus, compared to 69% of Sikhs and Muslims, received qualifying interview scores.[40] Fifty-two percent of Hindus passed the interview compared to 81% of non-Hindus in 1938.[41] Numbers were only comparable (62% for Hindus and 67% for non-Hindus) when the army was recruiting for the Second World War.[42] Some Indian politicians such as Motilal Nehru pushed back against the idea that a single, subjective interview could assess a potential officer's "personality" and "character" during the debates about Sandhurst. Those who supported "martial race" recruiting, by contrast, believed that interviews were important for exposing "racial" differences between candidates.[43] Military officials defended the practice vehemently.[44] Hindu boys and men, meanwhile, proved that colonial critiques about their lack of martial potential were unwarranted.

Dinesh Chandra Misra's perception that he was exceptional and unwelcome as a Hindu candidate was both overstated and well justified. His criticism of the Muslim interviewers who accused his community of being "bigoted pundits" captured his feelings of being a mistreated military minority. These types of comments also may have affected the scores of other Hindu candidates. If they became defensive about discriminatory interview questions they would have likely earned score reductions. Yet Misra's impression that 80% of the interviewees were from Punjab and the North-West Frontier Province was also inaccurate. The largest proportion of men came from the Punjab province but these were usually less than half. The second most well-represented province was not the North-West Frontier Province, but the United Provinces—Misra's own region of origin. By singling out boys and men from the North-West Frontier Province and Punjab, Misra revealed his own geopolitical biases. He equated the North-West Frontier Province/Punjab as Pakistan and hence Muslim. In reality, about half of the candidates were regularly Hindu. Although Misra overstated his own exceptionalism, British officials did give preference to Muslim candidates in interviews, giving credence to his sense of being out of place. Army inclusion did not come fast enough to prevent greater hostility based on the perception of exclusion. As Misra suggests, very real feelings of isolation continued to follow successful Hindu officers who served in the army. This shaped their narratives of service even after their military careers. Hindu officers endured continued discrimination and institutional biases, which perpetuated a defensive response to the "martial races" that outlasted colonial rule.[45]

SCAPEGOATING THE BANIA

Hindu successes in the interwar Indian Army should have resulted in the rejection of older "martial race" assumptions. What it did instead was create alternative rationales for army discrimination. Military education and physical culture made it less convincing to attack Hindu masculinity. The worldwide economic depression and bitter competition for employment made class-based arguments more persuasive. Many rural peasants relied on army recruitment to escape the hardships of their villages. Punjabi landlords with military connections, meanwhile, often condemned city-based politicians for intervening in rural affairs. Sikh and Muslim landowners who dominated the Unionist Party in Punjab from 1920 to 1937 feared losing influence to the middle-class urban elites who dominated elections and petitioned for changes amenable to city interests.[46]

As a result, army officials and Punjabi elites frequently caricatured Hindus generally—and western-educated or city-dwelling Hindus in particular—as over-educated and out of touch with the so-called martial classes. It became increasingly common to blame Hindu businessmen and politicians, rather than imperial agricultural management and taxation, for India's economic and political woes. This emboldened anti-Hindu attitudes within and beyond the army.

British officials frequently used class-based critiques to condemn Hindus who entered into military institutions. India's Central Legislative Assembly approved a motion to allow boys to attend the segregated King George's Military Schools "irrespective of caste or creed" in 1929.[47] Since opening in 1925, the Jhelum school offered positions to highly recruited Muslim communities, while Jullundur targeted Sikhs, Dogras, and Punjabi Hindus. The army did not view the Central Legislative Assembly's intervention as a positive step toward religious integration. The Military Committee believed that this would result in the schools getting "nothing but the sons of banias, shopkeepers & non-martial races who will never be of any use in the Indian Army."[48] Military Secretary to the India Office and former Commander-in-Chief (1925) General Claud R. Jacob believed that "Indian Officers will not send their sons to schools to which the non-martial classes like banias, babus etc send their sons." He accused the Central Legislative Assembly of attempting "to destroy all martial spirit in the country & to embarrass the military authorities in India."[49] In 1930 another British official feared that military schools might turn boys into "babu log" (clerky people).[50] "Babu" had become a derogatory term associated with Bengali clerks and civil servants.[51] Yet it was the figure of the "bania"—or moneylender—that became the prevalent "enemy" of the interwar army.

In the army, "babu" and "bania" were shorthand for the class-based fear of Hindus. Muhammad Ismail Khan, a Muslim officer from the North-West Frontier Province, gave a typical explanation of this view. His military family feared Indianization because "the middle class Hindu families who are called the Banias" would "join the army with no inherent qualities of leadership." Compared to these unqualified "banias," Khan believed that Muslim applicants were inherently superior because they came from the "landowner classes" who possessed "the qualities of leadership." Their experience "running their agricultural estates" and "commanding their servants and their tenants" made them "better suited" for being officers than their Hindu counterparts. While Dinesh Chandra Misra had found Muslim men unjustifiably exalted in the army, Khan was certain that Hindu "banias" were the most unqualified.[52]

Institutional suspicion about moneylenders stemmed from older fears about soldiers' difficulties retaining the financial benefits of military service. First World War Commander-in-Chief General Creagh (1909–14) worried that the "Sturdy peasant proprietor class" faced economic difficulties during the war despite their expectation to secure small landholdings for their military service. So-called "moneylenders" and "private enemies" apparently took advantage of their families and property while they were overseas.[53] Blaming these amorphous groups sidestepped British culpability in sending these men away or failing to provide social and economic protection to their families. By the interwar period, not all British officers were so willing to overlook army complicity. Former Indian army officer and British fascist Francis Yeats-Brown recognized that the army created economic hardships for its soldiers.[54] Writing shortly before his death in 1944, Yeats-Brown identified moneylenders as one of the major causes of the 1857 uprising. He believed that prior to colonization, Hindu moneylenders charged high interest but there was "always the chance that the flames of some local affray would cause them—or at least their books—to disappear in smoke." With the advent of the East India Company, moneylenders' debts gained "all the power of the State behind them." This led soldiers to wonder, in Yeats-Brown's view, "Was it to be made a bondslave to a bania, the sepoy asked himself, that he served the British?"[55] For Yeats-Brown, the rebellion of 1857 was the result of economic exploitation. South Asian peasant soldiers suffered from the collaboration between Hindu moneylenders and the colonial state's bureaucracy. These ideas resonated in the economic turmoil and political uncertainty of the 1930s and 1940s.

It was not coincidental that a British fascist critiqued Indian moneylenders. Condemnations of moneylenders in India echoed fairly standard European antisemitic arguments during the interwar period. Some

South Asians even found antisemitism useful to explain political and economic life in India. F. K. Khan Durrani, who identified as "A Muslim missionary," wrote in 1929 that Jews were "prototypes of Hindus in Europe." He felt that "We Muslims are a race of workers. The Hindus are a race of capitalists and money-lenders." Muslims, he alleged, held "usury" to be unclean but this was "the chief source of the Hindu's wealth." Durrani believed that for Hindus and Muslims: "The cultural ideals and entire outlook on life are different. Until a re-adjustment is effected in these, unity is unthinkable."[56] Durrani believed that socialist, communist, Bolshevik, and labor activism proved the incompatibility of workers with "usurers and capitalists."[57] Muslim League leader and founding father of Pakistan Mohammad Ali Jinnah echoed these sentiments when he condemned "landlords and capitalists" when he encouraged Muslims to support the formation of Pakistan.[58] However, soldiers' service to Britain left them with limited political options. Many came from families of peasant laborers whom Durrani exalted. Embracing socialist or communist ideas would have cost them their jobs in the army. The glorification of Punjabi peasants and condemnation of Hindu moneylenders remained.

Class-based critiques of religious difference were never just examples of Hindu-Muslim antagonism. Indian Army officer Douglas Sidney Frederick Stacey was certain that Sikhs also "despised" Bengalis "as a non-martial race." They apparently saw Bengalis as "profiteers" and money-lenders.[59] When Lt. Colonel W. L. Farrow conducted educational exercises with a Sikh regiment, he learned that "the men had little or no knowledge of Indian leaders such as Nehru, Gandhi, Jinnah, etc, [*sic*] or the precise role they played." Whenever "city dwellers of Bombay, Delhi or Calcutta" were mentioned, soldiers dismissed them as "just another 'babu.'"[60] Imperial clichés about "babus" and "banias" circulated between British and South Asian soldiers, fueling army discourses about moneylenders, politicians, and businessmen frequently characterized as Hindu. Anxieties about religious difference were often rooted in economic-political concerns that the army actively encouraged.

Slurs against "moneylenders" over-exaggerated interwar soldiers' actual experiences of economic exploitation. M. L. Darling visited the Punjab province in the interwar period and noted that "the prosperity of the soldier family is one of the most striking features of the Punjab landscape."[61] An inquiry into the economic status of South Asian veterans by Roshan Lal Anand similarly indicated that soldiers and their families were doing well financially. Most borrowed money to host weddings, to contribute to religious celebrations, or to buy and build houses. They did not borrow money for subsistence or through the trickery of outsiders, despite military clichés. In fact, military training got many soldiers into the habit of using banks to manage their money. The Indian Army Pensioners' Cooperative Thrift and Savings Society, or "Fauji bank," established in 1925, made it possible for soldiers to protect their financial interests.[62] Darling estimated that 90% of banking families in Punjab had military connections.[63] One Rajput veteran in Kangra even became a moneylender himself.[64] If soldiers had at one time been the victims of the "bania," they were using banks and moneylending to increase their own access to wealth and prosperity. Army condemnation of the "bania" was at the very least outdated. Nonetheless, it created a convenient scapegoat for military elites who did not want to question their own affluence during a period of global economic decline.

Critiques of the bania enabled British officials to portray military service as an escape from poverty and protection against urban—and allegedly Hindu—economic exploitation. The interwar tendency to demonize parasitic capitalism as endemic among Jewish and Hindu actors replaced longer critiques of the imperial drain of wealth and agricultural resources from the subcontinent generally and the Punjab in particular. In fact, the army often let antisemitic rhetoric pass into army discourses.[65] The first IMA entrance exam after the declaration of war against Germany expected prospective cadets to summarize a selection from *Across the Frontiers* (1938) by Philip Gibbs. The passage began by condemning "The extreme anti-Semites among the National Socialists" who mistreat Jews for their "penetrating influence . . . in foreign newspapers and foreign democracies." Rather than condemning this conspiratorial view of the press and politics, Gibbs suggested that "There is something in that. The Jews are not without influence, and exercise it in a thousand ways." Gibbs's passage explained that the "Jewish problem is not easy." He lamented Jewish interwar migration into Europe and Palestine. Their movements, he believed, made the Arab population "hostile, sullen, and murderous" because they lost what had been their "land for a thousand years." Jewish migration also displeased Germans who, despite the rise of Nazism, were apparently "over half a million souls of a most vital section of civilized humanity." According to Gibbs, Germans now faced diminished opportunities in "the land where their ancestors had been settled for centuries." The excerpt closed with the ominous lines: "The Jews had no peace throughout their history. There is no peace for them now."[66] Indian men who trained to become officers during the Second World War paraphrased and summarized a passage that took for granted that Jews represented a political and economic danger to the world. This, along with pervasive anxieties about "banias," suggests that the army found easy parallels in the political extremism of the fascist far right.

FASCISM AND IMPERIALISM

In order to make sense of the antisemitic logic creeping into the interwar Indian Army it is useful to examine in greater detail the relationship between fascism and imperial militarism. The creation of the Central Legislative Assembly, the greater autonomy for provinces, and the slow introduction of elections in the 1920s and 1930s introduced democratic systems, as well as bitterly divisive politics, to India at a tenuous global political moment.[67] Some soldiers and civilians believed that these institutions were destined to fail and that India should embrace a radical new political order. By 1937, retired officer Francis Yeats-Brown argued that India needed an "enlightened autocracy" because "Parliaments can't get things done: they debate too long."[68] Democratic institutions, he reasoned, were too slow to introduce positive and lasting change. By contrast, he hoped that strong leaders, such as Adolf Hitler, could turn global chaos into control.[69] Military education and imperial experience sometimes encouraged army men to embrace militant paternalism, anti-liberalism, anti-nationalism, antisemitism, and anti-communism. These ideas proved to be a dangerous cocktail in an army and empire built on racial and religious difference.

Like Yeats-Brown, several British officers with imperial experience articulated fascist sympathies in the interwar period. In a *Times* article in

1939, Major General J. F. C. Fuller declared that "I am called a 'Fascist'" because he privileged "the nation before individual rights." He found no objection to the label "Fascist" as long as "British is placed before this."[70] In other forums he blamed Jews for creating a "conspiracy" of "Race interests" across the world by backing anti-colonial movements.[71] He declined a high-level appointment in India because he believed that controlling India required actions similar to General Dyer's at Amritsar.[72] Fuller's experience as a soldier in India at the height of the "Great Game" against Russia convinced him that Russia—then the Soviet Union—was a greater threat to India than Hitler's Germany.[73] Yeats-Brown, who served as an officer in the 17th Lancers before, during, and after the First World War, similarly encouraged Britain to put its faith in Hitler or else "a shocking cataclysm is inevitable."[74] Other active and former British officers, including Henry Hamilton Beamish and Lieutenant-Colonel Graham Seton Hutchison, espoused antisemitic and pro-Nazi views in the 1930s. According to historian Thomas Linehan, "the composite [British] fascist leader in 1935 was a widely travelled, extremely restless, public-school-educated, middle-class ex-army officer in his late thirties."[75] Military ideals of corporate-ness encouraged officers to place individual desires beneath national goals. The frustration of serving an empire that was teetering on the verge of collapse made some believe that only extreme programs of national rejuvenation, militarism, and racial supremacy could secure Britain's place in the world.

Fascism was attractive in some British military circles because of the uncertain future of the interwar empire. Despite reaching its greatest territorial extent after the First World War, British power buckled under the pressure of rebellions, revolutions, and wars of independence as far afield as Ireland and Egypt, as well as India. Antisemitism became a convenient way to explain away imperial decline. Some blamed India's Jewish Secretary of State Edwin Montagu for the Amritsar Massacre because he failed to crush anti-colonialism, thereby forcing General Dyer to take violent action.[76] Antisemitic discourses also absolved Britain from blame for dividing the Ottoman Empire and using violence to control League of Nations mandates. Some accused Zionism of being the exclusive cause of instability in Palestine and portrayed the League of Nations as a Jewish conspiracy.[77] Many developed an embarrassed sympathy for Muslims and a cynically defensive antisemitic posture.[78] British residents and military families, meanwhile, forgave British leaders for authoritarianism in India because they believed that it was necessary to prevent another 1857-style rebellion. Sporting and private clubs provided political and social isolation where military elites and white settlers could remain inward-looking. Even those landed Indian elites who attended colonial schools, went on hunting trips, or participated in lavish social gatherings and sports with Britons tended to embrace similar ethics of conservative militancy.[79] Many shared colonial officials' distrust for urban politicians who challenged rural, landed interests. Few protested when All-India Radio head Lionel Fielden blocked Indian nationalist broadcasts but allowed fascist broadcasts to pass easily.[80] By the Second World War, Clive Branson, a communist soldier, observed that Hitler's *Mein Kampf* was available at every bookseller in India.[81] British officials and soldiers, therefore, found it easy to welcome fascist ideas into their colonial homes and outposts.

Theories of racial difference provided one of the strongest links between imperialism and fascism.[82] Retired officer and fascist Francis Yeats-Brown is a good indication of this trend. He became a best-selling author through the publication of his memoir, *The Lives of a Bengal Lancer* (1930), which inspired an Oscar-nominated film (1935) of the same name. He served briefly as editor of the *Spectator*, and was well-connected in elite circles in Britain. He also traveled widely and published numerous works about yoga that carried debts to the Indian Army's entangled theories of race and religion.[83] In one of his unpublished notebooks from a lecture by American yogi P. A. Bernard in 1924, he wrote that "Vedas are the scriptures of our own white Aryan race" and "to pull on pure energy requires a pure white or Aryan blood."[84] Although he described "white" and "Aryan" as interchangeable, his experience in India gave him a slightly more complex understanding of the term. In one notebook, he referred to Hindu men in 1930 as "Aryan brother[s]."[85] This echoed groups like the Hindu Mahasabha and the theosophical society, which defined "Hindus" as Aryans.[86] Some Indian soldiers agreed. IMA graduate Dinesh Chandra Misra described his community as a result of when "Aryans came to our country." He maintained that "the initial teaching of war was done by the Brahmans. My community."[87] Yeats-Brown fully embraced this narrative of martial Aryanism as well. In *Martial India* he described Garhwalis as having "racial affinities . . . with the Aryan race."[88] He believed that Marathas were a "master-race" because they once ruled half of India. The army's tendency to celebrate the martial races as natural and hereditary warriors fit seamlessly with racial theories of Aryanism—and martial Hinduism—gaining international political influence.

By the end of the 1930s, Yeats-Brown's view of Indian men as "Aryan brothers" may have faded when he wrote to his mostly white European and American audience in *Yoga Explained* that yoga was part of "our racial inheritance." Yoga, he believed, stemmed from "our family relationship with the first explorers of the Aryan Path." These explorers, he believed, were "blond invaders" who "were a beef-eating, beer-drinking, horse-loving, pastoral, and poetic folk."[89] Yeats-Brown recognized Indian men as "Aryan brothers" but his beef-eating Aryans sounded a lot more like India's British rulers than the Hindu Brahmans he had initially praised. His ultimate goal in practicing the yogic wisdom of "Aryans" was to reverse the "stagnation that has been the death of many races in the past."[90] He saw yoga as a key to "racial" regeneration in Europe and the United States, echoing Hindu nationalists in India. His celebration of elite Aryan warriors made sense within a context of both Hindu nationalist and martial race discourses.

Yeats-Brown's depictions of martial Hindus hints at the contradictions of imperial fascist sympathies. He blamed banias for the 1857 uprising but he also used the logic of the "martial races" to praise other Hindus, including Brahmans. He believed that Brahmans had "preserved their racial type" through social exclusivity and selective reproduction. He was certain that "it is to the good of the world that strong racial types should flourish."[91] England, he maintained, should follow a similar model by preventing Englishmen and women from becoming "adulterated" in their "blood" with "alien strains."[92] In *Martial India* he alleged that "the Hindu system is based on realities; the thoroughbred is a good horse, and the Rajput is a good soldier for reasons that have been tested and proved through centuries." While "Weaklings die in North India; the survivors are a fine stock."[93] His admiration for Hindu soldiers was *because of*, rather than despite, the exclusivity that early twentieth-century military officials condemned. His attitudes also demonstrated how quickly things had changed: while serving in 1909 India he had characterized Hindus as "a desperate race: accepting neither the iron bonds of Brahminism nor the higher ethics of the Arya Samaj."[94] By the 1930s, when Hindu nationalists encouraged a more militant and racialized interpretation of religious difference, they had finally become ideal martial men in Yeats-Brown's eyes. He believed that if India was going to thrive, it needed to embrace rather than reject racial and religious exclusivity.

Yeats-Brown's admiration for martial Hindus led him to believe that the army could and should be the foundation of political and economic reform in India. He hoped that "scientific selection" could be extended to "every walk of life" so that "the best men hold the best positions in politics."[95] He wondered "What might not be done in India if her fighting men, after their immediate task had been accomplished, were switched to the battle for the regeneration of the countryside?" He urged politicians in Britain and India to "Forget the financiers and lawyers and the toadies who haunt your Ministries in Delhi." Instead, they should support "the fighting peasant with better cattle, better seed, more credit; he is the hope of the future and the salt of the Indian earth." For Yeats-Brown, preserving imperial rule, and bringing India to its fullest potential, meant investing in the men of the Indian Army. He called this world a "vision of Utopia."[96] But this utopia was run by very specific men. His distrust of the "financiers and lawyers" echoed the army's class-based demonization of Hindus, betraying his utopian fantasies. Yet British military men, like Yeats-Brown, often saw themselves as the protectors of their peasant allies against elite, moneylending, and politically savvy opponents. Military education, political isolation from nationalism, and limited economic opportunities allowed some South Asian soldiers to believe that this might, in fact, be true.

INTERRACIAL INTIMACIES AND FASCISM

Yeats-Brown's education, military experience, and class position made him an influential author in and beyond India. His works were so readily available that working-class British soldier H. H. Somerfield called him "one of my favourite authors" after four years of service in India. Somerfield served in India from 1935 to 1940 and was a voracious reader. He consumed works by authors such as George MacMunn who wrote a classic text on the "Martial Races of India."[97] Yet it was not until he read Yeats-Brown's overtly fascist *European Jungle* in 1939 that he documented his political views. *European Jungle* condemned pacifism, characterized Russia as "unholy," took painstaking efforts to demonize Jews, and exalted Hitler's Germany. The book left Somerfield certain that Yeats-Brown's "temperament and view of European politics is mainly the same as mine."[98] Fascism, in some cases, was able to cross class lines among men-of-arms. Somerfield's life in India reveals that he did not merely absorb the ideas of a retired Indian Army officer. His rare working-class diary suggests that his repeated social encounters with South Asian men did as much to shape his political worldview as his readings of British military authors. British soldiers were not alone in finding fascism a logical complement to their military service.

In the years after his arrival in India in 1935, Somerfield immersed himself in the radically changed world of the 1930s Indian Army. He visited cinemas with soldiers Abdul Rehman and Sikh Havildar Pritan Singh while dressing in Indian clothing and darkening his skin.[99] He arranged for a "Chevrolet" for a night out of drinking and dancing alongside sixteen Indian soldiers who crammed into the car with him.[100] Soldiers Sher Singh and Sohan Singh joined him for hunting expeditions. Pakhar Singh accompanied him when he disguised himself in Indian clothing to attend a fair.[101] Somerfield visited a saloon with dancing girls alongside Naik Fagir Singh and Ujagir Singh who bragged (lied) that Somerfield was a captain with a large salary.[102] A private room above the post office became a drunken hideaway for Somerfield and soldiers such as Karnoul Singh and Kishan Singh. Hindu café owner Brij Lall gave Somerfield gifts of chocolate and advice about sodomy. They occasionally shared a bed.[103] He even found "kindred spirits" in two other British soldiers named Eric Hagill and Skellon; the latter helped him to rent the room above the post office.[104] Somerfield had seemingly endless sources of recreation, including modern conveniences such as cars and cinemas.

He had no shortage of social companions that included Hindu, Sikh, and Muslim men. In some ways this reflected the slow integration of spaces formerly shrouded in strict racial hierarchy. Yet this life of ease and plenty betrayed the anger and resentment that thrived within him.

Despite—or perhaps emboldened by—his interracial sociability, Somerfield became fervent in his admiration of fascism. He condemned Indian nationalism, stating that "I should like to see a really strong government in this country, which would send all these stupid agitators to jail." He believed that England, too, required "a rigid Dictatorship," which he called "the best form of government." He argued that politics "should be confined to an individual view to avoid different policies."[105] Compared to his clean and comfortable life of recreation and personal servants in the military cantonment, the "stupid agitators" in India were a source of annoyance and distraction. He worried about democracy's ability to defeat communism, which he found to be "a far greater danger than Fascism." Fascism, in his view, "aims at healthy nationalism."[106] Even though Somerfield had not lived in England for several years, he declared in 1939 that "some of us real English people stand to lose more by a British victory than a German one." He was certain that Germans would be sympathetic to "Anglo-Saxon people who are akin to them, but the people with hooked noses would probably suffer." He condemned "Jewish propaganda" in cinemas.[107] Somerfield's overt antisemitism was both an adoption of European ideas and a reflection of the colonial racism sanctioned within the Indian Army. His worldview and social encounters reveal how tenuous the army's vision of racial and interfaith harmony could be.

Despite his embrace of strong-man militarism, Somerfield detested many aspects of military life in India. He sometimes had difficulty evading the judgmental glances of his fellow British soldiers who scrutinized his interracial sociability. This may have contributed to his disdain for being in cinemas with "military audiences" whom he found obnoxious.[108] It may have also led him to become the "pet hate" of the commanding officer.[109] Worse still, he was frequently in and out of the hospital and lamented the lack of brothels.[110] His dissatisfaction inspired him to contemplate deserting in early 1938. He coded this desire in his diary in devanagari script (देसुरशन). By June, fellow signalman Sultan Mohammad gave him a reason to stay.[111] He explained that Sultan Mohammad "showed his goodwill towards me in various *practical* ways," which led to "jealousy from the others."[112] To escape this jealousy, Sultan Mohammed visited him on two occasions and "were it not for evil tongues in the lines we could be proper friends."[113] After meeting Sultan Mohammad, his outlook on life in India improved.

It was during his companionship with Sultan Mohammad from 1938 to 1940 that Somerfield made two radical declarations: he attempted to get circumcised and become a Muslim and also articulated his fascist views most fervently. His intimate relationship with a Punjabi Muslim soldier no doubt shaped his worldview in unexpected ways. Their attachment, at least from Somerfield's perspective, was undoubtedly intense in nature. Despite jealousies and "evil tongues" Somerfield believed that they had developed a close relationship. He explained his disappointment that he was going to be transferred to Lucknow because "Sultan Mohd, whom I had been meeting, will also be puzzled at my sudden absence." He hoped that "Fate will arrange a re-union for us, and also the numerous other I.O.R.'s [Indian Other Ranks] for whom I have a genuine liking."[114] He wondered frantically "whether he is my दोस्त [friend] in his दिल [heart]." He longed for them to get leave and "spend that time together." He worried that when he planned to visit Meerut, Sultan "has given no rendezvous where we could meet."[115] He was relieved to receive a letter suggesting that "he is all for the Somerfield Sahib." Somerfield continued to refer to Sultan Mohammad in his journal as *"mera piyare dost"* (my beloved/dear friend) in 1940.[116] In describing their relationship, he may have used devanagari words to affect a communion with Sultan Mohammed, conveying their closeness in words that they both could understand. Yet the only other instance in which Somerfield used devanagari in his diaries was to hide his plans for desertion, signaling that he used it as a code to avoid detection. After conversations with a minister and fellow British soldiers, Somerfield decided not to get circumcised and become a Muslim. But he did maintain his fascist views and his close affection for his *"piyare dost."*

Although Somerfield was an exceptional soldier, his frequent encounters with South Asian men sheds light on the paradoxes of life in colonial India. For example, his interracial encounters did little to upend his fascist worldview. Instead, they hint at the successes and failures of social engineering in the army. His only explicitly named Hindu companion was Brij Lall—a café owner rather than a soldier. Yet even this encounter could have nudged him toward his radical outlook. Shortly after visiting Brij Lall, with whom he discussed "sodomy" and texts such as the *Ramayana*, Somerfield went to an out-of-bounds bazaar and purchased a picture of the birth of Krishna.[117] Many Hindu nationalists followed Swami Vivekananda in exalting Krishna as a Hindu warrior with immense physical strength.[118] This was consistent with the army's emphasis on martial masculinity and the popularity of Hindu nationalist militancy in the 1920s and 1930s. Meanwhile, he argued that a German victory would be preferable because "if Germany took over our Empire there would be no salaaming of Indian officers."[119] Somerfield resented the upwardly mobile, well-educated Indian officers increasingly making their way into the army. Somerfield was, after all, a working-class soldier—the type of man British officials most worried would feel alienated by taking orders from Indian officers. His working-class origins and irregular education prevented him from training at Sandhurst. Indian officers, therefore, threatened his position of racial superiority. Low-ranking Indian soldiers did not.

Despite being a working-class man, racial and economic privilege were inherent in every aspect of Somerfield's social life. When Brij Lall, Kishan Singh, and Sultan Mohammad partook in Somerfield's charades of pretending to be an officer or an Indian soldier, they took money to help him find clothes or rent rooms. They also stayed near him to gain the attention of dancing girls and piled into his rented Chevrolet. Somerfield was, at least in part, buying the companionship of men whose pay and social standing was dramatically lower than his own. He even included cryptic references to enclosing an "envelope as usual" whenever he made plans to meet up with Sultan Mohammad, perhaps indicating that their "rendezvous" included economic exchange.[120] Somerfield's many Sikh and Muslim companions may have enjoyed the novelty—and opportunity— of keeping close association with a British soldier. Somerfield admitted this was true when he traveled throughout northwestern India. He admitted that "Being in the Army seems a definite asset in this region, even the coolies benefitting from my association."[121] Whenever "local lads" heard that his party was coming, "our resting place become the popular rendezvous for miles around." However, his "stock went down" when they found out that he was not an officer.[122] He still had many conversations including one with an "ambitious sepoy." Another young man with "military ambitions" saw Somerfield's presence as an opportunity to gain employment.[123] Merely being British in India gave men—including working-class men—the opportunity to enjoy elite status and make connections with South Asians that were otherwise impossible. Indianization threatened to challenge whiteness as an automatic ticket to privilege and prestige. This made Somerfield contemplate the value of an even more racialized assertion of European imperialism in fascism.

The recruiting patterns and institutional biases of the Indian Army meant that, despite Somerfield's interracial encounters, other hierarchies were still carefully intact. It was no accident that he most frequently spent his time with Punjabi Muslim and Sikh men. The Signal Corps explicitly declared its desire for "non-Brahmans" in its Urdu recruiting posters.[124] Another member of the 1930s Signals in India, Patrick Miles Pennington Hobson, also remembered being "very fond of Muslims and the Muslim belief" because it was "more akin to the Christian religion." Hinduism, by contrast, seemed to him "very foreign to a sort of Christian outlook." He echoed the anti-Hindu biases of army recruiting, stating that Madrassis were "babus" while Bengalis were suitable as "merchants but not army." He believed that Hindu politicians such as Gandhi made an "undue fuss." He condemned the Indian National Congress as a "Hindu organization" that was "not mixed up with the warrior caste so much."[125] Hobson felt more sympathetic to the Muslim League, by contrast, because he saw it as "more in tune with your own soldiers and their outlook." This suggests that both British and South Asian soldiers internalized army biases about nationalist politics. It was commonplace to exalt the Punjabi peasant laborer—and Muslim political organizations—while condemning Hindus and "Hindu" organizations as effeminate, upstart, and nonmartial. Indianization and racial integration made possible moments of interracial sociability unthinkable in prewar India (Figure 10). Yet this interracial intimacy also gave Punjabi Muslims like Sultan Mohammad

FIGURE 10 Unlabeled photograph of British and Indian men from the collection of H. H. Somerfield. The attire is consistent with 1930s India. Somerfield is likely the second man from the left. *Source*: H. H. Somerfield Papers, Documents, 10530, Imperial War Museum. Reprinted with permission.

and British working-class soldiers like Somerfield the chance to realize and reinforce their shared frustrations and biases.

SIKHS AND MUSLIMS IN THE FASCIST UTOPIA

Somerfield's repeated and meaningful encounters with Sikh men like Kishan Singh and Muslims like Sultan Mohammad provided only an illusion of interracial and interfaith solidarity. His Sikh, Hindu, and Muslim companions were rarely in the same place at the same time. This was the true consequence of interwar efforts to forge interfaith unity. Recruited men orbited around British soldiers' privileged status at the center of a military-imperial universe. South Asian officers such as Dinesh Chandra Misra and Mohammad Ismail Khan, by contrast, remembered slow-burning hostilities and resentments. Misra condemned the Muslim soldiers on his interview board and Khan challenged the right of "banias" to become officers. An Indian Catholic officer, Stanley Menezes, similarly condemned Sikh soldiers for following the army's martial race ethos by "trying to say . . . that they were a separate race."[126] Hindus, Sikhs, Christians, and Muslims increasingly competed for colonial favors with one another. This contributed to greater scrutiny between fellow army men. British soldiers and officers, by contrast, got to take the seemingly neutral position of paternally bestowing ranks and honors to the prize-winners. The result was greater tension and hostility between those competing for martial prestige.

In the 1930s two disputes about holy sites revealed the growing tensions between Sikh and Muslim visions of martial supremacy. In 1930, individuals inside of Delhi's Sisganj *gurdwara* (Sikh temple) allegedly threw objects at British officials. Troops and police entered and fired inside the holy place, dragging individuals into the streets.[127] This inspired an armed band (Akali *jatha*) of Sikhs to march to Peshawar. According to one report, "Sikh soldiers" and "other classes of Indian troops recruited in the Punjab" grew incensed by the disgrace.[128] However, civilians spurned soldiers' efforts to participate in the protests. A group of Sikh women occupied the Sisganj *gurdwara* and refused entry to anyone wearing foreign cloth, including Sikh soldiers in uniform. Meanwhile, activists outside of the Sisganj *gurdwara* distributed leaflets for the secular

Hindustan Socialist Republican Army.[129] The firing, they contended, demonstrated the excesses and evils of imperial militarism. They cast soldiers as imperial collaborators despite soldiers' important roles in the Akali activism of the 1920s.[130] Even though soldiers were infuriated by the firing, 1930s civilians rejected the possibility that peacetime soldiers could effectively criticize imperial rule.

The attack on the Sisganj *gurdwara* did not match the divisiveness of events surrounding Shahid Ganj in Lahore. East India Company officials gave the property to Sikh custodians in 1835 and British officials confirmed Sikh management in 1927.[131] The land was transferred to the Sikh Shiromani Gurdwara Parbandhak Committee (SGPC) in 1935. For many Sikhs this was a natural culmination of Sikh rights to a disputed property. However, both an active mosque and a Sikh *gurdwara* stood on the grounds. The SGPC proposed to destroy the mosque and build a wall. Sikh men occupied the grounds and armed themselves against backlash from local Muslims. The Punjab government feared violent escalation and sent the army, which opened fire on Muslims when they arrived. The Shahid Ganj mosque became a focus of renewed Punjabi Muslim anticolonialism in the 1930s. Sympathetic allies included the northwestern Muslim rebel the Faqir of Ipi, who participated in frequent campaigns against the Indian Army.[132] This deepened existing tensions in the Punjab province. The Lahore district magistrate prohibited Sikhs from carrying Sikh swords, or *kirpans*, in 1935. As a retort, the SGPC declared December 5th "Kirpan Day."[133] One Sikh protested that this ban enabled Muslim violence against Sikhs.[134] The dominant narrative of the conflict, therefore, shifted from a critique of imperial policy and violence to a struggle between Sikhs and Muslims. One Akali leader even described the conflict as part of perennial Sikh-Muslim competition. He believed that quarrels for possession of the Punjab province were inevitable as long as Sikhs lived in a province that the Muslim majority attempted to rule.[135] By the 1930s, Akali activists focused their energies on the Muslim-majority population in Punjab rather than the British-appointed "slow converts" that they opposed in the 1920s. This meant emphasizing precolonial Sikh spiritual heritage defined in opposition to the Mughal, rather than the British, Empire.[136]

During the agitation around Shahid Ganj, Sikh and Muslim activists asserted their superior militancy. According to Sikh author Ganda Singh writing in the *Civil and Military Gazette,* two hundred "irresponsible [Muslim] youths" marched in military formation supported by a crowd of three thousand. In response, an equal number of Akalis defended "Sikh rights against a show of force." Even more tellingly, Muslim activists wielded spiritual swords of their own. In addition to using stones and lathis against the police, they were "carrying spades"—or *belcha*—which, like *kirpans*, had power as a sacred symbol.[137] The Prophet had used *belcha* at Uhud to defend against the people of Mecca.[138] According to one Sikh writer in 1936, British authorities allowed seven thousand young Muslim men to march through Lahore with *belcha*.[139] Shaikh Muhammad Sadiq, a Muslim man from Amritsar City, predicted this level of escalation and competition during the *kirpan* debates. He had wondered, "Is it necessary that the Musalmans also should say that their religion enjoins them to wear talwars [long curved swords] before the Government would allow it in the case of Musalmans?"[140] His complaint had led the Legislative Assembly to grant rights to swords to all wealthy and influential men of the Punjab province in 1926. When Punjabi Muslims and Sikhs viewed one another as potential enemies rather than potential allies, the demand for spiritual swords increased.

The frequency of *belcha* in riots and fights with police was a result of yet another militant youth movement gaining traction in India.[141] The Khaksar (humble) developed under the leadership of Inayatullah Khan, or al-Mashriqi ("the Orientalist" or "the Sage"). Al-Mashriqi had studied at Cambridge and advocated a social Darwinist version of Islam. He believed, like Akali reformers, Hindu nationalists, British army officers, and fascist youth organizations, that military discipline should be a centerpiece of religious reform and revival. He developed the paramilitary Khaksars in 1931 when he retired from government service. Khaksars marched in parades and military formations and mocked *maulvis* (Muslim religious scholars) and ulema for having never handled swords.[142] They wore khaki uniforms, carried rifles in parades, adhered to strict military discipline, and carried *belcha*. Some even marched to Friday prayers in military formations, not unlike the British and South Asian cadets who marched to church, temple, and *gurdwara*. The growing tensions between Sikhs and Muslims were not simply the result of inevitable religious antagonism or recent legislative and political competition from the mid-1930s. It reflected the glorification of religious militarism in and beyond the Indian Army.

The rise of the Khaksar signaled the contested state of Muslim identities in interwar India. Hindu activists embraced militancy to compete with the "martial classes" but the Khaksars worried that South Asian Muslims had forgotten their own martial heritage. The movement peaked between 1935 and 1940, when debates about martial masculinity within and beyond the army were at their height. Their anxiety was rooted, in part, in the growing affiliation of Muslims with imperial rule. The Government of India set aside 50% of its official appointments for Muslims after 1932.[143] Hindu nationalists and Muslim reformers attacked a range of Muslim stereotypes in their efforts to reform, redefine, or undermine Muslim identities. Frequent targets of attack included wealthy landowning Muslim politicians, "dandy" Muslim cosmopolitans, and spiritual leaders such as ulema, *maulvis,* and mullahs regarded as "ignorant" by Muslim elites.[144] The homophobic tendencies of interwar militarism and nationalism would have condemned soldiers such as Sultan Mohammad as "collaborators" who had unhealthy attachments to British men.[145] Civilian-led militarism and public violence reasserted Muslim masculinity outside of colonial institutions.

Khaksar ascendancy reveals the tenuous position of South Asian Muslims in both the imperial state and anti-colonial movements. Hindu nationalists widely criticized Muslims' preferential recruitment while Sikhs undermined their dominant position in the Punjab province. Some Muslims looked to the northwest for the salvation of the community. Dr. Mohammad Iqbal famously declared in 1930 that the goal and destiny of Indian Muslims should be to create a state in India's northwest borderlands. A "Muslim Zion" in northwestern India gradually became the official position of many Indian Muslim politicians by the end of the decade.[146] This happened at a time when northwestern India was subject to considerable imperial violence. An invasion of Peshawar district in 1930 by Afridis revived fears of borderland activism. Abdul Ghaffar Khan became known as the "Frontier Gandhi" for his advocacy of nonviolence and support of social and rural reform. Ghaffar emerged from prison in 1931 and gained a following of thirty thousand Pathan nationalists known as the "Red Shirts." In turn, the years 1932 and 1933 witnessed some of the most brutal military and police actions along India's northwestern borders.[147] Making northwestern India into a Muslim homeland did more than challenge colonialism and Hindu-led nationalism. It proposed to extend the dominance of landed military rulers into areas of rebellion. Muslim men with experience living and serving in the army to "pacify" this region increasingly made their own plans to rule and tame it. Military service continued to divide communities internally, turn them against their perceived competitors, and convince soldiers and civilians that violence was a necessary arm of politics.

IMA graduate Muhammad Ismail Khan is a good example of the fraught nature of Muslim military identities on the eve of the Second World War. Originally from Peshawar in northwestern India, he found his calling in the Indian Army after failing to earn a position as an imperial policeman. He was a Pathan from a police and military family who followed his brother into the army. He trained at the IMA in 1939.[148] Like many British officers, he was attracted to "the romance attached" to military service based on what he had read about the First World War and northwestern border wars. He learned these lessons while studying at Islamia College in Peshawar, which was founded to educate Pathans. Looking back on the 1930s, he believed that there was "not much resentment" against the British even though "all of us wanted to be free one day." He believed that there was "sincerity" to British attempts to Indianize the army "from the very beginning." However, he remembered that anti-colonial Pathan activist Ghaffar Khan had "tremendous support" in his town. He was careful to distance himself from this admiration by claiming that Ghaffar was "violent and militant," despite his reputation as "Frontier Gandhi."[149]

Khan's condemnation of Ghaffar helped to rationalize his memories of colonial violence close to home. British officials opened fire on Ghaffar's Red Shirts in Peshawar and then laid the wounded in front of Khan's home. This placed his family in a politically contentious position. When his family doctor helped the wounded Red Shirts, his police officer father warned the doctor to "watch out." The doctor later was arrested.[150] This incident did not prevent Khan from seeing the army as a desirable career path. By the 1930s, middle-class and elite Muslims could benefit from connections to imperial rule through education and military service. As a member of a borderland community, however, Khan lived with the daily threat of violence in and near his town. He had internalized the idea that the reason for this violence was the misguided actions of his friends and neighbors. One of his few avenues of safety and security was imperial service. Having done so, Khan earned privileges not extended to those who endured the punishments, rather than beneficence, of imperial rule.

Even though Muhammad Ismail Khan earned a position at the IMA, the recruitment of Pathans and Afridis remained controversial throughout the 1930s. Some British officials proposed recruiting local communities into an irregular "frontier corps" to pacify the region with military force. This would, according to one official, keep "the tribesmen out of mischief" and provide additional defense in case of a Russian (USSR) attack against Afghanistan. Others maintained that such recruitment would open the ranks to unsuitable agitators.[151] Until 1940, the army halted borderland recruitment, owing to the fact that "men who received training in the Indian Army went back to their homes and used the training and our tactics against us in tribal warfare on the Frontier."[152] The provision to set aside 50% of government positions for Muslims therefore mostly benefited those groups—such as Punjabi Muslims—already enjoying privileged imperial status. Meanwhile, most of the Indian officers trained at Sandhurst or the IMA learned their military profession and earned honors in the northwestern campaigns of the 1930s.[153] In so doing, they inherited the Indian Army's desire to "pacify" borders with violent force. They believed that violence could check ideological differences or "civilize" the "untamed"—even near their own homes. Those who had not embraced the army's narratives of democracy, imperial upward mobility, and liberalization would be categorized as "tribes," "fanatics," or communists. Living in or near an imperial borderland limited the choices of soldiers and civilians alike.

Martial brotherhoods of arms became more exclusive in the era of the army's racial integration and India's tepid extension of imperial democracy. The divisions within communities, as well as those between different communities, grew more strained with the intensification of martial activism in the 1930s. A common ground between colonial and anti-colonial activists was faith in militant masculinity to achieve their goals and forge a new world order. This meant that communities that had fought side by side in the Indian Army for decades instead turned against one another in competition for political or economic opportunity. Many convinced themselves that religious and economic animosity was perennial and natural, rather than the result of recent tensions and failures.

MEMORIES OF THE RAJ
Despite the contentious state of nationalist politics and the dire economic conditions of the depression, many soldiers remembered 1930s army life in India as calm and placid. Mohammad Ismail Khan recalled "no resentment" toward the British even though "all of us wanted to be free one day." He noted that there were a few British "diehard types" who despised Indianization but he nonetheless characterized his training at the IMA as "perfect."[154] Kuldip Singh Bajwa agreed that racist behavior in 1930s British India was not the norm; some of his best friends were British cadets who traveled to his home on holidays.[155] Edwin John Watson, a teacher at the Royal Indian Military College, remembered similarly that men of different faiths messed together, lived together, and "got on extremely well." When an interviewer with the Imperial War Museum asked if there was ever religious tension, he responded, "None. None at all. Never."[156] This rosy view of military life reflected some of the realities of racial integration and interfaith collaboration. It was also part of a hazy memory of the British Raj. These men left their testimonies decades after the Second World War and the chaos, heartbreak, and turmoil of partition. The hope and enthusiasm of forming new nation states or breaking free from imperial rule had been eclipsed by the disillusionment of war, imperial decline, traumatic migration, and national division. Memories of life in the Indian Army seemed peaceful by comparison.

Toco Moses Stevens offers a slightly more telling account of army life in the 1930s. Like the others, he believed that there was no general hostility between soldiers and civilians. He described the relationship between

Britons and South Asians as "very good" because most South Asian soldiers behaved like "they were gentlemen." This meant that they had the respect to refer to British privates as sahib.[157] Peace and stability under the British Raj meant knowing one's place. Those who enjoyed imperial privilege had to maintain strict codes of conduct to retain it.

The Indian Army boasted a degree of racial inclusivity as *certain* Hindu, Sikh, and Muslim soldiers entered side by side into recreational, educational, and official spaces with their British counterparts. Yet this inclusivity was built on a sharply maintained foundation of religious, racial, and economic difference. Soldiers lived in clean and controlled spaces without feeling bothered by the "religious tensions" and "anti-colonial violence" about which they read in the paper. Such disturbances seemed like fantasies of an over-eager press or blunders of civilian government. If the army could successfully recruit Hindu, Muslim, and Sikh soldiers, they wondered, then why did the Indian government repeatedly fail to manage such divisions? The democratization of Indian politics after 1935, coupled with renewed rebellions in the northwest, appeared to be signs of imperial weakness and a call to arms for more radical solutions. Liberalism and secularism struggled to remedy the inequalities, hierarchies, and paradoxes of colonial rule. By contrast, the army's ability to provide employment, care, community, and welfare for certain South Asians made some believe that military discipline, anti-liberal nationalism, religious hierarchies, and military education would secure a stable future for both individuals and the nation. Some envisioned a future in which soldiers could rule the world. Nostalgia for this period reflects its novelty and fragility. In reality, the calm placidity of military life depended on the violent antagonisms that thrived outside the gates.

While soldiers struggled to carve out a place for themselves in India's rapidly changing political order, colonial officials failed to adapt to or understand the many innovative strategies of resistance and rebellion that characterized the period. Civil servant Sir William Barton, for example, could not fathom how it was possible that so many stereotypically martial Pathans supported Mohandas Gandhi, whom he described as "Faqir of the Hindu Bania caste." This slur made Gandhi simultaneously into two of the primary perceived threats to the imperial state in the 1930s—a

Muslim ascetic (faqir) and a Hindu bania.[158] The lived realities of military campaigns, economic hardship, and imperial rule meant that alliances and allegiances were always shifting and unstable. A former ally could become a friend, and a friend, a competitor. British efforts to fix soldiers as "martial races" were inherently flawed as soldiers' identities—or modes of expressing their identities—changed over time according to the varied needs of their families, communities, friends, lovers, allies, and enemies.

The army's "fascist utopia" proved to be an island of privilege in which the few gained at the expense of the many. It also, paradoxically, made many soldiers fear that they would be left behind in a world that was changing rapidly. They searched for new utopias as the dream—or nightmare—of Indian empire was fading. Most believed that the future needed to be seized by force. In the 1930s, colonial and anti-colonial actors agreed that violence and militarism were necessary to achieve political aims. Few could agree, however, on when, how, and against whom this violence should be implemented. Hindus, Muslims, Sikhs, and Christians all wrestled with how to participate in an increasingly divided world. The violence on the horizon of the 1940s was not the result of inevitable religious fissures. Instead, it was rooted in the militarization of economic, political, and cultural differences. Many British and South Asian soldiers and civilians embraced ideologies of exclusion and militant violence to achieve political ends. Cosmopolitan brotherhood, militant masculinity, and martial visions of unity became comforting sources of stability in an uncertain age.

CONCLUSION

IN NOVEMBER 2018, nearly one hundred years after the 1918 armistice, someone vandalized a statue of a Sikh soldier in Birmingham (UK).[1] Many in Britain, the United States, and the post-colonial world have criticized statues that commemorate colonialism, racial segregation, or white supremacy.[2] However, this statue was not a decades- or centuries-old relic from another era. It was unveiled by mostly non-white Sikh members of a British *gurdwara* in the same year that it was vandalized. The statue, much like the Sikh reenactors at the Royal Pavilion in Brighton, commemorated colonial subjects who fought and died in the First World War. The desire to remember their contributions comes at a time when non-white Britons face intense racial discrimination as "outsiders" in the British nation, revitalized by debates about Britain's exit from the European Union (Brexit). The vandalization, meanwhile, demonstrates how the colonial past, and the legacies of the First World War, remain sources of debate and controversy. The vandal struck through the words "Great War," adding instead "sepoys no more" and "1 jarnoil" in black letters. Multiple leading news outlets speculated that "1 jarnoil" referred to Jarnail Singh Bhindranwale, who was killed in 1984 by Government of India forces. He had occupied the Amritsar Golden Temple to protest Indian Prime Minister Indira Gandhi's anti-Sikh policies.[3] "Sepoys no more," by contrast, echoes critiques and questions of commemoration put forward by many First World War scholars: Is it possible to remember colonial soldiers without commemorating colonialism? Do these monuments create racialized expectations for non-white Britons to enlist in military service to claim citizenship and avoid harassment? Worse still, do they inadvertently support cultures of contemporary war-mongering in places—like Iraq and Afghanistan—formerly colonized or subject to continued international military violence and invasion?[4] These acts of commemoration—and "decommemoration" through vandalism—suggest that symbols of South Asian militarism remain just as controversial as they were during colonial rule.

Officers of the Indian Army, not unlike some contemporary politicians, hoped that hierarchical identities would differentiate the loyal from the disloyal, the initiate from the outcast(e). However, imperial categories failed to reflect the diversity and complexity of life under colonialism. Sikhs were never unquestioningly loyal. Nepali soldiers were more than proud and hearty fighters. Indian Hindus were not too "prejudiced" to serve. Muslims were more often loyal soldiers than "fanatics" waiting to cast out the infidels. Britons, too, were not a uniform mass of unquestioning imperial Christianity. The army's religiously tinged martial masculinity created unrealistic expectations for all soldiers. These reflected the values of the imperial, military, economic, and political powers that enforced them. Military rituals encouraged soldiers to mobilize their precolonial heritage to become strong, militant warriors ready to carry out acts of violence on behalf of the colonial state. Anti-colonial and nationalist actors adopted or reformed these codes and signifiers to undermine the moral authority of imperialism and reclaim precolonial heritage. Cultures of militarism ultimately encouraged further violence from soldiers and civilians alike. Military identities also became pathways for exclusion, fragmentation, and violence in post-colonial nations.

There was no inevitable outcome of "religious violence" or "communal antagonism" in the late colonial period. Hindus, Sikhs, Christians, and Muslims created anti-colonial alliances with one another before, during, and after the First World War. Competition between the "martial races," and the adoption of martial race logics in civilian life in the late days of empire were dramatic reversals from prewar and postwar interfaith alliances. It had not been long since British officials lamented the manufacture and sale of Sikh *kirpans* by Muslim proprietors or the circulation of Ghadar pamphlets between Sikh, Hindu, and Muslim men. Many of the widely recruited Muslims, Hindus, and Sikhs of the Indian Army shared common identities as Punjabis and had lived and served side by side as soldiers for decades. They should have been the simultaneous beneficiaries of army recruitment and educational opportunities. The army's ritualistic codes of belonging, however, deemphasized regional and linguistic commonalities and drew further attention to religious differences.

Racial integration could make differences between Indian communities more, rather than less, pronounced. For example, in 1908 Francis Yeats-Brown worried that he had "spoilt Khushal Khan by making too much of a friend of him." He sent this soldier, working as his bearer, "back to the lines" to prevent their "friendship" from affecting military discipline.[5] By the early 1920s, R. A. L. Moysey's close associations with Pathan soldiers led military and police officials to suspect disloyalty. In the 1930s, H. H. Somerfield, Sultan Mohammad, and countless other British and South Asian soldiers socialized publicly and had sex in military spaces.[6] The relative degree of cooperation and intimacy between British and South Asian soldiers built a myth of imperial racial inclusion. Nonetheless, the army still failed to address the lingering hierarchies of religious difference and "martial" fitness. Integration did not come to all equally. South Asian communities competed with one another to prove themselves as the fittest to survive and thrive in a world of war and empire.

Despite prevalent divisions, dissensions, and violence, India in the 1940s was, in some ways, more united than ever before. Faith in martial masculinity had become almost universal. Whether identities or movements were backed by Hindus, Muslims, Sikhs, communists, fascists, colonial officers, or imperial unionists, most found great value in spreading military discipline, martial education, and the virtues of strong warriors. This, they believed, was necessary to ensure unity and strength—however different their visions of unity might be. Those who knew how to wield weapons, control their bodies through physical exercise, and implement military discipline hoped to take up the mantle of political, national, and military leadership. Faith in the perfectibility of the masculine and disciplined soldier urged men—and women—to fight. The army's attempts to appropriate precolonial traditions and fortify cultural bonds through military training encouraged civilians to think and act like soldiers. Indianization was central to building, not an interracial and interfaith paradise, but a society in which many viewed militant violence and strict racial hierarchies as prerequisites of social order. Leela Gandhi has suggested that failing to recognize human imperfection and diversity supports fascistic regimes of power that restrict and constrain opponents, dissenters, and those deemed imperfect, often with violent force.[7] The Indian Army embodied the imperial demand for perfection and the violence that followed in its wake.

By the 1940s, the army's illusion of racial inclusivity cracked under the weight of imperial and global crisis. The Indian armed services recruited 2.4 million South Asians to serve from 1939 to 1945. This was roughly one million more than had served in the First World War and at least ten times the number of men serving in peacetime. Second World War forces proved to be vastly different from their interwar predecessors. The racialized recruiting of the "martial races" was all but abandoned to deal with significant manpower shortages. Indian officers who trained in British military academies found new opportunities for command and battlefield experience. By 1940 they stopped being sent exclusively to "Indianized" units and gained the ability to command British troops.[8] This often led them to reevaluate the racial hierarchies of imperial rule and articulate their own desires for greater political leadership. The rise of the anti-colonial Indian National Army under S. C. Bose in 1942, meanwhile, undermined the strength of the colonial army by allying with the Japanese and attracting Indian deserters, civilians, and prisoners of war.

Those who returned from the Second World War continued the interwar army's pattern of ritualizing martial faith. During the partition of India and Pakistan in 1947, returning soldiers seized property and carried out acts of violence on a massive scale. The militarily significant Punjab province faced far more violence than the simultaneous division of Bengal.[9] Some Hindu politicians attempted to backtrack on the anti-martial races rhetoric of the 1930s to undermine the threat of national division in the 1940s.[10] However, the hasty transition from war to partition made it all but impossible for this perspective to permeate colonial society. Religious militarism and anti-martial race discourses were too prevalent and entrenched. The rushed process of partition and independence under the last viceroy, Lord Louis Mountbatten, betrayed the multiple contending ideas about how, when, and to what extent India should become independent. It largely ignored the millions of soldiers, civilians, and activists still coping with the fallout of another traumatic and devastating global war.

Military rituals solidified militant masculinity as an ideal for internationally minded twentieth-century soldiers and civilians. In many ways, this helped to streamline the transition from the colonial army into the national forces of India and Pakistan, ensuring their continued alliances and political negotiations with British and American military forces after independence. Over several decades, military power in India had encouraged South Asian communities to view one another as impediments to martial prowess and political representation. These ideals encouraged South Asian officers who trained at British military academies to identify as part of a global cosmopolitan brotherhood, erected in opposition to identities that they found more divisive and limiting, such as caste, women's movements, nationalism, communism, and religious sectarianism. Although some soldiers and officers embraced a cosmopolitan identity, this only underlined their differences from civilian communities.[11] Cosmopolitanism, in fact, often served and replicated the inequalities of imperial rule. More than anything, the Indian Army gave men the tools to carry out violence on a massive scale and to see themselves as exceptional leaders, misunderstood by the majority of civilians. "Cosmopolitanism" also fit well within Britain's new geopolitical and military rebranding as a commonwealth. By using racial and religious difference as building blocks for military participation and social engineering, the Indian Army attempted to salvage and revive the imperial project. Instead, it polarized and militarized public opinion about racial and religious difference in Britain and South Asia. The colonial army's strength ensured imperial and national weakness. As the British fled from India, violence was directed from soldier to soldier, neighbor to neighbor.

The lived reality of racialized violence for many post-colonial subjects in and beyond modern Britain has made it essential for scholars and members of the public to remind the world of South Asian and other colonial and non-white military contributions to the world wars. This helps to undermine racist claims that only white citizens fought to defend the nation, and, by extension, deserve citizenship rights. At the same time, exalting the contributions of Black and colonial soldiers often replicates imperial narratives of loyalty and devotion. These implicitly or explicitly exclude women, workers, and colonial subjects who fought—or served—in noncombatant roles or on non-European fronts. It also reinforces longer patterns of exalting militarism, violence, and warfare that have deep colonial roots. Soldiers' and civilians' identities continue to negotiate power and citizenship, shaped by the difficult lived realities of imperialism and war.

The twentieth-century Indian Army offers the opportunity to reflect on the global legacies of imperial militarism. South Asian soldiers received simultaneous praise and condemnation for taking the violent actions that many British officials did not want to implement themselves. Yet soldiers came from communities that lived with the constant threat of imperial violence, few employment opportunities, discrimination, and political and economic systems deeply shaped by imperial control. Being a soldier meant, in part, being a waged laborer subject to the whims of imperial capital. This was especially true for those living at the borders and boundaries of imperial and national influence. Service in a military profession was never easy and did not always feel like a choice. While some soldiers experienced upward mobility, personal pride, and financial gain from military service, their options were always limited by the inequalities of race, class, religion, and (dis)ability.[12] This was true for those who shared the theoretically exalted position of ideal recruits. Religion may have been the language of recruitment and loyalty in the colonial army but it was not the only factor that shaped soldiers' service. Where and why nations and empires recruit their soldiers, and how they create different rules for some than others, reflects and often sets the terms for where and why military violence is permissible. The year 2019 brought a series of far less celebrated imperial centenaries than those of 2014 and 2018. As we reflect on the anniversaries of the Third Anglo-Afghan War and Amritsar Massacre, this work offers a timely reminder—and act of remembrance—of the global consequences of militarism and exclusion.

NOTES

INTRODUCTION

1. A walking tour about the Indian hospitals at the Royal Pavilion on February 28, 2015, detailed this event.

2. Research on the Indian Army has witnessed a recent resurgence that has added much to military histories of the army. I am especially indebted to the following works: Gajendra Singh, *The Testimonies of Indian Soldiers and the Two World Wars: Between Self and Sepoy* (London: Bloomsbury, 2014); Yasmin Khan, *India at War: The Subcontinent and the Second World War* (Oxford: Oxford University Press, 2015); Santanu Das, *India, Empire, and First World War Culture: Writings, Images, Songs* (Cambridge: Cambridge University Press, 2018); Santanu Das, *Race, Empire and First World War Writing* (Cambridge: Cambridge University Press, 2011); David Omissi, *Indian Voices of the Great War: Soldiers' Letters, 1914–18* (New York: Palgrave Macmillan, 1999); Daniel Marston, *The Indian Army at the End of the Raj* (Cambridge: Cambridge University Press, 2014); Heather Streets, *Martial Races: The Military, Race, and Masculinity in British Imperial Culture, 1857–1914* (Manchester: Manchester University Press, 2004). For additional excellent studies on non-Indian colonial soldiers, see also Michelle Moyd, *Violent Intermediaries: African Soldiers, Conquest, and Everyday Colonialism in German East Africa* (Athens: Ohio University Press, 2014); Richard Fogarty, *Race and War in France: Colonial Subjects in the French Army, 1914–1918* (Baltimore: Johns Hopkins University Press, 2008).

3. Army officials constantly monitored the "religious composition" of the Indian Army. For example, in 1912: Sikhs (32,702—20.5%), Punjabi Muslims (25,299—16%), Pathans (12,202—7.7%), Hindustani Muslims (9,054—5.7%), other Muslims (8,717— 5.5%) (Muslims = 34.5% total), Gurkhas (18,100—11.5%), Rajputs (12,051—7.7%), Garhwalis (10,421—6.1%), other Hindus (Ahirs, Gujars, Mers, Mians, Bhils, Parias, Tamils = 10,252—6.5%), Jats (9,670—6%), Marathas (5,685—3%), Brahmins (2,636—1.7%), Christians (1,800—1.2%). Kaushik Roy, *Hinduism and the Ethics of Warfare in South Asia: From Antiquity to the Present* (Cambridge: Cambridge University Press, 2012), 217; *Proceedings of the Army in India Committee, 1912*, vol. I-A, Minority Report (Simla, 1913), 156. These numbers changed during and after the First World War. See Satya M. Rai, *Legislative Politics and Freedom Struggle on [sic] the Panjab 1897–1947* (New Delhi: People's Publishing House, 1984), 179–80. The percentage of recruits from Punjab and the North-West Frontier Province rose from 46% to 58.5% in the twentieth century. The percentage from Nepal, Garhwal, and Kumaun rose from 14.8% to 22% in the same period. Nirad C. Chaudhuri, "The Martial Races of India," Part II, *Modern Review* 48, No. 285 (1930): 296.

4. There is a rich and robust scholarly dialogue about the "martial races." See, for example, Streets, *Martial Races*; Gavin Rand and Kim Wagner, "Recruiting the 'Martial Races': Identities and Military Service in Colonial India," *Patterns of Prejudice* 46, Nos. 3–4 (2012); Singh, *The Testimonies of Indian Soldiers*; David Omissi, *The Sepoy and the Raj: The Indian Army, 1860–1940* (London: Macmillan, 1994). The most famous text about the martial races written during the British Raj was George MacMunn, *The Martial Races of India* (London: Low, Marston & Co., 1933). Various military recruiting manuals both enforced and demonstrated the flexibility of the concept.

5. This will be explored in greater detail in the second chapter.

6. Seema Alavi, *The Sepoys and the Company: Tradition and Transition in Northern India, 1770–1830* (Delhi: Oxford University Press, 1998), 35.

7. I use the term "Panjab" when referring to the precolonial region and "Punjab" when speaking to the colonial period and term. For a greater understanding of the connections between precolonial, company, and colonial militaries, see Purnima Dhavan, *When Sparrows Became Hawks: The Making of the Sikh Warrior Tradition* (Oxford: Oxford University Press, 2011), 6–7; Dirk A. Kolff, *Naukar, Rajput and Sepoy: The Ethnohistory of the Military Labour Market in Hindustan, 1450–1850* (Cambridge: Cambridge University Press, 1990); Kaushik Roy, "The Hybrid Military Establishment of the East India Company in South Asia: 1750–1849," *Journal of Global History* 6, No. 2 (2011); Alavi, *The Sepoys and the Company*; Erica Wald, *Vice in the Barracks: Medicine, the Military and the Making of Colonial India, 1780–1868* (New York: Palgrave, 2014); William Pinch, *Warrior Ascetics and Indian Empires* (Cambridge: Cambridge University Press, 2006); Kaushik Roy, "The Construction of Regiments in the Indian Army: 1859–1913," *War In History* 8, No. 127 (2001).

8. Company officials often disagreed about the desirability or harm of spreading Christianity in the early years of Company rule. Nile Green, *Islam and the Army in Colonial India: Sepoy Religion in the Service of Empire* (Cambridge: Cambridge University Press, 2009), 72; Streets, *Martial Races*, 27.

9. For example, Brigadier Colin Mackenzie earned the nickname "Moollah" from his Afghan captors due to his religious fervor for Christianity. He refused to allow South Asian soldiers to participate in the festivities surrounding the holy month of Muharram. Green, *Islam and the Army*, 63; Streets, *Martial Races*, 28.

10. Antoinette Burton, *The First Anglo-Afghan Wars: A Reader* (Durham, NC: Duke University Press, 2014).

11. Susanne Hoeber Rudolph, Lloyd L. Rudolph, and Mohan Singh Kanota, eds., *Reversing the Gaze: Amar Singh's Diary, a Colonial Subject's Narrative of Imperial India* (Boulder, CO: Westview Press, 2002).

12. Streets, *Martial Races*, 28.

13. Cartridges were frequently greased to facilitate the easier entry of bullets into the barrel of rifles. Thanks to University of North Texas student and veteran Jason Maynard. What type of grease they used remains a source of debate and controversy. See below.

14. Debates about the causes of 1857 remain contentious. Many point to a mix of religious and secular causes but the cartridge story remains the most retold cause of the

1857 rebellion. S. L. Menezes, *Fidelity & Honour: The Indian Army from the Seventeenth to the Twenty-First Century* (New Delhi: Viking, Penguin Books India, 1993); Vera Nünning, "'Daß Jeder seine Pflicht thue': Die Bedeutung der Indian Mutiny für das nationale britische Selbstverständnis," *Archiv für Kulturgeschichte* 78 (1996): 373; Marina Carter and Crispin Bates, *Mutiny at the Margins: New Perspectives on the Indian Uprising of 1857* (New Delhi: Sage Publications, 2013); Streets, *Martial Races*, 28–29; Kim A. Wagner, *The Great Fear of 1857: Rumours, Conspiracies and the Making of the Indian Uprising* (Oxford: Peter Lang, 2010), 27–28; Avril Powell, *Muslims and Missionaries in Pre-Mutiny India* (New York and London: Routledge, 1995).

15. Powell, *Muslims and Missionaries*, 272.

16. Roy, "The Construction of Regiments," 143.

17. Powell, *Muslims and Missionaries*, 283; Streets, *Martial Races*, 32–33.

18. Streets, *Martial Races*, 20.

19. They also suggested doubling the number of British soldiers to eighty thousand and aimed to maintain a ratio of one British soldier for every two Indian soldiers. Syed Hussain Shaheed Soherwordi, "'Punjabisation' in the British Indian Army 1857–1947 and the Advent of Military Rule in Pakistan," *Edinburgh Papers in South Asian Studies* 24 (2010): 12; Streets, *Martial Races*, 24, 32.

20. See note 3.

21. Kaushik Roy, "Spare the Rod, Spoil the Soldier? Crime and Punishment in the Army of India, 1860–1913," *Journal of the Society for Army Historical Research* 84, No. 337 (Spring 2006): 9–33, at 26.

22. Roy, "The Construction of Regiments," 130, 146.

23. *The Eden Commission*, India Office Records, British Library (henceforth IOR), IOR/L/MIL/17/5/1687.

24. Tan Tai Yong, *The Garrison State: The Military, Government and Society in Colonial Punjab, 1849–1947* (New Delhi and London: Sage, 2005), 20.

25. The four commands were the Punjab Command, the Bengal Command, the Bombay Command, and the Madras Command, each of which had its own lieutenant general. The former Bengal Army was split between the Punjab and Bengal Commands. This period also witnessed a clash between civil and military power through Viceroy Lord Curzon and Commander-in-Chief Kitchener. Soherwordi, "'Punjabisation' in the British Indian Army 1857–1947," 5, 15; Tan, *Garrison State*, 32–33.

26. Most famously, Swami Vivekananda promoted football and encouraged a program of "Beef, Biceps and Bhagvat Gita." Quoted in Leela Gandhi, *Affective Communities: Anticolonial Thought, Fin-de-Siècle Radicalism, and the Politics of Friendship* (Durham, NC: Duke University Press, 2005), 82; Joseph Alter, "Yoga at the Fin de Siècle: Muscular Christianity with a 'Hindu' Twist," *International Journal of the History of Sport* 23, No. 5 (2006): 759–76; Mark Singleton, *Yoga Body: The Origins of Modern Posture Practice* (Oxford: Oxford University Press, 2010).

27. Joseph Alter, "Indian Clubs and Colonialism: Hindu Masculinity and Muscular Christianity," *Comparative Studies in Society and History* 46, No. 3 (2004): 497–534, at 517. The 1880s and 1890s were critical moments in theorizing who could be defined as

"martial." Mrinalini Sinha, *Colonial Masculinity: The "Manly Englishman" and the "Ef-feminate Bengali" in the Late Nineteenth Century* (Manchester: Manchester University Press, 1995), 3–4, 17, 21–23.

28. Sinha, *Colonial Masculinity*. Sinha's discussion of the volunteer movement is especially instructive.

29. The Bengal partition was under Viceroy Lord Curzon (1898–1905), who attempted to streamline India's large government bureaucracies and undermine growing threats of political activism in and around the imperial capital of Calcutta. Barbara D. Metcalf and Thomas R. Metcalf, *A Concise History of Modern India* (Cambridge: Cambridge University Press, 2012), 156–57.

30. Tan, *Garrison State*; Mark Condos, *The Insecurity State: Punjab and the Making of Colonial Power in British India* (Cambridge: Cambridge University Press, 2017).

31. This incident and the relevant literature will be discussed in greater detail in the next chapter. See, for example, Derek Sayer, "British Reaction to the Amritsar Massacre 1919–1920," *Past and Present* 131 (May 1991): 130–64.

32. See Chapter 2 for a further discussion of these dynamics.

33. See note 2 for a more detailed catalog of recent work.

34. Marston, *The Indian Army at the End of the Raj*; Khan, *India at War*.

35. Singh, *The Testimonies of Indian Soldiers*.

36. Shrabani Basu, *For King and Another Country: Indian Soldiers on the Western Front, 1914–18* (New Delhi: Bloomsbury India, 2015); Khan, *India at War*.

37. Omissi, *Indian Voices of the Great War*; Roy, *Hinduism and the Ethics of Warfare*; Das, *India, Empire, and First World War Culture*; Roy, "The Hybrid Military Establishment."

38. This represents just a few of the many ground-breaking scholars partaking in debates about the use of "religion" in South Asia: Talal Asad, *Genealogies of Religion: Discipline and Reasons of Power in Christianity and Islam* (Baltimore: Johns Hopkins University Press, 1993); Arvind-Pal S. Mandair, *Religion and the Specter of the West: Sikhism, India, Postcoloniality, and the Politics of Translation* (New York: Columbia University Press, 2009); Dhavan, *When Sparrows Became Hawks*; Richard King, *Orientalism and Religion: Postcolonial Theory, India and "the Mystic East"* (London and New York: Routledge, 1999); Peter Van der Veer, *Imperial Encounters: Religion and Modernity in India and Britain* (Princeton, NJ: Princeton University Press, 2001); Indrani Chatterjee, "Monastic Governmentality, Colonial Misogyny, and Postcolonial Amnesia in South Asia," *History of the Present: A Journal of Critical History* 3 (Spring 2013): 55–98.

39. See also Edmund Burke III, *The Ethnographic State: France and the Invention of Moroccan Islam* (Berkeley: University of California Press, 2014).

40. See also Junaid Rana, *Terrifying Muslims: Race and Labor in the South Asian Diaspora* (Durham, NC: Duke University Press, 2011).

CHAPTER 1

1. Major A. E. Barstow, 2/11th Sikh Regiment (late 15th Ludhiana Sikhs), *Handbooks for the Indian Army, Sikhs: Revised at the Request of the Government of India* (Calcutta: Government of India Central Publications Branch, 1928), 151.

2. Toco Moses Stevens, interviewed by Conrad Wood, Oral History 776, Imperial War Museum, June 14, 1976, Reel 6. Soldiers such as William Homer similarly admired Sikhs for being "hard fighters." William Homer, interviewed by Conrad Wood, August 4, 1976, Imperial War Museum Interview 792, Reel 12.

3. Lieut. Col. Alexander George Stuart, *The Indian Empire: A Short Review and Some Hints for the Use of Soldiers Proceeding to India* (Calcutta: Government of India Central Publication Branch 1932), 59. This work is also sometimes published under the title *Our Indian Empire*.

4. Stuart, *The Indian Empire.*

5. Gajendra Singh, *The Testimonies of Indian Soldiers and the Two World Wars: Between Self and Sepoy* (London: Bloomsbury Press, 2014), 29.

6. M. Macauliffe, "The Sikh Religion and Its Advantages to the State" (lecture delivered July 6, 1903), *Journal of the United Service Institution of India* 32, No. 153 (October 1903): 325.

7. Lord Kitchener's comments are included with the published edition of Macauliffe's speech. M. Macauliffe, "How the Sikhs Became a Militant Race" (lecture delivered July 6, 1903), *Journal of the United Service Institution of India* 32, No. 153 (October 1903): 330–58.

8. Macauliffe, "How the Sikhs Became a Militant Race."

9. Diary of J. P. Swindlehurst, entries for November 22, 23, 24, 1919, Imperial War Museum.

10. Diary of J. P. Swindlehurst, entries for November 22, 23, 24, 1919, Imperial War Museum.

11. Purnima Dhavan, *When Sparrows Became Hawks: The Making of the Sikh Warrior Tradition* (Oxford: Oxford University Press, 2011); J. S. Grewal, *History, Literature, and Identity: Four Centuries of Sikh Tradition* (New Delhi: Oxford University Press, 2012); Singh, *The Testimonies of Indian Soldiers*, 29.

12. Punjab Government Civil Secretariat, "Question Whether Students Who Solemnly Affirm Themselves to Be Sikhs but Do Not Wear the Prominent Symbol (Keshas) Can Be Admitted to the K. E. In. College, Lahore, as Sikh Students," Home: Medical 5796/71, file 48 B (1924), Panjab State Archives, henceforth PSA.

13. Malavika Kasturi, "'Asceticising' Monastic Families: Ascetic Genealogies, Property Feuds and Anglo-Hindu Law in Late Colonial India," *Modern Asian Studies* 43, No. 5 (2009): 1080; Charu Gupta, "Anxious Hindu Masculinity in Colonial North India: Shuddhi and Sangathan Movements," *Cross Currents* 61, No. 4 (December 2011): 441–54.

14. Brian P. Caton, "Social Categories and Colonisation in Panjab, 1849–1920," *Indian Economic and Social History Review* 41, No. 1 (2004): 190, 193–94; Maia Ramnath, *Haj to Utopia: How the Ghadar Movement Charted Global Radicalism and Attempted to Overthrow the British Empire* (Berkeley and Los Angeles: University of California Press, 2011), 18.

15. Grewal, *History, Literature, and Identity*, 294; see also Richard G. Fox, *Lions of Punjab: Culture in the Making* (Berkeley: University of California Press, 1985).

16. Bhai Kahn Singh's *Ham Hindū Nahīn* (We are not Hindu) promoted the concerns of the Singh Sabhas. It argued that Sikhs had their own scripture—the Guru

Granth Sahib—and were distinct from both Hindus and Muslims according to the Adi Granth. By 1920 *Ham Hindū Nahīn* became one of the leading Sikh publications and the Sikh Maharaja of Nabha became one of its most influential supporters. Grewal, *History, Literature, and Identity*, 275–79, 293–95; Dhavan, *When Sparrows Became Hawks*, 12.

17. Tan Tai Yong, *The Garrison State: The Military, Government and Society in Colonial Punjab, 1849–1947* (New Delhi and London: Sage, 2005), 193–94.

18. Tan, *Garrison State*, 192–93; Dhavan, *When Sparrows Became Hawks*.

19. Kaushik Roy, *Hinduism and the Ethics of Warfare in South Asia: From Antiquity to the Present* (Cambridge: Cambridge University Press, 2012), 217; See also *Proceedings of the Army in India Committee, 1912*, vol. I-A, Minority Report (Simla: Govt. Central Branch Press, 1913), 156; "The Sikh Question in the Punjab, 1919–1922," Home Department, Government of Punjab, file 31, June 1922, PSA; Navdeep S. Mandair, "Colonial Formations of Sikhism," in *Oxford Handbook of Sikh Studies*, ed. Pashaura Singh and Louis E. Fenech (Oxford: Oxford University Press, 2014), 71.

20. Alexander Bubb, "The Life of the Irish Soldier in India: Representations and Self-Representations, 1857–1922," *Modern Asian Studies* 46, No. 4 (2012): 1–45.

21. Sir James A. Douie, *Provincial Geographies of India: The Panjab, North-West Frontier Province, and Kashmir* (Cambridge: Cambridge University Press, 1916), 114, 117. https://archive.org/stream/provincialgeogra01holluoft#page/n13/mode/2up.

22. Arvind-Pal S. Mandair, *Religion and the Specter of the West: Sikhism, India, Postcoloniality, and the Politics of Translation* (New York: Columbia University Press, 2009), 17–18; see also Caton, "Social Categories and Colonisation in Panjab," 34.

23. Douie, *Provincial Geographies of India*, 114, 117.

24. David Petrie, *Developments in Sikh Politics* (Simla, 1911), 52.

25. Tan, *Garrison State*, 95.

26. Mark Condos, *The Insecurity State: Punjab and the Making of Colonial Power in British India* (Cambridge: Cambridge University Press, 2017); Richard J. Popplewell, *Intelligence and Imperial Defence: British Intelligence and the Defence of the Indian Empire 1904–1924* (London: Frank Cass, 1995).

27. Director Criminal Intelligence, Weekly Report (November 9, 1907), Home Political Department (December 1907), file 2–9 B, National Archives of India, henceforth NAI.

28. "Endeavours of Sikh Sepoys to Spread Sedition" (June 26, 1907), Home (Political) 'A' Pros(s), file 113 (August 1907), NAI.

29. Director, Criminal Intelligence, Weekly Reports (October 4, 1907), Home (Political), pros. 459/II and k.w., 1922, NAI.

30. "Endeavours of Sikh Sepoys to Spread Sedition" (June 26, 1907).

31. Director of Criminal Intelligence, Daily Report (July 6, 1907); Tan, *Garrison State*, 95.

32. "Daily Report on the State of Political Agitation in the Punjab" (July 5, 1907), Home (Political), August 1907, 5–90 B, NAI.

33. Petrie, *Developments in Sikh Politics*, 23.

34. Satya M. Rai, *Legislative Politics and Freedom Struggle on* [sic] *the Panjab 1897–1947* (New Delhi: People's Publishing House, 1984), 37–39, 41, 43–44, 50, 55.

35. Indian Army regimental Dussehra celebrations emphasized the slaughter of goats and buffalos with the soldiers' *khukri* to distance Nepali soldiers from Brahman rituals previously associated with Dussehra. Seema Alavi, *The Sepoys and the Company: Tradition and Transition in Northern India, 1770–1830* (Oxford: Oxford University Press, 1998), 278–79. Military officers believed that Gurkhas worshiped khukris because "it is to the favour of the sword they owe their prosperity." See also Major B. U. Nicolay, *Handbooks for the Indian Army: Gurkhas. Compiled Under the Orders of the Government of India by Lt-Col Eden Vansittart* (Calcutta: Government of India Press, 1915), 54.

36. Rajput officer Amar Singh recalled that confiscation of a soldier's sword caused "a great blow to our pride." Susanne Hoeber Rudolph, Lloyd L. Rudolph, and Mohan Singh Kanota, eds., *Reversing the Gaze: Amar Singh's Diary, a Colonial Subject's Narrative of Imperial India* (Boulder, CO: Westview Press, 2002), 187.

37. Boxers gained inspiration from the Big Sword Society, or Dadaohui. Gadadhar Singh, a Rajput soldier who served against the so-called Boxer rebellion in China (1899–1901), admired one Chinese Boxer who apparently fought off a sharpshooter's bullets with a sword. He wondered if the "sword of Punjab ruler Govind Singh" was "any less miraculous?" Anand A. Yang, "(A) Subaltern('s) Boxers: An Indian Soldier's Account of China and the World in 1900–1901," in *The Boxers, China, and the World*, ed. Robert Bickers and R. G. Tiedemann (Plymouth: Rowman & Littlefield, 2007), 43–64, at 46–47.

38. *The Indian Arms Act, 1878: As Modified Up to the 1st July, 1892* (Simla: Government Central Printing Office, 1892), 13–14, 19–20.

39. Mrinalini Sinha, *Colonial Masculinity: The "Manly Englishman" and the "Effeminate Bengali" in the Late Nineteenth Century* (Manchester: Manchester University Press, 1995), 4, 17, 21–23.

40. Editorial comment from *Mahratta* (April 9, 1922) quoted in "History of Kirpan (a Sample of British Government's Recent Persecution of the Sikh Religion)" (Hyderabad, Standard Printing Works, 1922), IOR/L/PJ/6/1808, file 3030, p. 23.

41. See Chapter 4 for an additional discussion of food and anti-Brahman attitudes in the army. Military officials described the mixture as "baptismal fluid," known as "Amrit." Barstow, *Handbooks for the Indian Army, Sikhs*, 8; Stuart, *The Indian Empire*, 66; Petrie, *Developments in Sikh Politics*, 23.

42. Broadsheets attributed to Jagat Singh, Updeshak of Lyallpur. Petrie, *Development in Sikh Politics*, 37.

43. The man was Harnam Singh of Batala. Petrie, *Development in Sikh Politics*, 33.

44. The man in question was named Fazal Ahmad. From F. H. Burton, ICS, Deputy Commissioner, Attock Division, at Campbellpore to the Commissioner, Rawalpindi Division (June 25, 1913), file 41 (1914), PSA.

45. Dhavan, *When Sparrows Became Hawks*.

46. Special branch report (June 7, 1907), Home (Political) A, file 113 (August 1907), NAI.

47. Director of Criminal Intelligence, Weekly Report (January 4, 1908), Home Department, Political (January 1908), file 111–118 B, NAI.

48. In 1913 the deputy commissioner of Amritsar described an unlicensed arms dealer possessing four daggers that he claimed "were not daggers within the meaning of the Arms Act, but *kirpans*, and were intended to be used at Sikh initiation ceremonies for the purpose of marking the sacred food." From C. M. King, ICS, Deputy Commissioner, Amritsar, to Commissioner, Lahore Division (July 2, 1913), file 41 (1914), PSA.

49. Captain R. W. Falcon, *Handbook on Sikhs for the Use of Regimental Officers* (Allahabad: Falcon Press, 1896); General Sir John J. H. Gordon, *The Sikhs* (Edinburgh and London: William Blackwood and Sons, 1904).

50. Punjab Government Civil Secretariat, "Note on the Sikh Question in the Punjab, 1919–1922," Home, file 31 (June 1922), Home Department Proceedings, PSA.

51. Shaikh Asghar Ali, CBE, ICS, Home Secretary to Government to All Deputy Commissioners in the Punjab (February 9, 1921), file 885/17, West Bengal State Archives, henceforth WBSA.

52. Teja Singh, *The Gurdwara Reform Movement and the Sikh Awakening* (Jullundur City, Punjab: Desh Sewak Book Agency, 1922), 464–65.

53. Singh, *Gurdwara Reform Movement*.

54. Singh, *Gurdwara Reform Movement*, 465.

55. The official was Arur Singh. Punjab Government Civil Secretariat, "The Kirpan Question," Home—Police, file 116, 1924, PSA; Derek Sayer, "British Reaction to the Amritsar Massacre 1919–1920," *Past and Present* 131 (May 1991): 130–64, at 144.

56. Punjab Government Civil Secretariat, Home—Police, file 116 (1924); Mandair, "Colonial Formations of Sikhism," 77.

57. The arrested man was Baba Nihal Singh Nihang. From Mohan Singh, Secretary, Khalsa Young Men's Association, Rawalpindi, to His Honour Sir Michael Francis O'Dwyer, Lt-Governor Punjab (August 20, 1913), file 41 (1914), PSA; From Teja Singh, Secretary, Khalsa Bhujangi Sabha, Lyallpur, to His Honour the Lt-Governor, Punjab (August 21, 1913), file 41 (1914), PSA. Those who put forward petitions and statements included the Khalsa Young Men's Association, Rawalpindi, Ramgarhia Sabha, the Chief Khalsa Diwan, and the Sabha at Rawalpindi. F. C. Isemonger and J. Slattery, *An Account of the Ghadr Conspiracy, 1913–1915* (Lahore: Superintendent, Government Printing, Punjab, 1919), 87.

58. These included the Khalsa Young Men's Association at Rawalpindi and Khalsa Bhujangi Sabha in Lyallpur. From Mohan Singh, Secretary, Khalsa Young Men's Association, Rawalpindi, to His Honour Sir Michael Francis O'Dwyer, Lt-Governor Punjab (August 20, 1913), file 41 (1914), PSA; From Teja Singh to the Lt-Governor, Punjab (August 21, 1913).

59. From C. M. King, ICS, Deputy Commissioner, Amritsar, to Commissioner, Lahore Division (July 2, 1913), file 41 (1914), PSA.

60. They consulted Takht Sahibs, *gurdwaras*, Singh Sabhas and Diwans about the matter. From C. M. King, ICS, Deputy Commissioner, Amritsar, to Commissioner, Lahore Division (July 2, 1913).

61. From Sunder Singh, Majithia, Honorary Secretary, Chief Khalsa Diwan, Amritsar, to the Chief Secretary to Government, Punjab, Lahore (February 13, 1914), file 41 (1914), PSA.

62. Punjab Government Civil Secretariat, Home—Police, file 116 (1924); Singh, *Gurdwara Reform Movement*, 466; quote is from Shaikh Asghar Ali to All Deputy Commissioners (February 9, 1921).

63. Shaikh Asghar Ali to All Deputy Commissioners (February 9, 1921).

64. Rai, *Legislative Politics and Freedom Struggle*, 79–80.

65. Sayer, "British Reaction to the Amritsar Massacre 1919–1920," 136.

66. Other estimates are that the province supplied 50%–60% of wartime recruits despite possessing only 7.5% of India's population. Excerpt from the *Morning Post* (November 28, 1916), IOR/L/PJ/6/1405, file 4095; A. E. Barstow estimated that Sikhs made up 12% of the population of the Punjab. The government of Punjab estimated in 1922 that the Sikh population in Punjab was about 10.5%. See "The Sikh Question in the Punjab, 1919–1922," Home Department, Government of Punjab, file 31, June 1922, PSA. Barstow estimates that 33,000 soldiers were Sikhs at the start of the war and no fewer than 88,925 Sikh combatants enlisted between 1914 and 1918; Barstow, *Handbooks for the Indian Army, Sikhs*, 4–5.

67. Ramnath, *Haj to Utopia*; Heather Streets-Salter, *World War One in Southeast Asia: Colonialism and Anticolonialism in an Era of Global Conflict* (Cambridge: Cambridge University Press, 2017); Seema Sohi, *Echoes of Mutiny: Race, Surveillance, and Indian Anticolonialism in North America* (Oxford: Oxford University Press, 2014).

68. Tan, *Garrison State*, 112; Rai, *Legislative Politics and Freedom Struggle*, 65.

69. Isemonger and Slattery, *An Account of the Ghadr Conspiracy*, 88.

70. Isemonger and Slattery, *An Account of the Ghadr Conspiracy*; refusal by the Canadian government to admit Sikh passengers arriving on the Komagata Maru, resolutions and protests from public meetings in India, IOR/L/PJ/6/1324, file 3461.

71. This happened on May 31, 1914, and was led by Balwant Singh. Isemonger and Slattery, *An Account of the Ghadr Conspiracy*, 38.

72. Lajpat Rai, *Young India* (New York: B. W. Huebsch, 1916), 21–23.

73. Isemonger and Slattery, *An Account of the Ghadr Conspiracy*, 127; Supplementary Lahore Conspiracy Case, IOR/L/PJ/6/1405, file 4095, p. 22.

74. Supplementary Lahore Conspiracy Case, IOR/L/PJ/6/1405, file 4095, pp. 22, 110–12, 127–29.

75. Supplementary Lahore Conspiracy Case, IOR/L/PJ/6/1405, file 4095, pp. 73, 110.

76. For a further discussion, see Ian Beckett, "The Singapore Mutiny of February 1915," *Journal of the Society for Army Historical Research* 62 (1984): 132–53; Streets-Salter, *World War One in Southeast Asia*.

77. See, for example, Staff Surgeon A. Grant, Medical Officer-in-Charge of the Johore Forces; No. 2637 Lance Naik Feroze, C Company, 5th Light Infantry; [108] Corporal J. A. Bews, RAMC; Quartermaster Sergeant W. W. Brown, RE [royal engineer], in Streets-Salter, *World War One in Southeast Asia*. See also Isemonger and Slattery, *An Account of the Ghadr Conspiracy*, 131; Singh, *The Testimonies of Indian Soldiers*.

78. From the General Officer Commanding the Troops, Straits Settlements to His Excellency the Governor & Commander-in-Chief, Straits Settlements (June 21, 1916),

"Mutiny of 5th Light Infantry at Singapore 1915," Part I—Proceedings of Court of Enquiry; Part II—"Report by His Excellency the Governor of the Straits Settlements and the General Officer Commanding at Singapore" (Simla: Government Central Branch Press, 1915), 143, IOR/L/MIL/7/7191: 1915–37.

79. Singh, *The Testimonies of Indian Soldiers*, 154.

80. Being the son of an Anglo-Irish landlord gave him confidence in ruling colonies with a firm hand. Sayer, "British Reaction to the Amritsar Massacre 1919–1920," 136.

81. Kalwant Singh, a student, to Kot Dafadar Ghamand Singh of the 3rd Skinner's Horse (April 2, 1916), Letter 280, reproduced in David Omissi, *Indian Voices of the Great War: Soldiers' Letters, 1914–18* (New York: Palgrave Macmillan, 1999), 170.

82. See, for example, Shrabani Basu, *For King and Another Country: Indian Soldiers on the Western Front, 1914–18* (New Delhi: Bloomsbury India, 2015). Basu includes several excellent wartime propaganda images, most of which prominently feature Sikhs.

83. See, for example, Radhika Singha, "Front Lines and Status Lines: Sepoy and 'Menial' in the Great War 1916–1920," in *The World in World Wars* (Leiden and Boston: Brill, 2010), 59; Basu, *For King and Another Country*, 88; Mulk Raj Anand depicted the bitterness that many Dogra soldiers felt about British gratitude and admiration for Sikhs and Gurkhas in Mulk Raj Anand, *Across the Black Waters* (New Delhi: Orient Paperbacks, 2008), 110, 214.

84. Geoffrey H. Malins and Edward G. Tong, "With the Indian Troops at the Front Part I" (British Topical Committee for War Films and War Office January 17, 1916), Imperial War Museum (henceforth IWM), online archive, 202–1, http://www.iwm.org .uk/collections/item/object/1060022700, accessed January 24, 2016.

85. Dafadar Nathan Singh (Sikh) to Sowar Paran [?] [*sic*] Singh (State Cavalry, Jind State, Punjab), Letter 295, reproduced in Omissi, *Indian Voices of the Great War*, 177.

86. A sepoy of the 47th Sikhs to a friend in India (December 14, 1915), Brighton, Letter 199, reproduced in Omissi, *Indian Voices of the Great War*, 126.

87. Leela Gandhi, *The Common Cause: Postcolonial Ethics and the Practice of Democracy, 1900–1955* (Chicago: University of Chicago Press, 2014), 93.

88. The 1919 Montagu-Chelmsford Reforms introduced separate representation for Sikhs, which was less than 20% of the seats in the Punjab Legislative Council. They requested one-third, which would have turned the Punjab province's Muslim majority into a political minority against Sikhs and Hindus. Rai, *Legislative Politics and Freedom Struggle*, 32, 71–72, 79–82.

89. Inspector-General of Civil Hospitals, Punjab, "Report on the Epidemic of Influenza in the Punjab During 1918," Home: Medical & Sanitary (March 1919), file 89–104, collection number 5207/63, PSA.

90. Xu Guoqi, *Asia and the Great War: A Shared History* (Oxford: Oxford University Press, 2017), 82.

91. Kamlesh Mohan, *Militant Nationalism in the Punjab, 1919–1935* (New Delhi: Manohar, 1985), 18; Rai, *Legislative Politics and Freedom Struggle*, 79–82.

92. The first bill passed into law on March 21 as the Anarchical and Revolutionary Crimes Act and gave no jury or right of appeal to political offenders. Sayer, "British Reaction to the Amritsar Massacre 1919–1920," 135.

93. Urdu poets urged people to have courage and sacrifice themselves for a noble cause. Urdu pamphlet, "Bande Mataram" (Delhi Home Rule Series/Bande Mataram Dilhi Swarajya) (Delhi, 1919), Urdu B 2867/2, British Library (henceforth BL).

94. Basu, *For King and Another Country*, 184–85.

95. Sayer, "British Reaction to the Amritsar Massacre 1919–1920," 130–64.

96. Ghadar-di-Gunj meant "Echoes of Mutiny" and was distributed by the Ghadar press. Quoted in Rai, *Legislative Politics and Freedom Struggle*, 58, 67; Sohi, *Echoes of Mutiny*, 60–61.

97. Rai, *Legislative Politics and Freedom Struggle*, 89, 111.

98. Sayer, "British Reaction to the Amritsar Massacre 1919–1920," 151.

99. V. W. Smith, Superintendent of Police (Political), Criminal Investigation Department, Punjab, "The Akali Dal and Shiromani Gurdwara Parbandhak Committee, 1921–22" (Lahore: Superintendent, Government Printing, Punjab 1922), Home (Political), pros. 459/II and k.w., 1922, p. 16, NAI.

100. Rai, *Legislative Politics and Freedom Struggle*, 89, 111; Punjab Government Civil Secretariat, "The Kirpan Question," 1924; Sayer, "British Reaction to the Amritsar Massacre 1919–1920," 144.

101. Petrie, *Developments in Sikh Politics*, 51.

102. From R. B. Hyde, Inspector General of Police, Bengal to Chief Secretary to the Government of Bengal, Political Department, file 885/17 (December 21, 1921), WBSA; Singh, *Gurdwara Reform Movement*, 466–67.

103. "Note on Sikh Enquiries," Intelligence Branch serial number 13/1916, file 454/16, WBSA.

104. Singh, *Gurdwara Reform Movement*, 467.

105. Singh, *Gurdwara Reform Movement*, 468; A. Shairp, Colonel, for Major-General, Secretary to the Government of India, to the Adjutant General in India (September 30, 1920), IOR/L/MIL/7/12459: 1920; "History of Kirpan," 2.

106. "History of Kirpan," 1922.

107. Mandair, "Colonial Formations of Sikhism," 78.

108. Many *gurdwara* managers (mahants) were Udasi Sikhs who were renowned for their asceticism but denigrated for collaborating with British officials. They were also largely *sahajdhari*—"slow converts" who cut their hair.

109. Tan, *Garrison State*, 194, 196, 201; Barstow, *Handbooks for the Indian Army, Sikhs*, 35–36; Amarjit Singh Narang, "The Shiromani Akali Dal," in *Oxford Handbook of Sikh Studies*, ed. Pashaura Singh and Louis E. Fenech (Oxford: Oxford University Press, 2014), 339–49, at 339.

110. For more about Pathans, see Chapter 2. V. W. Smith, "A Note on the Guru-Ka-Bagh Affair, 1922" (Lahore: Superintendent, Government Printing, Punjab, 1923), European Manuscripts (henceforth Mss Eur), BL, F161/11.

111. Punjab Government Civil Secretariat, "Note on the Sikh Question in the Punjab, 1919–1922" (June 1922).

112. Punjab Government Civil Secretariat, "Note on the Sikh Question."

113. Punjab Government Civil Secretariat, "Note on the Sikh Question."

114. Punjab Government Civil Secretariat, "Note on the Sikh Question"; Punjab Government Civil Secretariat, "The Kirpan Question," 1924; Rai, *Legislative Politics and Freedom Struggle*, 112.

115. "Report on the Political and Economic Situation in the Punjab for the Fortnight Ending the 15th of March, 1921," IOR/L/PJ/6/1776, file 7087.

116. Shaikh Asghar Ali to All Deputy Commissioners in the Punjab (February 9, 1921).

117. Shaikh Asghar Ali to All Deputy Commissioners in the Punjab.

118. One SGPC president was sentenced to one year of rigorous imprisonment for "manufacturing kirpans" when police found "179 swords of various sizes" at his factory. Police confiscated *kirpans* from many Sikh leaders including Giani Sher Singh, Sardar Labh Singh, and Sardar Dalip Singh of the SGPC in Ludhiana and Chaudhri Shamsher Singh, Secretary from the Singh Sabhas of Sitapur Singh. This even extended beyond Punjab, as Calcutta police arrested several men who carried swords between two and three feet in length. Punjab Government Civil Secretariat, "Notes on Government Evidence to Be Placed Before General Birdwood's Committee on Kirpans," Home—Police, file 116 (1924), PSA; Excerpt from "Sardar Kharak Sing's [*sic*] Case," *Amrita Bazar Patrika* (April 25, 1922), Serial 13/17, file 885/17 WBSA; Singh, *Gurdwara Reform Movement*, 389, 466; "History of Kirpan," 14–16; one 1922 pamphlet estimated that the number of arrests was 1,500 but the Government of India maintained that the number was less than 1,000; extract from "Sikhs and Their Kripans [*sic*]," *Amrita Bazar Patrika* (May 16, 1923), Serial 13/17, file 885/17, WBSA.

119. Singh, *Gurdwara Reform Movement*, 463

120. In 1922, one Lahore High Court judge admitted that *kirpan* was a Sanskrit word meaning "sword." He nonetheless upheld the government's arrest of a man wearing a 22-inch *kirpan*. "History of Kirpan," 4.

121. The men were Hari Singh and Kishan Singh. Extract from the Indian Law Reports, Before Mr. Justice Scott-Smith [*sic*] and Mr. Justice Harrison, March 18, 1924, Hari Singh and Kishan Singh—Petitioners, versus the Crown—Respondent, Criminal Revision No. 1612 of 1923, IOR/L/PJ/6/1776, file 7087.

122. Extract from the Indian Law Reports, Before Mr. Justice Scott-Smith [*sic*] and Mr. Justice Harrison, March 18, 1924, Hari Singh and Kishan Singh—Petitioners, versus the Crown—Respondent.

123. Roughly "200 Akalis, armed with lathis, axes and *kirpans*" marched to Baba Budha at Teja in Gurdaspur district in September 1921. "Brief Note on Trouble in Four Indian Units During February 1922," Home (Political), pros. 459/II and k.w., 1922, p. 2, NAI.

124. Copy of telegram from Viceroy, Home Department, to Secretary of State for India (November 28, 1921), IOR/L/PJ/6/1776, file 7087.

125. "Brief Note on Trouble in Four Indian Units During February 1922"; Smith, "The Akali Dal and Shiromani Gurdwara Parbandhak Committee, 1921–22," 27.

126. Tan, *Garrison State*, 207, 226.

127. Excerpt from the *Gazette of India* (February 25, 1922), Home Department: Establishments (February 20, 1922), IOR/L/PJ/6/1776, file 7087.

128. Smith, "The Akali Dal and Shiromani Gurdwara Parbandhak Committee, 1921–22" (1922).

129. H. D. Craik, Off. Chief Secretary to Government, Punjab, "Proceedings of the Governor of the Punjab in Council in the Home Department, No. 15150, Dated the 6th May 1922," Home Department Proceedings, May 1922, Part A, file 23, pp. 2–3, PSA.

130. Report from Officer Commanding 23 Sikh Pioneers (February 2, 1922), Army Department, note of 1922, Home (Political), file 415, NAI; Tan, *Garrison State*, 216.

131. Mandair, "Colonial Formations of Sikhism," 78–79; "Brief Note on Trouble in Four Indian Units During February 1922"; Tan, *Garrison State*, 212.

132. "Brief Note on Trouble in Four Indian Units During February 1922," 19, 23.

133. "Note on the Sikh Question in the Punjab, 1919–1922."

134. Tan, *Garrison State*, 198, 212.

135. Photographs of the Fourth Akali Jatha (1924), IOR/R/1/1/4903.

136. Gandhi, *The Common Cause*, chap. 3.

137. Smith, "A Note on the Guru-Ka-Bagh Affair"; Barstow, *Handbooks for the Indian Army, Sikhs*, 19.

138. "Brief Note on Trouble in Four Indian Units During February 1922," 19. Teja Singh also estimated that one-third of the Akali *jathas* had served in the First World War. Singh, *Gurdwara Reform Movement*, 422, 428.

139. They estimated that 1,270 out of 15,506 Akalis were military pensioners or discharged soldiers. "Brief Note on Trouble in Four Indian Units During February 1922."

140. "Brief Note on Trouble in Four Indian Units During February 1922," 10–11, 15.

141. These were Mota Singh of Patara and Kishan Singh "Gargaj." Report from Government of India, Activities of the Babbar Akali Movement, 1922, IOR/L/PJ/6/1851, file 3206.

142. Mohan, *Militant Nationalism in the Punjab*, 57.

143. Singh, *Gurdwara Reform Movement*, 432–33.

144. Singh, *Gurdwara Reform Movement*, 433–34.

145. Singh, *Gurdwara Reform Movement*, 433.

146. Extract from the General Staff (India) Summary of Intelligence for the week ending July 11, 1922, IOR/L/MIL/7/13768.

147. Tan, *Garrison State*, 216; Singh, *Gurdwara Reform Movement*, 467.

148. Singh, *Gurdwara Reform Movement*, 390.

149. "Prosecution for Sedition of the Zamindar, Bande Mataram and Akali Newspapers," IOR/L/PJ/6/1805, file 2598: February–August 1922.

150. Note by General Staff, India on Subject of Attempts to Tamper with the Loyalty of Indian Soldiers, 1922–1923, IOR/L/MIL/7/13768.

151. Smith, "A Note on the Guru-Ka-Bagh Affair," 1.

152. Smith, "A Note on the Guru-Ka-Bagh Affair."

153. Smith, "A Note on the Guru-Ka-Bagh Affair," 4, 13.

154. Mohan, *Militant Nationalism in the Punjab*, 52, 64.

155. *Tribune*, October 6, 1923, 10.

156. Mohan, *Militant Nationalism in the Punjab*, 71–72.

157. Rai, *Legislative Politics and Freedom Struggle*, 146.

158. Extract from *Amrita Bazar Patrika* (May 16, 1923); "Sikhs and Their Kripans [*sic*]." One pamphlet estimated that the number of arrests was 1,500 but the Government of India maintained that the number was less than 1,000. "History of Kirpan," 15.

159. "Prosecution for Sedition of the Zamindar, Bande Mataram and Akali Newspapers," IOR/L/PJ/6/1805, file 2598.

160. The homophobic undertones of these assertions also became increasingly common in interwar activism as nationalists associated same-sex acts with colonialism. Kate Imy, "Queering the Martial Races: Masculinity, Sex and Circumcision in the Twentieth-Century British Indian Army," *Gender and History* 27, No. 2 (August 2015): 374–96.

161. Aidan Forth, *Barbed-Wire Imperialism: Britain's Empire of Camps, 1876–1903* (Berkeley: University of California Press, 2017).

162. Smith, "A Note on the Guru-Ka-Bagh Affair," 9.

163. Smith, "A Note on the Guru-Ka-Bagh Affair," 3.

164. Singh, *Gurdwara Reform Movement*, 469.

165. "Adjustment of the Expenditure Incurred by the Military Authorities in the Nabha State in Connection with Possible Disturbances at the Time of the Departure of His Highness the Maharaja," IOR/R/1/1/1509(2): 1924–27.

166. "Extract from Moral & Material Progress Reports" (1924), 282–84, Mss Eur F161/111; Mandair, "Colonial Formations of Sikhism," 79.

167. "Copies of Two Notes on the Akali Agitation Given by V. W. Smith in Amplification of the Punjab Government Bluebook 'Guru-ka-Bagh,'" Mss Eur F161/111; "Extract from Moral & Material Progress Reports" (1924) 423/24, pp. 282–83, Mss Eur F161/111.

168. "Extract from Moral & Material Progress Reports," 423/24, p. 286, Mss Eur F161/111.

169. Louis E. Fenech has described Jaito as the "final victory" in 1924 that gave the Singh Sabhas movement its control over Sikh identity. Louis E. Fenech, "Contested Nationalism; Negotiated Terrains: The Way Sikhs Remember Udham Singh 'Shahid' (1899–1940)," *Modern Asian Studies* 36, No. 4 (2002): 827–70.

170. Photographs of the Fourth Akali Jatha, IOR/R/1/1/4903: 1924.

171. "Extract from Moral & Material Progress Report," 424/5, p. 342; Smith, "A Note on the Guru-Ka-Bagh Affair."

172. Tan, *Garrison State*, 341, 236.

173. Tan, *Garrison State*.

174. Rai, *Legislative Politics and Freedom Struggle*, 118–19.

175. The SGPC gained official recognition and status from the government. In turn, they threw their support behind the imperial state by rejecting all affiliation and association with more extreme factions such as the Babbar Akali. Rai, *Legislative Politics and Freedom Struggle*, 147.

176. Extract from *Pioneer Mail* (May 3) and extract from *New York Times* (November 12, 1921), "Gandhi Exhorts Hindus to Remove Lawrence Statue," IOR/L/PJ/6/1776, file 7098.

177. *Our Indian Empire: A Short Review and Some Hints for the Use of Soldiers Proceeding to India* (London: His Majesty's Stationery Office, n.d., ca. 1912), 51–52. The 1932 edition uses the title *The Indian Empire*.

178. Stuart, *The Indian Empire*, 67.

179. W. H. Barlow Wheeler, Lt, Adjutant, 4th Bn, 11th Sikh Regt, *Standing Orders, 4th Bn. 11th Sikh Regiment* (Landikotal, March 1939), 72.

180. Susan Kent, *Aftershocks: The Politics of Trauma in Britain, 1918–1931* (New York: Palgrave Macmillan, 2009); Sayer, "British Reaction to the Amritsar Massacre 1919–1920," 130–64; Jon Lawrence, "Forging a Peaceable Kingdom: War, Violence, and Fear of Brutalization in Post–First World War Britain," *Journal of Modern History* 75 (September 2003): 557–89; Kim A. Wagner, "'Calculated to Strike Terror': The Amritsar Massacre and the Spectacle of Colonial Violence," *Past and Present* 233, No. 1 (2016): 185–225.

181. For the public school comparison, see Sayer, "British Reaction to the Amritsar Massacre 1919–1920," 162–63.

CHAPTER 2

1. Kaushik Roy, *Hinduism and the Ethics of Warfare in South Asia: From Antiquity to the Present* (Cambridge: Cambridge University Press, 2012), 217. Roy provides a table of religious composition of the Indian Army in 1912. Punjabi Muslims total 16%, Pathans 7.7%, Hindustani Muslims 5.7%, and "other Muslims" 5.5%. See also *Proceedings of the Army in India Committee, 1912*, vol. I-A, Minority Report (Simla, 1913), 156.

2. They used Persianized Urdu language in the Company and Indian armies. Kaushik Roy, "The Hybrid Military Establishment of the East India Company in South Asia: 1750–1849," *Journal of Global History* 6, No. 2 (2011): 195–218.

3. Nile Green, *Islam and the Army in Colonial India: Sepoy Religion in the Service of Empire* (New York: Cambridge University Press, 2009), 18.

4. Anjali Arondekar, *For the Record: On Sexuality and the Colonial Archive in India* (Durham, NC: Duke University Press, 2009), 69, 85; Indrani Chatterjee, "When 'Sexuality' Floated Free of Histories in South Asia," *Journal of Asian Studies* 71, No. 4 (November 2012): 945–62, at 947.

5. Seema Alavi, *Muslim Cosmopolitanism in the Age of Empire* (Cambridge, MA: Harvard University Press, 2015); Barbara D. Metcalf and Thomas R. Metcalf, *A Concise History of Modern India* (Cambridge: Cambridge University Press, 2012).

6. Martin J. Bayly, *Taming the Imperial Imagination: Colonial Knowledge, International Relations, and the Anglo-Afghan Encounter, 1808–1878* (Cambridge: Cambridge University Press, 2016); Antoinette Burton, *The First Anglo-Afghan Wars: A Reader* (Durham, NC: Duke University Press, 2014).

7. See note 1.

8. Major F. C. C. Yeats-Brown, *The Star and Crescent: Being the Story of the 17th Cavalry from 1858 to 1922* (Allahabad: Pioneer Press, 1927), 130.

9. Francis Thackeray Warre-Cornish, Letter (September 2, 1895), quoted in Francis Yeats-Brown, *The Star and Crescent*, 39.

10. His attitude is reported in J. F. C. Fuller, "Report on India," J. F. C. Fuller Papers, Box 1, Envelope 10, Rutgers University Special Collections and University Archives, 13.

11. See Bernt Glatzer, "Being Pashtun—Being Muslim: Concepts of Person and War in Afghanistan," in *Essays on South Asian Society: Culture and Politics II*, ed. Bernt Glatzer (Berlin: Verlag Das Arabische Buch, 1998), 83–94; Brandon D. Marsh, "The North-West Frontier and the Crisis of Empire: Post-War India and the Debate over Waziristan, 1919–1923," *British Scholar* 1, No. 2 (March 2009): 197–221, at 198, 200; Elizabeth Kolsky, "The Colonial Rule of Law and the Legal Regime of Exception: Frontier 'Fanaticism' and State Violence in British India," *American Historical Review* 120, No. 4 (October 2015): 1218–46.

12. Leila Tarazi Fawaz, *A Land of Aching Hearts: The Middle East in the Great War* (Cambridge, MA: Harvard University Press, 2014), 214.

13. F. C. Isemonger and J. Slattery, *An Account of the Ghadr Conspiracy, 1913–1915* (Lahore: Superintendent, Government Printing, Punjab, 1919), 87.

14. Alavi, *Muslim Cosmopolitanism*.

15. Alexander George Stuart, *Our Indian Empire: A Short Review and Some Hints for the Use of Soldiers Proceeding to India* (Calcutta: Government of India Central Publication Branch, 1912), 66–67. This work was also published under the title *The Indian Empire*.

16. Home, Jails, file 7, part A (May 1915), PSA.

17. Green, *Islam and the Army*.

18. Thomas L. Hughes, "The German Mission to Afghanistan, 1915–1916," *German Studies Review* 25, No. 3 (October 2002): 447–76, at 450; Hew Strachan, *The First World War* (London: Simon & Schuster, 2006), 98; Fritz Fischer, *Germany's Aims in the First World War* (London: Chatto & Windus, 1967).

19. Mustafa Aksakal, "'Holy War Made in Germany'? Ottoman Origins of the 1914 Jihad," *War in History* 18, No. 2 (2011): 184–99, at 185–86.

20. Aksakal, "'Holy War'?," 191, 199.

21. Commander-in-Chief Lord Kitchener worried that the 5th Light Infantry was "too Mohammedan for service in Egypt." Letter from General Officer Commanding the Troops, Straits Settlements, to the Secretary, War Office (August 26, 1915), IOR/L/MIL/7/7191; *Report, in Connection with "Mutiny of 5th Light Infantry at Singapore 1915": Part I—Proceedings of Court of Enquiry* (Simla: Government Central Branch Press, 1915), section 7, IOR/L/MIL/7/7191; Nikolas Gardner, *The Siege of Kut-al-Amara: At War in Mesopotamia, 1915–1916* (Bloomington and Indianapolis: Indiana University Press), 2014.

22. The 15th Lancers petitioned the government and focused on the suffering that women and children would endure without the support of their sons, husbands, and fathers. Urdu petition related to mutiny of 15th Lancers, Collection 425/1155, IOR/L/MIL/7/18327: 1917–1920.

23. H. V. Cox, Minute Paper (July 17, 1918), IOR/L/MIL/7/18848.

24. Ayesha Jalal, *Partisans of Allah: Jihad in South Asia* (Cambridge, MA: Harvard University Press, 2008), 207; John Slight, *The British Empire and the Hajj, 1865–1956* (Cambridge, MA: Harvard University Press, 2015), 189.

25. Jalal, *Partisans of Allah*, 204–6.

26. Hughes, "The German Mission to Afghanistan, 1915–1916."

27. Jalal, *Partisans of Allah*, 207–8.

28. "Translations of the 'Ghadr'" (November 1915), Mss Eur E288/3.

29. Letters that made religious appeals for soldiers to drop out of British service became coded as the "snowball." Gajendra Singh, *The Testimonies of Indian Soldiers and the Two World Wars: Between Self and Sepoy* (London: Bloomsbury Press, 2014), 99–128.

30. Hughes, "The German Mission to Afghanistan, 1915–1916," 454.

31. This is mentioned in a discussion of sending men to East Africa after 1908. To the Secretary of State for India from the Army Department (September 7, 1911), Proceedings of the Government of India in the Army Department for the Month of January 1912, NAI.

32. Tan Tai Yong, *The Garrison State: The Military, Government and Society in Colonial Punjab, 1849–1947* (New Delhi and London: Sage, 2005), 253–54.

33. Tan, *Garrison State*.

34. Singh, *The Testimonies of Indian Soldiers*, 124–25.

35. Many thanks to Mohammad Ali Raza, Language Must, for his assistance translating and analyzing this document with me. 'Abd al-Hakim, *Fauj aur-Police ki Mulazamat Musalmanan I Hind ke Liye Mazhaban ja'iz aur-zaruri hai* [On the necessity of Indian Musalmans joining the army and the police] (Lahore, 1923), U.D. 2231, BL.

36. He also felt that Indianization was a sign that the British Empire was willing and eager to restore power to Indians. 'Abd al-Hakim, *Fauj aur-Police*, 8.

37. 'Abd al-Hakim, *Fauj aur-Police*, 12, 18–19, 2–3.

38. IOR/L/PS/11/129, file 5094.

39. For additional details about Ramzan, see Chapter 4; IOR/L/PS/11/129, file 5094. See also Kate Imy, "Kidnapping and a 'Confirmed Sodomite': An Intimate Enemy on the Northwest Frontier of India, 1915–1925," *Twentieth Century British History* 28, No. 1 (March 2017): 29–56.

40. Dom Bede Camm, *Pilgrim Paths in Latin Lands* (London: MacDonald & Evans, 1923).

41. Letter from Everard Digby to E. S. Montagu (November 9, 1918), Collection 425/1449, IOR/L/MIL/7/18619.

42. Letter from Everard Digby to E. S. Montagu.

43. Draft Letter to War Office from H. V. Cox (October 30, 1918); Letter to Colonel S. D. Gordon, India Office, from Clive Wigram (November 19, 1918), IOR/L/MIL/7/18619.

44. R. W. Headly, Draft Letter to the Secretary to the Government of India Army Department, undated, IOR/L/MIL/7/18619.

45. Singh, *The Testimonies of Indian Soldiers*, 117.

46. Santanu Das, "Indians at Home, Mesopotamia and France, 1914–1918: Towards an Intimate History," in *Race, Empire and First World War Writing*, ed. Santanu Das (Cambridge: Cambridge University Press, 2011); Fawaz, *A Land of Aching Hearts*.

47. Abdul Rauf Khan, 21st Combined Field Ambulance, Mesopotamia, to Lance Dafadar Abdul Jabar Khan (Hindustani Muslim, 6th Cavalry, France), March 7, 1916, reproduced in David Omissi, *Indian Voices of the Great War: Soldiers' Letters, 1914–18* (New York: Palgrave Macmillan, 1999), letter 261.

48. Anwar Shah to Aurangzeb Shah (Punjabi Muslim, Signal Troop, Lucknow Cavalry Brigade, France), Camel Corps, Suez, August 18, 1916, reproduced in Omissi, *Indian Voices of the Great War*, letter 383.

49. From Saif Ali, serving in France, either 40th Pathans or 129th Baluchis, to Kazim Din, 19th Punjabis, Robat, Seistan, Persia (Urdu, August 17, 1915), Military Dept. Censor of Indian Mails, 1914–1915, Pt. 5 FF. 713–869, IOR/L/MIL/5/825.

50. Secret Despatch from GHQ Egypt to DMI, despatched May 3, 1919, received May 5, 1919, IOR/L/MIL/7/18619.

51. Mario M. Ruiz, "Manly Spectacles and Imperial Soldiers in Wartime Egypt, 1914–19," *Middle Eastern Studies* 45, No. 3 (2009): 351–71, at 357, 365.

52. Letter from the War Office to the Under Secretary of State, India Office (June 24, 1921), IOR/L/MIL/7/18619.

53. Minute to Mr. Stewart signed H. V. Cox, January 27, 1919; Secret Despatch from GHQ Egypt to War Office, IOR/L/MIL/7/18619.

54. "The Arrangement of Islam: The Caliphate," translated by M.I.7c. War Office, No. 53 (August 8, 1916), "Hostile Oriental Propaganda Pamphlets," Mss Eur E288: 1914–19.

55. Jalal, *Partisans of Allah*, 209.

56. Slight, *The British Empire and the Hajj*.

57. Selections from the "Vernacular Newspapers Published in the North-Western Provinces & Oudh," vol. 33–34 (1900), Uttar Pradesh State Archives; Slight, *The British Empire and the Hajj*, 9.

58. One War Office official stated that the Hijaz railway was "destroyed over a considerable extent," which made it difficult for soldier-pilgrims to travel there. Letter to the Under Secretary of State, India Office on War Office, London, signed B. B. Cubitt (January 6, 1919), IOR/L/MIL/7/18619.

59. Letter dated "Received India Office" on November 20, unsigned, IOR/L/MIL/7/18619.

60. Captain Ajab Khan to the BGI, GHQ, EEF, dated Cairo, October 2, 1919, IOR/L/MIL/7/18619.

61. Secret Despatch from War Office to GHQ Egypt (December 24, 1918), IOR/L/MIL/7/18619.

62. Secret Despatch from GHQ Egypt to War Office (December 30, 1918), IOR/L/MIL/7/18619.

63. Minute to Gen Sir H. Cox (January 23, 1919); Secret Despatch from GHQ Egypt to War Office (January 21, 1919), IOR/L/MIL/7/18619.

64. When the second party arrived, the first departed, giving each group of men roughly one month to undertake the pilgrimage. Secret letter to Secretary, War Office (April 26, 1919), IOR/L/MIL/7/18619.

65. From India Office to Lt. Col. C. Colonel Wigram at Buckingham Palace (May 2, 1919), IOR/L/MIL/7/18619.

66. Statement of Subedar Major Sirdar Khan, 121st Pioneers, translated by H. P. Keelan Lt. Col. Cdg. 121st Pioneers, IOR/L/MIL/7/18619.

67. Hakim Said Hasan, "Report on Indian Troops Pilgrimage," IOR/L/MIL/7/18619.

68. To the British Agent, Jeddah, signed H. Said Hassan, Indian Police Officer, British Agency (January 30, 1919); Report to the British Agent, Jeddah, from H. Said Hassan (February 8, 1919). Hakim Said Hasan is listed as both Hasan and Hassan in British sources.

69. Statement of Subedar Major Sirdar Khan, IOR/L/MIL/7/18619.

70. Despite wearing their uniforms, they carried no arms, according to officials in Cairo. Copy of telegram from Egypforce [*sic*], to S. of S., dated Cairo (March 11, 1920).

71. The men received the direct order that they must stay in uniform during their entire stay with the exception of visiting "the holy place. If this order is disobeyed the man concerned will be severely punished." Statement of Subedar Major Sirdar Khan.

72. Copy of telegram from Viceroy Army Dept. (February 27, 1920) to Cairo, Constantinople, repeated Secretary of State, IOR/L/MIL/7/18619.

73. From the General Officer Commanding, EEF, to the Secretary, War Office, London (October 13, 1920).

74. To the British Agent, Jeddah, from H. Said Hassan, Indian Police Officer, British Agency (January 30, 1919); Report on first batch of Indian Muslim troops, from Sub, Maj. Jalal Khan, 2/19th Punjabis, to Officer Commanding, 2nd Mecca Party, and from General Officer Commanding, Egyptian Expeditionary Force, to Secretary, War Office, London (December 11, 1919); W. N. Congreve, Lt-Gen, General Officer Commanding Egyptian Expeditionary Force, IOR/L/MIL/7/18619.

75. According to Captain Ajab Khan, "the men became very fond of these guides." To the AAG (Indian), General Headquarters, Egyptian Expeditionary Force, Ajab Khan, Report (October 15, 1919).

76. They received greetings from Sheikh Suleman Kabil, the Rais-El-Baladia (chairman of Municipal Committee) of Jeddah, Rushdi Bey, the officer commanding Jeddah troops, and one Lt. Kamal, who received the troops on behalf of the Arab government. To the British Agent, Jeddah, from H. Said Hassan (January 30, 1919).

77. Khan to the AAG (Indian) (October 15, 1919), IOR/L/MIL/7/18619.

78. Statement of Subedar Major Sirdar Khan; Subedar Major Jalal Khan to the Officer Commanding, 2nd Mecca Party.

79. H. Said Hasan to the British Agent, Jeddah (February 1, 1919).

80. From Jalal Khan to Officer Commanding, 2nd Mecca Party, IOR/L/MIL/7/18619.

81. H. Said Hassan (January 30, 1919); Statement of Subedar Major Sirdar Khan, 121st Pioneers.

82. Medical Report by Captain J. M. Shah, IMS MO i/c 2nd Mecca Party, IOR/L/MIL/7/18619.

83. Statement of Subedar Major Sirdar Khan.

84. H. Said Hassan, Report to British Agent (February 19, 1919), IOR/L/MIL/7/18619.

85. Hakim Said Hassan, Report on Indian Troops Pilgrimage to His Excellency, Mahmud Pasha Kaisuni, MC Minister of War, Mecca (February 6, 1919).

86. H. Said Hassan, Report to British Agent, Jeddah (February 19, 1919); Statement of Subedar Major Sirdar Khan.

87. Statement of Subedar Major Sirdar Khan. Shah noted that several men got fevers and dysentery as a result of being fatigued from the journey. Medical Report by Captain J. M. Shah, IMS MO i/c 2nd Mecca Party; on the 1920 journey men caught no contagious diseases but many suffered from dysentery and diarrhea. From the General Officer Commanding, EEF, to the Secretary, War Office, London (October 13, 1920), IOR/L/MIL/7/18619.

88. From the General Officer Commanding, Egyptian Expeditionary Force, to the Secretary, War Office, London (December 11, 1919).

89. J. M. Shah, Medical Report, IOR/L/MIL/7/18619.

90. J. M. Shah, Medical Report.

91. From the General Officer Commanding, Egyptian Expeditionary Force, to the Secretary, War Office, London (December 11, 1919).

92. To Lt. Col. C. Colonel Wigram at Buckingham Palace, from the India Office (May 2, 1919); From Clive Wigram to Major G. L. Pepys, India Office (May 3, 1919), IOR/L/MIL/7/18619.

93. From Khan to the BGI, GHQ, EEF (October 2, 1919).

94. H. Said Hasan, Report to British Agent, Jeddah (February 4, 1919).

95. Report on Indian Troops Pilgrimage, IOR/L/MIL/7/18619.

96. Captain J. H. L. Hindmarsh, 8th Rajputs, attached to 2nd Battalion QVO Corps of Guides (FF) and organized the party's journey from Suez to Jeddah. From the Commander-in-Chief, Egyptian Expeditionary Forc,e to the Secretary, War Office, London (June 12, 1919).

97. J. M. Shah, Medical Report (October 21, 1919).

98. H. Said Hassan, Report to British Agent (February 19, 1919).

99. J. M. Shah, Medical Report (October 21, 1919).

100. Hasan, Report (February 1, 1919).

101. Speech by Captain Salamat Ulla Khan to King Hussein (January 31, 1919), IOR/L/MIL/7/18619.

102. H. Said Hassan, Report to the British Agent, Jeddah (February 8, 1919).

103. Hasan, Report (February 4, 1919).

104. Medical Report by Captain J. M. Shah.

105. Hasan, Report (February 4, 1919).

106. Statement of Subedar Major Sirdar Khan.

107. Hassan, Report (February 8, 1919).

108. Hasan, Report (February 4, 1919).

109. Hassan, Report (February 8, 1919).

110. Hassan, Report (February 19, 1919).

111. Statement of Subedar Major Sirdar Khan.

112. Ajab Khan to the AAG (Indian) (October 15, 1919), IOR/L/MIL/7/18619.

113. Report on Indian Troops Pilgrimage.

114. Ajab Khan to the AAG (Indian) (October 15, 1919).

115. Ajab Khan to the BGI, GHQ, EEF (October 2, 1919).

116. Statement of Subedar Major Sirdar Khan.

117. Ajab Khan to the AAG (Indian) (October 15, 1919).

118. Ajab Khan to the BGI, GHQ, EEF (October 2, 1919).

119. Ajab Khan to the AAG (Indian) (October 15, 1919).

120. David Arnold, "Touching the Body: Perspectives on the Indian Plague, 1896–1900," *Selected Subaltern Studies* (1988): 391–426.

121. From Sub. Maj. Jalal Khan, 2/19th Punjabis, to Officer Commanding, 2nd Mecca Party; Ajab Khan to the BGI, GHQ, EEF (October 2, 1919).

122. Ajab Khan to the BGI, GHQ, EEF (October 2, 1919).

123. *Straits Times* (September 27, 1916): 10, accessed November 21, 2013, http://newspapers.nl.sg/Digitised/Article/straitstimes19160927-1.2.63.aspx.

124. Tan, *Garrison State*, 254.

125. Slight, *The British Empire and the Hajj*, 208.

126. Medical Report by Captain J. M. Shah.

127. From the General Officer Commanding, EEF, to the Secretary, War Office, London (October 13, 1920).

128. Letter from B. B. Cubitt, War Office, to the Under Secretary of State, India Office (April 29, 1921).

129. From J. E. Shuckburgh to the Secretary, War Office (June 6, 1921), IOR/L/MIL/7/18619.

130. Letter from War Office to the Under Secretary of State, India Office (June 24, 1921).

131. Letter from J. E. Shuckburgh to the Under Secretary of State, India Office (March 27, 1922).

132. For additional citations on the German mission, see notes 18 and 19. Shrabani Basu, *For King and Another Country: Indian Soldiers on the Western Front, 1914–1918* (London: Bloomsbury, 2015), 118; Report on Deserters List A, BL/IOR/L/MIL/17/5/2403; Report of the death from influenza of the deserter Mir Mast (Public Records Department), Foreign & Political (Public Records), Frontier File No. Progs., No. 70 (May 1919), Part B, NAI.

133. Glatzer, "Being Pashtun—Being Muslim," 83–94; Kolsky, "The Colonial Rule of Law"; Marsh, "The North-West Frontier and the Crisis of Empire," 198, 200.

134. British authors regarded them as more brave, manly, and chivalric than other South Asians. They also feared their alleged uncontrollability and cruelty. Stuart, *The Indian Empire* (1932), 66; Singh, *The Testimonies of Indian Soldiers*, 45; Edmund Candler, *The Sepoy* (London, 1919), 63.

135. Parliamentary Notice Session 1920, Undersecretary, dated July 28, 1920, HVC; Question by Mr. Allen Parkinson to the Secretary of State for India, No. 425, file 1607, IOR/L/MIL/7/18846.

136. He believed that "this feeling has hardly touched Punjabi Mussulmans." Copy of telegram from Viceroy (January 29, 1915), No. 425, file 1607, IOR/L/MIL/7/18846.

137. Heather Streets-Salter, *World War One in Southeast Asia: Colonialism and Anti-colonialism in an Era of Global Conflict* (Cambridge: Cambridge University Press, 2017).

138. Daily Report of the Director of Criminal Intelligence, dated Simla, July 20, 1907, NAI.

139. Copy of telegram from Viceroy (January 29, 1915).

140. Gardner, *The Siege of Kut-al-Amara*, 21, 171.

141. Minute Paper by H. V. Cox (July 17, 1918), "Insubordination Among Trans-Frontier Pathans," Collection 425/1603, IOR/L/MIL/7/18848.

142. See, for example, Pathan (Afridi) from ——, serving with 57th Rifles in France, to ——, Khyber Rifles, Peshawar (Urdu, August 30, 1915), Copies of "Supplementary Letters" from censored Indian mails, Mss Eur F143/93; Pathan (Afridi) from ——, Camp Chakdarra, to ——, 4th Cavalry (Urdu, August 17, 1915), Copies of "Supplementary Letters" from censored Indian mails, Mss Eur F143/93: September 1915–June 1916.

143. Cox, Minute Paper (July 17, 1918).

144. As Ressaidar Husyar Singh lamented, the land in Mesopotamia was "desolate." Ressaidar Hushyar Singh, Sikh, 16th Cavalry, Mesopotamia, to Jemadar Harband Singh, 9th Hodson's Horse, France, January 30, 1916, reproduced in Omissi, *Indian Voices of the Great War*, letter 230. Fawaz, *A Land of Aching Hearts*, 209.

145. Gardner, *The Siege of Kut-al-Amara*, 125, 170; Fawaz, *A Land of Aching Hearts*, 226; Charles Townshend, *Desert Hell: The British Invasion of Mesopotamia* (Cambridge, MA: Belknap Press of Harvard University Press, 2011), 244.

146. Townshend, *Desert Hell*, 23; Fawaz, *A Land of Aching Hearts*, 223; Lawrence James, *The Golden Warrior: The Life and Legend of Lawrence of Arabia* (New York: Sky-horse Publishing, 2008).

147. Fawaz, *A Land of Aching Hearts*, 211, 223.

148. F. James, *Faraway Campaign* (London: Grayson and Grayson, 1934), 17.

149. Quoted in DeWitt C. Ellinwood Jr., *Between Two Worlds: A Rajput Officer in the Indian Army, 1905–21* (Lanham, MD: Hamilton Books, 2005), 398.

150. Sir Krishna G. Gupta, Annexure I, Minute, *Report of the Committee Appointed by the Secretary of State for India to Enquire into the Administration and Organisation of the Army in India*, Chairman: Lord Esher (London: His Majesty's Stationery Office, 1920).

151. Copies of "Supplementary Letters" from censored Indian mails, Mss Eur F143/93: September 1915–June 1916.

152. Cox, Minute Paper (July 17, 1918).

153. Major R. T. I. Ridgway, 40th Pathans, Late Recruiting Staff Officer for Pathans, *Handbooks for the Indian Army, Pathans* (Calcutta: Superintendent, Government Printing, India, 1910).

154. Gardner, *The Siege of Kut-al-Amara*, 11.

155. Military Secret, from Viceroy, February 15, 1916, IOR/L/MIL/7/18848; Gardner, *The Siege of Kut-al-Amara*, 13.

156. Maia Ramnath, *Haj to Utopia: How the Ghadar Movement Charted Global Radicalism and Attempted to Overthrow the British Empire* (Berkeley and Los Angeles: University of California Press, 2011), 196, 200.

157. Jalal, *Partisans of Allah*, 209.

158. Jalal, *Partisans of Allah*, 210.

159. The Waziristan campaign lasted formally from 1919 to 1920 and posed similar challenges to the Mesopotamia campaign in the First World War. Marsh, "The North-West Frontier and the Crisis of Empire," 198; Kaushik Roy, "Indian Cavalry from the First World War till the Third Afghan War," in *The Indian Army in the Two World Wars*, ed. Kaushik Roy (Leiden: Brill, 2012), 191–222.

160. Pathan (Afridi), from ——, Camp Chakdarra, to ——, 4th Cavalry (Urdu, August 17, 1915), Copies of "Supplementary Letters" from censored Indian mails, Mss Eur F143/93: September 1915–June 1916.

161. Lilian A. Starr, *Frontier Folk of the Afghan Border and Beyond* (London, 1920), 62.

162. Priya Satia, "The Defense of Inhumanity: Air Control and the British Idea of Arabia," *American Historical Review* (February 2006): 16–51, at 26; David E. Omissi, *Air Power and Colonial Control: The Royal Air Force, 1919–1939* (Manchester, 1990), 12.

163. "Afghan Versus Aeroplane," *The Sphere* (June 14, 1919): 224.

164. Sirdar Ikbal Ali Shah, "Confessions of an Afghan Brigand," *Graphic* 117, No. 3010 (August 20, 1927): 288.

165. Diary of Private J. P. Swindlehurst (March 29, 1920), Imperial War Museum. See also W. F. Raper, *Hints for Soldiers Proceeding to India: A Common-Sense Health Lecture* (London: Gale & Polden, Ltd., 1911), 42.

166. Singh, *The Testimonies of Indian Soldiers*, 38–39.

167. Jalal, *Partisans of Allah*, 211.

168. Jalal, *Partisans of Allah*, 210.

169. Yeats-Brown, *The Star and Crescent*, opposite title page.

170. Ramnath, *Haj to Utopia*, 202.

171. Swindlehurst, Diary (March 29, 1920).

172. Swindlehurst, Diary (March 29, 1920).

173. One British officer turned over a detailed operation for an attack on the depot that was supposedly prepared by Moysey. D. S. Hadow, Report on the actions of Lt. Moysey, late 1/22nd Punjabis, during the last year (November 22, 1921), BL, India Office Records, IOR/L/E/7/1259, file 458; From H. A. Smith, Deputy Commissioner, Rawalpindi, to H. P. Tollinton, Commissioner, Rawalpindi (November 23, 1921), IOR/L/E/7/1259, file 458; Hadow, Report (November 22, 1921).

174. Smith to Tollinton (November 23, 1921).

175. *Indian Army List* (July 1921), 1104.

176. Moysey was twenty-three when this adoption took place. Muzaffar Shah, Nur Hussein's father, signed an adoption certificate giving Moysey permission to act as his son's "guardian" giving him control over the boy "as if he were his father." From

Lt. R. A. L. Moysey, 1/22nd Punjabis, Rawalpindi, to the General Officer Commanding, Rawalpindi District (November 21, 1921), IOR/L/E/7/1259, file 458. Copy of an
agreement made between Muzaffar Shah and Lieut. Moysey, regarding the adoption of
Nur Hussein Shah (November 27, 1920), IOR/L/E/7/1259, file 458.

177. Hadow, Report (November 22, 1921).

178. Hadow, Report (November 22, 1921).

179. From Moysey to the General Officer Commanding (November 21, 1921); From
Smith to Tollinton (November 23, 1921).

180. Hadow, Report (November 22, 1921).

181. From Smith to Tollinton (November 23, 1921); Hadow, Report (November 22,
1921).

182. Arondekar, *For the Record*, 39; Douglas M. Peers, "The Raj's Other Great Game:
Policing the Sexual Frontiers of the Indian Army in the First Half of the Nineteenth
Century," in *Discipline and the Other Body: Correction, Corporeality, Colonialism*, ed. An-
upama Rao and Stephen Pierce (Durham, NC: Duke University Press, 2006), 115–50.

183. Richard Francis Burton claimed that sodomy was one among many "vices specific
to Muslims." Later British officials considered it one factor influencing Muslim soldiers'
supposed tendencies toward desertion and religious radicalism. Singh, *The Testimonies of
Indian Soldiers*, 39, 44; Mrinalini Sinha, *Colonial Masculinity: The "Manly Englishman" and
the "Effeminate Bengali" in the Late Nineteenth Century* (Manchester: Manchester University
Press, 1995), 19. See also Imy, "Kidnapping and a 'Confirmed Sodomite,'" and Kate Imy,
"Queering the Martial Races: Masculinity, Sex and Circumcision in the Twentieth-
Century British Indian Army," *Gender and History* 27, No. 2 (August 2015): 374–96.

184. I am referring to R. A. L. Moysey as Moysey in keeping with standard practices for writing European names and referring to Nur Hussein Shah as Nur to keep with
standard practice in India to use first names even when using honorifics.

185. From Moysey to the General Officer Commanding, Rawalpindi District
(November 21, 1921), IOR/L/E/7/1259, file 458.

186. From Moysey to the General Officer Commanding, Rawalpindi District
(November 21, 1921).

187. From Hadow to the IG of Police, Punjab, the DIG of Police, Western Range,
the Deputy Commissioner, Police Office, Rawalpindi (November 22, 1921).

188. From Hadow to the IG of Police, Punjab, the DIG of Police, Western Range,
the Deputy Commissioner, Police Office, Rawalpindi (November 22, 1921); From Smith
to Tollinton (November 23, 1921).

189. From Hadow to the IG of Police, Punjab, the DIG of Police, Western Range,
the Deputy Commissioner, Police Office, Rawalpindi (November 22, 1921); see also from
Smith to Tollinton (November 23, 1921); Copy No. 1, Operation Order No. 1 by Lt.
Col. Moysey, Commanding the "Last Hope Relief Force," B. 281, Peshawar Road,
Rawalpindi (November 21, 1921), IOR/L/E/7/1259, file 458.

190. From Smith to Tollinton (November 23, 1921).

191. From Hadow to the IG of Police, Punjab, the DIG of Police, Western Range,
the Deputy Commissioner, Police Office, Rawalpindi (November 22, 1921).

192. Kabul Diary, No. 42, for Week Ending October 29, 1923, IOR/L/PJ/12/67.

193. From the India Office to the Under Secretary of State, Foreign Office, Secret Draft Paper (July 19, 1922), IOR/L/E/7/1259, file 458.

194. Copy of letter from Secretary to the Government of the Punjab, Home Department, to the Secretary to the Government of India, Home Department (December 7, 1921), IOR/L/E/7/1259, file 458; From Hadow to the IG of Police, Punjab, the DIG of Police, Western Range, the Deputy Commissioner, Rawalpindi (November 22, 1921).

195. From Smith to Tollinton (November 23, 1921); see also Deportation to England under the Defence of India (Consolidation) Rules of one R. A. L. Moysey, Department (Public Records) Home Branch (Public Records), Political File No. 433, Year 1921, NAI.

196. From Secretary to the Government of the Punjab (December 7, 1921).

197. Declaration to be made by Applicant for Passport (May 15, 1922), completed by Rex (Reginald) Abel Lewis Moysey, IOR/L/E/7/1259, file 458.

198. Passport Office Minute (July 4, 1922), FO 7947/7947/334, National Archives (UK).

199. From the India Office to the Under Secretary of State, Foreign Office (July 19, 1922); Letter from M. Villiers of the Foreign Office to the Under-Secretary of State, India Office (July 31, 1922), IOR/L/E/7/1259, file 458. Letter from R. A. L. Moysey to Chief Passport Officer, Passport Office, Westminster (August 8, 1922), IOR/L/E/7/1259, file 458.

200. Letter from New Scotland Yard to J. W. Hose (January 1, 1924), IOR/L/PJ/12/67; L. D. Wakely, Minute Paper (February 5, 1924), IOR/L/PS/11/243, P 533/1924.

201. Kabul Diary (October 29, 1923); see also FO 371/9288 (1923).

202. His stepfather, Colonel Rattray, had served in the Indian Army, including during the Second Anglo-Afghan War.

203. Kabul Diary (October 29, 1923).

204. Copy of telegram from Viceroy, Home Department, to Secretary of State for India (December 11, 1923), IOR/L/PJ/12/67.

205. For more on the orientalist trope of "dressing up," see, for example, Michael Silvestri, "The Thrill of 'Simply Dressing Up': The Indian Police, Disguise, and Intelligence Work in Colonial India," *Journal of Colonialism and Colonial History* 2 (2001); Edward Said, *Culture and Imperialism* (New York: Vintage, 1993), 161; Dane Kennedy, *The Highly Civilized Man: Richard Burton and the Victorian World* (Cambridge, MA: Harvard University Press, 2007), 69; Kaja Silverman, "White Skin, Brown Masks: The Double Mimesis, or with Lawrence in Arabia," *Differences* 1, No. 3 (1989): 19.

206. When she was too injured to make a speedy escape, they left her. "Murder by Raiders," *Pioneer Mail and Indian Weekly News* 47 (November 26, 1920): 27.

207. Claud Dangerfield, "Frontier Life in North-West India," *The Field* 142 (July 26, 1923): 122.

208. Alfred Ollivant, "Kidnapping a Memsahib," *The Sphere* 93, No. 1215 (May 5, 1923): 140.

209. Laurence Frederic Rushbrook Williams, *India: A Statement Prepared for Presentation to Parliament in Accordance with the Requirements of the 26th Section of the*

Government of India Act (1924). Thank you to Elizabeth Kolsky for reminding me of the Ellis case.

210. Shah, "Confessions of an Afghan Brigand," 288.

211. This is true for the National Archives (Kew) copies.

212. Marsh, "The North-West Frontier and the Crisis of Empire," 208–9.

213. Minute Paper, P. & J. (May 22, 1924), IOR/L/PJ/12/67; From the India Office, Public and Judicial (June 26, 1924), Home Political 28/II/1925, NAI.

214. One Indian cantonment schoolmaster was sentenced to seven years' rigorous imprisonment for sending a series of lurid and explicit letters to an English officer's wife threatening to kidnap her. Unlike Moysey, the man never approached her place of residence. Copy of the Judgment in King Emperor versus Kandhar Singh Rangin charged under Sections 506 and 507 IPC, IOR/R/1/1/1285: 1909.

CHAPTER 3

1. See, for example, the pamphlet *Our Indian Empire*, which describes Nepali men as preferring "the society of Europeans" and despising "all other eastern races." The Indian Army handbook on Gurkhas suggests similarly that "They despise the natives of India, and look up to and fraternize with Europeans, whom they admire for their superior knowledge, strength, and courage." Alexander George Stuart, *Our Indian Empire: A Short Review and Some Hints for the Use of Soldiers Proceeding to India* (Calcutta: Government of India Central Publication Branch, 1912), 35; Major B. U. Nicolay, *Handbooks for the Indian Army: Gurkhas. Compiled Under the Orders of the Government of India by Lt-Col Eden Vansittart* (Calcutta: Government of India Press, 1915), 58.

2. Nicolay, *Handbooks for the Indian Army: Gurkhas*, 54.

3. Seema Alavi, *The Sepoys and the Company: Tradition and Transition in Northern India, 1770–1830* (Oxford: Oxford University Press, 1998), 266, 268–69, 282, 291.

4. David Arnold, "Touching the Body: Perspectives on the Indian Plague, 1896–1900," *Selected Subaltern Studies* (1988): 391–426, at 393.

5. Michael Fisher, *Counterflows to Colonialism: Indian Travellers and Settlers in Britain, 1600–1857* (Delhi: Permanent Black, 2004), 92, 97, 223.

6. Loomarsh Roopnarine, "The Indian Sea Voyage Between India and the Caribbean During the Second Half of the Nineteenth Century," *Journal of Caribbean History* 44, No. 1 (2010): 48–74.

7. Mulk Raj Anand, *Across the Black Waters* (New Delhi: Orient Paperbacks, 2008), 169.

8. Havildar Fazl Mehdi (Punjabi Muslim) to Subedar Muhammad Nawaz Khan (28th Punjabis, attached 57th Rifles, France, 34), 28th Punjabis, Colombo, June 28, 1915, reproduced in David Omissi, *Indian Voices of the Great War: Soldiers' Letters, 1914–18* (New York: Palgrave Macmillan, 1999), letter 86, p. 72.

9. A South Indian Muslim to a friend in India, hospital ship, February 9, 1915, in Omissi, *Indian Voices of the Great War*, letter 18, p. 35.

10. Sanjog Rupakheti, "Reconsidering State-Society Relations in South Asia: A Himalayan Case Study," *Himalaya* 35, No. 2 (2015): 73–86, at 74, 76.

11. Alavi, *The Sepoys and the Company*, 270–71.

12. John Pemble, "Forgetting and Remembering Britain's Gurkha War," *Asian Affairs* 40, No. 3 (November 2009): 361–76, at 375; Mary Katherine Des Chene, "Relics of Empire: A Cultural History of the Gurkhas, 1815–1987," PhD Diss., Stanford University, 1991, 24.

13. Alavi, *The Sepoys and the Company*, 275, 277, 280. For more about the war, see John Pemble, *The Invasion of Nepal: John Company at War* (Oxford: Clarendon Press, 1971).

14. Sanjeev Uprety, "Masculinity and Mimicry: Ranas and Gurkhas," Baha Occasional Papers 5 (2011): 1–48, at 8.

15. Pemble, "Forgetting and Remembering Britain's Gurkha War," 375.

16. Lionel Caplan, *Warrior Gentlemen: "Gurkhas" in the Western Imagination* (Kathmandu: Berghahn Books, 2009); Uprety, "Masculinity and Mimicry," 8.

17. Alavi, *The Sepoys and the Company*, 265–67, 276, 285, 287–91.

18. Uprety, "Masculinity and Mimicry," 4; Des Chene, "Relics of Empire,"143.

19. Nepali soldiers initially had to take their discharge from British forces before reentering their homelands but Jung Bahadur eventually permitted their return if they wore civilian attire. Caplan, *Warrior Gentlemen*, 28–29; Des Chene, "Relics of Empire," 145; Uprety, "Masculinity and Mimicry," 4–6.

20. Caplan, *Warrior Gentlemen*, 29; Des Chene, "Relics of Empire," 1, 3, 146.

21. For further discussions of the Arya Samaj and the army, see Chapters 1 and 4. Barbara D. Metcalf and Thomas R. Metcalf, *A Concise History of Modern India* (Cambridge: Cambridge University Press, 2012), 141.

22. Bhuwan Lal Joshi and Leo E. Rose, *Democratic Innovations in Nepal: A Case Study of Political Acculturation* (Berkeley: University of California Press, 1966), 51.

23. Uprety, "Masculinity and Mimicry," 28.

24. Des Chene, "Relics of Empire," 148–49; Kapileshwar Labh, "China as a Factor in the Policy of British India Toward Nepal," *Journal of Indian History* 55, No. 3 (1977): 177–88, at 186.

25. Uprety, "Masculinity and Mimicry," 38, 40.

26. Uprety, "Masculinity and Mimicry," 28, 41.

27. Uprety, "Masculinity and Mimicry," 28.

28. Labh, "China as a Factor in the Policy of British India Toward Nepal," 177, 184–85.

29. The dowager empress, Tz'u-his, signed the Peking Protocol, agreed to pay an annual indemnity to the "Great Powers," and permitted foreign troops in China. Susanne Hoeber Rudolph, Lloyd L. Rudolph, and Mohan Singh Kanota, eds., *Reversing the Gaze: Amar Singh's Diary, a Colonial Subject's Narrative of Imperial India* (Boulder, CO: Westview Press, 2002), 135–36; Anand A. Yang, "China and India Are One: A Subaltern's Vision of 'Hindu China' During the Boxer Expedition of 1900–1901," in *Asia Inside Out: Changing Times*, ed. Eric Tagliacozzo, Helen F Siu, and Peter C. Perdue (Cambridge, MA: Harvard University Press, 2015), 207–25, at 207, 212; Anand A. Yang, "(A) Subaltern('s) Boxers: An Indian Soldier's Account of China and the World in 1900–1901," in *The Boxers,*

China, and the World, ed. Robert Bickers and R. G. Tiedemann (Plymouth: Rowman & Littlefield, 2007), 43–64.

30. From the Resident in Nepal (July 6, 1900), Foreign Department, Secret—E, August 1900, file 208–15, NAI; From Lieutenant Colonel D. C. F. MacIntyre, OC 1/4th Gurkhas, to Resident in Nepal, undated, ca. 1906, Foreign and Political Extl. (October 1906), file 51–53, NAI.

31. From the Resident in Nepal (June 25, 1900) to the Secretary to the Government of India, Foreign Department, Secret—E, August 1900, file 208–215, NAI.

32. A. P. Palmer, Note (July 1, 1900), Foreign Department, Secret—E, August 1900, file 208–15, NAI.

33. Lord Curzon, Note (July 1, 1900), Foreign Department, Secret—E, August 1900, file 208–15, NAI.

34. Telegram from agent to the Governor-General in Central India, Indore, to the Foreign Secretary, Simla (June 30, 1900), Foreign Department, Secret—E, August 1900, file 208–15, NAI.

35. From the Resident in Nepal Foreign Department (June 25, 1900).

36. Lord Curzon, Note (June 30, 1900), Foreign Department, Secret—E, August 1900, file 208–15, NAI.

37. Compiled by 1st Battalion Major D. G. J. Ryan, 2nd Battalion Major G. C. Strahan, 3rd Battalion Captain J. K. Jones, *Historical Record of the 6th Gurkha Rifles*, vol. 1, *1817–1919* (1925), 64–65, Gurkha Memorial Museum (Pokhara, Nepal).

38. Reproduced in Rudolph, Rudolph, and Kanota, *Reversing the Gaze*, 174, 182, 187–88, 191.

39. Yang, "China and India Are One," 207–25, at 207, 212; Yang, "(A) Subaltern('s) Boxers," 45–47, 56, 59–60.

40. From Major J. Manners-Smith, Officiating Resident in Nepal, to His Excellency Maharaja Sir Chandra Shamsher Jang Bahadur Rana, GCSI, Prime Minister and Marshal of Nepal (April 7, 1906), Foreign and Political Extl. (October 1906), file 51–53, NAI.

41. From Major J. Manners-Smith, VC, CIE, Resident in Nepal, to Sir L. W. Dane, CSI, KCIE, Secretary to the Government of India, Foreign Department (April 18, 1906), Foreign and Political Extl. (October 1906), file 51–53, NAI.

42. From MacIntyre to Resident in Nepal, undated, ca. 1906.

43. From Officer Commanding, 1/7th Gurkha Rifles, to the Brigade-Major, 1st Quetta Infantry Brigade (June 4, 1913), Army Department, file 1466–68, Part B (November 1913), NAI.

44. From Manners-Smith to Dane (April 18, 1906). The 1915 Army handbook on Gurkhas maintained that this was standardized to a payment of Rs. 3 for all soldiers returning from overseas. Nicolay, *Handbooks for the Indian Army: Gurkhas*, 50.

45. From Officer Commanding, 1/7th Gurkha Rifles, to the Brigade-Major (June 4, 1913).

46. From His Excellency Maharaja Sir Chandra Shamsher Jang Bahadur Rana, GCSI, Prime Minister of Nepal, to Major J. Manners-Smith, VC, CIE, Officiating Res-

ident in Nepal, Dated Camp (February 11, 1906), Foreign and Political Extl. (October 1906), file 51–53, NAI.

47. C. W. G. Richardson, Note (June 8, 1906), Foreign and Political Extl. (October 1906), file 51–53, NAI.

48. From Manners-Smith to Dane (May 12, 1906).

49. A. R. Martin, Note (July 12, 1906), Foreign and Political Extl. (October 1906), file 51–53, NAI.

50. From Major J. Manners-Smith, VC, CIE, Officiating Resident in Nepal, to Sir L. W. Dane, CSI, KCIE, Secretary to the Government of India, Foreign Department (May 12, 1906), Foreign and Political Extl. (October 1906), file 51–53, NAI.

51. "Appointment of the Prime Minister of Nepal, Sir Chandra Shamsher Jung, as Honorary Colonel of the 4th Gurkhas, and Grant to Him of the Honorary Rank of Major-General in the British Army: Visit of His Excellency the Commander-in-Chief to Nepal," Foreign and Political External—A, May 1907, file 54–72, p. 87, NAI.

52. *A Short History of the 3rd Queens Own Gurkha Rifles* (London: Hugh Rees Lt., 1907), 12; see also Gavin Rand and Kim Wagner, "Recruiting the 'Martial Races': Identities and Military Service in Colonial India," *Patterns of Prejudice* 46, Nos. 3–4 (2012): 236.

53. Nicolay, *Handbooks for the Indian Army: Gurkhas*, 54.

54. Caplan, *Warrior Gentlemen*, 30–31.

55. From the Officer Commanding, 1st Battalion, 1st KGO, Gurkha Rifles, to the Staff Captain, Jullundur Brigade (May 30, 1913), Army Department, file 1466–68, Part B (November 1913), NAI; Officer Commanding, 2nd Battalion, 1st KGO Gurkha Rifles, to the Staff Captain, Jullundur Brigade (June 3, 1913), Army Department, file 1466–68, Part B (November 1913), NAI.

56. Translation of a petition from discharged Rifleman Durga Mal, late 1st Battalion, 2nd Gurkha Rifles, to Lieutenant Saunders, Adjutant, 1st Battalion, 2nd Gurkha Rifles (August 6, 1913), Army Department, file 1466–68, Part B (November 1913), NAI.

57. From the Officer Commanding, 1/2nd Gurkha Rifles, to the Brigade-Major (May 26, 1913), NAI.

58. Letter from Lieutenant Colonel H. L. Showers, CSI, CIE, Officiating Resident in Nepal, to the Honorable Lieutenant Colonel Sir A. H. McMahon, GCVO, KCIE, CSI, Secretary to the Government of India in the Foreign Department, Simla (April 4, 1913), Army Department, file 1466–68, Part B (November 1913), NAI.

59. From Major C. Wigram, Equerry to His Majesty the King, to Sir James DuBoulay, Private Secretary to His Excellency the Viceroy (May 15, 1913), Army Department, file 1466–68, Part B (November 1913), NAI.

60. From the Officer Commanding, 1/2nd Gurkha Rifles, to the Brigade-Major (May 26, 1913).

61. From Wigram to DuBoulay (May 15, 1913).

62. From DuBoulay to Wigram (June 12, 1913).

63. Telegram from the Resident in Nepal, to the Secretary to the Government of India in the Foreign Department (November 10, 1913), Foreign and Political, External (December 1914), file 1–15 A, NAI.

64. From Lt-Col J. Manners-Smith, VC, CVO, CIE, Resident in Nepal, to Prime Minister and Marshal of Nepal (October 30, 1913), Foreign and Political, External (December 1914), file 1–15 A, NAI; From the Officer Commanding, 1st Battalion, 4th Gurkha Rifles, to the Staff Captain, Jullundur Brigade (May 30, 1913), Army Department, file 1466–68, Part B (November 1913), NAI.

65. Translation of a speech made by His Excellency Maharaja Sir Chandra Shamsher Jang Bahadur Rana, GCSI, Prime Minister of Nepal, Foreign and Political Extl. (October 1906), file 51–53, NAI.

66. From Major-General His Excellency Maharaja Sir Chandra Shumshere [*sic*] Jung Bahadur Rana, Prime Minister and Marshal of Nepal, to the Resident in Nepal (November 6, 1913), Foreign and Political, External (December 1914), file 1–15 A, NAI.

67. Letter from the Resident in Nepal (January 14, 1914), Foreign and Political, External (December 1914), file 1–15 A, NAI.

68. L. W. Reynolds, Note (November 19, 1913), Foreign and Political, External (December 1914), file 1–15 A, NAI.

69. From the General Officer Commanding, Burma Division, to the Adjutant General in India, Simla (June 12, 1913), Army Department, file 1466–68, Part B (November 1913), NAI; F. J. Aylmer, Note (August 2, 1913).

70. From the Officer Commanding, 1st Battalion, 4th Gurkha Rifles, to the Staff Captain, Jullundur Brigade (May 30, 1913).

71. B. Duff, Note (May 17, 1914), Foreign and Political, External (December 1914), file 1–15 A, NAI.

72. From the Officer Commanding, 2/7th Gurkha Rifles, to the Brigade Major, 1st Quetta Infantry Brigade (May 23, 1913), Army Department, file 1466–68, Part B (November 1913), NAI.

73. From Lieutenant Colonel J. Manners-Smith, VC, CVO, CIE, Resident in Nepal, to A. H. Grant, Esq, CIE, Officiating Secretary to the Government of India, Foreign and Political Department (February 26, 1914), Foreign and Political, External (December 1914), file 1–15 A, NAI; From the Secretary to the Government of India, Foreign and Political Department, to Lt-Col J. Manners-Smith, VC, CVO, CIE, Resident in Nepal, Katmandu (March 5, 1914), Foreign and Political, External (December 1914), file 1–15 A, NAI.

74. From Manners-Smith to Grant (February 26, 1914).

75. From the Foreign Secretary to the Government of India in the Foreign and Political Department to Lieutenant Colonel J. Manners-Smith, VC, CVO, CIE, Resident in Nepal (June 26, 1914), Foreign and Political, External (December 1914), file 1–15 A, NAI.

76. Lord Crewe, Military Department, India Office (September 18, 1914), IOR/L/MIL/7/5867: 1914–22.

77. From the Army Department Simla to the Most Honourable the Marquess of Crewe, KG, Secretary of State for India (July 23, 1914), IOR/L/MIL/7/5867: 1914–1922.

78. R. A. Cassels, Note (October 22, 1914), Foreign and Political, External (December 1914), file 1–15 A, NAI.

79. J. M. Walter, Note (October 23, 1914), Foreign and Political, External (December 1914), file 1–15 A, NAI.

80. F. J. Aylmer, Note (October 24, 1914), Foreign and Political, External (December 1914), file 1–15 A, NAI.

81. Caplan, *Warrior Gentlemen*, 31; Des Chene, "Relics of Empire," 150.

82. Des Chene, "Relics of Empire," 151.

83. Letter from Lieutenant-Colonel Manners-Smith, VC, CVO, CIE, to the Secretary to the Government of India (January 20, 1915), Army Department: War, file 21459–673, Appx. Part B, 1914–15, NAI.

84. By February 1915, commanding officers received orders to send all Gurkhas to Dehra Dun. Telegram to the General Officers Commanding, 2nd (Rawal Pindi) Division, 3rd (Lahore) Divisional Area, 4th (Quetta) Division, 6th (Poona) and 7th (Meerut) Divisional Areas, and 8th (Lucknow) and Burma Divisions, No. 24091 (January 28, 1915), Army Department: War, file 21459–673, Appx. Part B, 1914–1915, NAI; J. M. Walter, Quartermaster-General's Branch, Note (February 28, 1915), Army Department: War, file 21459–673, Appx. Part B, 1914–15, NAI.

85. From the Director, Medical Services in India, to the officer in charge, Indian Troops Hospital at Allahabad, Ambala, Bombay, Dehra Dun, Jhansi, Lahore, Lucknow, Meerut, Poona, Rurki and Secunderbad, and the officer in charge, Lady Hardinge War Hospital Bombay, Sassoon Hospital Bombay, King George's Hospital Lucknow, Civil Hospital Julundur, Civil Hospital Lahore, Civil Hospital Secunderbad (March 3, 1915), Army Department: War, file 21459–673, Appx. Part B, 1914–15, NAI; Walter, Quartermaster-General's Branch (February 28, 1915); From Major-General F. J. Aylmer, VC, CB, Adjutant-General in India, to General Baber Shumsher [*sic*] Jung, Bahadur Rana "Northbank" (July 16, 1915), Army Department: War, file 21459–673, Appx. Part B, 1914–15, NAI; From Adjutant General in India, to the General Officer Commanding, 7th Meerut Divisional Area, Meerut No. 21481 Dated Delhi (March 4, 1915), Army Department: War, file 21459–673, Appx. Part B, 1914–15, NAI.

86. From Brigadier-General N. Woodyatt, Commanding Dehra Dun Brigade, to the Adjutant General in India (April 7, 1915) Army Department: War, file 21459–673, Appx. Part B, 1914–15, NAI.

87. For arrangements about certificates, see, for example, Letter from the General Officer Commanding, Dehra Dun Brigade, No. 6-62—S.S. (June 29, 1915), Army Department: War, file 21459–673, Appx. Part B, 1914–15, NAI.

88. From the Adjutant General in India to the General Officer Commanding 7th Meerut Divisional Area (July 20, 1915), Army Department: War, file 21459–673, Appx. Part B, 1914–15, NAI.

89. Captain G. Hacknett, "Proceedings of a Board Assembled at Meerut, Indian General Hospital, on the 22nd March 1915, by Order of Officer Commanding, Meerut Indian General Hospital, for the Purpose of Reporting as to the Measures Necessary to Safeguard in Every Way Possible the Caste of Gurkhas," Army Department: War, file 21459–673, Appx. Part B, 1914–15, NAI.

90. Board Assembled on March 24, 1915, at Lady Hardinge Hospital, Army Department: War, file 21459–673, Appx. Part B, 1914–15, NAI.

91. Proceedings of a Board of Officers Assembled at Barton-on-Sea, Army Department: War, file 21459–673, Appx. Part B, 1914–15, NAI.

92. Proceedings of a Board Assembled at Milford-on-Sea, Army Department: War, file 21459–673, Appx. Part B, 1914–15, NAI.

93. S. G. Ranaday, Proceedings of the Board Assembled to Enquire into the Matter of Gurkha's Arrangements Overseas, Army Department: War, file 21459–673, Appx. Part B, 1914–15, NAI; From B. B. Cubitt, Secretary, War Office, London, to the Under Secretary of State for India, Military Department, India Office, Whitehall, SW (April 6, 1915), Army Department: War, file 21459–673, Appx. Part B, 1914–15, NAI.

94. Lt-Col F. S. Poynder, *The 9th Gurkha Rifles* (London: Royal United Services Institute, 1937), 75.

95. From Adjutant General in India to General Officer Commanding 8th Lucknow Division (September 15, 1915), Army Department: War, file 21459–673, Appx. Part B, 1914–15, NAI.

96. From the Prime Minister in Nepal to the Resident in Nepal (July 12, 1915), Army Department: War, file 21459–673, Appx. Part B, 1914–15, NAI.

97. From Lt-Col J. Manners-Smith, VC, CVO, CIE, Resident in Nepal, to Secretary to the Government of India in the Foreign and Political Department (July 30, 1915), Army Department: War, file 21459–673, Appx. Part B, 1914–15, NAI.

98. Woodyatt to the Adjutant General in India (April 7, 1915).

99. From Major General E. S. May, Commanding, 8th Lucknow Divison, to Adjutant General in India (August 10, 1915), Army Department: War, file 21459–673, Appx. Part B, 1914–15, NAI.

100. From Major-General His Excellency Maharaja Sir Chandra Shumshere [*sic*] Jung, Bahadur Rana, to Lt-Col J. Manners-Smith, VC, CVO, CIE, Resident in Nepal (August 5, 1915), Army Department: War, file 21459–673, Appx. Part B, 1914–15, NAI; From R. E. Holland, Deputy Secretary to the Government of India, Foreign and Political Department, to Lt-Col J. Manners-Smith, VC, CVO, CIE, Resident in Nepal (September 7, 1915), Army Department: War, file 21459–673, Appx. Part B, 1914–15, NAI.

101. From Lieutenant Colonel A. Wilson, Commanding, 1/8th Gurkha Rifles, to Adjutant General in India (August 9, 1915) Army Department: War, file 21459–673, Appx. Part B, 1914–15, NAI.

102. From the Adjutant General in India to the Officer Commanding, 1st Battalion, 8th Gurkha Rifles (August 14, 1915), Army Department: War, file 21459–673, Appx. Part B, 1914–15, NAI.

103. From the Officer Commanding Depot to the Deputy Assistant Adjutant and Quarter-Master General, Presidency Brigade, undated, Army Department: War, file 21459–673, Appx. Part B, 1914–15, NAI.

104. From C. A. F. Hocken, GOC, 7th Meerut Divisional Area (January 11, 1916), Foreign and Political—Internal "B," February 1916, file 317–20, NAI.

105. Copy of letter from Captain R. J. Macbrayne, Inspecting Officer, Kashmir Imperial Service Infantry, to the Bde Major, Dehra Dun (December 4, 1915) (December 8, 1915), Foreign and Political—Internal "B," February 1916, file 317–20, NAI.

106. Translation of the proceedings of a Gorkha [*sic*] Panchait held on the 9th Maghar 19172 (November 24, 1915), Foreign and Political—Internal "B," February 1916, file 317–20, NAI.

107. Copy of a letter from Lt. General His Excellency Maharaja Sir Chandra Shumshere [*sic*] Jung Bahadur Rana, Prime Minister and Marshal of Nepal to Lt-Col J. Manners-Smith, Resident in Nepal (February 7, 1916), Foreign and Political—Internal "B," February 1916, file 317–20, NAI.

108. From Major General F. J. Aylmer, VC, CB, Adjutant General in India, to the General Officers Commanding, 2nd, 4th, 8th, and Burma Divisions, 3rd Lahore, 6th Poona, and 7th Meerut Divisional Areas, and Dehra Dun Brigade, Army Department: War, file 21459–673, Appx. Part B, 1914–15, NAI.

109. C. A. F. Hocken, Note (February 2, 1916), War: 1916–17 B, file 13094–149, NAI; C. W. G. Richardson, Note (February 8, 1916), War: 1916–17 B, file 13094–149, NAI.

110. C. A. F. Hocken, Note (February 8, 1916), War: 1916–17 B, file 13094–149, NAI.

111. Telegram from the Resident in Nepal to the Secretary to the Government of India in the Foreign and Political Department, Delhi (February 21, 1916), War: 1916–17 B, file 13094–149, NAI; Copy of a letter from Lieutenant General His Excellency Maharaja Sir Chandra Shumshere [*sic*] Jung Bahadur Ran, GCB, GCSI, GCVO, DCL, Prime Minister and Maeshal [*sic*] of Nepal, to Lt-Col J. Manners-Smith, VC, CVO, IE, Resident in Nepal (February 16, 1916), War: 1916–17 B, file 13094–149, NAI.

112. From Adjutant General in India to the General Officer Commanding, 1st Peshawar Division, to General Officer Commanding, 3rd Lahore Divisional Area, and General Officer Commanding, 7th Meerut Divisional Area (February 24, 1916), War: 1916–17 B, file 13094–149, NAI.

113. These were to the men of the 1/6th, 2/8th, and 1/5th Gurkha Rifles. From the Adjutant-General in India to the Officer Commanding, 1/5th Gurkha Rifles, Peshawar (March 3, 1916); From Adjutant-General in India to the Officer Commanding, 2/8th Gurkha Rifles (March 2, 1916); From Adjutant-General in India to Officer Commanding, 1/6th Gurkha Rifles, Peshawar (March 6, 1916), War: 1916–17 B, file 13094–149, NAI.

114. From Adjutant General in India to Officer Commanding, 2/2nd Gurkha Rifles, Dehra Dun (March 10, 1916), War: 1916–17 B, file 13094–149, NAI.

115. From General Officer Commanding 1st Peshawar Division (March 6, 1916), War: 1916–17 B, file 13094–149, NAI; From Adjutant-General in India, Delhi, to General Officer Commanding, 1st Peshawar Division (March 6, 1916), War: 1916–17 B, file 13094–13149, NAI; Telegram from General Officer Commanding, 1st Peshawar Division, to Adjutant General in India, Delhi (March 9, 1916), War: 1916–17 B, file 13094–149, NAI.

116. These were the 2/10th, the 1/9th, and the 1/1st Gurkha Rifles.

117. From GOC Burma (September 5, 1916), Foreign and Political—Internal "B," October 1916, file 303–14 B, NAI.

118. See various telegrams dated September 1916 between the Government of India in Simla and the Nepal Residency, Foreign and Political—Internal "B," October 1916, file 303–14 B, NAI.

119. A. H. P. Harrison, Note (February 18, 1919), Foreign and Political Department Internal "B" Pros (June 1919), file 242–44, NAI.

120. Adjutant General's Branch, unsigned and undated, Foreign and Political Internal Part B, August 1918, file 351–53, NAI.

121. Telegram from L. B. Ginns, Embarkation Commandant, Bombay (February 15, 1919), Foreign and Political Department Internal "B" Pros (June 1919), file 242–44, NAI.

122. Letter from Lieutenant General His Excellency Maharaja Sir Chandra Shumshere [sic] Jang Bahadur Rana to Lt-Col W. F. O'Connor, CIE, Resident in Nepal (March 16, 1919), Foreign and Political Department Internal "B" Pros (June 1919), file 242–44, NAI.

123. From Army Department Simla to Secretary, Military Department, India Office Staff, and Establishments for the Pani Patya Camp, Dehra Dun (September 21, 1922), IOR/L/MIL/7/5867: 1914–22.

124. From Lieutenant Colonel S. F. Bayley, Resident in Nepal, to the Secretary to the Government of India in the Foreign and Political Department, Simla (May 31, 1918), Foreign and Political Internal Part B, August 1918, file 351–53, NAI.

125. Copy of a letter from Lt. General His Excellency Maharaja Sir Chandra Shumshere [sic] Jang Bahadur Rana to Lt-Col S. F. Bayley, Resident in Nepal (November 29, 1916), Foreign and Political Internal Part B (February 1917), file 24–25, NAI.

126. Copy of confidential letter from his Excellency the Prime Minister of Nepal to the Resident in Nepal (October 16, 1917), Foreign and Political International Part B (April 1918), file 106–9, NAI.

127. "Hostile Oriental Propaganda Pamphlets," Mss Eur E.288/Vols 1, 2, 3, and 4, numbers 63 and 119.

128. Copy of letter from the GOC Meerut Division to the Adjutant General in India, Army HQ, Delhi (January 29, 1918), Foreign and Political International Part B (April 1918), file 106–9, NAI.

129. Shrabani Basu, *For King and Another Country: Indian Soldiers on the Western Front, 1914–1918* (London: Bloomsbury, 2015), 107.

130. Basu, *For King and Another Country*, 155.

131. Eventually Ali Mardan fatally wounded the Nepali soldier. Dafadar Ali Mardan to Risaldar Mirza Khalilulla Khan, April 20, 1916, included in Omissi, *Indian Voices of the Great War*, 178.

132. Basu, *For King and Another Country*, 88.

133. Anand, *Across the Black Waters*, 110, 214.

134. English translation of anonymous letter, n.d., Foreign and Political International Part B (April 1918), file 106–9, NAI.

135. English translation of anonymous letter, undated, Foreign and Political International Part B (April 1918).

136. To Lieutenant Colonel S. F. Bayley Resident in Nepal (February 20, 1918), Foreign and Political International Part B (April 1918), file 106–109, NAI; Copy of letter from Lt-Gen Maharaja Sir Chandra Shumshere [*sic*] Jung Bahadur Rana, PM and Marshal of Nepal, to Lt-Col S. F. Bayley, Resident in Nepal (March 7, 1918), Foreign and Political International Part B (April 1918), file 106–109, NAI.

137. From the GOC Meerut Division to the Adjutant General in India (January 29, 1918).

138. Major General Nigel Woodyatt, *Under Ten Viceroys: The Reminiscences of a Gurkha* (London: Herbert Jenkins, Ltd., 1922), 164–65.

139. Colonel L. W. Shakespear, *History of the 2nd King Edward's Own Goorkhas (The Sirmoor Rifle Regiment)*, vol. 2, *1911–1921* (Aldershot: Gale & Polden Ltd., n.d.), 13–14.

140. Major H. R. K. Gibbs, *The Gurkha Soldier* (Calcutta: Thacker, Spink & Co., 1944), 43, 45.

141. Des Chene, "Relics of Empire," 141, 152.

142. Uprety, "Masculinity and Mimicry," 29; Rishikesh Shaha, *Modern Nepal: A Political History, 1769–1885*, vols. 1 and 2 (New Delhi: Manohar Books, 1996).

143. Brigadier Commander, HQ 48, Gurkha Brigade (June 15, 1960), BG/67, the Gurkha Museum (Winchester, UK), henceforth TGM.

144. He made this observation while passing through the headquarters of British Gurkhas in Barrackpore, West Bengal, in 1960. From HQ British Gurkhas India, Barrackpore, West Bengal, to HQ Brigade of Gurkhas Rasah Camp Malaya 14 (April 1960), BG/67, TGM.

145. 1/6th QEO Gurkha Rifles, Kluang, Johore, Malaya (June 29, 1960), BG/67, TGM.

146. Anand, *Across the Black Waters*, 8.

147. Anand, *Across the Black Waters*, 116.

148. For instances of Gurkha troops participating in the suppression and pacification of rebellions, protests, and demonstrations, see, for example, "Punjab Disturbances," reprinted from the Civil and Military Gazette, Mss Eur F138/193: 1919; photographs of the Fourth Akali Jatha, IOR/R/1/1/4903 1924.

149. Pratyoush Onta, "Creating a Brave Nepali Nation in British India: The Rhetoric of Jāti Improvement, Rediscovery of Bhanubhakta and the Writing of Bīr History," *Studies in Nepali History and Society* 1, No. 1 (1996): 37–96, at 44, 65.

150. This remained true in 1931 when military officials considered opening opportunities to soldiers from Nepal and Burma. To Secretary, Military Department, India Office, from the Government of India, Army Dept. (Simla, August 6, 1931), Collection 210/45, IOR/L/MIL/7/9321: 1923–46.

CHAPTER 4

1. CUL/MD, Hardinge Papers: Willcocks Letter to Hardinge, December 5, 1914, quoted in George Morton-Jack, *The Indian Army on the Western Front: India's Expeditionary*

Force to France and Belgium in the First World War (Cambridge: Cambridge University Press, 2014), 197.

2. Sir James Willcocks, *From Kabul to Kumassi: Twenty-Four Years of Soldiering and Sport* (John Murray, 1904), 91.

3. Willcocks, *From Kabul to Kumassi*.

4. General Sir James Willcocks, *With the Indians in France* (London: Constable and Company, 1920), 97.

5. For more on food in the First World War, see Rachel Duffett, *The Stomach for Fighting: Food and the Soldiers of the Great War* (Manchester: Manchester University Press, 2012).

6. Major R. T. I. Ridgway, *Handbooks for the Indian Army, Pathans* (Calcutta: Superintendent, Government Printing, India, 1910), 116.

7. Leila Shaheen "Manners in the Middle East," *Saudi Aramco World* (March/April 1965), available at http://www.aramcoworld.com/issue/196502/manners.in.the .middle.east.htm, accessed January 31, 2016.

8. Kaushik Roy, *Hinduism and the Ethics of Warfare in South Asia: From Antiquity to the Present* (Cambridge: Cambridge University Press, 2012), xvi, 183–84.

9. Dirk A. Kolff, *Naukar, Rajput and Sepoy: The Ethnohistory of the Military Labour Market in Hindustan, 1450–1850* (Cambridge: Cambridge University Press, 1990), 20.

10. From "Punjabi Musalman" Cavalry, Poonch State, Kashmire, to —— and —— 41st Dogras (Urdu, May 1915), Copies of "Further Extracts" from censored Indian mails, Mss Eur F143/92: June 1915–October 1916.

11. From Subedar Mir Dast, VC, to Naik Nur Zada, 55th Rifles, Kohat (Urdu, August 27, 1915), Military Dept. Censor of Indian Mails, 1914–15, Pt. 5, FF. 713–869, IOR/L/MIL/5/825.

12. "Song by a Sikh Soldier," Military Dept. Censor of Indian Mails, 1914–15, Pt. 5, FF. 713–869, letter number 849/L45, IOR/L/MIL/5/825.

13. From Sepoy Chutar Singh, IGH, Brighton, to Sowar Rajan Singh, 27th Light Cavalry, Bolarum (Urdu, August 1915), Military Dept. Censor of Indian Mails, 1914–15, Pt. 5, FF. 713–869, letter number 860/L66, IOR/L/MIL/5/825.

14. Lord Kitchener's comments are included with the published edition of Macauliffe's speech. M. Macauliffe, "How the Sikhs Became a Militant Race" (second lecture, July 6, 1903), *Journal of the United Service Institution of India* 32, No. 153 (October 1903): 330–58.

15. "Translation of Leaflet: The Hindostani Army of the British Government— Bande Mataram!" (ca. 1907), IOR/L/PJ/6/798, file 453.

16. Such arguments are similar to those put forth by the Ghadar "mutiny" conspiracy. See Chapter 1.

17. Miles Ogborn, *Global Lives: Britain and the World, 1550–1800* (Cambridge: Cambridge University Press, 2008), 93–94.

18. Mike Davis, *Late Victorian Holocausts: El Niño Famines and the Making of the Third World* (London and New York: Verso, 2001); Sunil M. Amrith, "Food and Welfare in India, c. 1900–1950," *Comparative Studies in Society and History* 50, No. 4 (2008): 1013;

James Vernon, *Hunger: A Modern History* (Cambridge, MA: Belknap Press of Harvard University Press, 2007), 42, 48–49.

19. Barbara D. Metcalf and Thomas R. Metcalf, *A Concise History of Modern India* (Cambridge: Cambridge University Press, 2012), 154.

20. These were Romesh Dutt and William Digby. Vernon, *Hunger*, 49–52.

21. Tan Tai Yong, *The Garrison State: The Military, Government and Society in Colonial Punjab, 1849–1947* (New Delhi and London: Sage, 2005), 90–91; Satya M. Rai, *Legislative Politics and Freedom Struggle on [sic] the Panjab 1897–1947* (New Delhi: People's Publishing House, 1984), 1.

22. The most controversial were the 1900 Land Alienation Act, 1906 Colonization Bill, and Bari Doab Canal scheme. Maia Ramnath, *Haj to Utopia: How the Ghadar Movement Charted Global Radicalism and Attempted to Overthrow the British Empire* (Berkeley and Los Angeles: University of California Press, 2011), 18.

23. Indian migrants and activists in the United States contrasted the wealth and prosperity in independent nations like the United States with India's recurring famines. Ramnath, *Haj to Utopia*, 29, 33; Seema Sohi, *Echoes of Mutiny: Race, Surveillance, and Indian Anticolonialism in North America* (Oxford: Oxford University Press, 2014).

24. Vernon, *Hunger*, 52.

25. Superintendent of Police, Jhang, "Endeavours of Sikh Sepoys to Spread Sedition," June 26, 1907, Home (Political) "A" Pros(s). 113, August 1907, NAI.

26. A. E. Barstow, *Handbooks for the Indian Army, Sikhs* (Calcutta: Government of India Central Publications Branch, 1928), 180.

27. W. F. Raper, *Hints for Soldiers Proceeding to India: A Common-Sense Health Lecture* (London: Gale & Polden, Ltd., 1911), 11–13.

28. Lieut. Col. Alexander George Stuart, *The Indian Empire: A Short Review and Some Hints for the Use of Soldiers Proceeding to India* (Calcutta: Government of India Central Publication Branch 1932), 89, 101–2, 111–13. This work was also published under the title *Our Indian Empire*.

29. Patrick Miles Pennington Hobson, interviewed by Conrad Wood, August 17, 1977, Reel 2, Imperial War Museum Interview 966; Edwin John Watson, March 22, 1977, Reel 1, Imperial War Museum Interview 903.

30. About meat being a luxury, see J. M. Wikeley, *Hand Books for the Indian Army: Punjabi Musalmans* (1927; repr., New Delhi: Government of India Press, 1936), 34; Lt.-Col. W. B. Cunningham, 17th Dogra Regiment, *Handbooks for the Indian Army, Dogras* (Calcutta: Government of India Central Publication Branch, 1932), 91.

31. M. Macauliffe, "The Sikh Religion and Its Advantages to the State" (lecture at the United Service Institution, July 6, 1903), *Journal of the United Service Institution of India* 32 (October 1903): 300–329, at 315–16.

32. From Brigadier General W. H. H. Waters, Commanding Troops, North China, to Secretary of the Army Council, War Office (December 4, 1906); Extract from Report by Captain W. St. C. Muscroft, Chief Supply & Transport Officer, North China Command (May 12, 1906), IOR/L/MIL/7/16648.

33. Anand A. Yang, "(A) Subaltern('s) Boxers: An Indian Soldier's Account of China and the World in 1900–1901," in *The Boxers, China, and the World*, ed. Robert Bickers and R. G. Tiedemann (Plymouth: Rowman & Littlefield, 2007), 43–64, at 46.

34. Mrinalini Sinha, *Colonial Masculinity: The "Manly Englishman" and the "Effeminate Bengali" in the Late Nineteenth Century* (Manchester: Manchester University Press, 1995), 21; Srinivas Aravamudan, *Guru English: South Asian Religion in a Cosmopolitan Language* (Princeton, NJ: Princeton University Press, 2006), 56.

35. Metcalf and Metcalf, *A Concise History of Modern India*, 151.

36. Macauliffe, "The Sikh Religion and Its Advantages to the State."

37. Cow protection societies were known as Gaurakshini Sabhas. Metcalf and Metcalf, *A Concise History of Modern India*, 151–53.

38. A 1931 Punjab periodical, *Comrade*, stated that "It is the English who eat the largest quantity of pork and beef." Excerpt from Punjab "Comrade" (Lahore) (December 6, 1931), Government of India, Home Department, file no. 13/6 and (unprinted) K.-W. 1931, Ordinance, X of 1930, 62, NAI.

39. The allegation was raised by Narayan Shivram Barve. Daily report on the state of political agitation in the Punjab, dated Simla, July 11, 1907, NAI.

40. Weekly Report of the Director of Criminal Intelligence, Simla, for the week ending March 12, 1910, NAI.

41. Major Kemp's project re: Beef supply in India, Home, Pol. "B" S., No. 413, F. No. 175, NAI.

42. For additional details about Hewett, see *The Cyclopedia of India: Biographical, Historical, Administrative, Commercial*, vol. 2 (Calcutta: Cyclopedia Press, 1908), 143.

43. Major Kemp's project re: Beef supply in India, Home, Pol. "B" S., No. 413, F. No. 175, NAI.

44. They received additional payments based on fluctuations in food prices. Wikeley, *Hand Books for the Indian Army: Punjabi Musalmans*, 33–34; Gajendra Singh, *The Testimonies of Indian Soldiers and the Two World Wars: Between Self and Sepoy* (London: Bloomsbury Press, 2014), 55.

45. Khan Bahadur Risaldar Shahzad Mir Khan, *A Right Royal World Tour*, translated by Lt. Col. C. A. Boyle (Simla: Army Press, 1934), Urdu Manuscripts, 14110, Cc23, British Library, 7–8.

46. Abdur Razzak, *The Native Officer's Diary* (Madras: Higgenbotham and Co., 1894), 1, 4–5.

47. Khan, translated by Boyle, *A Right Royal World Tour*, 32–33, 55.

48. DeWitt C. Ellinwood Jr., *Between Two Worlds: A Rajput Officer in the Indian Army, 1905–21* (Lanham, MD: Hamilton Books, 2005). Excerpt from diary dated December 29, 1905.

49. "Minute Paper" (March 8, 1907), IOR/L/PJ/6/798, file 453.

50. See the introduction and Thomas Trautmann, *Aryans and British India* (Berkeley: University of California Press, 1997).

51. The population estimate in 1912 was that 207 million out of 300 million were Hindu. *Our Indian Empire: A Short Review and Some Hints for the Use of Soldiers Proceed-*

ing to India (London: His Majesty's Stationery Office, n.d., ca. 1912), 56. This work was also published under the title *The Indian Empire*.

52. Kaushik Roy, "The Construction of Regiments in the Indian Army: 1859–1913," *War in History* 8, No. 127 (2001): 129; Seema Alavi, *The Sepoy and the Company: Tradition and Transition in Northern India, 1770–1830* (Delhi: Oxford University Press, 1998), 71.

53. Vera Nünning highlights the missionary, land, and economic causes of the revolt that have been erased beneath narratives of the cartridges. "'Daß Jeder seine Pflicht thue': Die Bedeutung der Indian Mutiny für das nationale britische Selbstverständnis," *Archiv für Kulturgeschichte* 78 (1996): 373. See the introduction for further discussion of 1857.

54. Kaushik Roy, "The Hybrid Military Establishment of the East India Company in South Asia: 1750–1849," *Journal of Global History* 6, No. 2 (2011): 205, 209.

55. E. M. Collingham, *Imperial Bodies: The Physical Experience of the Raj c. 1800–1947* (Cambridge: Polity Press, 2001), 27.

56. Indian officers noted Company hostility to Brahman dietary practice, which included forcing them to take food from the hands of Muslims. Sheik Hedayat Ali, "On Origins of Mutiny," United Service Institution Library, 24/4/140; "Extracts from Proceedings of the Hon'ble the President of the Council of India in Council in Home Dept, Fort William" (October 26, 1858), United Service Institution Library.

57. Sections from this text appeared in British soldiers' language exams and in the Urdu-language army periodical *Fauji Akhbar*. See also Alison Safadi, *"From Sepoy to Subedar/Khvab-o-Khyal* and Douglas Craven Phillott," *Annual of Urdu Studies* 25 (2010): 43.

58. A. H. Bingley and A. Nicholls, *Brahmans* (Simla: Government Central Printing Office, 1897); Singh, *The Testimonies of Indian Soldiers*, 43.

59. Revised by Major B. U. Nicolay, *Handbooks for the Indian Army. Gurkhas. Compiled Under the Orders of the Government of India by Lt-Col Eden Vansittart* (Calcutta: Government of India Press, 1915), 54.

60. *Our Indian Empire*, 58.

61. Major S. H. E. Nicholas, 95th Russell's Infantry, "Indian Army Castes: Ahirs," *Journal of the United Service Institution of India* 40, No. 183 (April 1911): 73.

62. Singh, *The Testimonies of Indian Soldiers*, 41.

63. Captain C. Watson Smyth, 1st Brahmans, "Indian Army Castes: Brahmans," *Journal of the United Service Institution of India* 40, No. 183 (April 1911): 205–11.

64. Smyth, "Indian Army Castes: Brahmans," 205–11.

65. Willcocks, *From Kabul to Kumassi*, 91.

66. Smyth, "Indian Army Castes: Brahmans," 209.

67. Anand A. Yang, "China and India Are One: A Subaltern's Vision of 'Hindu China' During the Boxer Expedition of 1900–1901," in *Asia Inside Out: Changing Times*, ed. Eric Tagliacozzo, Helen F Siu, and Peter C. Perdue (Cambridge, MA: Harvard University Press, 2015), 207–25, at 219.

68. Arya Samaj member Sant Ram argued cynically in 1907 that "many people became Christians for the sake of their stomachs." "Weekly Report of the Director of

Criminal Intelligence," November 23, 1907, Home Department, Political Branch (December 1907), 2–9 B, NAI; Lala Lajpat Rai, *The Arya Samaj: An Account of Its Origin, Doctrines, and Activities: With a Biographical Sketch of the Founder* (London: Longmans, Green and Co., 1915), 252.

69. Pandit Sant Ram was a member of the Arya Prabha. "Weekly Report on the Director of Criminal Intelligence," October 11, 1910, NAI.

70. From Lloyd to the Assistant Director (April 6, 1915); From B. B. Cubitt, esq., Secretary, War Office, London, to the Under Secretary of State for India, Military Department, India Office, Whitehall, SW (April 6, 1915), Army: War 1914–15, 21459–673, Appx. Part B, NAI.

71. Revised by Captain F. M. Wardle, *The Sepoy Officer's Manual: A Book of Reference for Infantry Officers of the Indian Army* (Calcutta and Simla: Thacker, Spink & Co., 1922), 163. Officers noted that Dogras preferred Brahman cooks "when they can afford them." Cunningham, *Handbooks for the Indian Army, Dogras*, 91.

72. Indian Military Hospital, Royal Pavilion, Brighton, *A Short History in English, Gurmukhi and Urdu of the Royal Pavilion, Brighton, and a Description of It as a Hospital for Indian Soldiers* [illustrated], Mss Eur F143/94: 1915, 17.

73. Letter from Private Ratan Lal, Brahman Clerk, Post Office, Basra, to Rai Sahab Private Prabhu Dayal, Sonipat, published in *Jat Gazette* (March 26, 1918): 10. Thanks to Professor K. C. Yadav of Haryana Academy of History and Culture in Gurgaon, India, for assisting me in locating and translating this document.

74. Gugan Singh retells the story of Dalip Singh. From Gugan Singh (Jat), 20th Deccan Horse France, to Mular Singh (Editor, *Jat Gazette*, Rohtak, Punjab), Urdu (April 8, 1917), in David Omissi, *Indian Voices of the Great War: Soldiers' Letters, 1914–18* (New York: Palgrave Macmillan, 1999), letter 504, p. 284.

75. From M. L. Tilhet (Hindustani Hindu) to Pyari Lal Tilhet (Muzaffarnagar, UP), Indian Convalescent Home, New Milton (Urdu, February 21, 1916), in Omissi, *Indian Voices of the Great War*, letter 251, p. 155.

76. Quoted in Ellinwood, *Between Two Worlds*, 438–39.

77. Francis Yeats-Brown, *Martial India* (London: Eyre & Spottiswoode, 1945), 18.

78. Morton-Jack, *The Indian Army on the Western Front*, 197–98.

79. H. V. Cox, Military Department Note (May 28, 1917), Subject: Conduct of the 3rd Brahman Regiment in Mesopotamia, IOR/L/MIL/7/7277.

80. Scholars such as Gajendra Singh, David Omissi, and George Morton-Jack have cited these cases as evidence of Brahman particularity and unsuitability for military service. Singh, *The Testimonies of Indian Soldiers*; Omissi, *Indian Voices of the Great War*; Morton-Jack, *The Indian Army on the Western Front*.

81. Copy of Telegram from Viceroy Army Department (May 24, 1917), IOR/L/MIL/7/7277.

82. Singh, *The Testimonies of Indian Soldiers*, 43.

83. Stuart, *The Indian Empire*, 65.

84. *Our Indian Empire*, 36, expresses that they are freer from prejudice, while the 1932 edition chooses the words "broad-minded." Stuart, *The Indian Empire*, 64.

85. From the Officer Commanding, 2/9th Gurkha Rifles, to the Brigadier-Major, Dehra Dun Brigade (May 30, 1913), Army Department (November 1913), Part B, file 1466–68, NAI.

86. From Lt-Colonel R. A. Lloyd, IMS, Commanding, Meerut Indian General Hospital, to the Assistant Director of Medical Services, Indian Medical Establishments (April 6, 1915), Army: War, file 21459–673, Part B, 1914–15, NAI.

87. Memorandum from the General Officer Commanding, Indian Army Corps, to the Deputy Adjutant-General 3rd Echelon, Indian Section (March 12, 1915), Army: War, 21459–673, Appx. Part B, 1914–15, NAI.

88. From Lloyd to Assistant Director (April 6, 1915), NAI.

89. From the Honorable Mr. H. Wheeler, CSI, CIE, Secretary to the Government of India, Home Department, to the Chief Secretary to Government, Punjab, "Distribution of the Illustrated Record Published in English, Gurmukhi and Urdu Languages by the Brighton Corporation of a Year's Work at the Pavilion Hospital for Indian Soldiers" (Delhi, November 15, 1915), Home Department Proceedings, December 1915, Medical and Sanitary, File No. 82, Panjab State Archives.

90. Indian Military Hospital, *A Short History in English*, 6–8, 15.

91. From Said Ahmad Khan, KIH, Brighton, to Sahib Nur, 26th Punjabis Tank, India, Urdu (September 3, 1915), letter number 831/12, IOR/L/MIL/5/825.

92. Letter from G. Lowan, Kitchener Indian Hospital, Brighton, to Tukaram Chowan, Big Saraffa, Indore City (Marathi, August 25, 1915), letter number 815/42, IOR/L/MIL/5/825.

93. Copy of Lt. Col. Allanson's Diary, p. 13, 6GR/302, TGM.

94. After the Siege of Kut, Indian and Nepali prisoners of war received hard-baked coarse barley biscuits, which included husks and straw. These left "disastrous" effects on the stomach. Account by Lt Col. W. R. B. Williams of the Fall of Kut, 7GR/207, TGM.

95. Nikolas Gardner, *The Siege of Kut-al-Amara: At War in Mesopotamia, 1915–1916* (Bloomington and Indianapolis: Indiana University Press, 2014), 155–70.

96. Gardner, *The Siege of Kut-al-Amara*, 6.

97. Account of Operations Kurdistan, July–October 1919, includes "Resume of the Medical Aspect of the Operation of Nightengale's Column from 31st July '19 to 15th Oct," 7GR/326, TGM.

98. A Sikh to his father (Punjab), a hospital in England, February 20, 1915, reprinted in Omissi, *Indian Voices of the Great War*, letter 24, p. 39.

99. For a chart on the specific distribution in 1912, see Roy, *Hinduism and the Ethics of Warfare*, 217; Proceedings of the Army in India Committee, 1912, vol. I-A, Minority Report (Simla: Govt. Central Branch Press, 1913), 156.

100. Wikeley, *Hand Books for the Indian Army: Punjabi Musalmans*, 98.

101. See Chapter 2.

102. From Hoffman Philip, Embassy of the United States of America, to the Secretary of State, Washington (September 15, 1916), Army: War, September 1918, A 2221–49, Pay and Allowances—Indian Army—A, NAI.

103. Gardner, *The Siege of Kut-al-Amara*, 124.

104. When describing the fast of Ramzan, the Reverend Alban Butler argued that "None is excused fasting, neither Women, Soldiers, Travellers, Labourers, nor Artificers; neither poor nor rich; the Sultan himself fasts like others." Reverend Alban Butler, *The Moveable Feasts and Fasts and Annual Observances of the Catholic Church* (Dublin: James Duffy, 1839), 155.

105. John Murdoch, *Hindu and Mohammadan Festivals* (Christian Literature Society of India, 1904), 77.

106. Mrs. Meer Hasan Ali, *Observations on the Mussulmans of India* (London: Oxford University Press, repr. 1917), 104.

107. Major W. Fitz G. Bourne, *Hindustani Musalmans and Musalmans of the Eastern Punjab* (Calcutta: Superintendent, Government Printing, India, 1914), 11.

108. Wikeley, *Hand Books for the Indian Army: Punjabi Musalmans*, 27–28.

109. Ja'far Sharif, *Islam in India; or The Qanun-i-Islam*, translated by G. A. Herklots (Oxford University Press, 1921), 112.

110. Joseph Alter, *Gandhi's Body: Sex, Diet, and the Politics of Nationalism* (Philadelphia: University of Pennsylvania Press, 2000), 28.

111. Mohandas Gandhi, *An Autobiography: The Story of My Experiments with Truth* (Boston: Beacon Press, 1994), 331–32.

112. H. A. Walter, *The Religious Life of India: The Ahmadiya Movement* (Calcutta: Association Press; London: Oxford University Press, 1918), 58. See also Rudy Bell's *Holy Anorexia* for a similar rationale among medieval Europeans. Rudy Bell, *Holy Anorexia* (Chicago: University of Chicago Press, 1987).

113. From Nur Mohamed, Pathan, 38 Central India Horse, France, to Sultan Mohamed Khan, Turangazai, Peshawar, North-West Frontier Province, India, July 26, 1916; CIM 1915–16, Part 6, quoted in Singh, *The Testimonies of Indian Soldiers*, 133.

114. Letter from Badshah Khan (Afridi) to Torai Khan (57th Rifles, France) dated July 26, 1915, Meerut Stationary Hospital. Originally written in Urdu. Quoted in Omissi, *Indian Voices of the Great War*, letter 104, p. 81. Badshah Khan's assertions that "the Punjabis" were lax in the fast likely related to the fact that Punjabi Muslims formed the largest proportion of combatants recruited during the First World War, totaling 136,126 out of 657,739. Only 13% of combatants were Muslims from other provinces; Singh, *The Testimonies of Indian Soldiers*, 127, 129.

115. From Pir Dil Khan, 129th Baluchis, serving at the front to Naik Mir Gul Khan, Secunderabad Hospital, France (Urdu, September 2, 1915), letter number 828/9, IOR/L/MIL/5/825. See Chapter 2 and Singh, *The Testimonies of Indian Soldiers*, for a more in-depth analysis of Muslim soldiers' wartime anxieties about Mecca and Medina.

116. From Driver Lal Din (Punjabi Muslim) to Manlair Karim Bakhsh (Sialkot District, India), U Battery RHA, 1st Indian Cavalry Division, France (July 14, 1916), quoted in Omissi, *Indian Voices of the Great War*, letter 353, pp. 206–7.

117. From Zabu Shah (Hindustani Muslim) to his mother (Farrukhabad District, UP), 6th Cavalry, France (July 17, 1917), quoted in Omissi, *Indian Voices of the Great War*, letter 547, pp. 303–4.

118. For further discussions of the mutiny, see Chapters 1 and 2.

119. Statement of Subedar Major Khan Mohamed Khan, Section 7: Indian Officers, Report, in Connection with "Mutiny of 5th Light Infantry at Singapore 1915," Part I— Proceedings of Court of Enquiry; Part II—"Report by His Excellency the Governor of the Straits Settlements and the General Officer Commanding at Singapore" (Simla: Government Central Branch Press, 1915), 143, IOR/L/MIL/7/7191: 1915–37, henceforth Singapore Mutiny Report.

120. Singapore Mutiny Report, 194, 292, 378.

121. Statement by Lt-Colonel E. V. Martin, Singapore Mutiny Report, 294, 300.

122. Ali, *Observations on the Mussulmans of India*, 7–8.

123. From Abdul Ali Khan (Hindustani Muslim) to Fazl Ali Khan (33rd Cavalry, Multan, Punjab), Urdu, July 22, 1917, 6th Cavalry, France, in Omissi, *Indian Voices of the Great War*, letter 554, p. 307.

124. From No. 13128, Havaldar Ahdurehman Khan, 5th Brigade, Ammunition Column, Force A, France, August 13, 1915, letters about the twice-weekly Hindi and Urdu paper *Akbar-i-Jang*, with copies of letters written by Indian soldiers to the paper, Mss Eur F143/75: 1915.

125. From Abdul Ali Khan to Fazl Ali Khan (July 22, 1917), 307.

126. *Nottingham Evening Post*, August 14, 1915, 2.

127. Major R. S. Waters, *History of the 5th Battalion (Pathans) 14th Punjab Regiment, Formerly 40th Pathans* (London: James Bain Limited, 1936), 156.

128. Waters, *History of the 5th Battalion*, 156.

129. From Havildar Ghufran Khan (Afridi, 129th Baluchis) to Subedar Zaman Khan (Depot, 129th Baluchis, Karachi, 43) dated August 4, 1915, Pavilion Hospital Brighton in Omissi, *Indian Voices of the Great War*, letter 113, p. 86.

130. Havildar Mohamad Sofid, 82 Punjabis, attached to 58 Rifles, wounded, Pavilion Hospital, Section C, England (July 24, 1915), countersigned by Mir Dast Subedar Khan Bahadur, Translation, "Protection of Religions by English Government and Its Officers" (July 30, 1915), letter to editor of the *Akbar-i-Jang*, Mss Eur F143/75: 1915.

131. Willcocks, *With the Indians in France*, 62.

132. Cunningham, *Handbooks for the Indian Army, Dogras*, 91–92.

133. From Jemadar Tek Chand from the Battlefield in France to Chhotu Ram, Rohtak, published in Urdu in the *Jat Gazette* (June 4, 1918): 8. Thanks to Professor K. C. Yadav of Haryana Academy of History and Culture in Gurgaon, India, for assisting me in locating and translating this document.

134. S. M. Jafri, "In One of the Largest Camps in France," n.d., IOR/L/MIL/7/18577.

135. Wardle, *The Sepoy Officer's Manual*, 233–34. See also Wikeley, *Hand Books for the Indian Army: Punjabi Musalmans*, 23: "A Muslim (in theory) cannot object to feed with a Christian so long as the food he eats is 'halal.' Any objection to do so must arise from ignorance, or, in the case of Indian Muhammadans from a lingering adherence to the caste prejudices of his Hindu ancestors." *The Hints for Soldiers Proceeding to India* reported similarly in 1912 that Dogras, "In common with all high caste Hindus, . . . are very particular about matters connected with food and drink." *The Hints for Soldiers Proceeding to India* (1912), 33.

136. Wardle, *The Sepoy Officer's Manual*, 222.

137. Barstow, *Handbooks for the Indian Army, Sikhs*, 19–20.

138. Indianization will be discussed further in Chapter 5.

139. Pradeep Barua, *Gentlemen of the Raj: The Indian Army Officer Corps, 1817–1949* (Westport, CT: Praeger, 2003), 59.

140. From the Secretary to the Government of India, Army Department, to Rao Bahadur Pandurang Chimnaji Patil, Deputy Director of Agriculture, Poona (December 12, 1924), papers of Lt. Gen S. P. P. Throat, RR 375, S. No. 6, Miscellaneous Files, Nehru Memorial Library.

141. Barua, *Gentlemen of the Raj*, 70.

142. Sukhwant Singh, *Three Decades of Indian Army Life* (Sterling Publishers Ltd., 1967), 41.

143. Patrick Miles Pennington Hobson, interviewed by Conrad Wood, August 17, 1977, Reel 2, Imperial War Museum Interview 966; Stanley Menezes, interviewed by Peter M. Hart, September 2003, Reel 2, Imperial War Museum Interview 25448.

144. Barua, *Gentlemen of the Raj*, 70–71.

145. Singh, *Three Decades of Indian Army Life*, 28.

146. Stuart, *The Indian Empire*, 62.

147. William Homer, interviewed by Conrad Wood, August 4, 1976, Imperial War Museum Interview 792, Reel 10.

148. Quoted in Barua, *Gentlemen of the Raj*, 70.

149. Gandhi also quoted the Sermon on the Mount, during which Jesus proclaimed, "Blessed are the poor . . . Ye are the salt of the earth." Quoted in Robert Young, *Postcolonialism: An Historical Introduction* (Malden, MA: Blackwell, 2001), 332.

150. Gandhi fasted thirteen times between 1913 and 1948. Alter, *Gandhi's Body*.

151. An author in the Lahore *Comrade* of 1930 protested that "Indians die with empty stomachs" while the English eat "the largest quantity of pork and beef." The author only implicitly called upon the soldiers of the army by wondering about those who died "in foreign lands" and others who "died after drenching in blood for the honour of the country, nation and religion." "Comrade" (Lahore), December 6, Extracts File no. 13/6 and (unprinted) K.-W. 1931, Government of India, Home Department, Promulgation of the Indian Press and Unauthorised News-sheets and Newspapers Ordinance, X of 1930, NAI.

152. "An Appeal to Police Brethren" (translation, 1930), Home Department Branch, Home Special, File 748—B, Maharashtra State Archives, henceforth MSA.

153. Excerpt from Kushalbhai Madhubhai Patel, ed., *Police Patrika* 1, No. 1 (Surat, August 6, 1930), MSA.

CHAPTER 5

1. Indian Sandhurst Committee, "Volume II: Evidence" (Calcutta: Government of India Central Publication Branch, 1926), IOR/26/280/13.

2. "Reports on the Prince of Wales's Royal Indian Military College, Dehra Dun. 1st and 2nd Terms, 1922" (Simla: Superintendent, Government Monotype Press, 1923), 2, IOR/L/MIL/7/19133.

3. *Our Indian Empire: A Short Review and Some Hints for the Use of Soldiers Proceeding to India* (London: His Majesty's Stationery Office, n.d., ca. 1912), 74. This work is also sometimes titled *The Indian Empire*.

4. Joseph Alter, "Indian Clubs and Colonialism: Hindu Masculinity and Muscular Christianity," *Comparative Studies in Society and History* 46, No. 3 (2004): 502; Peter van der Veer, *Imperial Encounters: Religion and Modernity in India and Britain* (Princeton, NJ: Princeton University Press, 2001), 85–86.

5. Francis Yeats-Brown, *Martial India* (London: Eyre & Spottiswoode, 1945), 35.

6. M. L. Darling, *Wisdom and Waste in the Punjab Village* (Oxford: Oxford University Press, 1934), 88.

7. Roshan Lal Anand, under the supervision of F. L. Brayne, "Soldiers' Savings and How They Use Them" (Board of Economic Inquiry, Punjab, 1940, held at Panjab University), 9.

8. For example, the pamphlet *Our Indian Empire* (1912) describes education as unfit for warriors. *Our Indian Empire*, 31. See also Mrinalini Sinha, *Colonial Masculinity: The "Manly Englishman" and the "Effeminate Bengali" in the Late Nineteenth Century* (Manchester: Manchester University Press, 1995).

9. Chandar Sundaram, "Grudging Concessions: The Officer Corps and Its Indianization, 1817–1940," in *A Military History of India and South Asia*, ed. Daniel P. Marston and Chandar S. Sundaram (Westport, CT: Praeger Security International, 2007), 88–100, at 92–93.

10. Susanne Hoeber Rudolph, Lloyd L. Rudolph, and Mohan Singh Kanota, eds., *Reversing the Gaze: Amar Singh's Diary, a Colonial Subject's Narrative of Imperial India* (Boulder, CO: Westview Press, 2002).

11. Enclosure to para. 17 of General Despatch No. 114 (Army) (August 27, 1914), IOR/L/MIL/7/9314.

12. H. J. Hanham, "Religion and Nationality in the Mid-Victorian Army," in *War and Society: Historical Essays in Honor and Memory of J. R. Western*, ed. M. R. D. Foot (New York: Barnes & Noble Books, 1973), 159–81, at 159.

13. To the Most Honourable the Marquis of Crewe, K. G., His Majesty's Secretary of State for India (October 5, 1911), IOR/L/MIL/7/12353.

14. M. A. Khan Haidari, *Selections from Fauji Akhbar for Preliminary and Interpreters Examinations in Hindustani* (Delhi: Oriental Book Depot, 1923), 50.

15. Army Department, Confidential Despatch, to the Most Honourable the Marquis of Crewe, K. G., His Majesty's Secretary of State for India Separate (September 14, 1911), IOR/L/MIL/7/7162.

16. Army Department to Crewe (September 14, 1911).

17. This phrase is used in the Singapore Mutiny Report, 301–4. "Mutiny of 5th Light Infantry at Singapore 1915," Part I—Proceedings of Court of Enquiry; Part II—"Report by His Excellency the Governor of the Straits Settlements and the General Officer Commanding at Singapore" (Simla: Government Central Branch Press, 1915), 143, IOR/L/MIL/7/7191: 1915–37, henceforth Singapore Mutiny Report. See also Nile Green, *Islam and the Army in Colonial India: Sepoy Religion in the Service of Empire*

(New York: Cambridge University Press, 2009); William Pinch, *Warrior Ascetics and Indian Empires* (Cambridge: Cambridge University Press, 2006).

18. F. C. Isemonger and J. Slattery, *An Account of the Ghadr Conspiracy, 1913–1915* (Lahore: Superintendent, Government Printing, Punjab, 1919), 4.

19. Some argued that Gurkha religious teachers should be paid less because they were "not so liable to be influenced by the fanatical or unorthodox teaching of outsiders." Army Department to Most Honourable the Marquis of Crewe, K. G., His Majesty's Secretary of State for India (May 16, 1912), IOR/L/MIL/7/7162.

20. See Army Department Index, "Ecclesiastical," 1913, NAI; Captain F. M. Wardle, *The Sepoy Officer's Manual: A Book of Reference for Infantry Officers of the Indian Army* (Calcutta and Simla: Thacker, Spink & Co., 1922), 75.

21. Translation of a query and the replies made by Asghar Ali, *Roohi*, and Abdul Wahid, *Khatib* (Imam) of the Chinian Mosque, Lahore, Army Department (March 1919), file 3514–15, NAI; Reply of Abdul Wahid, of Ghazni, Imam of Chinian Mosque, Lahore, Army Department (March 1919), file 3514–15, NAI.

22. Statement of Subadar-Major Khan Mohamed Khan, Section 7, Indian Officers, Singapore Mutiny Report.

23. Section 9, Miscellaneous, Including 2 Secret Agents, Singapore Mutiny Report.

24. Statement of Suleman Khan, village of Dojana of Rohtak District, India, Singapore Mutiny Report, 143.

25. Letter from General Officer Commanding the Troops, Straits Settlements, to the Secretary, War Office, Whitehall, London, SW, Headquarters, Singapore, August 26, 1915, 22–23, IOR/L/MIL/7/7191.

26. Statement of Colour Havildar Mahboob, C Company, 5th Light Infantry, from Khanung Village, District Hissar, Singapore Mutiny Report; Statement of Subadar-Major Khan Mohamed Khan, Singapore Mutiny Report.

27. Statement of Subadar Sharf-ud-din, H Company, Singapore Mutiny Report.

28. Statement of Mr. Purshotamdas Thakurdas, "Civil Administrative Departments: Ecclesiastical Expenditure," contained in *The Report of the Indian Retrenchment Committee, 1922–23*, JEF, March 28, 1923. See also "Civil Administrative Departments: Ecclesiastical Expenditure," contained in *The Report of the Indian Retrenchment Committee, 1922–23*, part VI, p. 175, IOR/L/MIL/7/3123.

29. Telegram from Secretary of State for India (December 21, 1922), Home Department, Political file no. (1923), NAI.

30. Note by General Staff, India, on subject of attempts to tamper with the loyalty of Indian soldiers, n.d., ca. 1922–23, IOR/L/MIL/7/13768.

31. In the nineteenth century, religious teachers received Rs. 8 per month compared to Rs. 7 for Indian "sepoys." By 1911, sepoys had received pay raises of Rs. 11, while most Indian religious teachers continued to be paid just Rs. 8. Sikhism's "military value," and extra ceremonial responsibility, meant that Sikh granthis received a minimum of Rs. 10, or up to Rs. 15 if they had accompanied troops on field service. Religious teachers were paid Rs. 15 after 1912 but the pay of the lowest-ranking Indian soldiers was raised to

Rs. 16 after the war. India Office Minute Paper, undated and unsigned, ca. 1910, IOR/L/ MIL/7/7162; Wardle, *The Sepoy Officer's Manual*, 75.

32. Sundaram, "Grudging Concessions," 94.

33. "Regulations for King George's Royal Indian Military Schools, Jhelum, Jullundur and Ajmer, 1933" (New Delhi: Manager of Publications, Delhi, 1933), 2–3, IOR/L/ MIL/17/5/2303: 1933–39.

34. Tarak Barkawi characterizes Indian soldiers as cosmopolitan in *Soldiers of Empire: Indian and British Armies in World War II* (Cambridge: Cambridge University Press, 2017); Kaushik Roy, "The Hybrid Military Establishment of the East India Company in South Asia: 1750–1849," *Journal of Global History* 6, No. 2 (2011): 195–218; Sundaram, "Grudging Concessions."

35. Army Department to Viscount Peel, His Majesty's Secretary of State for India (September 20, 1923), IOR/L/MIL/7/9321: 1923–46.

36. Statement of Lt-Col H. L. Haughton, Commandant, RIMC Dehra Dun, Indian Sandhurst Committee, Volume II, Evidence (Calcutta: Government of India Central Publication Branch, 1926), 27–31, IOR/26/280/13.

37. Army Department to the Right Honourable Viscount Peel, PC, GBE, His Majesty's Secretary of State for India, Dated Simla (September 20, 1923), Collection 210/45, Scheme for provision of educational facilities for children of Indian Army soldiers: King George's Indian Military Schools, IOR/L/MIL/7/9321: 1923–46.

38. Army Department to the Right Honourable Viscount Peel, 2.

39. Hanham, "Religion and Nationality in the Mid-Victorian Army," 172–75.

40. Examination of Mr. Littlehailes, Officiating Educational Commissioner with the Government of India (August 28, 1925), Indian Sandhurst Committee, Volume II, Evidence (Calcutta: Government of India Central Publication Branch, 1926), 39–41, IOR/26/280/13.

41. The age at entry was later raised to twelve or thirteen. "Regulations for King George's Royal Indian Military Schools, 1933," 2–3.

42. "Regulations for King George's Royal Indian Military Schools, 1933," 2–3.

43. Letter from J. A. Simpson (August 8, 1930); Government of India, Army Department, Army Instructions (India) (Simla, June 9, 1925), p. 1103–1104, IOR/L/ MIL/7/9321: 1923–46.

44. Government of India, Army Dept., Simla (August 6, 1931), to Secretary, Military Dept., India Office; India Office to Private Secretary to His Royal Highness the Prince of Wales, Enclosure (November 22, 1928), IOR/L/MIL/7/9321: 1923–46; see also *Sydney Morning Herald* (February 20, 1922): 9, accessed at National Library of Australia online, July 18, 2017, http://trove.nla.gov.au/newspaper/article /15970298.

45. For height and weight requirements, see "Regulations for King George's Royal Indian Military Schools, 1933," 19, and "Regulations for King George's Royal Indian Military Schools, Jhelum, Jullundur and Ajmer, 1939" (New Delhi: Manager of Publications, Delhi, 1939), 7, IOR/L/MIL/17/5/2303: 1933–39.

46. "Regulations for King George's Royal Indian Military Schools, 1939," 19, 41–43.

47. Government of India, Army Dept., Simla, to Secretary, Military Dept., India Office (August 6, 1931), IOR/L/MIL/7/9321: 1923–46.

48. Parliamentary Notice Question by Major Graham Pole (March 10, 1930), IOR/L/MIL/7/9321: 1923–46; "Military Schools in India," *Morning Post* (September 18, 1929), IOR/L/MIL/7/9321: 1923–46.

49. Government of India, Army Department, *Army Instructions (India)* (Simla, June 9, 1925), 1123, IOR/L/MIL/7/9321: 1923–46; "Regulations for King George's Royal Indian Military Schools, 1933," 19; "Regulations for King George's Royal Indian Military Schools, 1939."

50. India Office, London, to His Excellency the Right Honorable Gov. Gen. of India in Council (October 9, 1930), IOR/L/MIL/7/9321: 1923–46.

51. "Regulations for King George's Royal Indian Military Schools, 1933," 5, 7–8.

52. "Educational Training, Indian Army" (Calcutta: Government of India Central Publication Branch, 1932), 20, 37–38, IOR/L/MIL/17/5/2272.

53. "Educational Training, Indian Army," 20, 22.

54. Excerpt, "Statement of Case," IOR/L/MIL/7/19133; "Information Respecting Conditions of Admission to the Prince of Wales's Royal Indian Military College, Dehra Dun," IOR/L/MIL/7/19133.

55. To the Right Honouable Viscount Peel, PC, GBE, His Majesty's Secretary of State for India (November 8, 1923), IOR/L/MIL/7/19133.

56. Letter from Government of India, Army Department, Simla, to Sec. of State for India, Military Department, India Office, London (July 9, 1925), IOR/L/MIL/7/19133.

57. Copy of telegram from Viceroy, Army Department, to Sec. of State for India, dated Simla (August 10, 1921), IOR/L/MIL/7/19133.

58. "Administrative Report on the Prince of Wales's Royal Indian Military College, Dehra Dun," December 1922, IOR/L/MIL/7/19133.

59. "Regulations for the Prince of Wales's Royal Indian Military College, Dehra Dun, 1934" (Delhi: GSI, 1938), 9, IOR/L/MIL/17/5/2285.

60. British women missionaries had long emphasized the need to bring home comforts into British soldiers' military spaces, which the army supported to encourage sobriety and lawfulness. The absence of British women in Indian men's military spaces and lack of military influence among Indian women changed army strategies. Kenneth Hendrickson, "Winning the Troops for Vital Religion: Female Evangelical Missionaries to the British Army, 1857–1880," *Armed Forces and Society* 23, No. 4 (Summer 1997): 615–34, at 622.

61. Statement of Lt-Col H. L. Haughton, 25–26.

62. "Regulations for the Prince of Wales's Royal Indian Military College," 15. The College Committee recommended that during terms "the number of religious and other holidays should be reduced to a minimum." Even during observed holidays "cadets should not be permitted to absent themselves from College." Report of the Indian Military College Committee (July 15, 1931), 12–13, IOR/L/MIL/17/5/1790.

63. To Peel (November 8, 1923).

64. For a later exploration of this dynamic, see Barkawi, *Soldiers of Empire*.

65. Statement of Lt-Col H. L. Haughton, Commandant, RIMC Dehra Dun, Indian Sandhurst Committee, Volume II, Evidence (Calcutta: Government of India Central Publication Branch, 1926), 27, IOR/26/280/13.

66. "Regulations for the Prince of Wales's Royal Indian Military College," 4, 9.

67. Yeats-Brown, *Martial India*, 35.

68. Examination of Mr. Littlehailes (August 28, 1925), 48–49.

69. Sundaram, "Grudging Concessions," 94.

70. Military Department, Government of India, Telegram (May 26, 1926), IOR/L/MIL/7/13079: 1924–27.

71. Sundaram, "Grudging Concessions," 97.

72. Military Department paper regarding Prince of Wales's Royal India Military College, Dehra Dun, expansion in number of cadets from 120 to 130, sent to Under Secretary (February 21, 1933), IOR/L/MIL/7/19133.

73. Appendix I, His Excellency the Commander-in-Chief's address (May 25, 1931), "Report of the Indian Military College Committee" (July 15, 1931), 24, IOR/L/MIL/17/5/1790.

74. Sundaram, "Grudging Concessions," 96.

75. Statement of Lt-Col H. L. Haughton, 16.

76. Sundaram, "Grudging Concessions," 88.

77. Pamphlet of the Competitive Examination for Admission to the Indian Military Academy, Dehra Dun, and the Royal Indian Marine, Held in March–April 1935 (Delhi: Manager of Publications, 1935), ii, IOR/L/MIL/17/5/2282.

78. Daniel Marston, *The Indian Army and the End of the Raj* (Cambridge: Cambridge University Press, 2014), 23.

79. Sundaram, "Grudging Concessions," 98.

80. Report of the Indian Military College Committee (July 15, 1931), 20, IOR/L/MIL/17/5/1790.

81. Sundaram, "Grudging Concessions," 95, 99.

82. Sundaram, "Grudging Concessions," 99.

83. Twenty-five South Asians received commissions between 1918 and 1926. Minute and Suggested Reply to Parliamentary Notice, Session 1930–31, Question by Major Graham Pole for Monday (March 23, 1931); Statement of Lt-Col H. L. Haughton.

84. Statement of Mr. E. Littlehailes, Officiating Educational Commissioner with the Government of India, Indian Sandhurst Committee, Volume II, Evidence (Calcutta: Government of India Central Publication Branch 1926), 27–31, IOR/26/280/13.

85. "Pamphlet of the Competitive Examination . . . Held in October 1932" (Delhi: Manager of Publications, 1933), 35–36, IOR/L/MIL/17/5/2282.

86. Military Department paper regarding RIMC expansion (February 21, 1933).

87. "Pamphlet of the Competitive Examination . . . Held in March–April 1933" (Delhi: Manager of Publications, 1933), 20–21, IOR/L/MIL/17/5/2282.

88. *The Prince of Wales's Royal Indian Military College* (Dehra Dun, February 1933), 6, 8, 11, 15, IOR/L/MIL/17/5/2286.

89. Dinesh Chandra Misra, interviewed by Christopher Somerville, Oral History 18370, IWM, 1995, Reel 2–3.

90. Kristen Tewari, interviewed by Christopher Somerville, Oral History 18396, IWM, 1995.

91. "Pamphlet of the Competitive Examination . . . October 1937" (Delhi: Manager of Publications, 1938), 34; Aditya Sondhi, *The Order of the Crest: Tracing the Alumni of Bishop Cotton Boys' School, Bangalore (1865–2015)* (Gurgaon: Penguin Books India, 2014), 16.

92. Sondhi, *The Order of the Crest*, 16, 24.

93. "Pamphlet of the Competitive Examination . . . March–April 1938" (Delhi: Manager of Publications, 1938), 40.

94. Pradeep Barua, *Gentlemen of the Raj: The Indian Army Officer Corps, 1817–1949* (Westport, CT: Praeger, 2003), 49–50.

95. Hayden Bellenoit, "Missionary Education, Religion and Knowledge in India, c. 1880–1915," *Modern Asian Studies* 41, No. 2 (2007): 369–94.

96. The Cotton School educated European, Eurasian, and South Asian students since its earliest days. Abraham Ebenezer, *Eton of the East: The Story of Bishop Cotton Boys School, 1865–1998* (Bangalore: WorkMakers Publishing, 1998), 23, 35, 119.

97. Gauri Viswanathan, *Masks of Conquest: Literary Study and British Rule in India* (New York: Columbia University Press, 2014).

98. Also included is Government of India, Army Dept., Simla, to Sec., Military Dept., India Office, London, "Provisional Regulations Respecting the Admission of Indian Gentlemen to the Royal Military College, Sandhurst" (September 23, 1926), IOR/L/MIL/7/13079: 1924–27.

99. Barua, *Gentlemen of the Raj*, 51.

100. Indrani Chatterjee, "Colouring Subalternity: Slaves, Concubines and Social Orphans Under the East India Company," *Subaltern Studies* 10 (1999): 49–97.

101. Jeffrey Cox, *Imperial Fault Lines: Christianity and Colonial Power in India, 1818–1940* (Stanford: Stanford University Press, 2002), 254.

102. About chaplains for Indian Christians, see Question by Mr. M. Ruthnaswamy, extract from Official Report of the Legislative Assembly Debates (March 21, 1927), 2450, IOR/L/MIL/17/5/541; about pariahs, see "A Grave Injustice to Indian Christians," Army Part B (July 1918), file 40–42, NAI.

103. Francis Yeats-Brown, *The Lives of a Bengal Lancer* (London: Victor Gollancz, 1930), 138.

104. Green, *Islam and the Army*.

105. Report of the Indian Military College Committee (July 15, 1931), 11, IOR/L/MIL/17/5/1790.

106. "Pamphlet of the Competitive Examination . . . Held in March–April 1939" (Delhi: Manager of Publications, 1939), 36.

107. In the spring exam 1937, one Indian Christian and one Anglo-Indian applied and both earned passing interview scores. In the fall, an Anglo-Indian candidate made it into the top ten of all candidates on the exam. Another did not pass the exam overall but earned a perfect interview score. All three of the Anglo-Indians who interviewed

received qualifying interview scores, as did one of the two Indian Christians. The spring 1938 exam produced similar results. "Pamphlet of the Competitive Examination for Admission to the Indian Military Academy, Dehra Dun, and the Royal Indian Marine: Held in March–April 1937" (Delhi: Manager of Publications, 1937), 35; "Pamphlet of the Competitive Examination . . . March–April 1938" (Delhi: Manager of Publications, 1938), 53; "Pamphlet of the Competitive Examination . . . March–April 1939" (Delhi: Manager of Publications, 1939), 36, 49; "Pamphlet of the Competitive Examination . . . October 1937" (Delhi: Manager of Publications, 1938), 34–36, 48; "Pamphlet of the Competitive Examination . . . October 1939" (Delhi: Manager of Publications, 1940), 43; "Pamphlet of the Competitive Examination . . . October 1938" (Delhi: Manager of Publications, 1939), 51.

108. *Provisional Regulations Respecting Admission to the Indian Military Academy Dehra Dun, 1932* (Calcutta: Government of India Central Publication Branch, 1932), 22, IOR/L/MIL/17/5/2284.

109. The Committee of Enquiry upon Religion, *The Army and Religion: An Enquiry and Its Bearing upon the Religious Life of the Nation* (London: Macmillan & Company, 1919), 9.

110. Erica Wald, "From Begums and Bibis to Abandoned Females and Idle Women: Sexual Relationships, Venereal Diseases and the Redefinition of Prostitution in Early Nineteenth-Century India," *Indian Economic and Social History Review* 46, No. 5 (January/March 2009): 5–25; Erica Wald, *Vice in the Barracks: Medicine, the Military and the Making of Colonial India, 1780–1868* (New York: Palgrave, 2014).

111. The secretary of state for war argued that "It is to the credit of popular education" that soldiers are no longer "men without either education or ambition" who can only be "found in the canteen or the public house." Memorandum by the Secretary of State for War, the Cabinet, Recruiting for the Army (1936). See Hanham for details about Irish recruits in the nineteenth century: Hanham, "Religion and Nationality in the Mid-Victorian Army," 161, 170.

112. As the King's Regulations expressed: "A soldier's religious denomination will be classified, for all purposes, in accordance with his own declaration on the subject, under one of the following denominations:- Church of England; Presbyterian (including Church of Scotland, United Free Church of Scotland, Free Church of Scotland, Presbyterian Church of England, Presbyterian Church in Ireland, and Welsh Calvinistic Methodist Church); Roman Catholic; Wesleyan; Baptist; Congregationalist; Primitive Methodist; United Methodist; Jewish; or other denomination as stated by the soldier." Quoted in the Metropolitan's Chaplain, Bishop's House, Calcutta, *The Chaplain's Handbook India: A Guide to the Military, Civil and Ecclesiastical Rules in Force in India* (Calcutta: Baptist Mission Press, 1926), 8. This section is from "The King's Regulations," Section XII: General Duties, 1268, Religious Denominations.

113. *Our Indian Empire*, 57, 70.

114. Government of India, Military Department, *Army Regulations, India*, vol. 13, *British Army Schools* (Calcutta: Office of the Superintendent of Government Printing, India, 1900), 22, IOR/L/MIL/17/5/640; Government of India, Military Department

Army Regulations, India, vol. 12, *Barracks* (Calcutta: Government of India Central Printing Office, 1900), 174, 177, IOR/L/MIL/17/5/633.

115. Letter to Sir C[harles] J. Lyall from Secretariat (February 2, 1907); Letter from W. R. Bombay to Mr. R. E. Enthoven, Secretary to Government, Use of Roman Catholic Churches in India, Ferozepore, February 1893 (January 19, 1907), IOR/L/PJ/6/799, file 520 & 528.

116. Roman Catholics were 15%–20%, Presbyterians 8%, and Wesleyans 4%–5% from 1897 to 1921. Denominational census of British troops in India taken January 1897, March 1910, and December 1921 included in Army Department to the Right Honorable Viscount Peel, Secretary of State for India (July 12, 1923), IOR/L/MIL/7/3123.

117. Presbyterian and Anglican chaplains were appointed by the Indian Ecclesiastical Establishment, but Roman Catholic priests were appointed by their own ecclesiastical superiors. Their pay was supplemented by the Government of India when they ministered to the troops. Army Department to the Right Honorable Viscount (July 12, 1923).

118. Application of the Roman Catholic Chaplain, Lahore, for an Increase in His Present Allowance, Government of Punjab, Home Department, file 22 (March 1915), Panjab State Archives; Army Department, Despatch to His Majesty's Secretary of State for India (October 9, 1924), IOR/L/MIL/7/3123; see also Government of Punjab, Revised Regulations for the Appointment of Anglican and Presbyterian Chaplains, file 12 (January 1915), p. 27, Panjab State Archives; Extract from Department of Education Resolution (November 18, 1920), IOR/L/MIL/7/3123.

119. Army Department, Despatch to His Majesty's Secretary of State for India (February 25, 1926), IOR/L/MIL/7/3123; the 1920 Esher committee had recommended hiring British priests instead of foreign priests: "Report of the Committee Appointed by the Secretary of State for India to Enquire into the Administration and Organisation of the Army in India," Chairman: Lord Esher, Presented to Parliament by Command of His Majesty (London: printed and published by His Majesty's Stationery Office, 1920), 100.

120. William Keatinge, Bishop, Principal Chaplain to the Forces (Roman Catholic), Enclosure to the Secretary, War Office (October 23, 1923), IOR/L/MIL/7/3123.

121. He estimated his necessary expenditures amounted to approximately Rs. 807 per mensem, far exceeding his monthly salary of Rs. 675. Rev. J. Bell, Chaplain, Indian Ecclesiastical Establishment, Statement of Evidence, IOR/Q/11/15.

122. Maurice Boxall, letter to parents, n.d. (sent while in attendance at Cadet College, Quetta, ca. 1916), Private Papers of Captain M. W. J. Boxall, Documents 11286, IWM.

123. Minute Paper Financial Department, Referred to Military Secretary, IOR/L/MIL/7/3123. There were fourteen posts for Wesleyan chaplains for 2,516 soldiers, five United Board chaplains for 1,479 adherents, seventy-six Roman Catholic priests for 7,000–9,000 Roman Catholic soldiers, 166 chaplaincies for over 40,000 Anglican troops, and eighteen chaplains for approximately 5,000 Presbyterian troops.

124. G. M. Davies, *A Chaplain in India* (London and Edinburgh: Marshall, Morgan & Scott, Ltd., ca. 1933), 118; Interview with Arthur William Ford, interview by H. Campbell McMurray, Oral History 719, IWM, 1975, Reels 2–3.

125. For additional details about challenges for non-Anglican soldiers, see Government of India, Finance Department, *Army Regulations, India*, vol. 1, *Pay and Allowances and Non-effective Pay* (Calcutta: Superintendent, Government Printing, India, 1912), IOR/L/MIL/17/5/541; India Office to His Excellency the Right Honourable the Governor General of India in Council (February 7, 1924), IOR/L/MIL/7/3123; Army Department to the Right Honorable Viscount Peel (July 12, 1923); Army Department Despatch to His Majesty's Secretary of State for India (October 9, 1924); Nathan, Memorandum (October 21, 1899); Hanham, "Religion and Nationality in the Mid-Victorian Army," 159.

126. *Our Indian Empire*, 104; Royal Army Temperance Association, "Annual Report for the Official Year 1909–1910" (Simla: Royal Army Temperance Association Press, Simla), 55, IOR/L/MIL/7/9993; Hendrickson, "Winning the Troops for Vital Religion," 622.

127. Toco Moses Stevens, interviewed by Conrad Wood, Oral History 776, IWM, June 14, 1976, Reel 4.

128. The RATA maintained that it was "undenominational" and encouraged "Chaplains of the several persuasions" to "work amongst the men in the way they think best." Frederick Roberts, Temperance Speech at Meerut, March 3, 1888, IOR/L/MIL/7/9998.

129. Davies, *A Chaplain in India*, 149.

130. Form of Testimonial to the Right Reverent Arthur Foley (June 20, 1914), IOR/L/PJ/6/1324, file 3533.

131. Cox, *Imperial Fault Lines*, 254.

132. Others embraced imperial racial hierarchies. Quoted in Harald Fischer-Tiné, "'Unparalleled Opportunities': The Indian Y.M.C.A.'s Army Work Schemes for Imperial Troops During the Great War (1914–1920)," *Journal of Imperial and Commonwealth History* (2018): 1–38 at 7, https://doi.org/10.1080/03086534.2018.1511245.

133. S. M. Jafri, "In One of the Largest Camps in France," n.d., IOR/L/MIL/7/18577.

134. Closing down of Royal Army Temperance Association in India, IOR/L/MIL/7/10084.

135. William Homer, interviewed by Conrad Wood, August 4, 1976, IWM Interview 792, Reel 10.

136. Charles Crossland, interviewed by Conrad Wood, August 16, 1976, IWM Interview 797, Reels 2, 4.

137. William Homer, IWM Interview, Reel 10.

138. S. P. P. Thorat, *From Reveille to Retreat* (New Delhi: Allied Publishers Private Limited, 1985), 39.

139. Thorat, *From Reveille to Retreat*, 15–16.

140. Thorat, *From Reveille to Retreat*, 15–16.

141. "Regulations for King George's Royal Indian Military Schools, 1933 [and 1939]," 7.

142. Educational Training, Indian Army (Calcutta: Government of India Central Publication Branch, 1932), 24, IOR/L/MIL/17/5/2272.

143. *Prince of Wales' Royal Indian Military College* (Calcutta: Government of India Press, n.d.), 5–6, IOR/L/MIL/17/5/2283; Sukhwant Singh, *Three Decades of Indian Army Life* (Sterling Publishers Ltd., 1967), 28.

144. *Prince of Wales' Royal Indian Military College*, 5.

145. Educational Training, Indian Army (Calcutta: Government of India Central Publication Branch, 1932), 24, IOR/L/MIL/17/5/2272.

146. Vinayak Chaturvedi, "Rethinking Knowledge with Action: V. D. Savarkar, the Bhagavad Gita, and Histories of Warfare," *Modern Intellectual History* 7, No. 2 (2010): 425–27; Shruti Kapila, "A History of Violence," *Modern Intellectual History* 7, No. 2 (2010): 439, 447–48; Shruti Kapila and Faisal Devji, "Introduction: The Bhagavad Gita and Modern Thought," *Modern Intellectual History* 7, No. 2 (2010): 273, 271.

147. Included in question-and-answer portion of Statement of Lt-Col H. L. Haughton, 26–27.

148. Question by Nawab Sir Sahibzada Abdul Qaiyum to Lt. Col. H. L. Haughton, Indian Sandhurst Committee, Volume II, Evidence (Calcutta: Government of India Central Publication Branch, 1926), IOR/26/280/13.

149. Statement of Lt-Col H. L. Haughton, 26–27; "Regulations for the Prince of Wales's Royal Indian Military College," 11.

150. Edwin John Watson, interviewed by Conrad Wood, Oral History 903, IWM, March 22, 1977, Reel 1.

151. *Prince of Wales' Royal Indian Military College*.

152. *Prince of Wales' Royal Indian Military College*.

153. At the same time, instructors needed to avoid injuring "racial or religious susceptibilities" in their presentation of events. Educational Training, Indian Army (Calcutta: Government of India Central Publication Branch, 1932), 5, 12, 20, 22, 24, 92, IOR/L/MIL/17/5/2272.

154. Statement of Lt-Col H. L. Haughton, 26–27.

155. Statement of Lt-Col H. L. Haughton, 26–27.

156. Thomas Wentworth Nickalls, interviewed by Conrad Wood, Oral History 962, IWM, August 11, 1977, Reel 2.

157. "The King's Regulations," Section XII: General Duties, quoted in Metropolitan's Chaplain, *The Chaplain's Handbook India*, Section 1599, 8.

158. About pews, see Patrick Miles Pennington, interviewed by Conrad Wood, Oral History 966, August 17, 1977, IWM, Reel 4.

159. Thomas Nickalls, Toco Moses Stevens, and William Homer all recount near identical versions of this practice and its connection to 1857. Interview with Toco Moses Stevens, Interviewed by Conrad Wood, Oral History 776, IWM, June 14, 1976, Reel 7; Homer, IWM Interview, Reel 8; Nickalls, IWM Interview.

160. Memorandum from Godber to the Secretary to the Government of India (January 8, 1920).

161. After 1860 it was possible to change religious designations through a vocal affirmation but Somerfield was visited by a chaplain repeatedly until he changed his mind. See Chapter 6 for a greater discussion of Somerfield. See also Hanham, "Religion and Nationality in the Mid-Victorian Army," 163.

162. Homer, IWM Interview, Reel 8.

163. Letter from the Most Reverend A. E. J. Kenealy, D.D. Catholic Archbishop of Simla, to Lieutenant Colonel A. Shairp, Additional Deputy Secretary to the Government of India, Army Department (January 12, 1920), Army Department (May 1921), file 197–239, NAI.

164. Rev. Dr. McKelvie and the Venerable G. C. A. Smith, "Military Chaplaincies," in *Priest and Parish in India (European Congregations)*, ed. G. A. A. Wright (printed in India by George Kenneth at the Diocesan Press, 1928), 116–31, at 126.

165. Singh, *Three Decades of Indian Army Life*, 36.

166. This is according to William Homer, who served with the 2nd Battalion Royal Fusiliers in India. Homer, IWM Interview, Reel 3.

167. Misra, IWM Interview, Reels 2–3.

CHAPTER 6

1. H. H. Somerfield, unpublished diary, various entries, H. H. Somerfield Papers, henceforth HHS, IWM.

2. Barbara D. Metcalf and Thomas R. Metcalf, *A Concise History of Modern India* (Cambridge: Cambridge University Press, 2012); for examples of interwar moral critiques of imperialism, see Seth Koven, *The Matchgirl and the Heiress* (Princeton, NJ: Princeton University Press, 2015).

3. Christopher Pinney, "The Body and the Bomb: Technologies of Modernity in Colonial India," in *Picturing the Nation: Iconographies of Modern India*, ed. Richard H. Davis (Andhra Pradesh: Orient Longman, 2007), 51; Kama Maclean, *A Revolutionary History of Interwar India: Violence, Image, Voice and Text* (Oxford: Oxford University Press, 2015).

4. Brandon Marsh, *Ramparts of Empire: British Imperialism and India's Afghan Frontier, 1918–1948* (New York: Palgrave Macmillan, 2015); Sugata Bose, *His Majesty's Opponent: Subhas Chandra Bose and India's Struggle Against Empire* (Cambridge, MA: Belknap Press, 2011).

5. Mrinalini Sinha, *Colonial Masculinity: The "Manly Englishman" and the "Effeminate Bengali" in the Late Nineteenth Century* (Manchester: Manchester University Press, 1995).

6. Charu Gupta, "Anxious Hindu Masculinity in Colonial North India: Shuddhi and Sangathan Movements," *Cross Currents* 61, No. 4 (December 2011): 441–54, at 446.

7. Peter van der Veer, *Imperial Encounters: Religion and Modernity in India and Britain* (Princeton, NJ: Princeton University Press, 2001), 102; Mark Singleton, *Yoga Body: The Origins of Modern Posture Practice* (Oxford: Oxford University Press, 2010).

8. Mrinalini Sinha, *Specters of Mother India: The Global Restructuring of an Empire* (Durham, NC: Duke University Press, 2006).

9. Joseph Alter, *Gandhi's Body: Sex, Diet, and the Politics of Nationalism* (Philadelphia: University of Pennsylvania Press, 2000).

10. Pinney, "The Body and the Bomb," 51; Christopher Pinney, *Camera Indica: The Social Life of Indian Photographs* (Chicago: University of Chicago Press, 1998), 59–60; Maclean, *A Revolutionary History of Interwar India*.

11. Lata Mani, *Contentious Traditions: The Debate on Sati in Colonial India* (Berkeley: University of California Press, 1998); Sikata Banerjee, "Armed Masculinity, Hindu Nationalism and Female Political Participation in India: Heroic Mothers, Chaste Wives and Celibate Warriors," *International Feminist Journal of Politics* 8, No. 1 (2006): 62–83.

12. Examination of Mr. Littlehailes, Officiating Educational Commissioner with the Government of India (August 28, 1925), "Indian Sandhurst Committee. Volume II. Evidence" (Calcutta: Government of India Central Publication Branch, 1926), 40, IOR/26/280/13.

13. Contribution of Diwan Bahadur Ramachandra Rao during the questioning of Lt. Col. H. L. Haughton, "Indian Sandhurst Committee."

14. Contribution of Captain Banerjee included in the questioning of Lt. Col. Haughton, "Indian Sandhurst Committee."

15. Statement of Lt-Col H. L. Haughton, "Indian Sandhurst Committee."

16. Minute by Sir Abdur Rahim and Mr. S. N. Mukarji, "Report of the Indian Military College Committee" (July 15, 1931), 39–42, IOR/L/MIL/17/5/1790.

17. Minute by Sir P. S. Sivaswamy Aiyer and Major-General Raja Ganpat Rao Raghunath Rao Rajwade (July 2, 1931), "Report of the Indian Military College Committee," 87–89.

18. Extract from Indian Information Series 1939, IOR/L/MIL/7/19156: 1935–41.

19. Minute by B. S. Moonje (July 3, 1931), "Report of the Indian Military College Committee," 56. A similar attitude is expressed at the outset of the Second World War by Mr. Govind V. Deshmukh, Extract from Legislative Assembly (March 10, 1941), IOR/L/MIL/7/19156: 1935–41.

20. Minute by B. S. Moonje, 57.

21. "Indian Sandhurst, Numbers of Officers to Be Trained," *Times* (May 26, 1931), IOR/L/MIL/7/19112.

22. This name likely refers to the Bhonsale dynasty of Nagpur, which led the Maratha Empire in the eighteenth century. Govind V. Deshmukh argued in the Legislative Assembly during the Second World War that Hindus and Muslims served side by side under these leaders. Moonje, however, does not seem to emphasize this point in the 1930s. Deshmukh, Extract from Legislative Assembly (March 10, 1941).

23. Commander-in-Chief's Message (Nagpur, November 24, 1935), *Times of India* (November 26, 1935), reprint from the *Mahratta* (May 14, 1937), Home (Special), Sr. 989, File 812-A H.D. 1935, MSA.

24. Reprint from the *Mahratta* (May 21, 1937), MSA.

25. Gupta, "Anxious Hindu Masculinity."

26. Covering Minute by General Philip W. Chetwode, "Report of the Indian Military College Committee," 31.

27. "New Army of Indians, Full Division to Be Indianised," *Manchester Guardian* (May 26, 1931), IOR/L/MIL/7/19112.

28. See, for example, "Pamphlet of the Competitive Examination for Admission to the Indian Military Academy, Dehra Dun, and the Royal Indian Marine. Held in October 1934" (Delhi: Manager of Publications, 1935), 49, IOR/L/MIL/17/5/2282.

29. Extract from the Bombay Presidency Weekly Letter No. 18, dated May 4, 1935, Home (Special), Sr. 989, File 812-A H.D. (SPL) 1935, MSA.

30. *Bombay Chronicle* (September 9, 1935) (Special), Sr. 989, File 812-A H.D. (SPL) 1935, MSA.

31. *Bombay Chronicle*, September 9, 1935.

32. Document simply labeled "Dharwar, September 7th," Home (Special), Sr. 989, File 812-A H.D. (SPL), 1935, MSA.

33. Dinesh Chandra Misra, interviewed by Christopher Somerville, Oral History 18370, IWM, 1995, Reels 2–3.

34. "Pamphlet of the Competitive Examination . . . March–April 1935" (Delhi: Manager of Publications, 1935), 37.

35. "Pamphlet of the Competitive Examination . . . October 1932" (Delhi: Manager of Publications, 1933), 31–32.

36. "Pamphlet of the Competitive Examination . . . October 1934" (Delhi: Manager of Publications, 1935), 28–29.

37. "Pamphlet of the Competitive Examination . . . March–April 1935" (Delhi: Manager of Publications, 1935), 28.

38. "Pamphlet of the Competitive Examination . . . October 1935" (Delhi: Manager of Publications, 1936), 26; "Pamphlet of the Competitive Examination . . . March–April 1936" (Delhi: Manager of Publications, 1936), 26.

39. "Pamphlet of the Competitive Examination . . . March–April 1937" (Delhi: Manager of Publications, 1937), 35.

40. Twelve out of seventeen Muslims and eighteen out of twenty-six Sikhs passed the exam compared with thirty-four out of sixty-four Hindus. The rate for all non-Hindus on the interview, including Anglo-Indians, Christians, etc., was 72%. "Pamphlet of the Competitive Examination . . . October 1937" (Delhi: Manager of Publications, 1938), 48.

41. "Pamphlet of the Competitive Examination . . . October 1938" (Delhi: Manager of Publications, 1939), 51. Fifty-seven percent of Hindus compared with 66% of non-Hindus passed the interview in the spring. "Pamphlet of the Competitive Examination . . . March–April 1938" (Delhi: Manager of Publications, 1938), 53.

42. "Pamphlet of the Competitive Examination . . . October 1939" (Delhi: Manager of Publications, 1940), 43. Spring 1939 results were 39% passing Hindus and 56% of non-Hindus.

43. Nawab Sir Sahibzada Abdul Qaiyum served on several selection board committees for Sandhurst and asked British officials repeatedly about the "racial difference" of candidates. Haughton emphasized educational backgrounds and tentatively answered that "On the whole I should say that the boys from the North are probably physically stronger and harder." Qaiyum's exchange with Littlehailes was more telling. He asked whether there is "anything deeper in the character and qualifications of the boys, which enables you to decide between boys. Can you, even without putting a question, say whether a boy is drawn from a martial race, from a non-military class, from an urban population or from some other class?" Littlehailes responded that "You can make a shrewd guess as to the type which is suitable for a military career." "Indian Sandhurst Committee Report" (1926), 21–22, 46–48.

44. Examination of Mr. Littlehailes, 38–39.

45. While I was researching at the United Service Institution in New Delhi in 2014, a few high-ranking retired Indian Army officers came up to me to reiterate that they would not have been eligible for recruitment under the British because they were Hindu.

46. Tan Tai Yong, *The Garrison State: The Military, Government and Society in Colonial Punjab, 1849–1947* (New Delhi and London: Sage, 2005), 254–55.

47. "Military Schools in India," *Morning Post* (September 18, 1929), IOR/L/MIL/7/9321: 1923–46.

48. From S. K. B. to Claud W. Jacob and Military Committee, Military Department (October 16, 1929), IOR/L/MIL/7/9321.

49. Note by Claud W. Jacob, IOR/L/MIL/7/9321.

50. Letter from J. A. Simpson (August 8, 1930), IOR/L/MIL/7/9321.

51. Sinha, *Colonial Masculinity*.

52. Muhammad Ismail Khan, interviewed by Conrad Wood, IWM Interview 11748, 1990.

53. Indian Soldiers (Litigation) Laws, IOR/L/PJ/6/1355, file 846: October 1914–June 1918.

54. Kate Imy, "Fascist Yogis: Martial Bodies and Imperial Impotence," *Journal of British Studies* 55, No. 2 (April 2016): 320–43.

55. Francis Yeats-Brown, *Martial India* (London: Eyre & Spottiswoode, 1945), 64.

56. F. K. Khan Durrani, *The Future of Islam in India: A Warning and a Call* (Lahore, 1929), 18–19.

57. Durrani, *The Future of Islam in India*.

58. Excerpt from Jinnah, *Speeches and Writing*, reproduced in Stephen Hay, ed., *Sources of Indian Tradition*, 2nd ed., vol. 2 (New York: Columbia University Press, 1988), 231.

59. Douglas Sidney Frederick Stacey, interviewed by Conrad Wood, IWM Interview 10633, 1989, Reel 2.

60. Private Papers of Lieutenant Colonel W. L. Farrow, Documents 3598, Box No. 95/33/1, IWM.

61. M. L. Darling, *Wisdom and Waste in the Punjab Village* (Oxford: Oxford University Press, 1934), 23.

62. Roshan Lal Anand, under the supervision of F. L. Brayne, "Soldiers' Savings and How They Use Them" (Board of Economic Inquiry, Punjab, 1940, held at Panjab University), 18, 30–31.

63. Darling, *Wisdom and Waste in the Punjab Village*, 51.

64. Anand, "Soldiers' Savings," 9.

65. They also included passages by Zionists that condemned communism. For example, in 1938, candidates for the IMA summarized a lengthy passage from "This Freedom" by Zionist and Liberal politician Sir Herbert Samuel. Samuel denounced fascism as too extreme, but was also critical of communism and British socialism. "Pamphlet of the Competitive Examination . . . October 1938."

66. The original text is from Philip Gibbs, *Across the Frontiers* (Doubleday, Doran, 1938), reproduced in "Pamphlet of the Competitive Examination . . . October 1939" (Delhi: Manager of Publications, 1940), 1.

67. Metcalf and Metcalf, *A Concise History of Modern India.*

68. Francis Yeats-Brown, *Lancer at Large* (New York: Garden City Publishers, 1937), 213–14.

69. Francis Yeats-Brown, *European Jungle* (Philadelphia: Macrae-Smith Company, 1940), 120–21.

70. Fuller received numerous letters of thanks and support for expressing his opinions. J. F. C. Fuller, "Letter to the Editor," *Times* (April 24, 1939), J. F. C. Fuller Papers, Box 2, Envelope 18, Rutgers University Archives.

71. Richard C. Thurlow, *Fascism in Britain: From Oswald Mosley's Blackshirts to the National Front* (London: I. B. Tauris, 1998), 100, 128; J. F. C. Fuller, "The Cancer of Europe," *Fascist Quarterly* 1, No. 1 (January 1935): 66–81, quoted in Thomas Linehan, *British Fascism 1918–39: Parties, Ideology and Culture* (Manchester: Manchester University Press, 2000), 193.

72. Letter from Fuller (February 28, 1931), J. F. C. Fuller Papers, Box 2, Envelope 13, Rutgers University Archives.

73. J. F. C. Fuller, *India in Revolt* (London: Eyre & Spottiswoode, 1931), 216. See also J. F. C. Fuller, "Report on India," J. F. C. Fuller Papers, Box 1, Envelope 10, 24, Rutgers University Archives.

74. Francis Yeats-Brown, "Persons and Personages," *The Living Age* (August 1938): 354, 4463, 512. Yeats-Brown was an active member of the fascist-leaning January Club. He attended various fascist lectures and events in the United Kingdom and Europe. His *Dogs of War* in 1934 proudly lambasted pacifism in Britain; Imy, "Fascist Yogis"; Thurlow, *Fascism in Britain*, 69.

75. Linehan, *British Fascism 1918–39*, 49–50, 162; Ina Zweiniger-Bargielowska, "Building a British Superman: Physical Culture in Interwar Britain," *Journal of Contemporary History* 41, No. 4 (October 2006): 595–610, at 600, 604.

76. Derek Sayer, "British Reaction to the Amritsar Massacre 1919–1920," *Past and Present* 131 (May 1991): 130–64, 157.

77. See, for example, Paul Stocker, "'The Imperial Spirit': British Fascism and Empire, 1919–1940," *Religion Compass* 9, No. 2 (2015): 45–54, at 50. See, for example, IMA exams for March/April 1936, March/April 1933, October 1933, October 1937, and March/April 1939, "Pamphlet of the Competitive Examination . . ." (Delhi: Manager of Publications).

78. Joselyn Zivin, "'Bent': A Colonial Subversive and Indian Broadcasting," *Past and Present* 162 (February 1999): 195–220, at 201.

79. David Cannadine, *Ornamentalism: How the British Saw Their Empire* (Oxford: Oxford University Press, 2002).

80. Zivin, "Bent," 195–220.

81. Linehan, *British Fascism 1918–39*, 162.

82. Liam J. Liburd, "Beyond the Pale: Whiteness, Masculinity and Empire in the British Union of Fascists, 1932–1940," *Fascism: Journal of Comparative Fascist Studies* 7, No. 2 (October 2018), https://brill.com/view/journals/fasc/7/2/article-p275_275 .xml#d1611169e415.

83. Imy, "Fascist Yogis."

84. Francis Yeats-Brown, unpublished yoga notebook from a lecture of P. A. Bernard, November 29, 1924, Yoga Notebooks, Misc. 9.3, 1924–25, Harry Ransom Center, henceforth HRC. An identical claim also appears in the same notebook on December 14, 1924; Francis Yeats-Brown, "Unpublished Yoga Notebook," January 3, 1925, Yoga Notebooks, Misc. 9.3, 1924–25, HRC. See also Robert Love, *The Great Oom: The Improbable Birth of Yoga in America* (New York: Viking, 2010).

85. Francis Yeats-Brown, unpublished notebook written during travels in India, Indian Notebooks, Misc. 7.8, Notebook 2, part 1, HRC.

86. Ashwin Desai and Goolam Vahed, *The South African Gandhi: Stretcher-Bearer of Empire* (Stanford: Stanford University Press, 2015); David Chidester, *Empire of Religion: Imperialism and Comparative Religion* (Chicago: University of Chicago Press, 2013); Van der Veer, *Imperial Encounters.* For further discussions about the longer precolonial history of the term Aryan, see Donald S. Lopez Jr., *Buddhism and Science* (Chicago: University of Chicago Press, 2008), 83. For early twentieth-century examples of the use of Aryanism, see Swami Abhedananda, *How to Be a Yogi* (New York, 1903); Annie Besant, *Annie Besant: An Autobiography* (London, 1908), 352.

87. Dinesh Chandra Misra, interviewed by Christopher Somerville, Oral History 18370, IWM, 1995, Reels 2–3.

88. Yeats-Brown, *Martial India*, 35.

89. Francis Yeats-Brown, *Yoga Explained* (New York, 1937), 38.

90. Francis Yeats-Brown, "Yoga's Path to Heaven," *Nash's Pall Mall Magazine* 88, No. 462 (November 1931): 44–47, 110, at 47.

91. Yeats-Brown, *Lancer at Large*, 64–65.

92. The country, in his view, needed to be "regenerated" so that "the Jews will not rule the world." Yeats-Brown, *Lancer at Large*, 179; Yeats-Brown to Henry Williamson, November 24, 1942, quoted in Evelyn Wrench, *Francis Yeats-Brown* (London: Eyre & Spottiswoode, 1948), 258.

93. Yeats-Brown, *Martial India*, 35, 39.

94. Francis Yeats-Brown, Diary (March 20, 1909), Private Papers 13088, HRC.

95. Yeats-Brown, *Martial India*, 49.

96. Yeats-Brown, *Martial India*, 49.

97. Somerfield read MacMunn's works on India's "Frontier" and "Underworld." Kate Imy, "Queering the Martial Races: Masculinity, Sex and Circumcision in the Twentieth Century British Indian Army," *Gender and History* 27, No. 2 (August 2015): 374–96.

98. H. H. Somerfield, unpublished diary (November 30, 1939), HHS, IWM.

99. For more about the racial performance and appropriation of this act, see Imy, "Queering the Martial Races"; H. H. Somerfield, unpublished diary, October 19, 1938, January 1, 1938, November 26, 1937, December 30, 1937.

100. H. H. Somerfield, unpublished diary, October 30, 1938.

101. H. H. Somerfield, unpublished diary, December 16, 1938, March 31, 1938.

102. He reported attending with Skellon, Ujagir Singh, and Kahmira Singh, where he had "a bottle of brandy and 2 bottles of beer" with "the 2 Sikhs." H. H. Somerfield, unpublished diary, October 19, 1938, October 13, 1938.

103. H. H. Somerfield, unpublished diary, January 3, 1937.

104. H. H. Somerfield, unpublished diary, December 3, 1939, November 27, 1937.

105. H. H. Somerfield, unpublished diary, November 30, 1939.

106. H. H. Somerfield, unpublished diary, November 30, 1939

107. H. H. Somerfield, unpublished diary, November 30, 1939, January 1, 1935.

108. He described staying in a hotel and visiting the cinema with two British soldiers in Secunderabad. H. H. Somerfield, unpublished diary, December 11, 1939. See also entries for April 4 and 5, 1940.

109. H. H. Somerfield, unpublished diary, February 3, 1939.

110. H. H. Somerfield, unpublished diary, January 1, 1938.

111. H. H. Somerfield, unpublished diary, December 20 and 21, 1937. He initially expressed that he "was disturbed to receive none of the OR's [other ranks] as visitors. Sat and nattered with Kishan Singh and Skellon. Decided to try and get new quarters."

112. His emphasis. H. H. Somerfield, unpublished diary, June 14, 1938.

113. H. H. Somerfield, unpublished diary, November 11, 1938.

114. H. H. Somerfield, unpublished diary, October 14, 1939.

115. H. H. Somerfield, unpublished diary, November 25, 1938.

116. For "mera piyare dost," see H. H. Somerfield, unpublished diary, January 3, 1940. For the reference to Sultan Mohammad's letter, see H. H. Somerfield, unpublished diary, May 12, 1938.

117. H. H. Somerfield, unpublished diary, March 28, 1937.

118. Ugra hinted at the homoerotic behavior of Krishna with other warrior heroes such as Arjun and Surdas. Ruth Vanita, "The New Homophobia: Ugra's Chocolate," in *Same-Sex Love in India: Readings from Literature and History*, ed. Ruth Vanita and Saleem Kidwai (New York: Palgrave, 2000); Charu Gupta, "(Im)possible Love and Sexual Pleasure in Late-Colonial North India," *Modern Asian Studies* 36, No. 1 (2002): 198; Joseph Alter, "Yoga at the Fin de Siècle: Muscular Christianity with a 'Hindu' Twist," *International Journal of the History of Sport* 23, No. 5 (2006): 759.

119. H. H. Somerfield, unpublished diary, November 30, 1939.

120. H. H. Somerfield, unpublished diary, March 21, 1940.

121. H. H. Somerfield, unpublished diary, July 10, 1938.

122. H. H. Somerfield, unpublished diary, July 11, 1938.

123. H. H. Somerfield, unpublished diary, July 12, 1938.

124. "Recruitment Poster for the Boys Company of the Indian Signal Corps with Covering Note," Mss Eur F172/79: February 9, 1937.

125. Patrick Miles Pennington Hobson, interviewed by Conrad Wood, IWM Interview 966 (1977), Reel 4.

126. Stanley Menezes, interviewed by Peter M. Hart, IWM Interview 25448 (2003), Reel 2.

127. "Extracts from the Municipal Report on the Happenings in Delhi on May 6, 1930" (published by Shiromani Gurdwara Prabandhak Committee, Chauburji, Lahore), IOR/L/PJ/6/2005, file 2097: May 1930–March 1931.

128. Report ending May 15, 1930, IOR/L/PJ/12/705.

129. Report on the political situation in the Punjab for the fortnight ending November 15, 1930, IOR/L/PJ/12/705.

130. Report ending September 30, 1930, IOR/L/PJ/12/705.

131. "Shahidgang Mosque Dispute Between Sikhs and Moslems in the Punjab" (July 9, 1935–May 29, 1940), IOR/L/PJ/7/886; Sunil Chander, "Congress-Raj Conflict and the Rise of the Muslim League in the Ministry Period, 1937–39," *Modern Asian Studies* 21, No. 2 (1987), 303–28, at 307.

132. Chander "Congress-Raj Conflict and the Rise of the Muslim League," 308; William Barton, *India's North-West Frontier 1939* (London: John Murray, 1939), 177.

133. Cutting from the Delhi Police, First Incident Reports (December 21, 1935), file no. Sikh-7, Nehru Memorial Library (New Delhi), henceforth NML.

134. It was Dr. Mool Singh. Delhi Police, First Incident Reports (December 21, 1935), NML.

135. Delhi Police, First Incident Reports (December 21, 1935).

136. "Report on the Firing into the Gurdwara Sis-Ganj, Delhi" (May 1930–March 1931), IOR/L/PJ/6/2005, file 2097; Purnima Dhavan, *When Sparrows Became Hawks: The Making of the Sikh Warrior Tradition* (Oxford: Oxford University Press, 2011).

137. Ganda Singh, *History of the Gurdwara Shahidganj, Lahore, from Its Origin to November 1935 Compiled from Original Sources, Judicial Records and Contemporary Materials* (Lahore, 1935), 70, https://archive.org/details/HistoryOfTheGurdwaraShahidganjLahoreFromItsOriginToNovember1935.

138. Chander, "Congress-Raj Conflict and the Rise of the Muslim League," 307.

139. Dr. Mool Singh, Cutting from the Delhi Police Abstract of Intelligence, First Incident Reports (January 4, 1936), NML.

140. Excerpt from the Punjab Legislative Council (October 23, 1926), 1785, IOR/L/PJ/6/1776, file 7087.

141. Markus Daechsel, "Scientism and Its Discontents: The Indo-Muslim 'Fascism' of Inayatullah Khan al-Mashriqi," *Modern Intellectual History* 3, No. 3 (2006): 443–72, at 450, 468.

142. Chander, "Congress-Raj Conflict and the Rise of the Muslim League," 306–7.

143. Satya M. Rai, *Legislative Politics and Freedom Struggle on [sic] the Panjab 1897–1947* (New Delhi: People's Publishing House, 1984).

144. Prominent Muslims who held both desirable positions and intimate attachments to British men faced the contempt of those espousing a heteronormative ideal of nationalist masculinity. Zivin, "'Bent," 204.

145. Somerfield had described Khaksar activists as "a Moslem political group run on fascist lines" while he was embracing fascism and contemplating conversion to Islam. He made note of when twenty-six were killed in a fight with police. H. H. Somerfield, unpublished diary, October 7, 1939, October 10, 1939, and March 21, 1940, HHS, IWM.

146. Faisal Devji, *Muslim Zion: Pakistan as Political Idea* (Cambridge, MA: Harvard University Press, 2013).

147. Marsh, *Ramparts of Empire*, 126, 134, 138; Foreign Secretary to the Government of India, 1931, Letter to Chief Commission and Agent to Governor General, North-West Frontier Province (March 16, 1931), British Library, IOR/L/PS/12/3163; Barton, *India's North-West Frontier 1939*, 186; Elizabeth Kolsky, "The Colonial Rule of Law and the Legal Regime of Exception: Frontier 'Fanaticism' and State Violence in British India," *American Historical Review* 120, No. 4 (October 2015): 1218–46.

148. Khan, interviewed by Conrad Wood, Reel 1.

149. Khan, interviewed by Conrad Wood, Reel 1.

150. Khan, interviewed by Conrad Wood, Reel 14.

151. Letter to Mr. Walton from India Office Seal (June 22, 1940), IOR/L/PS/12/3163; Letter from L. S. A. to Sir Firoz Khan Noon, High Commissioner of India to UK from 1936 to 1941 (June 28, 1940), IOR/L/PS/12/3163; Letter from Honorable Sir Steuart Pears [*sic*], KCIE, CSI, Chief Commissioner, North-West Frontier Province, to the Foreign Secretary to the Govt. of India, Foreign and Political Department (September 3, 1931), IOR/L/PS/12/3163.

152. India house, Aldwych, from Firoz Noon to Rt. Hon. L. S. Amery, PC, MP, India Office London (June 21, 1940), IOR/L/PS/12/3163.

153. Marsh, *Ramparts of Empire*, 126; Kolsky, "The Colonial Rule of Law."

154. Khan, interviewed by Conrad Wood.

155. Kuldip Singh Bajwa, interviewed by Mark Tully, Oral History 28855, BBC (January 14, 2005), held by IWM.

156. Edwin John Watson, interviewed by Conrad Wood, Oral History 903, IWM (March 22, 1977), Reel 1.

157. Toco Moses Stevens, IWM, Reel 6.

158. Barton, *India's North-West Frontier 1939*, 186.

CONCLUSION

1. Thanks to Sara Black for bringing this story to my attention.

2. See, for example, Amit Chaudhuri, "The Real Meaning of Rhodes Must Fall," *The Guardian* (March 16, 2016), https://www.theguardian.com/uk-news/2016/mar/16/the -real-meaning-of-rhodes-must-fall, accessed December 30, 2018; Kristina Killgrove, "Scholars Explain the Racist History of UNC's Silent Sam Statue," *Forbes* (August 22, 2018), https://www.forbes.com/sites/kristinakillgrove/2018/08/22/scholars-explain-the -racist-history-of-uncs-silent-sam-statue/#2e5a77a6114f, accessed December 30, 2018.

3. "Sikh Soldier Memorial Statue in Smethwick Vandalized," *BBC* (November 10, 2018), https://www.bbc.com/news/uk-england-birmingham-46160028, accessed November 11, 2018; "Statue of Sikh Soldier Vandalised in Smethwick," *The Guardian* (November 11, 2018), https://www.theguardian.com/uk-news/2018/nov/10/statue-sikh-soldier -vandalised-smethwick-birmingham-war-memorial, accessed November 11, 2018.

4. I am grateful to Santanu Das for reflecting on some of these themes at the 2018 "Empire, Armistice, Aftermath" conference in Singapore.

5. Francis Yeats-Brown, Diary, November 2, 1908, HRC.

6. H. H. Somerfield, diaries, Imperial War Museum, May 12, 1938.

7. Leela Gandhi, Keynote Lecture at the Modern British Studies conference, Birmingham, UK, 2017.

8. Chandar Sundaram, "Grudging Concessions: The Officer Corps and Its Indianization, 1817–1940," in *A Military History of India and South Asia*, ed. Daniel P. Marston and Chandar S. Sundaram (Westport, CT: Praeger Security International, 2007), 88–100, at 100.

9. For a more comprehensive discussion of the 1940s, see Yasmin Khan, *India at War: The Subcontinent and the Second World War* (Oxford: Oxford University Press, 2015); Daniel Marston, *The Indian Army at the End of the Raj* (Cambridge: Cambridge University Press, 2014); Yasmin Khan, *The Great Partition: The Making of India and Pakistan* (New Haven, CT: Yale University Press, 2008); Gajendra Singh, *The Testimonies of Indian Soldiers and the Two World Wars: Between Self and Sepoy* (London: Bloomsbury Press, 2014).

10. For an example of a politician emphasizing unity in the 1940s, see Mr. Govind V. Deshmukh, Extract from Legislative Assembly (March 10, 1941), IOR/L/MIL/7/19156: 1935–41. Gandhi maintained the importance of Hindu-Muslim unity throughout the interwar period. See also Barbara D. Metcalf and Thomas R. Metcalf, *A Concise History of Modern India* (Cambridge: Cambridge University Press, 2012).

11. Tarak Barkawi characterizes Indian soldiers as cosmopolitan in his excellent study *Soldiers of Empire: Indian and British Armies in World War II* (Cambridge: Cambridge University Press, 2017).

12. For an examination of colonial soldiers and narratives of disability, see Hilary Buxton, "Imperial Amnesia: Race, Trauma and Indian Troops in the First World War," *Past and Present* 241, No. 1 (November 2018): 221–58.

SELECT BIBLIOGRAPHY

ARCHIVES
British Library
Gurkha Memorial Museum (Pokhara, Nepal)
Gurkha Museum (Winchester, UK)
Harry Ransom Center (Austin, Texas)
Imperial War Museum (London, UK)
Maharashtra State Archives
National Archives (Kew, UK)
National Archives of India
National Army Museum (Chelsea, UK)
Nehru Memorial Library
Panjab State Archives
Rutgers University Special Collections and Archives
Tamil Nadu State Archives
United Service Institution Library (New Delhi, India)
West Bengal State Archives

PRINTED PRIMARY SOURCES AND MEMOIRS
'Abd al-Hakim. *Fauj aur-Police ki Mulazamat Musalmanan I Hind ke Liye Mazhaban ja'iz aur-zaruri hai* [On the necessity of Indian Musalmans joining the army and the police]. Lahore, 1923.
Ali, Mrs. Meer Hasan. *Observations on the Mussulmans of India.* Repr., London: Oxford University Press, 1917.
Anand, Mulk Raj. *Across the Black Waters.* New Delhi: Orient Paperbacks, 2008.
Anand, Roshan Lal, under the supervision of F. L. Brayne. "Soldiers' Savings and How They Use Them." Punjab: Board of Economic Inquiry, 1940.
Barstow, A. E. *Handbooks for the Indian Army, Sikhs.* Calcutta: Government of India Central Publications Branch, 1928.
Barton, William. *India's North-West Frontier 1939.* London: John Murray, 1939.
Bingley, A. H., and A. Nicholls. *Brahmans.* Simla: Government Central Printing Office, 1897.
Bourne, W. Fitz G. *Hindustani Musalmans and Musalmans of the Eastern Punjab.* Calcutta: Superintendent, Government Printing, 1914.
Butler, Reverend Alban. *The Moveable Feasts and Fasts and Annual Observances of the Catholic Church.* Dublin: James Duffy, 1839.

Camm, Dom Bede. *Pilgrim Paths in Latin Lands.* London: MacDonald & Evans, 1923.

Candler, Edmund. *The Sepoy.* London, 1919.

Chaudhuri, Nirad C. "The Martial Races of India." Part II. *Modern Review* 48, No. 285 (1930): 296.

Committee of Enquiry upon Religion. *The Army and Religion: An Enquiry and Its Bearing upon the Religious Life of the Nation.* London: Macmillan & Company, 1919.

Cunningham, Lt.-Col. W. B. *Handbooks for the Indian Army, Dogras.* Calcutta: Government of India Central Publication Branch, 1932.

Darling, M. L. *Wisdom and Waste in the Punjab Village.* Oxford: Oxford University Press, 1934.

Davies, G. M. *A Chaplain in India.* London and Edinburgh: Marshall, Morgan & Scott, Ltd., ca. 1933.

Douie, James A. *Provincial Geographies of India: The Panjab, North-West Frontier Province, and Kashmir.* Cambridge: Cambridge University Press, 1916.

Falcon, Captain R. W. *Handbook on Sikhs for the Use of Regimental Officers.* Allahabad: Falcon Press, 1896.

Fuller, J. F. C. *India in Revolt.* London: Eyre & Spottiswoode, 1931.

Gandhi, Mohandas. *An Autobiography: The Story of My Experiments with Truth.* Boston: Beacon Press, 1994.

Gibbs, Major H. R. K. *The Gurkha Soldier.* Calcutta: Thacker, Spink & Co., 1944.

Gordon, General Sir John J. H. *The Sikhs.* Edinburgh and London: William Blackwood and Sons, 1904.

Haidari, M. A. Khan. *Selections from Fauji Akhbar for Preliminary and Interpreters Examinations in Hindustani.* Delhi: Oriental Book Depot, 1923.

Indian Military Hospital, Royal Pavilion, Brighton. *A Short History in English, Gurmukhi and Urdu of the Royal Pavilion, Brighton, and a Description of It as a Hospital for Indian Soldiers.* 1915.

Isemonger, F. C., and J. Slattery. *An Account of the Ghadr Conspiracy, 1913–1915.* Lahore: Superintendent, Government Printing, Punjab, 1919.

James, F. *Faraway Campaign.* London: Grayson and Grayson, 1934.

Khan, Khan Bahadur Risaldar Shahzad Mir. *A Right Royal World Tour.* Translated by C. A. Boyle. Simla: Army Press, 1934.

Lawrence, T. E. *Seven Pillars of Wisdom.* Ware, Hertfordshire, 1997.

Macauliffe, M. "How the Sikhs Became a Militant Race." *Journal of the United Service Institution of India* 32, No. 153 (October 1903): 330–58.

———. "The Sikh Religion and Its Advantages to the State." *Journal of the United Service Institution of India* 32, No. 153 (October 1903): 300–329.

MacMunn, George. *The Martial Races of India.* London: Low, Marston & Co., 1933.

———. *The Underworld of India.* London: Hutchinson, 1933.

Mayo, Katherine. *Mother India.* New York: Harcourt, Brace and Company, 1927.

Menezes, S. L. *Fidelity & Honour: The Indian Army from the Seventeenth to the Twenty-First Century.* New Delhi: Viking, Penguin Books India, 1993.

Nicholas, S. H. E. "Indian Army Castes: Ahirs." *Journal of the United Service Institution of India* 40, No. 183 (April 1911).

Nicolay, B. U. *Handbooks for the Indian Army: Gurkhas. Compiled Under the Orders of the Government of India by Lt-Col Eden Vansittart.* Calcutta: Government of India Press, 1915.

Norgate, Lieutenant-Colonel, trans. *From Sepoy to Subadar: Being the Life and Adventures of a Native Officer of the Bengal Army Written and Related by Himself.* Calcutta: Girish Irish Printing Works, 1922.

Petrie, D. *Developments in Sikh Politics.* Edited by S. Nahar Singh. Originally published in Simla, 1911. Republished by Chief Khalsa Diwan. https://archive.org/details/Deve lopmentsInSikhPolitics19101911DPetrie/page/n1.

Rai, Lala Lajpat. *The Arya Samaj: An Account of Its Origin, Doctrines, and Activities: With a Biographical Sketch of the Founder.* London: Longmans, Green and Co., 1915.

Raper, W. F. *Hints for Soldiers Proceeding to India: A Common-Sense Health Lecture.* London: Gale & Polden, Ltd., 1911.

Razzak, Abdur. *The Native Officer's Diary.* Madras: Higgenbotham and Co., 1894.

Ridgway, R. T. I., 40th Pathans, Late Recruiting Staff Officer for Pathans. *Handbooks for the Indian Army, Pathans.* Calcutta: Superintendent, Government Printing, India, 1910.

Shakespear, L. W. *History of the 2nd King Edward's Own Goorkhas (The Sirmoor Rifle Regiment).* Vol. 2, *1911–1921.* Aldershot: Gale & Polden Ltd., n.d.

Sharif, Ja'far. *Islam in India; or The Qanun-i-Islam.* Translated by G. A. Herklots. London: Oxford University Press, 1921.

Singh, Ganda. *History of the Gurdwara Shahidganj, Lahore, from Its Origin to November 1935 Compiled from Original Sources, Judicial Records and Contemporary Materials.* Lahore, 1935. https://archive.org/details/HistoryOfTheGurdwaraShahidganjLahor eFromItsOriginToNovember1935.

Singh, General Mohan. *Soldiers' Contributions to Indian Independence: The Epic of the Indian National Army.* New Delhi: S. Attar Singh, Army Educational Stores, 1974.

Singh, Sukhwant. *Three Decades of Indian Army Life.* Sterling Publishers Ltd., 1967.

Singh, Teja. *The Growth of Responsibility in Sikhism.* Amritsar: Shiromani Gurdwara Parbandhak Committee, n.d.

———. *The Gurdwara Reform Movement and the Sikh Awakening.* Jullundur City, Punjab: Desh Sewak Book Agency, 1922.

Smyth, Captain C. Watson, 1st Brahmans. "Indian Army Castes: Brahmans." *Journal of the United Service Institution of India* 40, No. 183 (April 1911): 205–11.

Starr, Lilian A. *Frontier Folk of the Afghan Border and Beyond.* London, 1920.

Stuart, Lieut. Col. Alexander George. *The Indian Empire: A Short Review and Some Hints for the Use of Soldiers Proceeding to India.* Calcutta: Government of India Central Publication Branch, 1932.

Thorat, S. P. P. *From Reveille to Retreat.* New Delhi: Allied Publishers Private Limited, 1985.

Walter, H. A. *The Religious Life of India: The Ahmadiya Movement.* Calcutta: Association Press; London: Oxford University Press, 1918.

Wardle, Captain F. M. *The Sepoy Officer's Manual: A Book of Reference for Infantry Officers of the Indian Army.* Calcutta and Simla: Thacker, Spink & Co., 1922.

Waters, R. S. *History of the 5th Battalion (Pathans) 14th Punjab Regiment, Formerly 40th Pathans.* London: James Bain Limited, 1936.

Wheeler, W. H. Barlow. *Standing Orders, 4th Bn. 11th Sikh Regiment.* Landikotal, March 1939.

Wikeley, J. M. *Hand Books for the Indian Army: Punjabi Musalmans.* 1927; repr., New Delhi: Government of India Press, 1936.

Willcocks, James. *From Kabul to Kumassi: Twenty-Four Years of Soldiering and Sport.* John Murray, 1904.

———. *With the Indians in France.* London: Constable and Company, 1920.

Woodyatt, Nigel. *Under Ten Viceroys: The Reminiscences of a Gurkha.* London: Herbert Jenkins, Ltd., 1922.

Yeats-Brown, Francis. *European Jungle.* Philadelphia: Macrae-Smith Company, 1940.

———. *Lancer at Large.* New York: Garden City Publishers, 1937.

———. *The Lives of a Bengal Lancer.* London: Victor Gollancz, 1930.

———. *Martial India.* London: Eyre & Spottiswoode, 1945.

———. *The Star and Crescent: Being the Story of the 17th Cavalry from 1858 to 1922.* Allahabad: Pioneer Press, 1927.

SECONDARY SOURCES

Aksakal, Mustafa. "'Holy War Made in Germany'? Ottoman Origins of the 1914 Jihad." *War in History* 18, No. 2 (2011): 184–99.

Alavi, Seema. *Muslim Cosmopolitanism in the Age of Empire.* Cambridge, MA: Harvard University Press, 2015.

———. *The Sepoys and the Company: Tradition and Transition in Northern India, 1770–1830.* Delhi: Oxford University Press, 1998.

Alter, Joseph. *Gandhi's Body: Sex, Diet, and the Politics of Nationalism.* Philadelphia: University of Pennsylvania Press, 2000.

———. "Indian Clubs and Colonialism: Hindu Masculinity and Muscular Christianity." *Comparative Studies in Society and History* 46, No. 3 (2004): 497–534.

———. "Yoga at the Fin de Siècle: Muscular Christianity with a 'Hindu' Twist." *International Journal of the History of Sport* 23, No. 5 (2006): 759–76.

Amrith, Sunil M. "Food and Welfare in India, c. 1900–1950." *Comparative Studies in Society and History* 50, No. 4 (2008): 1010–35.

Aravamudan, Srinivas. *Guru English: South Asian Religion in a Cosmopolitan Language.* Princeton, NJ: Princeton University Press, 2006.

Arnold, David. "Touching the Body: Perspectives on the Indian Plague, 1896–1900." *Selected Subaltern Studies* (1988): 391–426.

Arondekar, Anjali. *For the Record: On Sexuality and the Colonial Archive in India.* Durham, NC: Duke University Press, 2009.

Asad, Talal. *Genealogies of Religion: Discipline and Reasons of Power in Christianity and Islam.* Baltimore: Johns Hopkins University Press, 1993.

Banerjee, Sikata. "Armed Masculinity, Hindu Nationalism and Female Political Participation in India: Heroic Mothers, Chaste Wives and Celibate Warriors." *International Feminist Journal of Politics* 8, No. 1 (2006): 62–83.

———. *Muscular Nationalism: Gender, Violence, and Empire in India and Ireland, 1914–2004*. New York: NYU Press, 2012.

Barkawi, Tarak. *Soldiers of Empire: Indian and British Armies in World War II*. Cambridge: Cambridge University Press, 2017.

Barua, Pradeep. *Gentlemen of the Raj: The Indian Army Officer Corps, 1817–1949*. Westport, CT: Praeger, 2003.

Basu, Shrabani. *For King and Another Country: Indian Soldiers on the Western Front, 1914–18*. New Delhi: Bloomsbury India, 2015.

Bayly, Martin J. *Taming the Imperial Imagination: Colonial Knowledge, International Relations, and the Anglo-Afghan Encounter, 1808–1878*. Cambridge: Cambridge University Press, 2016.

Beckett, Ian. "The Singapore Mutiny of February 1915." *Journal of the Society for Army Historical Research* 62 (1984): 132–53.

Bose, Sugata. *His Majesty's Opponent: Subhas Chandra Bose and India's Struggle Against Empire*. Cambridge, MA: Belknap Press, 2011.

Burton, Antoinette. *The First Anglo-Afghan Wars: A Reader*. Durham, NC: Duke University Press, 2014.

Buxton, Hilary. "Imperial Amnesia: Race, Trauma and Indian Troops in the First World War." *Past and Present* 241, No. 1 (November 2018): 221–58.

Caplan, Lionel. *Warrior Gentlemen: "Gurkhas" in the Western Imagination*. Kathmandu: Berghahn Books, 2009.

Carter, Marina, and Crispin Bates. *Mutiny at the Margins: New Perspectives on the Indian Uprising of 1857*. New Delhi: Sage Publications, 2013.

Caton, Brian P. "Social Categories and Colonisation in Panjab, 1849–1920." *Indian Economic and Social History Review* 41, No. 1 (2004).

Chander, Sunil. "Congress-Raj Conflict and the Rise of the Muslim League in the Ministry Period, 1937–39." *Modern Asian Studies* 21, No. 2 (1987): 303–28.

Chatterjee, Indrani. "Colouring Subalternity: Slaves, Concubines and Social Orphans Under the East India Company." *Subaltern Studies* 10 (1999): 49–97.

———. "Monastic Governmentality, Colonial Misogyny, and Postcolonial Amnesia in South Asia." *History of the Present: A Journal of Critical History* 3 (Spring 2013): 55–98.

———. "When 'Sexuality' Floated Free of Histories in South Asia." *Journal of Asian Studies* 71, No. 4 (November 2012): 945–62.

Chaturvedi, Vinayak. "Rethinking Knowledge with Action: V. D. Savarkar, the Bhagavad Gita, and Histories of Warfare." *Modern Intellectual History* 7, No. 2 (2010).

Chidester, David. *Empire of Religion: Imperialism and Comparative Religion*. Chicago: University of Chicago Press, 2013.

Collingham, E. M. *Imperial Bodies: The Physical Experience of the Raj c. 1800–1947*. Cambridge: Polity Press, 2001.

Condos, Mark. *The Insecurity State: Punjab and the Making of Colonial Power in British India*. Cambridge: Cambridge University Press, 2017.

Cox, Jeffrey. *Imperial Fault Lines: Christianity and Colonial Power in India, 1818–1940*. Stanford: Stanford University Press, 2002.

Daechsel, Markus. "Scientism and Its Discontents: The Indo-Muslim 'Fascism' of Inayatullah Khan al-Mashriqi." *Modern Intellectual History* 3, No. 3 (2006): 443–72.

Das, Santanu. *India, Empire, and First World War Culture: Writings, Images, Songs*. Cambridge: Cambridge University Press, 2018.

———, ed. *Race, Empire and First World War Writing*. Cambridge: Cambridge University Press, 2011.

———. *Touch and Intimacy in First World War Literature*. Cambridge: Cambridge University Press, 2005.

Davis, Mike. *Late Victorian Holocausts: El Niño Famines and the Making of the Third World*. London and New York: Verso, 2001.

Des Chene, Mary Katherine. "Relics of Empire: A Cultural History of the Gurkhas, 1815–1987." PhD Diss., Stanford University, 1991.

Desai, Ashwin, and Goolam Vahed. *The South African Gandhi: Stretcher-Bearer of Empire*. Stanford: Stanford University Press, 2015.

Devji, Faisal. *Muslim Zion: Pakistan as a Political Idea*. Cambridge, MA: Harvard University Press, 2013.

Dhavan, Purnima. *When Sparrows Became Hawks: The Making of the Sikh Warrior Tradition*. Oxford: Oxford University Press, 2011.

Duffett, Rachel. *The Stomach for Fighting: Food and the Soldiers of the Great War*. Manchester: Manchester University Press, 2012.

Ellinwood, DeWitt C., Jr., *Between Two Worlds: A Rajput Officer in the Indian Army, 1905–21*. Lanham, MD: Hamilton Books, 2005.

Ellinwood, DeWitt C., Jr., and S. D. Pradhan, eds. *India and World War I*. Delhi: Manohar, 1978.

Farwell, Byron. *Armies of the Raj: From the Mutiny to Independence, 1858–1947*. New York: W. W. Norton & Company, 1989.

Fawaz, Leila Tarazi. *A Land of Aching Hearts: The Middle East in the Great War*. Cambridge, MA: Harvard University Press, 2014.

Fenech, Louis E. "Contested Nationalism; Negotiated Terrains: The Way Sikhs Remember Udham Singh 'Shahid' (1899–1940)." *Modern Asian Studies* 36, No. 4 (2002): 827–70.

Fischer, Fritz. *Germany's Aims in the First World War*. London: Chatto & Windus, 1967.

Fischer-Tiné, Harald. "'Unparalleled Opportunities': The Indian Y.M.C.A.'s Army Work Schemes for Imperial Troops During the Great War (1914–1920)." *Journal of Imperial and Commonwealth History* (2018): 1–38. https://doi.org/10.1080/03086534.2018.1511245.

Fisher, Michael. *Counterflows to Colonialism: Indian Travellers and Settlers in Britain, 1600–1857*. Delhi: Permanent Black, 2004.

Fogarty, Richard. *Race and War in France: Colonial Subjects in the French Army, 1914–1918.* Baltimore: Johns Hopkins University Press, 2008.

Forth, Aidan. *Barbed-Wire Imperialism: Britain's Empire of Camps, 1876–1903.* Berkeley: University of California Press, 2017.

Fox, Richard G. *Lions of Punjab: Culture in the Making.* Berkeley: University of California Press, 1985.

Gandhi, Leela. *Affective Communities: Anticolonial Thought, Fin-de-Siècle Radicalism, and the Politics of Friendship.* Durham, NC: Duke University Press, 2005.

———. *The Common Cause: Postcolonial Ethics and the Practice of Democracy, 1900–1955.* Chicago: University of Chicago Press, 2014.

Gardner, Nikolas. *The Siege of Kut-al-Amara: At War in Mesopotamia, 1915–1916.* Bloomington and Indianapolis: Indiana University Press, 2014.

Glatzer, Bernt. "Being Pashtun—Being Muslim: Concepts of Person and War in Afghanistan." In *Essays on South Asian Society: Culture and Politics II,* edited by B. Glatzer, 83–94. Berlin: Verlag Das Arabische Buch, 1998.

Green, Nile. *Islam and the Army in Colonial India: Sepoy Religion in the Service of Empire.* Cambridge: Cambridge University Press, 2009.

Grewal, J. S. *History, Literature, and Identity: Four Centuries of Sikh Tradition.* New Delhi: Oxford University Press, 2012.

Guha, Sumit. *Beyond Caste: Identity and Power in South Asia, Past and Present.* Leiden and Boston: Brill, 2013.

Gupta, Charu. "Anxious Hindu Masculinity in Colonial North India: Shuddhi and Sangathan Movements." *Cross Currents* 61, No. 4 (December 2011): 441–54.

———. "(Im)possible Love and Sexual Pleasure in Late-Colonial North India." *Modern Asian Studies* 36, No. 1 (2002): 195–221.

———. *Sexuality, Obscenity and Community: Women, Muslims, and the Hindu Public in Colonial India.* New York: Palgrave, 2002.

Heathcote, T. A. *The Military in British India: The Development of British Land Forces in South Asia, 1600–1947.* Manchester: Manchester University Press, 1995.

Hendrickson, Kenneth. "Winning the Troops for Vital Religion: Female Evangelical Missionaries to the British Army, 1857–1880." *Armed Forces and Society* 23, No. 4 (Summer 1997): 615–34.

Houlbrook, Matt. *Queer London: Perils and Pleasures in the Sexual Metropolis, 1918–1957.* Chicago: University of Chicago Press, 2005.

Hughes, Thomas L. "The German Mission to Afghanistan, 1915–1916." *German Studies Review* 25, No. 3 (October 2002): 447–76.

Imy, Kate. "Fascist Yogis: Martial Bodies and Imperial Impotence." *Journal of British Studies* 55, No. 2 (April 2016): 320–43.

———. "Kidnapping and a 'Confirmed Sodomite': An Intimate Enemy on the Northwest Frontier of India, 1915–1925." *Twentieth Century British History* 28, No. 1 (March 2017): 29–56.

———. "Queering the Martial Races: Masculinity, Sex and Circumcision in the Twentieth-Century British Indian Army." *Gender and History* 27, No. 2 (August 2015): 374–96.

Jalal, Ayesha. *Partisans of Allah: Jihad in South Asia.* Cambridge, MA: Harvard University Press, 2008.

James, Lawrence. *The Golden Warrior: The Life and Legend of Lawrence of Arabia.* New York: Skyhorse Publishing, 2008.

Kapila, Shruti, and Faisal Devji, eds. "Forum: The Bhagavad Gita and Modern Thought." *Modern Intellectual History* 7, No. 2 (2010).

Kent, Susan. *Aftershocks: The Politics of Trauma in Britain, 1918–1931.* New York: Palgrave Macmillan, 2009.

Khan, Yasmin. *The Great Partition: The Making of India and Pakistan.* New Haven, CT: Yale University Press, 2008.

———. *India at War: The Subcontinent and the Second World War.* Oxford: Oxford University Press, 2015.

King, Richard. *Orientalism and Religion: Postcolonial Theory, India and "the Mystic East."* London and New York: Routledge, 1999.

Kolff, Dirk A. *Naukar, Rajput and Sepoy: The Ethnohistory of the Military Labour Market in Hindustan, 1450–1850.* Cambridge: Cambridge University Press, 1990.

Kolsky, Elizabeth. *Colonial Justice in British India: White Violence and the Rule of Law.* Cambridge: Cambridge University Press, 2011.

———. "The Colonial Rule of Law and the Legal Regime of Exception: Frontier 'Fanaticism' and State Violence in British India." *American Historical Review* 120, No. 4 (October 2015): 1218–46.

Labh, Kapileshwar. "China as a Factor in the Policy of British India Toward Nepal." *Journal of Indian History* 55, No. 3 (1977): 177–88.

Lawrence, Jon. "Forging a Peaceable Kingdom: War, Violence, and Fear of Brutalization in Post–First World War Britain." *Journal of Modern History* 75 (September 2003): 557–89.

Levine, Philippa. *Prostitution, Race and Politics: Policing Venereal Disease in the British Empire.* New York: Routledge, 2003.

Liburd, Liam J. "Beyond the Pale: Whiteness, Masculinity and Empire in the British Union of Fascists, 1932–1940." *Fascism: Journal of Comparative Fascist Studies* 7, No. 2 (October 2018).

Linehan, Thomas. *British Fascism 1918–39: Parties, Ideology and Culture.* Manchester: Manchester University Press, 2000.

Maclean, Kama. *A Revolutionary History of Interwar India: Violence, Image, Voice and Text.* Oxford: Oxford University Press, 2015.

Mandair, Arvind-Pal S. *Religion and the Specter of the West: Sikhism, India, Postcoloniality, and the Politics of Translation.* New York: Columbia University Press, 2009.

Mandair, Navdeep S. "Colonial Formations of Sikhism." In *Oxford Handbook of Sikh Studies,* edited by Pashaura Singh and Louis E. Fenech, 70–81. Oxford: Oxford University Press, 2014.

Mani, Lata. *Contentious Traditions: The Debate on Sati in Colonial India.* Berkeley: University of California Press, 1998.

Markovits, Claude. "Indian Soldiers' Experiences in France During World War I: Seeing Europe from the Rear of the Front." In *The World in World Wars: Experiences, Perceptions and Perspectives from Africa and Asia*, edited by Heike Liebau et al., 27–53. Leiden: Brill, 2010.

Marsh, Brandon D. "The North-West Frontier and the Crisis of Empire: Post-War India and the Debate over Waziristan, 1919–1923." *British Scholar* 1, No. 2 (March 2009): 197–221.

———. *Ramparts of Empire: British Imperialism and India's Afghan Frontier, 1918–1948.* New York: Palgrave Macmillan, 2015.

Marston, Daniel. *The Indian Army at the End of the Raj.* Cambridge: Cambridge University Press, 2014.

———. *Phoenix from the Ashes: The Indian Army in the Burma Campaign.* Westport, CT: Praeger, 2013.

Mason, Philip. *A Matter of Honour: An Account of the Indian Army, Its Officers and Men.* New York: Holt, Rinehart and Winston, 1974.

McLaine, Robert. "The Indian Corps on the Western Front: A Reconsideration." In *War in the Age of Technology: Myriad Faces of Modern Armed Conflict*, edited by Geoffrey Jensen and Andrew Wiest, 167–193. New York: NYU Press, 2001.

Metcalf, Barbara D., and Thomas R. Metcalf. *A Concise History of Modern India.* Cambridge: Cambridge University Press, 2012.

Mitcham, John. *Race and Imperial Defence in the British World, 1870–1914.* Cambridge: Cambridge University Press, 2016.

Mohan, Kamlesh. *Militant Nationalism in the Punjab, 1919–1935.* New Delhi: Manohar, 1985.

Morton-Jack, George. *The Indian Army on the Western Front: India's Expeditionary Force to France and Belgium in the First World War.* Cambridge: Cambridge University Press, 2014.

Moyd, Michelle. *Violent Intermediaries: African Soldiers, Conquest, and Everyday Colonialism in German East Africa.* Athens: Ohio University Press, 2014.

Nünning, Vera. "'Daß Jeder seine Pflicht thue': Die Bedeutung der Indian Mutiny für das nationale britische Selbstverständnis." *Archiv für Kulturgeschichte* 78 (1996).

Omissi, David. *Indian Voices of the Great War: Soldiers' Letters, 1914–18.* New York: Palgrave Macmillan, 1999.

———. *The Sepoy and the Raj: The Indian Army, 1860–1940.* London: Macmillan, 1994.

Onta, Pratyoush. "Creating a Brave Nepali Nation in British India: The Rhetoric of Jāti Improvement, Rediscovery of Bhanubhakta and the Writing of Bīr History." *Studies in Nepali History and Society* 1, No. 1 (1996): 37–96.

Peers, Douglas M. *Between Mars and Mammon: Colonial Armies and the Garrison State in India, 1819–1835.* London: I. B. Tauris, 1995.

———. "Martial Races and South Asian Military Culture in the Victorian Indian Army." In *A Military History of Modern India*, edited by Daniel Marston and Chandar Sundaram, 34–52. Westport, CT: Praeger Security International, 2007.

Pemble, John. "Forgetting and Remembering Britain's Gurkha War." *Asian Affairs* 40, No. 3 (November 2009): 361–76.

———. *The Invasion of Nepal: John Company at War.* Oxford: Clarendon Press, 1971.

Pinch, William. *Warrior Ascetics and Indian Empires.* Cambridge: Cambridge University Press, 2006.

Pinney, Christopher. "The Body and the Bomb: Technologies of Modernity in Colonial India." In *Picturing the Nation: Iconographies of Modern India,* edited by Richard H. Davis, 51–65. Andhra Pradesh: Orient Longman, 2007.

———. *Camera Indica: The Social Life of Indian Photographs.* Chicago: University of Chicago Press, 1998.

Popplewell, Richard J. *Intelligence and Imperial Defence: British Intelligence and the Defence of the Indian Empire 1904–1924.* London: Frank Cass, 1995.

Powell, Avril. *Muslims and Missionaries in Pre-Mutiny India.* New York: Routledge, 1995.

Rai, Satya M. *Legislative Politics and Freedom Struggle on [sic] the Panjab 1897–1947.* New Delhi: People's Publishing House, 1984.

Ramnath, Maia. *Haj to Utopia: How the Ghadar Movement Charted Global Radicalism and Attempted to Overthrow the British Empire.* Berkeley and Los Angeles: University of California Press, 2011.

Rana, Junaid. *Terrifying Muslims: Race and Labor in the South Asian Diaspora.* Durham, NC: Duke University Press, 2011.

Rand, Gavin, and Kim Wagner. "Recruiting the 'Martial Races': Identities and Military Service in Colonial India." *Patterns of Prejudice* 46, Nos. 3–4 (2012).

Roopnarine, Loomarsh. "The Indian Sea Voyage Between India and the Caribbean During the Second Half of the Nineteenth Century." *Journal of Caribbean History* 44, No. 1 (2010): 48–74.

Roy, Kaushik. *Brown Warriors of the Raj: Recruitment & the Mechanics of Command in the Sepoy Army, 1859–1913.* New Delhi: Manohar, 2008.

———. "The Construction of Regiments in the Indian Army: 1859–1913," *War in History* 8, No. 127 (2001).

———. *Hinduism and the Ethics of Warfare in South Asia: From Antiquity to the Present.* Cambridge: Cambridge University Press, 2012.

———. "The Hybrid Military Establishment of the East India Company in South Asia: 1750–1849." *Journal of Global History* 6, No. 2 (2011): 195–218.

———. *The Indian Army in the Two World Wars.* Leiden: Brill, 2012.

———. "Spare the Rod, Spoil the Soldier? Crime and Punishment in the Army of India, 1860–1913." *Journal of the Society for Army Historical Research* 84, No. 337 (Spring 2006): 9–33.

Rudolph, Susanne Hoeber, Lloyd L. Rudolph, and Mohan Singh Kanota, eds. *Reversing the Gaze: Amar Singh's Diary, a Colonial Subject's Narrative of Imperial India.* Boulder, CO: Westview Press, 2002.

Ruiz, Mario M. "Manly Spectacles and Imperial Soldiers in Wartime Egypt, 1914–19." *Middle Eastern Studies* 45, No. 3 (2009): 351–71.

Rupakheti, Sanjog. "Reconsidering State-Society Relations in South Asia: A Himalayan Case Study." *Himalaya* 35, No. 2 (2015): 73–86.

Safadi, Alison. "*From Sepoy to Subadar/Khvab-o-Khyal* and Douglas Craven Phillott." *Annual of Urdu Studies* 25 (2010).

Said, Edward. *Culture and Imperialism*. New York: Vintage, 1993.

———. *Orientalism*. New York: Vintage, 1979.

Satia, Priya. *Spies in Arabia: The Great War and the Cultural Foundations of Britain's Covert Empire in the Middle East*. Oxford: Oxford University Press, 2008.

Sayer, Derek. "British Reaction to the Amritsar Massacre 1919–1920." *Past and Present* 131 (May 1991): 130–64.

Shaha, Rishikesh. *Modern Nepal: A Political History, 1769–1885*. Vols. 1 and 2. New Delhi: Manohar Books, 1996.

Sherman, Taylor. *State Violence and Punishment in India*. New York: Routledge, 2010.

Silverman, Kaja. "White Skin, Brown Masks: The Double Mimesis, or with Lawrence in Arabia." *Differences* 1, No. 3 (1989).

Silvestri, Michael. "The Thrill of 'Simply Dressing Up': The Indian Police, Disguise, and Intelligence Work in Colonial India." *Journal of Colonialism and Colonial History* 2 (2001).

Singh, Gajendra. *The Testimonies of Indian Soldiers and the Two World Wars: Between Self and Sepoy*. London: Bloomsbury Press, 2014.

Singh, Pashaura, and Louis E. Fenech, eds. *Oxford Handbook of Sikh Studies*. Oxford: Oxford University Press, 2014.

Singha, Radhika. "Finding Labor from India for the War in Iraq: The Jail Porter and Labor Corps, 1916–1920." *Comparative Studies in Society and History* 49, No. 2 (April 2007): 412–45.

Singleton, Mark. *Yoga Body: The Origins of Modern Posture Practice*. Oxford: Oxford University Press, 2010.

Sinha, Mrinalini. *Colonial Masculinity: The "Manly Englishman" and the "Effeminate Bengali" in the Late Nineteenth Century*. Manchester: Manchester University Press, 1995.

———. *Specters of Mother India: The Global Restructuring of an Empire*. Durham, NC: Duke University Press, 2006.

Slight, John. *The British Empire and the Hajj, 1865–1956*. Cambridge, MA: Harvard University Press, 2015.

Smith, Richard. *Jamaican Volunteers in the First World War: Race, Masculinity and the Development of National Consciousness*. Manchester: Manchester University Press, 2004.

Smith, Saumarez. *Rule by Records: Land Registration and Village Custom in Early British Panjab*. Delhi: Oxford University Press, 1996.

Soherwordi, Syed Hussain Shaheed. "'Punjabisation' in the British Indian Army 1857–1947 and the Advent of Military Rule in Pakistan." *Edinburgh Papers in South Asian Studies* 24 (2010).

Sohi, Seema. *Echoes of Mutiny: Race, Surveillance, and Indian Anticolonialism in North America*. Oxford: Oxford University Press, 2014.

Sondhi, Aditya. *The Order of the Crest: Tracing the Alumni of Bishop Cotton Boys' School, Bangalore (1865–2015).* Gurgaon: Penguin Books India, 2014.

Stocker, Paul. "'The Imperial Spirit': British Fascism and Empire, 1919–1940." *Religion Compass* 9, No. 2 (2015): 45–54.

Strachan, Hew. *The First World War.* London: Simon & Schuster, 2006.

Streets, Heather. *Martial Races: The Military, Race, and Masculinity in British Imperial Culture, 1857–1914.* Manchester: Manchester University Press, 2004.

Streets-Salter, Heather. *World War One in Southeast Asia: Colonialism and Anticolonialism in an Era of Global Conflict.* Cambridge: Cambridge University Press, 2017.

Sundaram, Chandar. "Grudging Concessions: The Officer Corps and Its Indianization, 1817–1940." In *A Military History of India and South Asia,* edited by Daniel P. Marston and Chandar S. Sundaram, 88–101. Westport, CT: Praeger Security International, 2007.

Tan Tai Yong. *The Garrison State: The Military, Government and Society in Colonial Punjab, 1849–1947.* New Delhi and London: Sage, 2005.

Thurlow, Richard C. *Fascism in Britain: From Oswald Mosley's Blackshirts to the National Front.* London: I. B. Tauris, 1998.

Townshend, Charles. *Desert Hell: The British Invasion of Mesopotamia.* Cambridge, MA: Belknap Press of Harvard University Press, 2011.

Trautmann, Thomas. *Aryans and British India.* Berkeley: University of California Press, 1997.

Trench, Charles Chenevix. *The Indian Army and the King's Enemies 1900–1947.* London: Thames and Hudson, 1988.

Ulrichsen, Kristian Coates. "The British Occupation of Mesopotamia, 1914–1922." *Journal of Strategic Studies* 30, No. 2 (April 2007): 349–77.

Uprety, Sanjeev. "Masculinity and Mimicry: Ranas and Gurkhas." Baha Occasional Papers 5 (2011): 1–48.

Van der Veer, Peter. *Imperial Encounters: Religion and Modernity in India and Britain.* Princeton, NJ: Princeton University Press, 2001.

Vanita, Ruth. "The New Homophobia: Ugra's Chocolate." In *Same-Sex Love in India: Readings from Literature and History,* edited by Ruth Vanita and Saleem Kidwai, 246–52. New York: Palgrave, 2000.

Vernon, James. *Hunger: A Modern History.* Cambridge, MA: Belknap Press of Harvard University Press, 2007.

Wagner, Kim A. "'Calculated to Strike Terror': The Amritsar Massacre and the Spectacle of Colonial Violence." *Past and Present* 233, No. 1 (2016): 185–225.

———. *The Great Fear of 1857: Rumours, Conspiracies and the Making of the Indian Uprising.* Oxford: Peter Lang, 2010.

Wald, Erica. *Vice in the Barracks: Medicine, the Military and the Making of Colonial India, 1780–1868.* New York: Palgrave, 2014.

White, David. *The Alchemical Body: Siddha Traditions in Medieval India.* Chicago: University of Chicago Press, 1998.

Winegard, Timothy C. *Indigenous Peoples of the British Dominions and the First World War.* Cambridge: Cambridge University Press, 2012.

Xu Guoqi. *Asia and the Great War: A Shared History.* Oxford: Oxford University Press, 2017.

Yang, Anand A. "China and India Are One: A Subaltern's Vision of 'Hindu China' During the Boxer Expedition of 1900–1901." In *Asia Inside Out: Changing Times,* edited by Eric Tagliacozzo, Helen F. Siu, and Peter C. Perdue, 207–25. Cambridge, MA: Harvard University Press, 2015.

———. "(A) Subaltern('s) Boxers: An Indian Soldier's Account of China and the World in 1900–1901." In *The Boxers, China, and the World,* edited by Robert Bickers and R. G. Tiedemann, 43–64. Plymouth: Rowman & Littlefield, 2007.

Young, Robert. *Postcolonialism: An Historical Introduction.* Malden, MA: Blackwell, 2001.

Zivin, Joselyn. "'Bent': A Colonial Subversive and Indian Broadcasting." *Past and Present* 162 (February 1999): 195–220.

Zweiniger-Bargielowska, Ina. "Building a British Superman: Physical Culture in Interwar Britain." *Journal of Contemporary History* 41, No. 4 (October 2006): 595–610.

INDEX

'Abd al-Hakim, 58–59
Across the Black Waters (Anand), 89, 109, 112
Afghanistan, 25, 57, 72–78, 81–84. *See also* Anglo-Afghan Wars; borderlands; Pathans
Afghan Mission (Indo-German), 57, 76
Ahmad, Mirza Ghulam, 58, 137
Ahmadiyya movement, 58, 137
Akali movement, 33–50, 207–9; Akali Dal, 37, 42; Akali *jathas*, 33–35, 37–39, 41–44, 46, 207; at Jaito, 35, 41–42, 44, 47, 236n169
al-Mashriqi (Inayatullah Khan), 209
Amritsar massacre, 9, 13, 31–32, 39, 50, 113, 197, 222
Anand, Mulk Raj, 89, 109, 112
Anglo-Afghan Wars, 4, 6, 9, 13, 54, 75–77, 82, 83, 120, 222
Anglo-Indians, 163, 166–68, 172, 272–73n107
anti-colonialism, 2–3, 7–15, 182–83, 218, 220; education and, 159, 180; food and, 125, 128, 146–47; masculinity and, 184, 185, 187, 213; Muslim soldiers and, 54, 55, 60, 62, 70, 71, 75, 77, 208, 210, 211; Nepali soldiers and, 87, 113–14; in Punjab, 23, 50, 197, 208; "religious teachers" and, 153, 174; Sikh soldiers and, 24, 25, 28, 31, 33, 153, 207. *See also* Arya Samaj; Ghadar; nationalism; pan-Islam
antisemitism, 57, 68, 193–98, 202, 282n92

Aryan race theory, 125, 198–99, 282n86. *See also* fascism
Arya Samaj, 21–23, 91, 128, 200

Bengal Partition (1905), 55, 96, 226n29
Bhonsala Military School, 186–87, 278n22
Birdwood, Judith, 80, 82, 84
Birdwood, William, 80
black waters. See *Across the Black Waters* (Anand); *kala pani*
borderlands, 6, 54, 77, 84, 110, 124, 210, 212. *See also* Anglo-Afghan Wars; North-West Frontier Province; Waziristan
Bose, S. C., 220
Boxer Rebellion, 24, 92, 94, 128, 229n37, 249n29
Boy Scouts, 156, 158, 166
Brahmans, 21; food and, 117, 125–32, 133–34, 143, 199–200, 229n35; Indianization and, 165, 179, 188; role in debates about purity in Nepal, 89–91, 93, 96, 98, 99, 100, 102. *See also* caste; Hindus
Brighton Pavilion. *See* Royal Pavilion

caliphate, 55, 56, 60, 62, 68, 71, 77. *See also* Khilafat movement
caste, 4–5, 14, 111, 115; attempts for unity, 142, 176, 186–87; Brahmans and, 19, 89–90, 98, 117, 125–32, 189; food and, 117, 123, 125–29, 131, 133–34, 142–43, 145, 150; *kala pani*